The Collected Writings of Walt Whitman

WALT WHITMAN

Daybooks and Notebooks

VOLUME II: DAYBOOKS,
December 1881-1891

Edited by William White

 NEW YORK UNIVERSITY PRESS 1978

© 1977 BY NEW YORK UNIVERSITY PRESS

LIBRARY OF CONGRESS CATALOG CARD NUMBER: 75–27382

MANUFACTURED IN THE UNITED STATES OF AMERICA

ISBN: 0–8147–9176–X–Vol. II

The Collected Writings of Walt Whitman

GENERAL EDITORS

Gay Wilson Allen and Sculley Bradley

ADVISORY EDITORIAL BOARD

Roger Asselineau   *Harold W. Blodgett*

Charles E. Feinberg   *Clarence Gohdes*

Emory Holloway   *Rollo G. Silver*   *Floyd Stovall*

GRATEFUL ACKNOWLEDGMENT IS MADE TO

Mr. Charles E. Feinberg,

WHOSE ASSISTANCE MADE POSSIBLE THE ILLUSTRATIONS
IN THIS VOLUME AND WHO ALSO MADE
AVAILABLE TO THE PUBLISHER THE RESOURCES OF
THE FEINBERG COLLECTION.

THE PREPARATION OF THIS VOLUME,
AND COSTS ASSOCIATED WITH ITS PUBLICATION,
WERE SUPPORTED THROUGH GRANTS FROM THE

Editing and Publication Programs
of the National Endowment for the Humanities,

AN INDEPENDENT FEDERAL AGENCY.

CONTENTS

Volume I

Volume II

Volume III

The Collected Writings of Walt Whitman

[217]

1881 – Dec: (and Jan '82) – in Camden

Dec 21 – Sent Mary $10 and pictures   mother's &c[1443]

" Hannah $10

wrote to W S Kennedy, Cambridge, Mass[1444]

22   sent letter to Rolleston, Dresden[1445]

sent <u>Merry Christmas</u> card to Mrs Stafford – sent Chainey's sermons

wrote to C H Farnam New Haven Conn in answer to his
     letter, about Whitman genealogy[1446]

23   sent papers to W S Kennedy – 5

24 – photos to Standish O'Grady, 11 L'r FitzWilliam
     st. Dublin[1447]

papers to Sister Mary — pict. card to Alice Barr

25 – L of G to Wm O'Connor[1448]

wrote to Ruth Stafford that I would come down
     Thursday[1449]

papers to Wm Wood

27   sent L of G to Arthur E Lebknocker,[1450] 450   sent
[first word in blue pencil:]   [in red ink:]   postal
     sent   Washington st Newark N J recd — paid   March 19
                              [in pencil:] $2 due   '82

1442. For an account of the Christmas gloves, see footnotes 550 and 1061a.
1443. The pictures were those Whitman got on 21 November 1881 from F. Gutekunst (see above); the money the poet sent to his sisters Mary Van Nostrand and Hannah Heyde was obviously for Christmas.
1444. Letter: *The Correspondence of Walt Whitman*, III, 260. Whitman thought Kennedy's "A Study of Walt Whitman," *The Californian*, III (February 1881), 149–158, "noble."
1445. Letter: *The Correspondence of Walt Whitman*, III, 260–261. Rolleston's translation, the subject of the letter, was finished later, with Karl Knortz; Walt Whitman's *Grashalme* (Zurich, 1889) — see footnote 2662. There are numerous others in German.
1446. Letter lost, but for genealogy, see footnotes 1297 and 1369.
1447. See footnote 1422.
1448. Although Whitman was still not yet reconciled with William Douglas O'Connor, it was the suppression of this edition of *Leaves of Grass* in 1882 that brought the two men back into a close relationship.
1449. Whitman stayed with the Staffords at Kirkwood, Glendale, New Jersey, from 29 December 1881 until 9 January 1882 (see first entry for 1882, below).
1450. See footnote 1385.

sent Press Dec 23 to Dr Bucke – also Osgood

sent card of thanks &c to Press[1451]

28 – made a bargain with Dr Babbitt – Gutekunst's
  – 1100 copies each head — (200 for me) — for Dr Bucke[1452]

sent letter to Dr Bucke – quite long – [1453]   – price $80

     <u>1882</u>   [year in red ink]
[three lines on slip pasted on page:]
29th Dec. to Jan 9 '82 – (11 days) down at Glend[ale]

Jan 1 – Sent letter to Herbert Gilchrist [1454]

2 – Jan 9 – Sent letters to Sister Hannah – Dr Bu[cke] [1455]

["Sent" in blue pencil:]   [in blue pencil:]
Jan. 10. Sent   Horace H Martin 1927 Michigan av   recd
        Chicago, Ill. a set Cent: Ed. 2 Vols. – ~~10 due~~ paid

"   Sent <u>Two Rivulets,</u> also card of thanks to Editor
      <u>Advance</u> newspaper Worthington Nobles co. Minn:

11   Sat to Mr Weld, (Scholl's 112 north 9th) (Mr Houseworth)
      for photos[1456]

(Oscar Wilde) Mr Stoddart's invitation (through Mr Winner)
      to drive with Mr Wilde in Phila[1457]

1451. See the Philadelphia *Press,* 23 December 1881.
1452. These 1100 copies "each head — (200 for me) — for Dr Bucke" must mean a photograph which Gutekunst had printed for the Bucke book, *Walt Whitman,* which was published by David McKay in 1883; but the book contained reproductions of Herbert Gilchrist's drawing and a photo taken by Edy Brothers in London, Ontario, and six other illustrations.
1453. Letter lost.
1454. Letter to Herbert H. Gilchrist, 30 December 1881: *The Correspondence of Walt Whitman,* III, 261–262.
1455. Both letters lost.
1456. Emil Scholl was the Philadelphia photographer; Weld and Householder may well have worked for him, though I have found no photo with either name on it. In *Specimen Days* is a short piece, "Only a New Ferry Boat," dated *Jan. 12, '82,* referring to a show on the Delaware "before sundown yesterday," not mentioned in the *Daybook* in any way. See *Prose Works 1892,* I, 283–284.
1457. For Stoddart, see footnote 1439; a letter, of this date, on the office stationery of J. M. Stoddart and Company, Philadelphia, now in the Library of Congress, reads: "Oscar Wilde has expressed his great desire to meet you socially. He will dine with me Saturday afternoon when I shall be most happy to have you join us. The bearer, Mr. Wanier, will explain at greater length any details which you may wish to know, and will be happy to bring me your acquiescence." (Printed in Clara Barrus, *Whitman and Burroughs: Comrades* [Boston and

[218]

--- Howland – reporter, <u>Press</u> from Springfield Mass

Walter Jones, young man at Scovel's | Paymaster
  convoyed me home   John S Cunningham U S N [1458]
    Sunday night   N a v y   P a y   O f f i c e,   [3
        425 Chestnut Street,   lines
Mrs Lydia Hamilton   Philadelphia   printed]
  253 Cherry St   Camden

       [Diagonally (in red) across card:]
Socrates Townsend Church   Transferr'd
  driver, Stevens st. (Cape May
March '82   boy

W^m   Pettit, the new carrier

   Herbert Harlakenden Gilchrist[1459] [printed]   Geo. G. Clapp[1460] [not
                  WW's hand]

      My address is ——
       Academy of Art
        630 Washington St
         Boston   Mass. — [4 lines
           not in WW's hand]

     Rev. James Morrow[1461]
     1341 N. 12th St. [name and address not in
            WW's hand]

New York, 1931], p. 235n.) This letter is, without question, Stoddart's invitation, which Whitman did not accept (see entry for 18 January 1882, below); but Stoddart and Wilde did spend much of that afternoon with Whitman in Camden. A transcript of Whitman's letter to Stoddart, 11 January 1882 (from *The Collector*, LVII [1943], 38) is in *The Correspondence of Walt Whitman*, III, 263.

  1458. See Whitman's letter to John S. Cunningham, 26 January 1882 (not listed below) in *The Correspondence of Walt Whitman*, III, 265, in which he thanks Cunningham for sending a clipping from the Washington *Star* about Wilde on Whitman. See Whitman's notation, below, on Cunningham's printed card, "June 22 '82 / Wakefield, / Rhode Island," which ties in with Whitman's note above, "Transferr'd."

  1459. Herbert Gilchrist was, at this time, in Hampstead, London, England, with his mother, Anne Gilchrist, whose portrait (now in the University of Pennsylvania) he was painting: see *The Letters of Anne Gilchrist and Walt Whitman*, pp. 205–206.

  1460. For George G. Clapp, see end of footnote 1096: Clapp may well have visited Whitman and written his new address in the *Daybook*.

  1461. The Rev. James Morrow, "a prominent Methodist," was quoted at length in the Philadelphia *Press* of 15 July 1882 on the front page, defending *Leaves of Grass* against the Boston censor, who had forced Osgood to drop the 1881 edition, of which Rees Welsh & Company, Philadelphia, became the publisher. See *The Correspondence of Walt Whitman*, III, 297n; and Horace Traubel, *With Walt Whitman in Camden*, II, 60–61.

[219]

Jan   Jan: 1882 – in Camden

18 – Oscar Wilde here[1462] – rec'd cordial inv. from Mr & Mrs Childs
to dine to-night, but declined – (also invitations from Mr Stoddart
                                                    & Mr Davis

Oscar Wilde here a good part of the   – declined [1463]
afternoon – J M Stoddart –

(in answer to application from him)
21 – Sent note ∧ to Daniel G Brinton, "Our Continent" [1464]
N W. Cor: Chestnut & 11 Sts. Phila. that I would fur
nish "Antecedents" for $50 – (rec'd answer) 24th

Sent N Y Times with Engineers' art. to Jeff.[1465]

1462. See footnotes 1439 and 1440, also *The Correspondence of Walt Whitman*, III, 263, 264, 266; and Wilde's letter to Whitman, 1 March 1882 (Feinberg Collection), in Horace Traubel, *With Walt Whitman in Camden*, II, 288, and Rupert Hart-Davis, editor, *The Letters of Oscar Wilde* (London, 1962), pp. 99–100 (see also pp. 15 and 451); see Lloyd Morris and Henry Justin Smith, *Oscar Wilde Discovers America* (New York, 1936), pp. 63–77; Gay Wilson Allen, *The Solitary Singer*, pp. 502–503; and *Walt Whitman Review*, VIII (December 1962), 93–94. Between Wilde's reference to Whitman as early as 1876 and as late as 1897, most significant is the British writer's remark in his letter to Whitman after they had spent the day together: "Before I leave America I must see you again. There is no one in this wide great world of America whom I love and honour so much." (He did not see Whitman again.) Of the several comments by the American in Traubel (II, 192, 279, 286, 288–289; III, 11, 276; IV, 79, 488), two seem to sum up his opinion of Wilde (1856–1900): "I never completely make Wilde out — out for good or bad. He writes exquisitely — is as lucid as a star on a clear night — but there seems to be a little substance lacking at the root — something — what is it? I have no sympathy with the crowd of scorners who want to crowd him off the earth" (II, 192); and "Wilde was very friendly to me — was and is, I think — both Oscar and his mother — Lady Wilde — and thanks be most to the mother, that greater, more important, individual. Oscar was here — came to see me — and he impressed me as a strong, able fellow, too" (V, 284). Whitman, of course, had been dead three years when Wilde's disgrace came in 1895.
1463. The reason Whitman turned down the invitations, one may infer from his letter to Harry Stafford — *The Correspondence of Walt Whitman*, III, 264 — is that the weather was "awfully cold here, this is now the third day"; anyway, Wilde and Whitman had spent an afternoon together in Camden, and he told Mrs G. W. Childs, "I am an invalid — just suffering an extra bad spell & forbidden to go out nights this weather." (*Ibid.*, III, 263.)
1464. Letter lost. Dr Daniel G. Brinton, author of "A Visit to West Hills," *The Conservator*, V (November 1894), 135–136; and "Whitman and Science," *The Conservator*, VI (April 1895), 20–21, became strongly attached to Whitman both before and after the poet's death; he spoke at his funeral, helped to organize the Walt Whitman Fellowship: International, was its first president, and was at work on a book about Whitman when he died in 1899. He achieved a considerable reputation as an anthropologist and specialists in the field still praise his studies. See his contribution to Charles N. Elliot's *Walt Whitman as Man, Poet and Friend* (Boston, 1915), pp. 37–40; and Charles B. Willard, *Whitman's American Fame: The Growth of His Reputation in America After 1892* (Providence, Rhode Island, 1950), p. 40. Brinton is often mentioned in Traubel's volumes, where Whitman expresses a high regard for him.
1465. Jefferson Whitman was, of course, the poet's brother in St Louis, who came to Camden three days later (see below, 24–25 January 1882).

[in blue pencil:]
25 – $16 to W V Montgomery for Ed's board   rec'd [1466]

letter to Harry Stafford [1467] {card-note to Paymaster
24th'5th – Jeff here   {Cunningham [1468]

26 – wrote to Mr Walsh, [1469] 715 Market st. declining

note to J H Johnston [1470]

☞ J H Johnson's letter – news from J H Osgood – O says has printed
& sold 2000 copies — ? in "three editions" [1471]

28 – sent to Josiah Child for two copies old preface [1472]

[in blue pencil:]
sent three photo-type portraits   rec'd 2 copies

Feb. 1 – reading Dr B's MS book (& a tough job it is) [1473]

2   picture to Mrs Kate Brownlee Sherwood office Journal
[in red ink:]
Toledo   Ohio   rec'd – (& hers sent me)

letter (card) to Dr Bucke [1474]

3   – sent letter to Ed Stafford, Indiana, Indianna Co: Penn. [1475]

5th – papers to Ed Stafford – Ruth [1476] – Sister Hannah

card to P M Boston, to send letters here [1477]

1466. As usual, for the care of Walt's feeble-minded brother, Edward.
1467. Letter: *The Correspondence of Walt Whitman*, III, 264. Also another letter, 31 January 1882, *ibid.*, III, 265–266.
1468. See footnote 1458.
1469. Letter to William S. Walsh lost.
1470. Note to John H. Johnston (?) lost.
1471. An excerpt from John H. Johnston's letter from James R. Osgood & Company is in *The Complete Writings of Walt Whitman* (1902), VIII, 288 (original in the Library of Congress).
1472. Letter lost.
1473. See *The Correspondence of Walt Whitman*, III, 266–267; and *Walt Whitman's Autograph Revision of the Analysis of Leaves of Grass* (for Dr. R. M. Bucke's *Walt Whitman*) (New York, 1974).
1474. Letter lost.
1475. There was an Edmund D. and an Edward L. Stafford, but this was apparently Edwin Stafford, Harry's brother.
1476. Ruth Stafford, sister to Harry and Edwin.
1477. Letter lost, though it cannot have been important.

7 sent Dr Bucke's MS back by Express
    sent long letter[1478]

papers to Harry – Geo & Susan Stafford –

9 sent card-letter to Mrs V O Coburn   Skowhegan   Maine
    in answer[1479]

13 – sent pictures to Miss Inman, Plainfield [1480]

16 down to Glendale
    return'd 6th March (2 weeks 4 days)[1481]

[220]

Dr. T. K. Reed, M.D.   [not in   Edward Carpenter[1483]   March '82
    Atlantic City   WW's
Box 50.   N. J.   hand]   Bradway   near Sheffield   Eng

Acc't   with Spieler[1484]
James Arnold [1482]   March   paid — $5
    531 Chestnut st: April 8   "   10
        Phila: recd   April 6 – 25 big head
                                    "   25 –¾   "
[On slip, not in WW's hand:]   "   50 profile
    If not called for return   paid all [in red ink]
to Helen Wiemans   [encircled in red ink]
[Letterhead, clipped: Rees Welsh & Co., Booksellers
and Publishers, no. 23 S. Ninth St., Philadelphia.]

[in pencil on slip:]   [in ink:]
    Nineteenth Century[1485]   Dec. '83

1478. See footnote 1473.
1479. Letters to and from Whitman lost. See footnote 1487.
1480. May well be related to the portrait painter John O'B. Inman (see footnote 567).
1481. This visit with the Stafford family at Kirkwood, Glendale, is a longer than ordinary one, though Whitman often was their guest.
1482. James Arnold had been the binder for Whitman's books for several years (see footnote 22).
1483. See footnote 20. Carpenter and Whitman were corresponding at this time.
1484. See end of footnote 8. Charles H. Spieler was a photographer at 722 Chestnut Street, Philadelphia, one of the several Whitman used; the hundred photographs which Whitman purchased he gave to relatives, friends, and others, as is seen in the letters that often accompanied them or as noted in the *Daybook*.
1485. These notes on the editor, publisher, and words-per-page in *The Nineteenth Century* (London) suggest that Whitman, following G. C. Macaulay's essay on *Leaves of Grass* in the issue of December 1882, XII, 903–918, planned to send James Knowles an article for

James Knowles
    Editor
Care Kegan Paul, Trench & Co.
    1 Paternoster row

about 480 words in	46
page of 19th Century	10½
the articles are signed same	480
as in N A Review	

(correction   page 31 L of G, "to a cent [1486]

[221]

1882

March 7 sent the two Vols. Cent. Ed'n to Mrs V. O. Coburn[1487]
                [in blue pencil:] sent photo type
    Skowhegan Maine – paid recd March 14 rec'd   [last word in
                                                 red ink]

" 8 – sent J R Osgood & Co: a letter (which see) ab't
    cancellation[1488]

publication; he did send "What Lurks Behind Shakspeare's Historical Plays" to *The Nineteenth Century* on 8 August 1884, asking $50 (see below, that date), but it was rejected, and was later published in *The Critic*. The British periodical did publish his long poem, "Fancies at Navesink" in August 1885, XVIII, 234–237, for which he received $145.20 (see entries, below, for 23 May and 15 August 1885).

1486. In the 1881 (Osgood) edition, this line 64 in "Song of Myself" (next to the last line in Section 3) reads "show to me a cent." This is in error for "show me to a cent," which Whitman corrected in the 1889 *Leaves of Grass*. See the Comprehensive Reader's Edition, p. 32.

1487. Mrs V. O. Coburn ordered the book on 9 February 1882 (see entry above). See Samuel A. Golden, "Whitman to Mrs Vine Coburn: Three Letters," *Walt Whitman Review*, IV (March 1969), 59–60.

1488. This was the beginning of the difficulties with James R. Osgood & Company and led to their ceasing to publish the 1881 edition of *Leaves of Grass*. Osgood wrote Whitman on 4 March 1882:

> We enclose a letter from the District Attorney, dated March 1st, and received by us yesterday, March 3d. Please read and return it, keeping copy of it if you so desire. We are not at present informed what portions of the book are objected to. We are, however, naturally reluctant to be identified with any legal proceedings in a matter of this nature. We are given to understand that if certain parts of the book should be withdrawn its further circulation would not be objected to. Will you advise us whether you would consent to the withdrawal of the present edition and the substitution of an edition lacking the obnoxious features?

The letter which the District Attorney sent to the publisher and which was sent to Whitman follows (both this and the above are printed in *The Complete Writings of Walt Whitman* [1902], VIII, 289–290):

Commonwealth of Massachusetts,
District Attorney's Office, Boston,
24 Court House, *March 1st, 1882.*

Messrs. Jas. R. Osgood & Co.:

Gentlemen: Our attention has been officially directed to a certain book entitled "*Leaves of Grass*: Walt Whitman" published by you.

We are of the opinion that this book is such a book as brings it within the provisions

sent Harry Stafford papers

sent Dr B "Sobbing of Bells"[1489] } ackn'd W J RR pass[1490]

11 – dinner with Mrs Stafford, at Mrs Rogers' 431 Linden[1491]

13 – Day's trip to Atlantic City   W J RR – dinner at Dr & Mrs Reed's[1492]

17 – Percy Ives here afternoon & evening[1493]

18 – big bundle papers, N J Letter, Saguenay do. "Poetry Future"

Critic notes &c. to Dr Reed, Atlantic City[1494]   rec'd thankful letter

[three words in red ink]

papers to Harry – Progress to Hannah[1495]

19   sent note to J R Osgood & Co.[1496]   (which see)

of the Public Statutes respecting obscene literature, and suggest the propriety of withdraw-ing the same from circulation and suppressing the editions thereof.
Otherwise the complaints which are proposed to be made will have to be entertained.
I am yours truly,
OLIVER STEVENS,
Dist. Att'y.
For Whitman's reply, saying that he didn't think the D. A.'s threat could amount to much but he might cancel ten lines or half a dozen phrases, see *The Correspondence of Walt Whitman,* III, 267–268.
1489. "The Sobbing of the Bells" dealt with President Garfield's death (see footnote 1346).
1490. Whitman's annual pass on the West Jersey and Seashore Railroad; his letter to the company is lost.
1491. Mrs Elizabeth Rogers, who lived on Linden Street, Camden, was Mrs Susan Stafford's widowed sister.
1492. The fact that Whitman could take a trip to Atlantic City to spend the day with Dr T. K. Reed and his wife (see the address on the previous page of the *Daybook,* written by Dr Reed?) indicated that he did not take the Osgood "problem" seriously at this time.
1493. For Percy Ives, the young artist, see footnotes 1007 and 1011.
1494. Dr Reed was a new acquaintance (see footnote 1492), to whom Whitman sent his pieces, "Summer Days in Canada," London (Ontario) *Advertiser,* 22 June 1880; "The Poetry of the Future," *North American Review,* February 1881; and some of the series, "How I Get Around at 60, and Take Notes," *The Critic,* 19 January, 9 April, 7 May, 26 July, and 3 December 1881.
1495. The *Progress,* the late Colonel John W. Forney's paper, may (or may not) have had something about Whitman in it (I doubt if there was anything by Whitman at this time); these went to Harry Stafford and Whitman's sister Hannah Heyde.
1496. Whitman wanted to know of Osgood's intention about continuing to sell *Leaves of Grass,* to which they replied they were wating to hear what the D.A. had decided about re-visions: see *The Correspondence of Walt Whitman,* III, 268.

21   sent letter to J R O & Co. about Dr Bucke's book
        & ab't my "Specimen Days" [1497]

                                        [in red ink:]   [in blue pencil:]
"   sent note to "Critic" for MSS for revision[1498]   rec'd   returned

        papers to Mary, Greenport [1499]

23 – sent J R Osgood letter, which see – also
        paper-bound L of G   with revisions prop:[1500]

24   down at Glendale from 24th to 31st inclusive – one week[1501]
31 – sent postal card to Herbert Gilchrist[1502]

31 – ~~sent postal to Herbert Gilchrist~~

April 2 – sent letter to C A Dana giving permission to
        extract poems in "Household Book" [1503]

Sent "How I still get around" No 6 (Death of
                        [in red ink:]   [two words in red ink:]
    Longfellow) to Critic[1504]   recd – paid $7   accepted
                                               paid

                ~~art~~ printed June No   [in red ink]
8 – Sent "A Memorandum at a Venture" to N. A. Review[1505]
                        paid $25 & 200 impressions   [line in red ink]

1497.   Letter: *The Correspondence of Walt Whitman,* III, 268–270. So sure was Whitman that all would blow over on the censorship matter that he offered Osgood the chance to publish both *Specimen Days* (his prose volume here first mentioned) and Dr Bucke's biography, which Osgood didn't want to read unless Whitman had approved of the book (he most assuredly had).

1498.   Letter: *The Correspondence of Walt Whitman,* III, 268. The MSS must mean Whitman's sixth part of "How I Get Around at 60, and Take Notes," to appear in *The Critic* on 15 July 1882.

1499.   Mary was Mrs Mary Van Nostrand, Whitman's sister.

1500.   Letter: *The Correspondence of Walt Whitman,* III, 270–271. The poet was willing to make changes on four pages, but the District Attorney wanted far more, which Whitman absolutely rejected: see *ibid.,* III, 270n, and the full story in Thomas B. Harned, "Walt Whitman and His Second Boston Publishers," *The Complete Writings of Walt Whitman* (1902), VIII, 275–300.

1501.   Whitman seems to be spending considerable time with the Stafford family.

1502.   Post card: *The Correspondence of Walt Whitman,* III, 272.

1503.   Letter: *The Correspondence of Walt Whitman,* III, 272. Charles A. Dana (1819–1897), editor of the New York *Sun,* included six Whitman poems in *The Household Book of Poetry* (1882).

1504.   "How I Get Around . . . ," No. 6, and "Death of Longfellow" were two different essays: the first was in *The Critic,* 15 July 1882; the Longfellow in *The Critic,* 8 April 1882, reprinted in *Essays from "The Critic"* (1882), pp. 41–45, and in *Specimen Days: Prose Works 1892,* I, 284–286.

1505.   "A Memorandum at a Venture," *The North American Review,* CXXXIV (June 1882), 546–550; reprinted in *Specimen Days: Prose Works 1892,* II, 491–497.

paid Spieler $15 – (10 to day & 5 some weeks ago)[1506]

Progress to Hannah – Paper to Harry[1507]

[222]

Major Drake, 2010 Diamond Street   SD

Joaquin Miller   109 West 33ᵈ Street[1508]

Mrs Mingle 114 north 32ᵈ st – Baring St cars[1509]

John A Marcus   book canvasses, dealer &c
    (call'd June 5 '82)   720 Christian St.   Phila

J L Brotherton – business office   134 South 2ᵈ
                        residence   553 north 16ᵗʰ   Phila

Linton W J   box 489 New Haven Conn[1510]

Wycliffe Stewart, at the gate W J Ferry

Sam Long 614 Sansom St – res: 3210 Race

Bender, hatter, 202 Race cor: 2ᵈ   1126 Columbia
                                        Av: [correction in red ink]

[On printed slip of J. M. Stoddart & Co., publishers, Philadelphia:][1511]

1018
Chestnut

[On printed card of John S. Cunningham, Pay Director, U. S. Navy:]

June 22 '82 [date in red ink]
Wakefield,
    Rhode Island.[1512]

[On slip of paper:]

bo't L of G

(live at Point Pleasant N J
Nestor Sanborn
                [not WW's hand]
Carrie V Sanborn

1506. This $15 was for photographs (see entry above and footnote 1484).
1507. See footnote 1495; Harry Stafford at this time was working in Clementon, New Jersey.
1508. See footnote 24.
1509. See footnote 693. Mrs Mingle had not been mentioned here for some time.
1510. See footnote 39.
1511. See footnotes 1439 and 1457.
1512. See footnote 1458.

Friends of Wyatt Eaton[1513]
July 7th 82

[223]

1882

April 9 – Sent back "Notes" No 6 MS. to Critic[1514]

Osgood gives up   L   of   G [1515]

[one word in red ink:]
accepted

17 – sent "Edgar Poe's Significance" to Critic – $10
asked [1516]

papers to Mr Nash[1517] – Harry Stafford

1513. Wyatt Eaton was a portrait painter Whitman met in June 1878 (see footnote 343). This left-hand page of the *Daybook*, like several others, is a grab-bag: names and addresses of old friends, some newly or casually met, and a businessman or tradesman (such as Bender, hatter) entered for some practical, immediate purpose.

1514. See footnotes 1498 and 1504.

1515. See footnotes 1488, 1496, 1497, and 1500. This bland remark in itself, "Osgood gives up L of G," is typical of the fairness, equanimity, and even good feeling toward the Boston publisher which Whitman displayed throughout the controversy. See *The Correspondence of Walt Whitman,* III, 273, for his telegram and letter, 5 and 12 April 1882, to Osgood refusing to make excisions in *Leaves* and suggesting calling off their arrangement. In the end, the firm paid Whitman $405.50 in royalties, plus $100 in cash, and turned over to him the plates, the steel portrait, and 225 copies of the book. See *The Complete Writings of Walt Whitman* (1902), VIII, 295–298, for the Osgood-to-Whitman letters, including this agreement of surrender:

Camden, N. J., May 17, 82.

Memorandum of Agreement between James R. Osgood & Co., of Boston, Mass., & Walt Whitman, of Camden, N. J. J. R. O. & Co. agree to surrender to W. W. the plates, dies, steel portrait, and 225 copies (more or less), in sheets of *Leaves of Grass,* and pay W. W. the sum of $100.00 in cash.

W. W. agrees to accept the same in lieu of all claims for copyright, &c., in full.

The publication of said work to be discontinued by J. R. O. & Co., the contract for the same to be cancelled, & no copies to be issued hereafter with their imprint.

JAMES R. OSGOOD & CO.
WALT WHITMAN

If Whitman remained unruffled, his friends were furious, denouncing both the District Attorney and the publisher. The one behind the attack on *Leaves of Grass* who first complained to State Attorney General George Marston, who turned to Boston District Attorney Oliver Stevens, is not definitely known. William Douglas O'Connor, coming back into friendly relations with Whitman after their ten years' estrangement, first suggested Anthony Comstock (1844–1915), secretary of the Society for the Suppression of Vice in New York, then Colonel Thomas Wentworth Higginson (1823–1911), the author, reformer, and editor who was always hostile toward Whitman. Thomas B. Harned, *The Complete Writings of Walt Whitman* (1902), VIII, 299, says "the real power — or man — back of the whole business will never be known." William Sloane Kennedy, *The Fight of a Book for the World* (1926), p. 248, says it was the "secretary of the [Boston] vice society, the Rev. Baylies Allen, who instigated the movement. Allen admitted it to me in his own parlor." Gay Wilson Allen, *The Solitary Singer* (1955), p. 589, footnote 185, says the person "was never definitely identified . . . . but some of Whitman's friends in Boston thought that it was a narrow-minded preacher."

1516. "Edgar Poe's Significance" appeared in *The Critic,* II (3 June 1882), 147, and was revised and reprinted in *Specimen Days,* with two paragraphs from the Washington *Star,* 18 November 1875: see *Prose Works 1892,* I, 230–233, 355.

1517. Michael Nash was an old Washington friend: see footnote 970.

1882

April 9 – sent back "Notes" No 8 MS. to Critic

Osgood gives up L of G

17 – sent "Edgar Poe's Significance" to Critic – (accepts / to be asked)

papers to Mr Nash – Harry Stafford

19 sent letter to Dr Bucke, announcing Osgood' withdrawal

" paid Montgomery $16 for Ed.

22 to 27 – 5 days – down at Glendale

27 – rec'd $25 from N A Review (with "sincere thanks")

for "Memorandum" (is to be in June number)

Emerson died aged 79

" sent long letter to Dr Bucke [death of Emerson]

28 sent letter to John Burroughs

29 sent "By Emerson's Grave" to Critic (printed May 6)

3

May 3 – rec'd Letter from John Burroughs – (answered)

" " " Dr Bucke

sent budget of Osgood & L of G letters to

O'Connor, tell'g him to forward them

finally to Dr Bucke – have gone to Dr B.

– all returned

May 2 – Visit from John Russell Young

4 sent letters "the Prairies in Poetry" to N A Review rec'd 50

returned to me

7th Sunday – wrote to Wm O'Connor

" " Dr Bucke

papers to Harry

8 1876 Edn L of G, 2 Vols. to Mr Stoddart, $10 paid

paid L/25 – pays to May 10

11 sent the Spieler profile to Wm O'Connor

" " Col Ingersoll

" Demorest's Magazine May to Ruthey

19 sent letter to Dr Bucke, announcing Osgood's withdrawal [1518]

"   paid Montgomery $16 for Ed: [1519]

22^{d} to 27 – 5 days – down at Glendale [1520]

27 – recd $25 from <u>N A Review</u> (with "sincere thanks")
    for "Memorandum" – (is to be in June number) [1521]

<u>Emerson died, aged 79</u>   [in red, with lines around in red ink,
――――――――――――   <u>death of Emerson</u> [1522]   also black ink:]
"   sent long letter to Dr Bucke

28 sent letter to John Burroughs [1523]

                                [in red ink:]
29 sent "<u>by Emerson's Grave</u>" to Critic   ℞ printed May 6 [1524]

   rec'd   3
May 3 – Letter from John Burroughs – (answered) [1525]

     "   "   "   Dr Bucke [1526]

   sent budget of Osgood & L of G letters to
   O'Connor, telling him to forward them

    1518. Letter unfortunately lost, as it may have dealt with William Douglas O'Connor and his part in the Osgood controversy: see *The Correspondence of Walt Whitman*, III, 275n.

    1519. See footnote 1177: William V. Montgomery was sent the $16 monthly to pay for Edward Whitman's care, as usual.

    1520. Another visit with the Stafford family.

    1521. "A Memorandum at a Venture," on Whitman's theory of sexual matter and "Children of Adam," *The North American Review*, CXXXIV (June 1882), 546–550; reprinted in *Specimen Days* — see *Prose Works 1892*, II, 491–497.

    1522. The fact that Whitman could write this down twice, and underline it with such a heavy mark is certainly significant: no man was more important in Whitman's literary life than R. W. Emerson, whose stirring 1855 letter was such a highpoint to *Leaves of Grass*. The sage of Concord died on 26 April 1882, while Whitman was with the Stafford's and he learned of it the next day; as noted here, he wrote Dr Bucke, and must have spoken of it, but this letter is lost.

    1523. Letter: *The Correspondence of Walt Whitman*, III, 274. On R.W.E., Whitman said only: "So Emerson is dead — the leading man in all Israel — If I feel able I shall go to his funeral — improbable though." He did not attend the funeral, but did write "By Emerson's Grave."

    1524. "By Emerson's Grave," showing the hold the man and the personality had on the aging Whitman, appeared in *The Critic*, II (6 May 1882), 123; reprinted with slight changes in *Specimen Days* — see *Prose Works 1892*, I, 290–291.

    1525. John Burroughs's letter, 1 May 1882, is in Horace Traubel's *With Walt Whitman in Camden*, III, 350–351, followed by William Douglas O'Connor's letter to Burroughs, 28 April 1882, *ibid.*, III, 351–352, both reacting strongly to the Osgood matter and mentioning Emerson's death; Burroughs also said he was sending a page or two on Emerson to *The Critic* (entitled "Emerson's Burial Day," it was in the 6 May 1882 issue, with Whitman's). Whitman's letter to Burroughs is lost.

    1526. Letter lost.

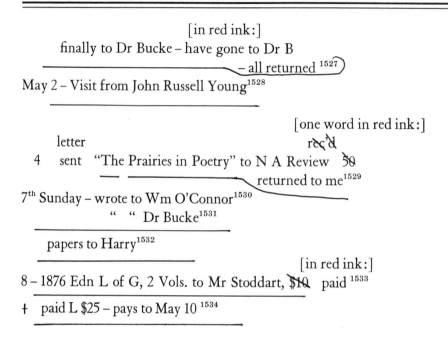

[in red ink:]
finally to Dr Bucke – have gone to Dr B
                        – all returned [1527]

May 2 – Visit from John Russell Young[1528]

                       [one word in red ink:]
   letter   rec'd
4   sent   "The Prairies in Poetry" to N A Review 5θ
                                 returned to me[1529]
7ᵗʰ Sunday – wrote to Wm O'Connor[1530]
      " " Dr Bucke[1531]

   papers to Harry[1532]

                            [in red ink:]
8 – 1876 Edn L of G, 2 Vols. to Mr Stoddart, $10 paid [1533]

† paid L $25 – pays to May 10 [1534]

1527. See footnote 1518; with this letter to O'Connor — see *The Correspondence of Walt Whitman,* III, 275 — the relationship between Whitman and O'Connor was finally renewed, O'Connor saying he was "thunderstruck" by Osgood, whom he called a "cowardly fool," and "infernal idiot," and "jackass." His letter to Burroughs is full of such terms as "outrage," "unlimited volcano," "crush" the District Attorney and "annul [his] action by a fulmin," and "I am trembling with fury, and with the fervor of my oration down stairs in the Department of Justice." (*With Walt Whitman in Camden,* III, 351–352.)

1528. John Russell Young (1840–1899), newspaper editor and Librarian of Congress, who went around the world with President Grant, and of whom Whitman said — when Young wrote from Peking in February 1883 to ask about the poet's health — "Dear Young! He is a lovable cuss . . . he is the higher type of newspaper man — a man with real guts to him – no mere penny a line liar as so many of the boys are: God bless 'em, too!" (Horace Traubel, *With Walt Whitman in Camden,* III, 310). Whitman said Young used to see him often after the Civil War, and he knew him pretty well; Young was "heartily" friendly towards *Leaves of Grass* and "seemed to find a good deal in it." See Traubel, IV, 40. See also footnote 3379, below. Young has a chapter on Whitman in his *Men and Memories: Personal Reminiscences,* edited by May D. Russell Young (New York, 1910), I, 76–109.

1529. "The Prairies in Poetry," rejected by *The North American Review,* was apparently not separately published, but as Whitman was preparing *Specimen Days* at this time, he included it under several consecutive headings: "The Prairies and Great Plains in Poetry (After Traveling Illinois, Missouri, Kansas and Colorado)," "The Spanish Peaks — Evening on the Plains," "America's Characteristic Landscape," "Earth's Most Important Stream," "Prairie Analogies — the Tree Question," and "Mississippi Valley Literature." The first section may well have been written in part on the poet's western trip in 1879. See *Prose Works 1892,* I, 219–224.

1530. Letter: *The Correspondence of Walt Whitman,* III, 276–277. Here begins (except for the two very short letters of 3 May 1882) a long correspondence between Whitman and O'Connor until the latter's death in 1889. Most of O'Connor's are in the Feinberg Collection (some in Yale and Syracuse University Libraries), and a number of them published in various Traubel volumes.

1531. Letter lost.

1532. Harry Stafford, apparently working as a telegrapher on the Camden & Atlantic Railroad.

1533. See footnote 1065.

1534. To Louisa Orr Whitman, his sister-in-law, for his board.

11 sent the Spieler profile to Wm O'Connor[1535]

"   "   "   Col Ingersoll [1536]

Democrat Magazine May to Ruthey[1537]

[224]

James Arnold, binder, 531 Chestnut st. Phila[1538]

visit June 6 Evening
Nath Haskell Dole[1539]
    of the Press
Mr Allen, of England

Rudolf Schmidt[1540]
    3 Baggesen's Gade N
        Copenhagen
        Denmark

[On slip, not in WW's hand:]

Afsender:
Rudolf Schmidt
    Baggesens 3 N

Oct 1883 [date in red ink]

[On card, in red ink, not in WW's hand:]

Wm. Hutchison
        "
    No. 197 Market St.
        Newark, N. J.
(To be called for.)

George
38 Walnut St

[On printed card of Charles G. Leland,
        in red ink:]

E B Haskell   Boston
    chief Editor (& an owner) Herald [1541]
    220 South Broad St
    [not in WW's hand]

1535. This was one of the photographs Whitman paid for on 8 April 1882.
1536. If Whitman included letters to O'Connor and Colonel Robert G. Ingersoll (see footnote 890), they are now lost.
1537. Ruthey was Harry Stafford's sister, 16 years old at this time.
1538. James Arnold, who bound earlier editions of Whitman's *Leaves*, had his address noted several times on these left-hand pages.
1539. Nathan Haskell Dole (1852–1935), author, editor, and translator of Tolstoy (Whitman called his translations "measurelessly poor, unequal, not to be considered" — Horace Traubel, *With Walt Whitman in Camden*, III, 371), who met Whitman in New York and saw him several times in Camden. At this time, 6 June 1882, Dole was on the Philadelphia *Press*, later went to *The Epoch*, then, says Whitman, he "went out on his own hook. He always displayed a very kindly and courteous spirit toward me, too — affable, a gentleman, generous — sent me a couple of his books" — i.e., the translations, which Whitman found dull, though he didn't blame Dole, whose best known books, such as *Not Angels Quite* (1893) and *Omar, the Tent-Maker* (1899), were written after Whitman's death. See Traubel, III, 272–273.
1540. For Rudolf Schmidt, Whitman's constant Scandinavian correspondent, see footnote 81, at the beginning.
1541. E. B. Haskell, editor and owner of the Boston *Herald,* supported Whitman against the Boston censors, 24 and 28 May 1882, and quoted Oscar Wilde in Whitman's defense on 2 June 1882. See *The Correspondence of Walt Whitman*, III, 283n.

[Classified ad of Magnolia
Hotel, Tom's River, Ocean
County, N. J.; and printed
slip of George Chainey, 51
Fort Ave. (Roxbury), Boston, Mass.] [1543]

[On slip, not in WW's hand:]
George S McWatters[1542]
221 East 18 st
New York

[225]

1882 – May –

17th – Ben Ticknor here – bargain L of G. plates $\frac{\&}{100}$ [1544]

18   Sent "Carlyle from American Points of View"   to

[in red ink:]
N A Review   returned [1545]

19 — sent order to Sanborn, Boston, to send the 225 sets
sheets to James Arnold [1546]

sent to Rand & Avery, ordering new title page[1547]

Herald –
23   letters to Whitelaw Reid – Boston ∧ Globe – Post[1548]
– C S Noyes[1549] – with Phil Press editorial May 22 [1550]

1542. George S. McWatters, whose letter to Whitman, 6 December 1867, is in the Fein-berg Collection, was the author of nonfiction books dealing with police work: *Detectives of Europe and America, or Life in the Secret Service; Forgers and Confidence-Men;* and *The Gambler's Wax Finger and other Startling Detective Experiences,* all published in the Pinker-ton Detective Series by Laird and Lee, Chicago, in 1892.
1543. George Chainey, publisher on *This World* (Boston), defended *Leaves of Grass* in a lecture, "Keep Off the Grass," which he printed in his issue of 17 June 1882, with Whitman's poem "To a Common Prostitute." Whitman, in appreciation, sent him a copy of *Leaves* on 26 June 1882: see *The Correspondence of Walt Whitman,* III, 294, 296n, 297n. Chainey's letter to Whitman, 27 July 1882, is in the Feinberg Collection.
1544. For the agreement of settlement, which was dated 17 May 1882, and brought by Benjamin H. Ticknor, of James R. Osgood & Company, see footnote 1515. See also Whitman to O'Connor, *The Correspondence of Walt Whitman,* III, 279. Ticknor wrote Whitman on 20 May 1882: "I am extremely sorry for the *contretemps* which has caused the change, but I am very glad of opportunity I have had of personal acquaintance with you. Hope to retain your goodwill in spite of our compulsory business separation." (*Complete Writings of Walt Whitman,* 1902, VIII, 299; the original is in the Library of Congress.)
1545. As with "The Prairies in Poetry" (see entry for 4 May 1882 and footnote 1529), "Carlyle from American Points of View" was rejected by *The North American Review* and went into *Specimen Days:* see *Prose Works 1892,* I, 254–262.
1546. Letter lost; Arnold was the binder of the 1876 *Leaves* who was to bind the books for Whitman to sell presumably as his own publisher, to be replaced by Rees Welsh in July.
1547. Letter: *The Correspondence of Walt Whitman,* III, 280. But see below, 8 June 1882, Whitman ordering 1000 copies printed of the 1881 *Leaves,* then the order "counter-manded" — for fear of legal action?
1548. Letter to Whitelaw Reid, New York *Tribune* in *The Correspondence of Walt Whitman,* III, 281; other letters lost.

– circ to Chs. W. Prynne   Springfield Rep – [1551]

– Mem's (N A Rev) to Dr Bucke[1552]

Mem to Dick Labar[1553]

26   Sent T E Callicot, Daily Times office Albany[1554]
                              [in blue pencil:]
            a copy – $3 due   paid

                                                [in blue pencil,
31   Sent L F deH Noble Elizabethtown N Y a set $10   sideways:]   paid [1555]
                                          [in blue pencil:]
       "   D[B] C Bass Rock Run Alabama one Vol   paid

June 8 – sent corrections to Rand & Avery
                              [in red ink:]
       – ordered 1000 copies printed   countermanded [1556]

10   sent letter to Dr Bucke, ab't "motif" of his book
            & a'bt printing in Phila[1557]

11   sent two copies new L of G to Fairman Rogers
                         [in blue pencil:]
            Newport R I –   paid $10 – recd

12   sent new L of G to F B Sanborn with "thanks & love" [1558]

1549. Crosby Stuart Noyes was an old friend and Washington *Evening Star* editor.
1550. The Camden *Daily Post,* 22 May 1882, reprinted the Philadelphia *Press* editorial defense of Whitman; see the list in *The Correspondence of Walt Whitman,* III, 281n, of those for and those against Whitman.
1551. "The Prurient Prudes and 'Leaves of Grass' " appeared in the Springfield *Republican,* 23 May 1882, on the same day a letter from Dr Bucke appeared; see Whitman's letter to O'Connor, 25 May 1882, in *The Correspondence of Walt Whitman,* III, 282–284.
1552. "Mem's" must refer to Whitman's piece, "A Memorandum at a Venture," in the June 1882 *North American Review* (see footnote 1521, above).
1553. The same piece (footnote 1552) went to Whitman's friend on the Philadelphia *Public Ledger.*
1554. Letter: *The Correspondence of Walt Whitman,* III, 284.
1555. Letter of 25 May 1882: *The Correspondence of Walt Whitman,* III, 282; letter of 31 May 1882: *ibid.,* III, 288.
1556. See footnote 1547.
1557. Rees Welsh & Co. had written to Whitman, 5 June 1882, offering to print *Leaves of Grass,* and he had suggested the Philadelphia firm also publish Dr Bucke's book on Whitman and *Specimen Days:* see Whitman's letter to Rees Welsh & Co., 17 June 1882, in *The Correspondence of Walt Whitman,* III, 291; the company's letter to Whitman is in the University of Pennsylvania.
1558. See footnote 1337 on Sanborn taking Whitman to visit Emerson in Concord on 17 September 1881.

[in blue pencil:]

"   "   Wm O'Connor ‾rec'd [1559]

"   "   Dr Bucke

Nautical Alm. office, Navy Dep't

20   sent new L of G to Prof: Loomis ∧Wash'n – $3 due   paid [1560]

[last word in red ink]

---

anniversary "Democrat" to Mrs Stafford   rec'd

---

26 sent George Chainey, Boston, new L of G [1561]

[226]

Miller (shirts &c) 129 s⊗ 10th

  Williams, engraver
    528 Walnut St
    558 Benson

John Smith, 2015 Winter st.

Mr & Mrs Dean (Walter's parents)
    756 Mt Vernon st.

G   F   Brinton   1531 Spring Garden St   Phila

---

wire beds – 829 no. 10th st.   my Welsh friend
                              J R Owens
    – (the flat style 1138 Market st)

Benj: R Tucker, box 3366 Boston

Hannah – 21 Pearl street   Burlington Vt

Wm Walker, printer, brings the proofs[1562]

1559. Whitman wrote (mainly) long letters to William Douglas O'Connor on 25, 28 and 30 May, 18, 22, 25 and 28 June 1882, none of which does Whitman mention in the *Daybook*: they are all in *The Correspondence of Walt Whitman*, III, 282–284, 285–286, 286–288, 291–292, 293, 293–294, 294–295. Similarly for the rest of 1882.

1560. Elias Loomis (1811–1889), astronomer, Yale professor, is mentioned in O'Connor's letter to Whitman, 19 June 1882: see Horace Traubel, *With Walt Whitman in Camden*, I, 312–314.

1561. See footnote 1543.

1562. Of the nine listed here on this all-purpose left-hand page of the *Daybook*, two, Hannah [Heyde], Whitman's sister, and Benjamin R. Tucker, can be identified beyond the information Whitman gives. For Tucker, translator, editor, and proposed publisher of *Leaves of Grass*, see *The Correspondence of Walt Whitman*, III, 348n–349n.

[227]

June, 1882 –

28th – Agreement with Rees Welsh & Co: 23 South 9th
    st: Phila: to publish <u>Leaves of Grass</u> and
    <u>Specimen Days</u> (35[cts] royalty)[1563]

sent Talcott Williams (Phil Press) author's L of G.[1564]

three days down at Glendale, 3[d], 4th, 5th July

July 15 sent P D Beckwith author's L of G, Dowagiac
                    [in blue pencil:]
      Michigan, $3 \ due paid – recd

19 – made a start on "Specimen Days" – left
    the first copy at Sherman & Co's., Printing
    office, cor: 7th & Cherry, Phila: [1565]

      first
    The ∧ Phila ed'n, (Rees Welsh & Co.) of
    1000 copies L of G. ready 18th – morning
    of 20th all exhausted = not a copy left [1566]

23[d] – read first pages proof "Specimen Days"

24 – paid Rand & Avery $13.75 [1567]

paid W. V. Montgomery $16 for Ed [1568]

Sent Megargee (Phil Press) author's ed'n L. of G.[1569]

1563. See Whitman's letter to Rees Welsh & Co., 20 June 1882, in *The Correspondence of Walt Whitman*, III, 292.

1564. See footnote 277; in his letter to O'Connor, 9 July 1882, Whitman called Williams "an ardent friend" — see *The Correspondence of Walt Whitman*, III, 297.

1565. This prose work is first mentioned as *Specimen Days & Thoughts* in Whitman's letter of 21 March 1882 to James R. Osgood & Company — see *The Correspondence of Walt Whitman*, III, 269 — as "about got into shape," so by "made a start" Whitman means in printing the book, not writing it; he called Sherman's "the best printing office in Philadelphia" (*ibid.,* III, 296); and though type-setting began at once, the book was not published until 1 October 1882 (see entry below).

1566. *Leaves of Grass* finally (after threats) having been declared mailable by Judge Charles A. Ray — see *The Correspondence of Walt Whitman*, III, 297n — there was no trouble with authorities, though discussion continued in newspapers.

1567. This amount to the Boston printers was for corrections they had made (see entry above for 8 June 1882).

1568. See footnotes 1177 and 1519.

1569. Usually when there is no notation that an amount is "due" and then followed by "paid" with the "due" crossed out, it means that Whitman presented *Leaves of Grass* to the recipient, in this case to someone on the Philadelphia *Press,* either because he had written something favorable or at the suggestion of Talcott Williams, also on the *Press* then.

Sent L of G to Rev: J. R. Dillon 1426 Warnock st.

[in blue pencil:]

Phil. St Mulachy's Ch. paid

Aug: 18 – sent W J Linton $18.50 for printing

head [1570]

[two words in red ink:]

Frank Patterson[1571] paid me $5, on the boat – owes $3

paid
all

Aug 27   paid James Arnold $60 [1572]

---

[228]

[On letterhead of Thomas Donaldson, agent Smithsonian Institution, No. 326
~~132~~ N. 40th St., Philadelphia, seven lines in red ink:]

my stout, gentlemanly friend, free talker, Baring street [1573]

— tells me (Oct. 10 '82

Baring st car front) so

much ab't

Fechter

– his draft

&c

[On card of J. Page Hopps, Lea Hurst, Stoneygate Road, Leicester, in red ink:]

call'd Sept: '82 [1574]

1570. William J. Linton was a wood-engraver: see footnote 39. This money was for an engraving of Whitman in the Author's Edition of *Leaves of Grass* (Camden, 1882), opp. p. 296; less than 100 copies of the edition were printed.

1571. Frank Patterson of the Camden *County Courier?*

1572. For binding copies of *Leaves of Grass.*

1573. Thomas Donaldson, a Philadelphia lawyer and author of *Walt Whitman, the Man* (1896), met Whitman on 10 October 1882, as seen here; and the poet dined with the Donaldsons on 4 December 1883 (see entry below). Donaldson got annual ferry passes for Whitman, offered him a rent-free house in Philadelphia (which was declined), was his host from time to time at his own home, organized the move in 1885 to obtain the horse and buggy for the poet, and served him in many ways (he was also a pallbearer at Whitman's funeral). Donaldson's book, full of first-hand details unavailable elsewhere on Whitman as his friend knew him, has little criticism of the poetry but does clearly evaluate his standing in 1896. Many do not read Whitman, Donaldson said, but some do: "Still he is a factor, in whatever light you look at him. Will he be in the future?" Not a disciple in the passionate sense of Dr Bucke, Harned, O'Connor, and Traubel — though he is mentioned about thirty times in the first five volumes of *With Walt Whitman in Camden* — Donaldson's final judgment is that if *Leaves of Grass* is to live for others beside "thinkers or expounders, or as a curiosity, the present [1896] public opinion of him must essentially change" — *Walt Whitman, the Man*, p. 114. See also Charles B. Willard, *Whitman's American Fame* (Providence, Rhode Island, 1950), pp. 50–51; and footnote 2389, below.

1574. See footnote 988.

Fitzgerald Molloy, 34 Woburn Place,
    Tavistock Square, London W C
author of the friendly article in "Modern Thought" '82 [1575]   [line in red ink]

Tasker Lay   416 West [1576]

Mr C Hine 432 Chapel st   New Haven[1577]
        Sent letter Nov. 3 '82   [in red ink]

Nov. 7. Mr Stowell, shoes – (business for Mrs. Alcott)
   — met on the ferry – talk about "John Darby" (Dr.
   Garrison.) [1578]

Alfred Tennyson, 86 Eaton Square S W
                   London
   (March '82) Farringford, Freshwater
           Isle of Wight [1579]

---

                 av:
Karl Knortz[1580] cor Morris   & 155th St   540
                          E 115th
                New York City   St

Robert Burroughs   boy 16, in notion store

1575. Fitzgerald Molloy, "Walt Whitman," *Modern Thought,* IV (1 September 1882), 319–326.

1576. See footnote 1152; Tasker Lay, whom Whitman met in 1881, died in March 1884; Whitman gave his grandfather, Alfred Lay, money for the rent on the house at 328 Mickle in the Spring of 1884 — see *The Correspondence of Walt Whitman,* III, 366n, and *Daybook* entries below for March 1884.

1577. See footnote 612 for Mrs Charles Hine, wife of the artist who painted Whitman's portrait; see also *The Correspondence of Walt Whitman,* III, 368n, 382n, 384n; and Horace Traubel, *With Walt Whitman in Camden,* III, 328–331, on John H. Johnston's purchase of the portrait for Whitman. As Hine died in 1871, this Mr C Hine must be his son; the letter of 3 November 1882 is lost.

1578. "John Darby" (Dr Garrison) not identified; this Darby might be the founder of the English religious group, though this does not seem to fit here.

1579. I cannot discover Tennyson's relationship to March 1882 and Whitman.

1580. Karl Knortz (1841–1918), who came to America from Prussia in 1863, wrote in New York on German-American affairs, taught German in Evansville, Indiana, 1892–1905, and was the author of "Walt Whitman," *Sonntagsblatt der New Yorker Staats-Zeitung,* 17 December 1882; *Walt Whitman* (New York, 1886), translated from the German by Alfred Forman and Richard Maurice Bucke for *In Re Walt Whitman* (Philadelphia, 1893), 215–230, and reprinted, with translations into German of *Leaves of Grass* (Leipzig, 1899); and *Walt Whitman und seine Nachahmer* [Carpenter, Traubel, Crosby] Leipzig, 1911). Whitman's eighteen letters to Knortz are in *The Correspondence of Walt Whitman,* III, 288–289, *et passim,* IV, 31–32, *et passim;* Knortz to Whitman, 14 September 1883, is in the Yale University Library.

Market st. Phila: lives in West
— on the boat Nov 9 [1581]

[On slip, not in WW's hand, from letter:]
Wm R Wood Warsaw Richmond & Co
dont forget paper = Love Pa [?]

~~W R W~~ [1582]

Work's office J H Johnson
121 So: 3d Phila:

[229]

1882 – Sept. 8 – sent to Tribune, N. Y. Times, Phil Press
Springfield Rep. N Y World [1583]
rec'd [in red ink]
Sept. 9 – Sent Rolleston roll pictures &c (Dresden Saxony) [1584]

---

15 sent L of G to Fitzgerald Molloy, care Editor
"Modern Thought," office of James ~~Tavistock~~
Wade, 18 Tavistock street, Covent Garden,
[two lines in red ink:]
W C – London England rec'd – & letter of thanks [1585]
(dated Oct 5) sent me

Sept 30 – Oct 1, 2, 3, — down at Glendale [1586]

1581. One more instance of Whitman recording a young man's name, age, and personal data in his *Daybook*.

1582. William R. Wood was among the numerous acquaintances Whitman wrote to on his trip to St Louis and the West: his letter of 31 October 1879 to Wood in Camden (see footnote 735) is lost.

1583. Of the five newspapers to which Whitman sent letters about *Specimen Days* — see *The Correspondence of Walt Whitman,* III, 304 — only the Springfield *Republican* on 10 September 1882 printed Whitman's announcement and two columns of excerpts, and the New York *World* printed a brief note.

1584. T. W. H. Rolleston had written Whitman on 14 August 1882, asking for "a few of your portraits, especially of the shirt-sleeves one," which was used in the first (1855) *Leaves of Grass* and in the second, sixth and seventh editions. See Horst Frenz, *Whitman and Rolleston: A Correspondence* (Bloomington, Indiana, 1951), pp. 64-66. Whitman's two post cards to Rolleston are lost — see Rolleston's reply, 24 September 1882, *ibid.,* pp. 67-68.

1585. See footnote 1575: Whitman sent *Leaves of Grass* in thanks for Molloy's article, which Whitman sent to O'Connor on 17 September 1882, and asked him to send it to Dr Bucke. See *The Correspondence of Walt Whitman,* III, 305. The letters to and from Molloy are lost.

1586. See Whitman's letter to Mrs Susan Stafford, 24 September 1882, in *The Correspondence of Walt Whitman,* III, 306-307, saying he was delayed in visiting the Staffords because of *Specimen Days* matters at Rees Welsh & Co. For some brief notes on this visit, see "Country Days and Nights," from *November Boughs* in *Prose Works 1892,* II, 581.

[two lines in red ink:]

26 Sept: D. McK.[1587] paid 300.   (270) printing <u>Specimen</u>

<u>Days</u>[1588]

_____

"S<u>pecimen D</u>ays" done – out to-morrow Oct. 1 '82

_____

[five lines in red ink:]

27 – paid Milliette $2 (pays in full to date)   rec'd $8.50

_____   from McKay

300 more altogether   in full for

Oct 5 & 4 – McKay paid me ∧ (600 – (540)   Milliette's

bill

_____

sent two copies   [in red ink]

"   5   Sent Mrs Gilchrist "Specimen Days"   [in red ink:]

recd   paid [1589]

_____

Oct 6 – sent "Specimen Days" to Hannah,   [in red ink:]   recd

Mary, & to Hattie & Jessie[1590]

"   9   sent Dr Bucke gilt-top "Specimen Days" [1591]

[in red ink:]   rec'd

_____

11   sent Isabella O Ford, Adel Grange, Leeds, Eng:

[in red ink:]   recd   <u>paid</u> [1592]

the two Vols. L of G and S D – £1 due

_____

10th Evn'g – J H Johnston call'd –with Australian friend [1593]

1587.   David McKay was the successor to Rees Welsh as Whitman's publisher until long after the poet's death in 1892; his papers, now in the University of Pennsylvania, show that Whitman received $1,091.30 in royalties for 3,118 copies of *Leaves* sold as of 1 December 1882. See *The Correspondence of Walt Whitman,* III, 310n.

1588.   Only 1,000 copies were printed, 925 sold, and Whitman's royalty was $203.50.

1589.   Whitman had written Mrs Anne Gilchrist on 22 July, 13 and 27 August 1882, and again on 8 October 1882, after he sent *Specimen Days*: see *The Correspondence of Walt Whitman,* III, 298–299, 302, 302–303, 309–310.

1590.   These copies went, of course, to Whitman's two sisters Hannah Heyde and Mary Van Nostrand, and his two nieces in St Louis.

1591.   See the letter from Dr R. M. Bucke, 11 October 1882, in the Feinberg Collection. Whitman's letter of 9 October 1882 is lost. Whitman also sent Sylvester Baxter, of the Boston *Daily Herald,* a paper-bound copy and a cloth-bound *Specimen Days,* along with a letter and a note on the book, which Baxter incorporated into his notice on *Specimen Days* in the *Herald* on 15 October 1882. See *The Correspondence of Walt Whitman,* III, 308–309.

1592.   Isabella Ford, her sister Elizabeth, and their friend Edward Carpenter, sent Whitman a gift of £50 in September 1885, and additional money in May 1886 and July 1887 (see entries, below, and *The Correspondence of Walt Whitman,* III, 400, 402).

1593.   The Australian friend of the New York jewelry merchant, according to Edwin Haviland Miller (*The Correspondence of Walt Whitman,* III, 311n), was John W. Tilton.

[in red ink:]   [in red ink:]

recd   recd

11   sent J H J.   L of G for Mr Tilton   and S D for Alma[1594]

[in red ink:]   recd   [four lines in red ink:]

13   sent S. D. to Rudolf Schmidt [1595]   sent

recd   postal

"   "   "   T W H Rolleston[1596]   cards

also

---

14   sent Ida Johnston "Specimen Days"   recd [1597]   [last work in red ink]

&c

17, 18, 19, 20 to 24, '5, '6, '7, ~~8~~   sick – liver – Dr Benjamin[1598]

---

24 – lent S S.   50 [1599]   [SS. in red ink]

[230]

J L Landis, representative of "Hill's Album"
22 North 10th Street   Phila

Henry Whitall, 1317 Brown St   Phila

[On slip, not in WW's hand: It is Charles Bright / Stanbrook / Cavendish
St / Stanmore / Sydney / Australia.] [In red ink:]

Liberal

newspaper office

New South Wales

1594. This copy of *Leaves of Grass* which Whitman sent to John H. Johnston was for his Australian friend, John W. Tilton, and *Specimen Days* was for Mrs J.H. (Alma) Johnston.

1595. See two letters to Rudolf Schmidt, Whitman's Copenhagen translator and friend, 8 and 13 October 1882, in *The Correspondence of Walt Whitman,* III, 310–311; and Schmidt's letter, 3 November 1882, in the Feinberg Collection.

1596. Post card to Rolleston lost; see footnote 1584. Rolleston's reply to Whitman, 29 October 1882, from Dresden, is in Horst Frenz, *Whitman and Rolleston: A Correspondence* (Bloomington, Indiana, 1951), pp. 69–70.

1597. Ida Johnston was the daughter of Colonel John R. Johnston of Camden, Whitman's artist friend.

1598. During Whitman's 12-day illness, which he described briefly in his letter of 25 October 1882 to William Douglas O'Connor — *The Correspondence of Walt Whitman,* III, 311 — he was attended by Dr Dowling Benjamin; a newspaper report called it Bright's disease and said he might not recover. See entries below about his recovery, and O'Connor's letter of 27 October 1882 (in Horace Traubel, *With Walt Whitman in Camden,* IV, 322–323) on hearing that Whitman was dying.

1599. Whitman here lends $50 to Mrs Susan Stafford, to whom he felt very kindly disposed and whose home in Glendale he frequently visited; her son Harry was a special favorite of Whitman's during this period.

John Newton Johnston[1600]   Mid   p. o.
Came to Camden ⎱   Marshall County   Alabama
  May & June '87 ⎰

Mrs: Ann Nash

[Slip, not in WW's hand:
Dr. I. Wealty-Gibson; and
printed: The Editor/Modern Thought/18, Tavistock St./Covent Garden,
W.C./.][1601]

[231]

Oct: 1882 – 24 – last five days laid by sick, sick – (no liver action)[1602]

---

26 – note to Chas S King & Co: Frisco, Beaver Co: Utah[1603]

~~Sept 8 — sent to Tribune, N Y Times, Phil Press~~

28 (Saturday) Beginning to be better – go out a little

  – sent tel: to Jeff[1604] – saw David McKay on Federal
  st. come over to see me,   two letters from Wm O'Connor[1605]

---

30   Am slowly getting better – sick two weeks –

  postal to Mrs Gilchrist[1606]

  Call from May Johnston and   Loag[1607]

---

  new suit   iron-grey – overcoat &c

1600. John Newton Johnson of Mid, Alabama (see footnote 9a), Whitman's colorful friend, whose visit is recorded here on a left-hand page of the *Daybook,* five years out of chronology (see entry below for 18–20 May 1887).
1601. This was the periodical, *Modern Thought,* in which Fitzgerald Molloy published his favorable article about Whitman (see footnote 1575).
1602. See footnote 1598.
1603. Letter lost.
1604. See Jefferson Whitman's letter, 29 October 1882, in the Feinberg Collection.
1605. See footnote 1598; these two letters and those of 18 and 19 December 1882, among many others, are in the Feinberg Collection. Whitman wrote O'Connor seven times before the end of 1882, a long letter on 12 November 1882: see *The Correspondence of Walt Whitman,* III, 311, 312, 313, 313–314, 318–319, 319–320, 321. Why were these not recorded in the *Daybook?*
1606. Letter: *The Correspondence of Walt Whitman,* III, 312.
1607. May Johnston was the daughter of the New York jewel merchant and manufacturer, John H. Johnston; Samuel Loag was a Philadelphia friend of theirs (see *The Bookman,* XLVI, 1917, 412).

Nov:

2   Percy Ives returned [1608]

6 – to-day, well as usual before sickness[1609]

"   sent W Hale White   Park Hill   Carshalton, Surrey[1610]
                                    [in red ink:]
        Eng. Gilt top S. D. $3 due   recd – paid

9   Sold the lot 460 Royden st: $525 — [1611]

"Walt Whitman's Illness" in "Progress"

sent the above (& "Illness & Recovery" in <u>Post</u>) to
many friends literary & personal [1612]

the Ezra Heywood arrest, Boston

                        with Heywood's letter[1613]
12 – sent quite long letter to O'Connor ʌ – Trelawny
                                            slip

papers to John Burroughs (Carlyle slip London Times[1614]
                                            good

      Nov
3ᵈ   paid Mrs Hassan $16 for Ed [1615] – $14 for suit clothes

1608.   See footnotes 1107, 1011, and 1493.
1609.   See entries, above, for 17–28 October, "Oct: 1882," and 30 October 1882.
1610.   William Hale White (1831–1913), an Englishman who wrote novels under the
pen name of Mark Rutherford, was the author of "The Genius of Walt Whitman," *Secular
Review*, 20 March 1880.
1611.   Whitman had bought this lot years before, intending to build a small house on it
but never did. See Gay Wilson Allen, *The Solitary Singer*, p. 515.
1612.   That two newspapers, the Philadelphia *Progress* (which had been published by
Whitman's good friend, Colonel John W. Forney) and the Camden *Daily Post*, could write
news stories merely about Whitman's illness is an indication of their regard for him in 1882.
1613.   Ezra H. Heywood (1829–1893), radical and free-love advocate, was arrested for
printing Whitman's "To a Common Prostitute" and "A Woman Waits for Me" in *The Word*
and mailing the magazine; Heywood's letter was "An Open Letter to Walt Whitman," a broad-
side distributed by *The Word*. A copy of this printed letter is in the Feinberg Collection;
Whitman's letter to W. D. O'Connor, 12 November, printed in *The Correspondence of Walt
Whitman*, III, 313–316, is in the Berg Collection, New York Public Library, with Whitman's
notation on Heywood's letter. By "Trelawny slip," Whitman refers to "Talks with Trelawny,"
in which Trelawny is quoted on *Leaves of Grass*, in *The Truth Seeker*, 4 November 1882, a
copy of which Whitman sent in the same O'Connor letter, now in the Berg Collection; see
The Correspondence of Walt Whitman, III, 314n.
1614.   This may well have been a notice in *The Times* of J. A. Froude's *Thomas Carlyle:
A History of the First Forty Years of His Life, 1795–1835*, published in 1882 in two volumes by
Longmans; Whitman called it "a precious book" in his letter to Franklin B. Sanborn, *The
Correspondence of Walt Whitman*, III, 316.
1615.   Mrs Hassan most likely was associated with W. V. Montgomery, to whom Whitman
was sending money for his brother Edward's board.

12   Dick Labar[1616] here – sent Mr Childs Specimen Days[1617]

13   dinner in Phila: with J H Johnston and Sam Loag[1618]

David McKay pays me 100 (94) [1619]

14, 15   sent Karl Knortz, books & papers – returned – [1620]
       "   "   "   Specimen Days

[232]

                   with G B Raum 1226 F St   Washington   [line in red ink]
Charles W Eldridge, ~~Internal Revenue Office~~   N W
room 55   28 School Street   Boston[1621]

R Pearsall Smith   4653 Germantown Av: [1622]

[On slip, printed, of Mark A. McGrillis, Ferry Agent, Camden & Philadelphia
Steamboat Ferry Co., Phila.:] [1623]

bo't Specimen Days
   Dec. '82

Jan 2,   '83 – Matt Biggs – new young man at Test's

1616. Whitman's friend on the Philadelphia *Public Ledger*.
1617. Josiah Child was handling Whitman's dealings with British publishers; in America, about this time, David McKay formally bought out Rees Welsh and became Whitman's publisher (see footnote 1587), as Whitman explained to W. D. O'Connor: see *The Correspondence of Walt Whitman*, III, 313–314.
1618. The Johnstons, from New York City, were apparently visiting Samuel Loag, as May Johnston, their daughter, and Loag called on Whitman on 30 October 1882 (see entry above).
1619. The amount of money in parentheses is apparently the sum Whitman received (see entries for 27 September and 5 October 1882, above), McKay retaining 6 per cent as his fee in the transaction.
1620. See footnote 1580.
1621. See footnote 116; Eldridge was Whitman's old friend from 1860 days of Thayer & Eldridge, and now a U.S. government employee.
1622. This is the first mention in the *Daybook* of R. Pearsall Smith (1827–1899), Quaker, connected with Whitall-Tatum Company in Milville, New Jersey, through his wife, Hannah Whitall Smith (1832–1911); father of Logan Pearsall Smith (1865–1946), the best known member of the family, Alys (1867–1951), the first wife of Bertrand Russell, and Mary (1864–1945), who became Mrs Bernard Berenson; Robert Pearsall Smith's brother was Lloyd (1822–1886), publisher and librarian. The full story of this remarkable family, all of whom except Hannah became good friends of Whitman's, is told in Robert Allerton Parker's *The Transatlantic Smiths* (New York, 1959); see also additional material in William White, "Mary Whitall Smith's Letters to Walt Whitman," *Smith Alumnae Quarterly*, XLIX (Winter 1958), 86–88. See entry below for 23–24–25 December 1882.
1623. McGrillis perhaps had something to do with Whitman's annual pass on the ferries.

(see circular)   [in red ink]
Chas. H. Farnam, p o box 91   New Haven   Conn[1624]
[three words and date in red ink:]
wrote to him   sent slips, genealogical pages – S D
     Jan 3 '83

Roth & Co.   Kindling Wood factory
     Cor 7th st & Kaign av

[On card, printed, of James W. Callahan, two lines in red ink:]
     W J RR office   foot of
     Market St: Phila

Edward P Mitchell   N Y Sun

Howard Paul Rambo, new driver Market st.   Jan 31

G. C. Macaulay Rugby, England
     recd   S D – sent Bible as Poetry[1625]

May 15 xx – 13 – '83 – Tom Jaggar, age 21 – blacksmith
     ————————   car   Camden
May 16 '83 – Frank Wagner, age 26, driver Market st

Walter Jones   May 18, '83 (on the ferry – high hat) is at R P
     Smith's

[233]

1882 – Nov: 18 to 27ᵗʰ inc.   down at Glendale, 9 days[1626]

                              1300 see next leaf
                                              back[1627]
Dec. 1.   David McKay pays me 570.78 – (1230.78 altogether)

    1624. Whitman's letters to Charles H. Farnam, 22 December 1881 and 3 June 1883, are both lost.
    1625. Among this curious melange of a kindling wood factory, a railroad official, a newspaperman, a blacksmith, two car drivers, and a man named Jones whom Whitman met at Robert Pearsall Smith's, one also finds G. C. Macaulay, whose "Walt Whitman," a review of *Leaves of Grass,* was in *The Nineteenth Century,* XII (December 1882), 903–918. Whitman asked Josiah Child, on 17 December 1882, to send Macaulay a copy of *Specimen Days:* see *The Correspondence of Walt Whitman,* III, 319. Whitman's essay "The Bible as Poetry" appeared in *The Critic,* III (3 February 1883), 39–40; see *Prose Works 1892,* II, 545–549.
    1626. Whitman's visit "in the Jersey wood" — his phrase for the times he spent with the Stafford family.
    1627. This was, financially, one of Whitman's successful years in book sales: see entries for 24 September, 5 October, 13 November 1882, above.

6 saw the transit of Venus over the Sun,
  11 a. m. through a piece of smoked glass,
  furnished me by a boy at the Camden ferry[1628]

———————————————————————

                              rec'd   with
10 Sent Rolleston full set loose leaves L of G. postal
——————————————————————————⌒ card [1629]
                              afterwards
16 – "Robert Burns" in <u>Critic</u> – $15 – paid N A Rev: in
                                          1886 [1630]

———————————————————————

17 – Sent special "Specimen Days" to Josiah Child ⎫ [in red ink:]
      ordinary   "   "   G C Macaulay ⎬ recd [1631]
    " Robert Burns" to O'Connor[1632]

18 – sent gilt-top L of G to L O Bliss Iowa Falls[1633]
                          recd [in red ink]
———————————————⌒ Iowa – paid
  sent "Robert Burns" in Critic
      also "Bible as Poetry" [1634]
  to Dowden   and   Rolleston – R Schmidt [1635]

———————————————————————

Karl Knortz's criticism N Y Staats-Zeitung Son-
    Tagsblatt Dec 17, 1882 – sent him my portrait [1636]
                          rec'd –

———————————————————————

          recd   recd   [two words in red ink]
20 – Sent Hannah $10 – Mary 10 – Ans. gloves[1637]

———————————————————————

1628. I can find nothing in Whitman's poetry or his prose referring to this "transit of Venus over the Sun" on 6 December 1882.

1629. See *The Correspondence of Walt Whitman*, III, 318.

1630. "Robert Burns," *The Critic*, II (16 December 1882), 337; revised and expanded as "Robert Burns as Poet and Person" for *The North American Review*, CXLIII (November 1886), 427–435, revised slightly in *Democratic Vistas and Other Papers* (London, 1888); see *Prose Works 1892*, II, 558–568.

1631. See footnote 1625.

1632. Letter: *The Correspondence of Walt Whitman*, III, 319–320.

1633. L. O. Bliss may be the person to whom Whitman wrote on 28 November 1882, though the letter deals only with an order of the 1882 *Leaves of Grass*: see *The Correspondence of Walt Whitman*, III, 317.

1634. For "Robert Burns" see footnote 1630; for "The Bible as Poetry" see the end of footnote 1625.

1635. If letters accompanied these two essays Whitman sent Edward Dowden (see footnote 9), T. W. H. Rolleston (see footnote 50), and Rudolf Schmidt (see beginning of footnote 81), they are now lost.

1636. See footnote 1580.

1637. Hannah Heyde and Mary Van Nostrand were Whitman's sisters; "Ans." refers to Ansel Van Nostrand, Mary's husband.

23 – 24 – 25 – Pleasant time at R. Pearsall
     Smith's and   his wife Mrs Hannah W Smith
     (& dear daughter Mary) at 4653 German-
     town avenue . . . . the fine, long, spirited
     drives along the Wissahickon, the rocks
     and banks, the hemlocks, Indian Rock —
     – Miss Willard, Miss Kate Sanborn, Lloyd
     Smith (R P's brother) the librarian[1638]

[234]

Jeff   2437 Second Carondelet Av: (2437)[1639]   [line in red ink]

Wilson & McCormick
     St Vincent street
          Glasgow   Scotland [1640]

Miss Mary W Smith
     Smith College
          Northampton   Mass:[1641]

"picture frames &c made while you wait"
     Forsyth & Bros: 54 and 141 North 2ᵈ Phila

---

513 So Broadway for sale   [five lines in red ink:]
[From corner of envelope, printed:]   Feb. 26 '83
     R. P. Smith [not WW's hand]   the 200 shares
Return to ~~Whitall, Tatum & Co.~~   Sierra Grande stock
     410 Race Street. — Lock-box P.   Mines at Lake Valley
     Philadelphia, Pa.   New Mexico[1642]
If not delivered within 10 days.

1638.   See footnote 1622. This first entry (apart from "R Pearsall Smith 4653 Germantown
Av:" on the opposite page, made at the same time) about the Smith family does not, of course,
tell us very much — in keeping with the nature of the entries in the *Daybook*. The full story,
though it is slightly misleading, is in Logan Pearsall Smith's "Knowing Walt Whitman,"
Atlantic Monthly, CLX (November 1937), 568–572, reprinted in his *Unforgotten Years* (Boston,
1939), pp. 92–108; but see William White, "Logan Pearsall Smith on Walt Whitman: A
Correction and Some Unpublished Letters," *Walt Whitman Review*, IV (June 1958), 87–90.
     1639.   Whitman wrote the St Louis address of his brother Jeff because Jeff was visiting
him and George at the time, January 1883.
     1640.   This was the name and address of British publishers of *Specimen Days*: see *The
Correspondence of Walt Whitman*, III, 323, 329, 329n.
     1641.   Mary Whitall Smith was of course the student at Smith College and daughter of
Robert Pearsall Smith and the one who insisted on going to visit Whitman in Camden, thus
beginning the long friendship: see footnotes 1622 and 1638.
     1642.   These two addresses, R. P. Smith's and Sierra Grande Mines's, are not unrelated,

Montgomery Stafford   714 King St   Wilmington
Del [1643]

[Printed:] F. Paxson & Co. 312 Stock Exchange Place, Philadelphia	[two lines in pencil:] J E Kelly 336 E 79th St artist New York [1644]
[Printed:] Phila. [WW's hand] F. Ehrlich, Bookseller and Importer, 413 Vine Street	Dr W F Channing [1645] No 98 Congdon St. Providence March 14'83 box 393 R I Pasadena Los Angeles County California

[Printed:]
American Bank Note Company
    53 Broadway, N.Y.
    P.O. Box 781.
D L Proudfit
    [WW's hand] [1646]

Rev L C Baker

[Printed:] The Boston Herald, 255 Washington St. Boston.	[Printed:] S. Weir Mitchell, M.D. [1647] 1524 Walnut St. Philadelphia.

[In WW's hand:]
Charles McFettridge
young conductor
car 28 – Market st.
May 19 '83

for Smith (see footnotes 1622 and 1638) gave Whitman the 200 shares of stock simply as a wealthy man's gesture of good will toward the poet, hoping it would bring him money from dividends; unfortunately, it did not work out that way, and the stock — after paying a few dividends — became worthless. See William White, "Walt Whitman and the Sierra Grande Mining Company," *New Mexico Historical Review*, XLIV (July 1969), 223–230.

1643. Montgomery Stafford, brother-in-law of Mrs Susan Stafford, visited Whitman in July 1883; he most likely was working in Wilmington at this time.

1644. James Edward Kelly (1855–1933), "sculptor of American history," was mentioned in a letter, dated 6 March 1883, to Joseph M. Stoddart, in which Whitman agreed to sit for him: see *The Correspondence of Walt Whitman*, III, 329–330.

1645. Dr William F. Channing (1820–1901), brother-in-law of W. D. O'Connor and a physician who conducted scientific experiments; Ellen O'Connor visited him in Providence, as did Whitman in 1868 (see *The Correspondence of Walt Whitman,* I, 241n, II, 60–66); in November 1882, Dr Channing asked Whitman to lecture in Boston, which he declined to do and said he would do nothing "to identify myself specially with free love" (see *ibid.,* III, 315); O'Connor was with the Channings in March 1883 — hence the Providence address here.

1646. Daniel L. Proudfit's letter, 14 March 1883, ordering books from Whitman, is in the Feinberg Collection; see entry below for 16 March 1883.

Frank – Lou's newsboy
    Market St Phila
        fine eyes[1648]

[235]

                        w
Dec. 26, '82 – Sent Gen: Sevell   L of G and S D .[1649]

        30 &
1883 –   Dec 31 and Jan 1 – 2 – at R P Smith's
    again, 4653 Germantown av – the eve-
    nings with Mary, Alice, Loyd and the others[1650]
    – my walks along Coulter street and in
    the Quaker grave yard

                            rec'd
Jan 23   sent L of G & S D to D M Zimmerman[1651]

                        rec'd
27.   returned $100 to John Burroughs – rec'd letter &
                                        wrote
        (Colonnade, 35 Lafayette Place,N Y)   one in
                                        answer[1652]

31   wrote letters to Mrs Stafford & to Harry[1653]

    Dr B's MS. sent over by McKay[1654]

Feb 7 – John Burroughs in Phila[1655]

1647. See middle of footnote 76.
1648. Another of the frequent entries, with brief comments, on young men Whitman meets or sees.
1649. See middle of footnote 76; Whitman most likely met General William J. Sewell in Washington during or just after the Civil War.
1650. The second of what were to be numerous visits with the Robert Pearsall Smith family in Philadelphia (see footnotes 1622 and 1638).
1651. See middle of footnote 76; Zimmerman was with the Camden & Atlantic Railroad.
1652. Both letters lost.
1653. Letter to Mrs Susan Stafford in *The Correspondence of Walt Whitman*, III, 323–324; to Harry Stafford, III, 322–323.
1654. Dr Richard Maurice Bucke's *Walt Whitman* (copyright recorded 18 April 1883) was published 20 June 1883 (see entry below for that date) by David McKay; the agreement between Dr Bucke and McKay, written entirely by Walt Whitman, signed by Dr Bucke and McKay, and witnessed by Whitman; endorsement on the verso of p. 2 reads: "Agreement Richard Maurice Bucke, David McKay. Copies interchanged. Feb. 19th 1883." MS now in the Feinberg Collection.
1655. See letter, 9 February 1883, in *The Correspondence of Walt Whitman*, III, 324–325.

recd
Feb. 8   Sent Dr B. back the $200 borrowed last fall[1656]

sent (through Gilders) "Bible as Poetry" to Mrs Gilchrist[1657]
(probably rec'd
Dowden, Rolleston, R Schmidt and G C Macaulay[1658]

recd [1659]
6th sent John Newton Johnson new ed L of G ∧

recd
sent Hannah $5 to get photo.[1660]

[six lines in pencil:]
14th – the group I saw this afternoon and
    to-night in the Phila. ferry house –
    – the two women – the three or four fine
    little children – that 12 or 13 year
    old boy that reminded me of myself,
    50 years ago[1661]

March 6 – rec'd first dividend Sierra Grande (50) [1662]

"   Dr Bucke's book now in the hands
        of the printers – Sherman & Co: Phila[1663]

" 5th   visit from Harry Stafford

[236]

April 22   83 – John L Sloan, boy 15, Jackson Prestwitch's friend

1656. Letter lost.
1657. For "The Bible as Poetry" see the end of footnote 1625; Mrs Anne Gilchrist had written Whitman on 27 January–13 February 1883 (both dates on the letter in *The Letters of Anne Gilchrist and Walt Whitman*, 1914, pp. 211–212), but his earliest letter to her that year was 27 February 1883: see *The Correspondence of Walt Whitman*, III, 328–329.
1658. Whitman sent Dowden, Rolleston, and Schmidt copies of "The Bible as Poetry" on 18 December 1882 (see entry above and footnote 1635), so why send it again? For Macaulay see footnote 1625; he may well have been sent the essay.
1659. See footnotes 9a and 1600.
1660. Whitman obviously wanted a photograph of his sister Hannah Heyde and did not feel either she or her husband could or would pay for it.
1661. For a diary with as little commentary as this *Daybook*, this is an unusual entry for Whitman; this time he did not record names and addresses.
1662. See footnote 1642.
1663. Whitman sent some galley-proofs to Dr Bucke on 9 March 1883 (see entry below).

Wm C Best, Chatham p o   Chester Co Penn [Printed on a slip:]

——————————————————————————— Roger Sherman,

[On a slip, in pencil, first line in WW's hand,   M. F. Benerman,
but not last four lines:]   Andrew Overend.

Elmer V Santee
Bush, Bull & Troth
36 Court St
Watertown
New York

Benj: R Tucker[1664]
  p o box 3366 Boston Mass

———————

Dr J H Wroth[1665]
  13 Cromwell B [?]
      Albuquerque

———————

[Three slips pinned on sheet, with recipe for doughnuts beneath, one in WW's
hand, in blue pencil:]

229 N 8ᵗʰ st
Shoes

[237]

1883 – March – 9 – sent to Dr B galleys 13 to 17–18 – in mail 1 o'c
——————————————————————————— also letter[1666]

March 16 – sent four Copies Auto L of G to D L
                 [in red ink:]   paid [1667]
      Proudfit, Am. Bank Note Co: 53 Broadway N Y

———————

March 15 to 31 – printing, proof – reading &c. Dr B's book
    proofs to Dr B at London Canada, & to Wm
    O'Connor at Providence R I Dr Bucke's Book[1668]
        [last three words in red ink]

1664. Benjamin R. Tucker, editor of the Boston *Globe,* was advertising *Leaves of Grass* in his newspaper, according to Ezra Heywood (see footnote 1613): see *The Correspondence of Walt Whitman,* III, 314n, 348n. On 25 May 1882 he wrote Whitman that he would publish Osgood's suppressed edition of *Leaves* to test the law; his letter is in Horace Traubel's *With Walt Whitman in Camden,* II, 253–254. Whitman said of Tucker: "he is remarkable for outright pluck — grit of the real sort: for loyalty, steadfastness" (*ibid.,* II, 241). Tucker is mentioned more than 25 times in the five Traubel volumes.
1665. Whitman wrote to Dr James Henry ("Harry") Wroth, Albuquerque, New Mexico on 17 September 1883 (see entry below), but the letter is lost.
1666. This letter to Dr Bucke, with proofs of his *Walt Whitman,* is lost.
1667. See footnote 1646.
1668. Letter to Dr Bucke lost, but letters to W. D. O'Connor at Dr Channing's in Provi-

31 – the type setting of Dr B's book all finished

---

sent 3 Vols. (& German Shakspere Essays)   G S
 to Wm O'Connor Providence[1669]   returned

---

read John Burroughs's "Carlyle" proof [1670]

April 14, 15, 16 – down at Glendale – Mrs. S. ill – [1671]
 Sunday, ride over to Clementon with Harry
 wrote postal card to Herbert

---

the Ezra Haywood acquittal – Boston – [1672]

---

21   sent Specimen Days to Edw'd Carpenter
 Bradway, near Sheffield, Eng[1673]

[two lines in ink, followed by rule in red:]
the next Sierra Grande divvy will be July 2
 (didn't come however till Oct 3ᵈ [1674]

May 3 – 10 to John Chew[1675]

---

10   Sent – J William Thompson[1676]
                 [in red ink:]
      6 Park Row   (rec'd

        Nottingham   England
3 Vols L of G – 3 of S D – six altogether   paid

---

dence, 15, 16, 18, 25, 29, and 31 March 1883, in *The Correspondence of Walt Whitman*, III, 332–336 (Whitman wrote O'Connor at least 30 letters in 1883, most of them not mentioned in the *Daybook*).

1669. Letter: *The Correspondence of Walt Whitman*, III, 335. G S refers to *Essays on Shakespeare* (in German) by Karl Elze (1821–1889).

1670. John Burroughs's "Carlyle" appeared in *The Century*, August 1883; and Burroughs said of it years later: "I guess I struck out most of what Walt marked — I usually did. He was a wonderful critic" — Clara Barrus, *Whitman and Burroughs: Comrades* (Boston and New York, 1931), p. 112. Whitman's letter to Burroughs, 29 March 1883, is in *The Correspondence of Walt Whitman*, III, 334–335.

1671. As Whitman wrote Herbert Gilchrist — mentioned two lines below — Mrs Susan Stafford was severely ill *"one week quite alarming"*: see *The Correspondence of Walt Whitman*, III, 339.

1672. The trial was for printing two Whitman poems: see footnote 1613.

1673. Carpenter (see footnote 20) was one of Whitman's staunchest British supporters.

1674. This postponement of payment was the first indication of the inevitable; failure of the Sierra Grande Mines (see footnotes 1642 and 1662).

1675. It is not clear what Whitman meant by "May 3 – 10 to John Chew": who is John Chew? did Whitman spend a week with him?

1676. On 16 June 1879 Whitman sent Thompson the 1876 two-volume *Leaves of Grass*

12, 13, 14 & 15   at Glendale[1677]

---

20 – paid Dr Benjamin $10 — pays up to date[1678]

June 1 – Dr Bucke's W W done at last – all bound
    & ready – seems to look very well – [1679]
— to-day I enter on my sixty-fifth year –

[238]

[Classified funeral notice:][1680]

VAN VELSOR. — At Newark   [?]   July 23, 1883,
ALONZO VAN VELSOR.
    Relatives and friends are invited to attend the funeral
services, at his late residence, No. 18 South-st., Newark, on
Wednesday, July 25, at 3 o'clock P. M. Interment in Ever-
green Cemetery.

Senator Conover[1681]
    1319 Arch Street – Phila
visit Sunday Sept 23, '83

Sierra Grande Mining Company
Geo: L Smedley   Secretary
18 Exchange Building[1682]

[Printed card of Dr William Carroll, South 16th St., Phila.;[1683] and one of
Jeneco M'Mullin, wholesale & retail boot and shoe manufacturer.]

(see entry above, that date); Thompson's 20 January 1880 letter, ordering books again, is in
the Feinberg Collection. He here, on 10 May 1883, orders three volumes each of *Leaves of Grass*
and *Specimen Days.*
    1677. Visiting the Stafford family.
    1678. Dr Dowling Benjamin, who attended Whitman during his illness on 17–28 October
1882 (see footnote 1598).
    1679. Dr Bucke's *Walt Whitman* was not officially published until 20 June 1883 (see
below, that date).
    1680. See footnote 1310; the date given there and in footnote 1369 is 22 July 1883.
    1681. As will be seen in entries below for 16 and 23 September 1883, Whitman met
Senator Simon B. Conover (1840–1908) at James Matlack Scovel's and had dinner at Conover's.
    1682. This was the Philadelphia office of the Mining Company (see footnote 1642).
    1683. Apparently Dr William Carroll was at Senator Conover's the same night Whitman
had dinner there.

C W Eldridge[1684]
    room 55   28 School Street
                    Boston
with G B Raum[1685]
    1226 F St.   Washington
    N W

[239]

1883 – June 8 – D McKay pays me $200 on acc't
    June 1, '83, payment of royalty —

[three lines in red ink, followed by rule in red ink:]
June 20 '83 – Dr Buckes <u>Walt Whitman</u> is
    published to-day ~~simultaneously in London~~
    in
    ~~and~~ Philadelphia[1686] – pub'd in London 15th

21   Sent Karl Knortz[1687]   Dr B's WW

24 – Sent Dr B's WW to Sister Hannah and John Burroughs[1688]

27 – Sent L of G. & S D. (two vols) to Bessie Ford[1689]
                                    [two words in red ink:]
    Adel Grange, near Leeds, Eng.   paid   recd

    Sent Dr B's W W to Hattie at St Louis
        "   "   " Mary,   Greenport[1690]

1684. Charles W. Eldridge (see footnote 116) had left government work and was going into law practice; W. D. O'Connor wanted him to become a book publisher again: see *The Correspondence of Walt Whitman*, III, 353n.

1685. G. B. Raum was to be Eldridge's law partner?

1686. See *The Correspondence of Walt Whitman*, III, 340n for details on reviews of Dr Bucke's *Walt Whitman* by William Sloane Kennedy and others.

1687. See footnote 1580; see Whitman's letters: *The Correspondence of Walt Whitman*, III, 343.

1688. Burroughs, in his letter to Whitman on 17 August 1883, said he did not care much for Dr Bucke's book: "he gives me no new hint or idea" — see Horace Traubel, *With Walt Whitman in Camden*, I, 403, and Clara Barrus, *Whitman and Burroughs: Comrades*, p. 244.

1689. Elizabeth (Bessie) and Isabella Ford, English friends of Edward Carpenter, ordered books on 16 June 1883 (letter in the Feinberg Collection); they contributed £50 to a fund for Whitman in August 1885, $216.74 in May 1886, and £20 in July 1887 (see *The Correspondence of Walt Whitman*, III, 370, 399, 400, and 402). Elizabeth Ford wrote Whitman in February 1875 and sent her picture to him in June 1877; see also footnote 1592 above.

1690. These gifts of Dr Bucke's *Walt Whitman*, just published by McKay, went to Whitman's niece, Mannahatta Whitman (Jeff's daughter), and Whitman's sister, Mary Van Nostrand.

July 3 to 17 – down at Glendale

    Eva Westcott – Mrs S's two boarders Wyld and
    Edwards – the rides over to "Charlestown" with
    Ed. evenings to engage "pea pickers" [1691]
    – hot weather –

---

19 Sent $10 to Hannah – (her photo's rec'd) [1692]

    Sent Dr Buckes W W to J H Johnston [1693]
    "   "   " " John Swinton [1694]

---

20 sent Wilson & McCormick Cent Ed'n L of G. 2
                                    Vols
                    [two lines in red ink:]
    with note asking their L of G – recd their
                                  L of G [1695]

Aug 2 – sent L of G & S D to Edw R Pease [1696]   [two words in red ink:]
                                                  paid
    17 Osnaburgh St Regents Park London   rec'd

Aug 4 to 28 – (24 days) at R P Smith's Germantown [1697]

1691. On this visit to Kirkwood, Glendale, at the home of George and Susan Stafford; in his letter to Mrs Stafford, 6 August 1883, Whitman wrote, "Love to Ruth — Ed also — (I havn't forgot those rides evenings off among the *pea-pickers*) — Respects to Messrs. Wyld and Edwards." (See *The Correspondence of Walt Whitman,* III, 346.) "Ed." apparently refers not to Edwards but to Edwin Stafford (1856–1906), Harry's brother and one of the seven Stafford children.

1692. These were the photographs Whitman asked his sister Hannah Heyde to have taken on 6 February 1883 and for which he sent her $5 (see entry above).

1693. Whitman was very good about constantly sending his New York jeweler friend his books as well as books and articles about him.

1694. John Swinton (see footnote 33), publisher (1883–1887) of his own newspaper *John Swinton's Paper,* wrote to Whitman on 20 July 1883: "A thousand thanks for the beautiful book" (William White, "Whitman and John Swinton: Some Unpublished Correspondence," *American Literature,* XXXIX [January 1968], 550).

1695. This letter to Wilson & McCormick, publishers, of Glasgow, Scotland, who published *Specimen Days* in Great Britain, is lost. See *The Correspondence of Walt Whitman,* III, 328n.

1696. See Whitman's letter of Edward R. Pease, 21 August 1883, in *The Correspondence of Walt Whitman,* III, 347–348; Pease was a friend of the Fords (footnote 1689, above), and visited Whitman in Camden in November or December 1888.

1697. On a slip of paper, possibly intended to be entered later in the *Daybook* (now in the Feinberg Collection), Whitman wrote:

                            24 Days at R P Smith's
                            4653 Germantown Av.
                            4th to 28th August, 1883

Aug 4 to 28 — '83 – Have been out in
Germantown, Philadelphia ~~in good most~~ pleasantly
quartered at the house of my friend R P S.

Hattie and Jessie here   came about 8th or 10^{th 1698}

[240]

Prospect Delgancy Co. Wicklow   [correction in pencil]
Rolleston – 28 Terrassen Ufer   Dresden
                                          Saxony[1699]

[On printed slip: Wilson & McCormick / Booksellers and Publishers / 120 Saint Vincent Street, Glasgow./:]   Frederick W Wilson[1700]   [in pencil]

Dr Gassoway & Senator Conover 410 Chestnut Street[1701]

John Rogers, (freight W J RR office Phil) model for studios[1702]

?

Paul (Genst) — one legged young fellow — German birth —
– at Market st. ferry – matches – [1703]

John Swinton's Paper   21 Park Row   N Y [1704]

    Fuetson [?]
Ed Watson, driver, 20 yrs – all lines – Camden

> — The family all away this summer at Newport
> – no one here only my friend at home, and he
> alway all day down town most of the day. A good
> long visit visit – just the place for the
> summer, and for my mood. ⨉ The large mansion –
> the ample, secluded great grass lawn and round.
> The in the rear with outlook so fresh and green, a
> with some trees and the old stone ivy-cover'd old
> stone wall

(See footnotes 1622 and 1638, and *Walt Whitman Review*, IV [June 1958], 90; Whitman also wrote to William D. O'Connor and John Burroughs, 14 and 21 August 1883, in much these same words as above — *The Correspondence of Walt Whitman*, III, 346–347.)

1698.   This was to be a long visit, for Whitman's two nieces (Jeff's daughters) did not return to St Louis until 1 December 1883; by "here" Whitman does not mean Germantown but George and Louisa Orr Whitman's, 431 Stevens Street, Camden, and they also went to Burlington, New Jersey, where Whitman's brother was moving permanently early in 1884.

1699.   T. W. H. Rolleston wrote to Whitman on 27 September and 22 November 1883 about a German translation of *Leaves of Grass*: see Horst Frenz, *Whitman and Rolleston: A Correspondence* (Bloomington, Indiana, 1951), pp. 77–79; Horace Traubel, *With Walt Whitman in Camden*, IV, 111–112; and *The Correspondence of Walt Whitman*, III, 349n.

1700.   Frederick W. Wilson was of course a member of the firm on Wilson & McCormick (see footnote 1695); Wilson's letter to Whitman, 27 February 1884, is in the Library of Congress.

1701.   See footnote 1681.

1702.   John M. Rogers's 1876 and 1878 letters to Whitman are in the Feinberg Collection, but this John Rogers, who worked in the freight office of the West Jersey Railroad, Philadelphia, and was also a model, was a different person. Whitman may have met him in Colonel John R. Johnston's studio.

1703.   Once again, a name and description of a young man Whitman met on the ferry.

1704.   See footnote 1694.

over
Al Bennett, 17–18 – comes ~~up~~   6.10 boat & up in the
                    cars with me

Miss Joe Barkaloo
        915 Third av.   Brooklyn

Nov 28 '83
James Murray W J RR hand
aged 18 or 19 – Cape May

Nov. 29 – on Market st cars
Robt Gilmore   driver
age 21 – from Woodbury[1705]

[241]

Sept: 1883

12th   sent L of G. and S D to Wm Brough, Franklin
        Penn. ~~$4 due   (no p o order rec'd)~~ paid all right[1706]
                [cancellation and three words in red]

17th – Sent Hannah's picture to Mary[1707]
    wrote to Harry Wroth, Albuquerque N M [1708]

16th (Sunday)   Dinner at Col. Scovel's – met Gov. Conover
    of Florida – Bates – Adams[1709]

18th gave L of G. to Harry Bonsall [1710]

1705. These four men, Fuetson, Bennett, Murray, and Gilmore are a further listing, similar to Genst (?) in footnote 1703; but Miss Josephine Barkaloo wrote to Whitman on 6 February 1884, thanking him for an article (letter in the Library of Congress).

1706. In using the *Daybook* as an account book for sales of *Leaves of Grass* and *Specimen Days,* Whitman would record when he sent books out, how much was due, and here that the money was not received; when it was paid, the poet seemed relieved and reported "paid all right."

1707. One of the pictures from his sister Hannah Heyde, which Whitman received on 19 July 1883 (see entry above), he sent to his other sister Mary Van Nostrand.

1708. Whitman took his meals in July 1881 with Mrs Caroline Wroth at 319 Stevens Street, Camden (see *The Correspondence of Walt Whitman,* III, 232n), and Harry Wroth may well have been a member of the family. This letter is lost; but it is odd that Whitman should have noted it and yet failed to mention those during September 1883 to Thomas Nicholson, William D. O'Connor (6 letters), and Karl Knortz.

1709. See footnote 1681 for Senator (not "Gov") Conover; I cannot identify Bates and Adams, though Whitman did write to a Robert Adams in Camden in 1890–91 (letters in the Feinberg Collection).

1710. Harry Bonsall (see near end of footnote 76) was the son of the editor of the Camden *Daily Post.*

22 – paid Ch: Spieler in full for Photos. & recd
them[1711]

Sunday
23   dinner at Senator Conover's[1712]
Dr Wm Carroll [1713]

Sept 26 to Oct 10. (two weeks) down at
Ocean Grove, "sea-side, N. J. at
Sheldon House – John Burroughs[1714] – Mrs Parks

Oct. 3.   50 dividend   Sierra Grande – rec'd [1715]

Sept 27, 8, 9, 30.   John Burroughs & I at
Sheldon House – Ocean Grove[1716]

1711.   Charles Spieler had been taking pictures of Whitman for years: see footnote 8; Whitman sent them to relatives, newspapers, friends, and those who bought his books.
1712.   Whitman had only met Senator Conover a week before (see entry above) at a dinner in the Camden home of Col. James Matlack Scovel (see footnote 71).
1713.   There is a previous mention in the *Daybook* (see footnote 1683) of Dr William Carroll, whom the poet may well have met at Senator Conover's house.
1714.   Whitman wrote a brief letter to William D. O'Connor, 30 September 1883, about his stay at Ocean Grove (see *The Correspondence of Walt Whitman*, III, 353–354); and Burroughs wrote at length about it in his journal, quoted by Clara Barrus, *Whitman and Burroughs: Comrades,* pp. 244–246, where Whitman's own remarks, from a MS in the Lion Collection, New York Public Library, are also given (p. 246n):
September 26, 1883, New Jersey Sea Coast, Ocean Grove. I write this on the beach, the husky surf rolling and beating a little way from my feet — the sun, half an hour after rising, a round red ball up in the heavens right before me east — the long line of sand and beach and beating surf as far as I can see on either hand north or south. I have come down here to be with my friend John Burroughs and for a sea change. Everything is soothing, monotonous, refreshing, a slight saline smell, the music of the rolling surf, the gold-shine of the sun on the water starting in brightness near me and gradually broadening the track leading away out to sea, and expanding there. Several sails in the distance. A fishing boat with three men just comes in and lands close by.
October 1, Still here. J. B. just left for New York. I walk long on the beach. A partial tempest of wind, from north, following a heavy rain storm last night. The waves rolling and dashing and combing. An unusual show of foam and white froth, not only on shore, but out everywhere as far as you can see; not a sail in sight. . . . The sea-beach and surf — its myriad ranks like furious white-maned racers, urged by demoniac emulation to the goal, the shore, breaking there ever and dissolving in other myriads pressing beyond and driving in the same, with husky guttural utterance of the sea, and ever its muffled distant lion roars.
In this same 13-page notebook, Whitman jotted down some of the phrases from the prose above for use in a poem that became "With Husky-Haughty Lips, O Sea!", several trial lines of which were also penciled on a page with a letterhead reading Sheldon House, Ocean Grove (now in the Feinberg Collection). See *Leaves of Grass,* Comprehensive Reader's Edition, pp. 517–518; the poem was first published in *Harper's Monthly,* LXVIII (March 1884), 607. See also Gay Wilson Allen, *The Solitary Singer,* pp. 512–514.
1715.   This was the second dividend; Whitman was to receive nine in all; see footnotes 1642, 1662, and 1674, and entires below for 21 August and 5 September 1884.
1716.   See footnote 1714.

<u>Scottish Review</u>   Criticism, quite
    ingenious – friendly – extracts –
    article headed with the names of
    L of G – S D – Dr B's book – & J B's Notes – [1717]
pub: Alex: Gardner, Paisley – & 12 Paternoster Row London

Sept 26 – T W H Rolleston's lecture on W W [1718]
    L of G. to the Dresden (Saxony) Literary
Society

[242]

H N Whitman, Stanbridge East
—————————————— Quebec, Canada[1719]
Mrs Townsend   parsonage
    525 Broadway   near Royden   C

---

good mattress & bed spring   store 163 Second St Phila

J H J & Alma Johnston   482 Mott av.
          near 149th St[1720]

[On card, printed, of Green B. Raum, attorney and counsellor at law, 1226 F
Street, N. W., Washington, D. C.:]

Charles W. Eldridge[1721]   [not WW's hand]
    now at Los Angeles, California   [five lines in red ink:]
            with   went Feb. '87
        Green B. Raum [printed]   (with W D O'C)
                         to Pasadena
                         Los Angeles Co:
                         California

1717. In a letter to John Burroughs — see *The Correspondence of Walt Whitman*, III,
355 — Whitman refers to this piece in *The Scottish Review*, II (September 1883), 281–300.
    1718. T. W. H. Rolleston wrote to Whitman about the lecture on 27 September 1883:
see Horst Frenz, *Whitman and Rolleston: A Correspondence*, pp. 77–79; the original lecture
was published in H. B. Cotterill and W. W. H. Rolleston, *Ueber Wordsworth und Walt Whitman* (Dresden, 1883), and a translation, by Horace L. Traubel's father of parts of it in "The
Old Gray Poet Penetrates Germany's Most Brilliant Literary Centre," Camden *Daily Post*, 13
February 1884 (reprinted in an appendix to Horst Frenz, *ibid.*, pp. 109–117); Whitman corrected the MS (now in the Feinberg Collection); translated again by Alfred Forman and
Richard Maurice Bucke as "Walt Whitman," it was included in *In Re Walt Whitman*, edited
by Horace L. Traubel, Richard Maurice Bucke, and Thomas B. Harned (Philadelphia, 1893),
pp. 285–295.
    1719. H. N. Whitman wrote to Walt Whitman on 20 November 1883, acknowledging
receipt of a book and asking for genealogical information (the letter is now in the Feinberg
Collection); Whitman's reply, 27 November 1883, is lost.
    1720. Whitman's New York friends with whom he stayed in that city and with whom he
was always in touch.
    1721. Charles E. Eldridge (see footnotes 116 and 1684) wrote to Whitman on 22 Septem-

In Boston   32 School st

[243]

Oct: 1883 – 12th, 13th &c – Hattie and Jessie at Burlington[1722]
    Lou gone east to Norwich, Conn – return'd 20th[1723]

---

sent package of papers, photos, &c to Mrs Parks[1724]

---

14 – three photos to T H Bartlett, 394 Federal
                    [in red ink:]
        st. Boston   rec'd [1725]

---

sent Rolleston (Dresden) Dr Knortz's translations
— also postal card [1726]   translations rec'd back
                [last three words in red ink]

20, 21, 22 at R P Smiths – Germantown[1727]

---

24 – Jessie's picture by Spieler – also WW head [1728]
        [in red ink:]   paid all

---

18 – Michael Nash (Pete's uncle) buried [1729]

---

26 – sent Jessie's photo to Jeff at St Louis
        "   "   Mary   Greenport
    both "   & Hatties to Hannah – Burlington[1730]

ber 1883 (letter at Yale University Library) about going into law — see *The Correspondence of Walt Whitman*, III, 353 — in Boston; hence the Boston address; but in February 1887, Whitman here has noted that Eldridge went to California, apparently to join Green B. Raum's firm.

1722. Mannahatta and Jessie Whitman, the daughters of Jefferson Whitman of St Louis, were visiting George and Louisa Orr Whitman in Camden (see footnote 1698); the latter were to move to Burlington, New Jersey, in 1884.

1723. Louisa Orr Whitman often visited her relatives, the F. E. Dow family, in Norwich.

1724. As Mrs Parks is mentioned above, under the entry for 26 September–10 October 1883, when Whitman was at the Sheldon House in Ocean Grove, New Jersey, she undoubtedly had something to do with that establishment.

1725. Letter: *The Correspondence of Walt Whitman*, III, 354. See footnotes 440 and 1097 for notes on Truman Howe Bartlett, the sculptor.

1726. Post card lost; see footnote 1718 and also Whitman's letter to Karl Knortz, 11 September 1883, in *The Correspondence of Walt Whitman*, III, 351; and T. W. H. Rolleston's letter to Whitman, 1 January 1884, in Horst Frenz, *Whitman and Rolleston: A Correspondence*, pp. 80–82.

1727. This visit with the Robert Pearsall Smith family in Philadelphia (see footnotes 1622, 1638, 1641, 1650, 1697) is described in Whitman's letter to Harry Stafford, 22 October 1883, in *The Correspondence of Walt Whitman*, III, 354–355.

1728. See footnote 1711.

1729. See footnote 970; Nash and his wife were old Washington friends.

1730. Jessie Whitman was Jeff's daughter, and thus Whitman's niece; Mary Van Nostrand was Walt's sister, Hattie (Mannahatta) was Jessie's sister, and Hannah Heyde of Burlington, Vermont, another sister of the poet.

Hatta and Jess visit Burlington, Norwich
    Boston and New York (N Y, Oct 30 '83)[1731]

---

30 – Harry Stafford here[1732]

Nov. 5 – Dr Bucke comes over from N Y & visits
    me afternoon & Evn'g — the supper, talk, &c at
    Continental Hotel – (call at McKay's)[1733]

---

7 – supper at J M S's[1734]

---

the two Vols. L of G and Two R.   (Cen'll Ed'n)

                                    [in red ink,
    to Porter & Coates[1735] – $7 due – if kept   sideways:]   paid

---

15   sent H N Whitman, Stanbridge East, P Q[1736]
                              [in blue pencil:]
    Canada, L of G, $3 due   paid

---

23 – Harry Stafford here – he starts
    for New York[1737]

[244]

Peter Doyle   616 South Broad
   M st   bet 4½ & 6th Wash[1738]

1731. Mannahatta and Jessie Whitman visited Burlington on 12–13 October 1883, but that was most likely Burlington, New Jersey (near Camden); this later trip was to Burlington, Vermont, where their aunt Hannah Heyde lived with her husband Charles L. Heyde; Norwich, Conn., was where the Francis E. Dowe and Emma Dowe, Louisa Orr Whitman's sister, lived; stops at Boston and New York were made while on their way to Vermont and Connecticut.

1732. Harry Stafford was the most important person to Whitman at this time (see *The Correspondence of Walt Whitman*, III, 2–9), and Whitman had written him on 22 October 1883 (*ibid.*, III, 354–355); he visited Whitman again on 23 November (see below) before leaving for New York, then for London, Ontario, to work for Dr Bucke; Harry was to marry on 25 June 1884 (see *ibid.*, III, 357n, 371n).

1733. David McKay had of course published Dr Richard Maurice Bucke's *Walt Whitman* in June 1883; this visit of Dr Bucke's was a short one.

1734. Supper with James Matlack Scovel was a long-time occurrence, not so frequent now as earlier.

1735. Porter & Coates, 9th and Chestnut Street, Philadelphia, was a bookstore, where, in 1880, Whitman had found Worthington's unauthorized editions of *Leaves of Grass*: see *The Correspondence of Walt Whitman*, III, 198.

1736. See footnote 1719.

1737. See footnote 1732.

1738. Peter Doyle, mentioned from time to time in the *Daybook*, was the Confederate prisoner-of-war who became a horsecar conductor in Washington and was Whitman's best known young friend during his days in Washington: see entry for 7 December 1883 below.

Walter R Thomas   205 north 9th st – Phila
author of the sonnet[1739]

G P Lathrop   80 Washington Sq. N Y City[1740]

Daniel Lelkens, boy, (15 or 16) on the boat – milk wagon
Jan 14   orphan – born in Baltimore[1741]

W<u>m</u> Harrison Riley, Townsend Harbor, Mass:[1742]

Mrs Elmina D Slenker, Snowville   Pulaski Co
Penn
H Buxton Forman, 46 Marlborough Street
St John's Wood, London   N W [1743]

[two lines in purple pencil:]
Frank and May Baker   26 C Street
N W
Washington D C [1744]

[On printed card of Herbert E. Wright:]   21 Federal

[Printed card of E. Haydon, practical locksmith and bell-hanger, speaking pipes put up, bronze door furniture made to order, and silver plating, 507 Mt. Vernon Street, Camden, N. J.]

[names, address, date in pencil:]
Bessie Ford   }
Isabella Ford   } 5 Hyde Park Mansions
Edward R. Pease }   London   N W (May '84) [1745]

1739. What sonnet by Walter R. Thomas does Whitman refer to?
1740. See footnote 1099.
1741. Daniel Lelkens must have been an orphan boy Whitman met on a ferry on 14 January 1884 and, as so often in the *Daybook*, wrote his name and brief description.
1742. See footnote 649; Riley, an English admirer, was most likely in this country at the time and may well have been responsible for *Specimen Days* and *Leaves of Grass* being sent to Emma Riley in London on 8 and 10 December 1883 (see entries below), although her letter, 23 November 1883, in the Feinberg Collection, asks for *Specimen Days*.
1743. See footnote 248; his name and address may be here in connection with Whitman sending his essay, "Our Eminent Visitors" to several English friends on 15 December 1883 (see entry below).
1744. A friend of Whitman's Washington days was Dr Frank Baker of the Smithsonian Institute, who married May Cole, a friend of Mrs William D. O'Connor (see Clara Barrus, *Whitman and Burroughs: Comrades,* pp. 9, 72, 369).
1745. For Elizabeth and Isabella Ford, and their friend Edward R. Pease, see footnotes 1689 and 1696.

[245]

Dec. (& Nov) '83 – Nov. 29 – death of Gen. Carse[1746]

Nov. 27, '8 – Dr Bucke here – our visit to R P.
     Smith's – Germantown[1747]

"   " Harry at London, Canada[1748]

Hatta and Jessie gone home to St Louis by way
     of Louisville – arrived in St L, Dec. 1 [1749]
                                                    Monthly   March   [in red ink]
sent Sea Sonnet to Harpers' — accepted₋50   paid 84 [1750]

Dec 3 – attended funeral Gen. Carse[1751]

8th   sent Specimen Days to Emma Riley, South
                                        [in blue pencil:]
     Heath, Hampstead N W   London, England   paid [1752]
                                        [in blue pencil, sideways:]
                                                    recd

Dec 4. Evn'g & supper at Mr and Mrs Donaldson's
     132 north 40th st. Phila. Curios, nuggets,
     historical M   momentos, a very enjoyable
     evening, warm hospitality – fine children.[1753]

5   McKay paid me 102.51 for royalty[1754]

1746. General Carse, whose funeral Whitman attended four days later, had a local reputation, but does not seem to have been well-known nationally.
1747. Dr Bucke, who was spending a month in New York, had visited Whitman less
than a month ago, on 5 November 1883, and Whitman had spent two days at the Robert
Pearsall Smith home on 20–21 November 1883, but Dr Bucke and Smith had probably not met
until now.
1748. See footnote 1732; Harry Stafford was working in Dr Bucke's asylum in London,
Ontario, but was not satisfied with his position — see Whitman's letters to Harry's parents, 1
December 1883, and to Harry, 8 December 1883, in *The Correspondence of Walt Whitman*, III,
356 and 357 (see also III, 357n).
1749. Mannahatta and Jessie Whitman were his nieces (see footnotes 1698, 1722, and
1731).
1750. "Sea Sonnet" was "With Husky-Haughty Lips, O Sea!" which Whitman began
writing at Ocean Grove, New Jersey, during his stay from 26 September to 10 October 1883;
the poem had given him a certain amount of difficulty — see footnote 1714, above, and *The
Correspondence of Walt Whitman*, III, 357, 357n.
1751. See footnote 1746.
1752. See footnote 1742.
1753. See a transcript of Whitman's letter to Thomas Donaldson, 2 December 1883, in
The Correspondence of Walt Whitman, III, 356; for details about Donaldson, see footnote 1573.
1754. Compared with 1882 — see entry for 1 December 1882 above — the royalty payments

8th   sent L of G and Sp Days (two vols) to

[two words in blue pencil:]

rec'd

Isabella Ford, Adel Grange, Leeds, Eng.   paid[1755]

---

7   Pete Doyle with me this afternoon[1756]

——————————————   [in blue pencil:]

9   sent Dr B's W W to John Newton Johnson   recd

also letter[1757]

---

recd   [in blue pencil]

10   sent L of G to Emma Riley (see above)   paid[1758]   [word in blue pencil]

---

rec'd Rolleston's lecture pamphlet "Wordsworth

and W W" from Dresden – sent one to W O'C[1759]

---

15 – sent "Eminent Visitors" to Dowden, Tennyson, Schmidt,

Symonds, H B Forman, Rolleston, Mrs Gilchrist[1760]

——————————————————   [three words in red ink:]

recd

sent O S Balwin, "An Indian Bureau Remniscence"   paid

$10[1761]

15, 16, 17 – At R P Smith's – Wm Horton Foster[1762]

---

for 1883 were not so large (see also footnote 1627); in addition to this $102.51, he got $200 on 8 June 1883, $100 in mining stock dividends, $50 from *Harper's Monthly* for his sea sonnet, and the money from his own sales of *Leaves of Grass* and *Specimen Days* — not a lot for a year's income.

1755. See footnote 1745.

1756. See footnote 1738; see also *The Correspondence of Walt Whitman,* III, 358n.

1757. Letter lost; for John Newton Johnson, of Mid, Alabama, see footnote 9a.

1758. See footnote 1742.

1759. This was the pamphlet in German, referred to in footnote 1718.

1760. Whitman's essay, "Our Eminent Visitors (Past, Present, and Future)," *The Critic,* III (17 November 1883), 459–460, was reprinted in *Democratic Vistas and Other Papers* (London, 1888), revised and reprinted in *November Boughs* (1888), and is in *Prose Works 1892,* II, 541–545; Edward Dowden, Alfred, Lord Tennyson, Rudolf Schmidt, H. Buxton Forman, T. W. H. Rolleston, and Mrs Anne Gilchrist were all well-known correspondents of Whitman abroad.

1761. O. S. Baldwin had written Whitman on 12 December 1883 (letter lost), asking for a piece; see Whitman's letters to Baldwin in *The Correspondence of Walt Whitman,* III, 358–359, sending "An Indian Bureau Reminiscence" and acknowledging payment. It was published in *Baldwin's Monthly* (New York), XXVIII (February 1884), 2; reprinted in *To-day, The Monthly Magazine of Scientific Socialism* (London), I (May 1884), 340–342, in *November Boughs* (1888); and in *Prose Works 1892,* II, 577–580. The title in its original publication is not the one Whitman gives in the *Daybook,* but was slightly changed to "Reminiscences of the Indian Bureau."

1762. William Horton Foster, whom Whitman undoubtedly met during this three-day visit at the home of Robert Pearsall Smith in Germantown, Philadelphia, is unidentified; see

recd   recd   [two words, sideways, in red ink]
21 – sent Hannah and Mary   each $10 [1763]

22   50 from G   W   C [1764]

[246]

Francis H Williams   209 S Third st – Phila.[1765]
Mrs Francis Howard Williams   Green st. below

Coulter

Germantown

F   Churchill Williams

Louis S Stern (660 n 8th) young man (17) on Chestnut [1766]

Jan 11 – Sent "A Backward Glance" [1767] to

– Dr Bucke, 2 copies   – Mrs Gilchrist
x – O'Connor   Joe Barkaloo

Whitman's brief letter, 11 December 1883, accepting the invitation, in *The Correspondence of Walt Whitman*, III, 358.

1763.   These were undoubtedly Christmas presents to his sisters Hannah Heyde and Mary Van Nostrand.

1764.   This $50 from George W. Childs, Philadelphia *Public Ledger* owner (see footnote 244), was a Christmas gift; Whitman was to borrow $500 from Childs in March 1884 to help pay for the house on Mickle Street, which he repaid (see Horace Traubel, *With Walt Whitman in Camden*, I, 291).

1765.   Francis Howard Williams (1844–1922), here first mentioned, was a poet and dramatist, who wrote on Whitman in *The American* in 1888, and after Whitman's death: "Walt Whitman as Deliverer," *Walt Whitman Fellowship Papers*, I (August 1894), 11–30; "A Woman Waits for Me," *Conservator*, VII (April 1896), 26–27; "Individuality as Whitman's Primary Motive," *Conservator*, XI (July 1900), 71–73; "An Appreciation of Walt Whitman," *Columbia Monthly*, May 1908; and two sonnets to Whitman in his *The Flute Player and Other Poems* (New York, 1894). He is referred to in the most friendly way more than forty times in Horace Traubel's *With Walt Whitman in Camden*, such as (II, 341): "I think I have told you how splendidly the Williamses have always received me in their home? Their home was a sort of asylum (like old churches, temples) when so many homes were closed against me. They were like the Gilders — they were not afraid even in the days of greatest outcry to ask me round, to have me cackle and rub feathers with them in their own coop." See Whitman's letter to Harry Stafford, 2 January 1884, in *The Correspondence of Walt Whitman*, III, 361, on his visit of 22–26 December 1883; and photograph of Whitman with the Williams family in the *Walt Whitman Review*, XIV (March 1968), 32. F. Churchill Williams, named here in the *Daybook*, was evidently a brother of Francis H. Williams, though a son of that name is shown in the picture.

1766.   Like the young man mentioned in footnote 1741, this is someone Whitman met, got his name and address, and recorded it.

1767.   Whitman's essay, "A Backward Glance on My Own Road," *The Critic*, IV (5 January 1884), 1–2 — not to be confused with "A Backward Glance O'er Travel'd Roads," which was included in *November Boughs* (1888) and was made up of this piece in *The Critic*, plus "How Leaves of Grass Was Made," New York *Star*, 1885 (according to Emory Holloway) and "My Book and I," *Lippincott's Magazine*, January 1887; it was reprinted in *Complete Poems & Prose* (1888 and *Leaves of Grass* (1892), but not in *Complete Prose Works* (1892). See *Prose Works 1892*, II, 711–732 for the text and notes of the later essay, and II, 768–771, for the deleted paragraphs from the essay in the 1884 *Critic*.

Dr Knortz	x – W S Kennedy
– G C Macaulay	George Chainey
Moncure D Conway	x Sister Hannah
– H Buxton Forman	– Wilson & McCormic[1768]
– J A Symonds	
x – Dowden	
x Rudolf Schmidt	
– Rolleston	

[247]

Dec. 1883

21 – sent "A Backward Glance at my Own Road" to
     N A Review – 40 asked – returned – [1769]

22 x 26 – at Mr Williams's Germantown[1770]

27   sent "A Backward Glance" to <u>Critic</u>   12 asked
                              [in red ink:]
               accepted – printed Jan 5 '84   paid [1771]
[year in red ink:]
1884 – Jan 5, 6, 7, 8, at R P Smith's Germantown

Jan. 9 – asked the <u>Critic</u> to send "A Backward Glance" to
                         [five words, two lines, in red ink]
                              not sent
     Dowden, Symonds, Schmidt, Rolleston & O'Connor I sent them[1772]

rec'd W J RR ticket for '84, from Gen: Sewell [1773]

Sunday 13 – dinner at J M S's – good time – Hines[1774]

1768. Of the 16 names here, all have been listed or identified several times in the *Daybook*, except Miss Josephine Barkaloo (see footnote 1705) of Brooklyn, George Chainey (see footnote 1543) of Boston (publisher of *This World*, who defended Whitman's *Leaves of Grass* in 1882), Wilson & McCormick of Glasgow (British publishers of *Leaves* and *Specimen Days*), and G. C. Macaulay (see footnote 1625) of Rugby, England (who reviewed *Leaves of Grass* in the December 1882 *Nineteenth Century*).
1769. See footnote 1767.
1770. See footnote 1765.
1771. See footnote 1767.
1772. These five friends of Whitman's are among those listed on the opposite page, to whom he sent copies of the essay on 11 January 1884.
1773. General William J. Sewell sent Whitman an annual pass to ride on the West Jersey and Seashore Railroad.
1774. J M S is James Matlack Scovel, with whom Whitman last had supper on 7 November 1883; he was an old Camden friend. I cannot identify Hines, unless he is "the

sent "An Indian Bureau Reminiscence" (pub.
in "Baldwin's Monthly," Feb.) to many persons[1775]

      Lawrence
Jan 30 – Saw ∧ Barrett in "Francesca da Rimini"
in Phila. B. sent for me behind the stage
& I went at the close of the play & had
a short interview with him in his dressing
room. Acting good, especially Francesca's
and her lover's.[1776]

---

31   paid Mrs Goodenough for Ed's board $16 [1777]

      Special
Feb. ⎫ Sent ~~Cent~~   L of G to Mrs James Barnard,
    ⎬   [two words in red ink:]
6 ⎭ Nashua, N. H.   paid 3   paid   rec'd

---

7   sent L of G to Priscilla Townsend, for Margaret
             rec'd   paid $2   Tripp[1778]

[two lines in purple pencil:]
9   Supper at Mr & Mrs Donaldson's[1779]
      capital good time – 4 or 5 hours

---

registered letter N Y   89385   [line in red ink]

---

13   abstract of Rolleston's Dresden lecture in
   Post. Sent it to many persons[1780]

money man" on *The Literary World* (see Horace Traubel, *With Walt Whitman in Camden,* III, 274).

1775. See footnote 1761.

1776. Lawrence Barrett (1838–1891) was an American Shakespearean actor; for Whitman's account of the play, see his letter to Harry Stafford in *The Correspondence of Walt Whitman,* III, 363–364.

1777. Whitman continued to pay this for his feeble-minded brother.

1778. See footnotes 285 and 352 for Priscilla Townsend; also *The Correspondence of Walt Whitman,* II, 214n; Mrs Margaret (Maggy) Tripp was Priscilla Townsend's sister (see *ibid.,* II, 215n).

1779. See footnote 1573; Whitman, visiting the Smiths, Williamses, as well as the Donaldsons, must have been in good health at this time, but became ill in mid-February for about two months.

1780. See footnote 1718; this version in the Camden *Daily Post* was translated from German by Horace L. Traubel's father and annotated by Whitman.

brain trouble &

17 to 24 – ill with ∧ bad cold – didnt go out – bad spell
[last two words in red ink]
two months [in red ink]   April [in red ink]
several days –∧miserable – up to March 4 – two mo[nths] [1781]
[last two words in red ink]

[248]

[Card of E. M. Turner, book and job printer, 327 Federal St., Camden:]
Eugene

Vincent S Cooke
Phil Press
News

[On slip about Carlyle Society, Hon. Sec., C. Oscar Gridley, 9, Duke Street,
London Bridge, London, S. E.:]

Called
   April '84 [1782]

May 9 '84 – Lougheeds young plumber   James Folwell [1783]   [line in pencil]

Benj R Tucker   p o box 3366   Boston Mass[1784]

[249]

1884   [in red ink]
Feb 24 – Sent the two Vols. Cent. Edition L of G &
   T R to Alfred G. Ginty, 45 S Salina
      [three words in red ink:]
   Street, Syracuse, N Y   paid 10 – rec'd – [1785]

24   Sent Rudolf Schmidt Dr Bucke's book[1786]

1781. Whitman wrote Robert Pearsall Smith, the Staffords, John Burroughs, and Anne Gilchrist about his illness: see *The Correspondence of Walt Whitman,* III, 365–368.
   1782. C. Oscar Gridley is listed among "some names of friends" in a letter to Herbert Gilchrist, 15 September 1885 (*The Correspondence of Walt Whitman,* III, 405); Gridley also contributed to the offering William Michael Rossetti collected in September and October 1885 (see Horace Traubel, *With Walt Whitman in Camden,* IV, 210).
   1783. Probably working on the house at 328 Mickle Street, into which Whitman had moved in March 1884.
   1784. See footnote 1664.
   1785. Whitman still had on hand, and continued to sell, copies of the 1876 Centennial Edition of *Leaves of Grass* and *Two Rivulets.*
   1786. Inasmuch as Dr Richard Maurice Bucke's *Walt Whitman* was published in June

Sick the last three weeks – get out (to p o) first time in over two weeks March 4 [1787]

March ————————————————————————

4   Sent Specimen   Days to Mrs Annie Bessey

———   [in red ink:]

March   paid

———   2 West Adams St. Syracuse   N Y. $2 –

letter to R P Smith – Mary & Logan call'd [1788]

March 8 – Saturday – Tasker Lay dying – I have been

died Sunday March 9

there (416 West st) all the day & evening ʌ ab't 12 M

[in red ink:]   buried March 12 [1789]

— R P Smith call'd – earnest & friendly, deeply so [1790]

for home in N J

Harry S. left London, Canada – ʌ now in Detroit [1791]

gave Mr L $10 – (15 altogether) – $20 more: (16 for the house) [1792]

—————————————   [in pencil:]

Mr Williams, (Germantown) called 16th (I was out) [1793]

[Two lines in pencil:]

21ˢᵗ   Geo Chainey called on me with two gen-

tlemen – actors, Irving's Company, &c [1794]

1883, it is surprising that Whitman waited until the end of February 1884 before sending a copy to Rudolf Schmidt in Copenhagen, to whom he had been sending other things.

1787. See entry for 17–24 February 1884.

1788. Letter: *The Correspondence of Walt Whitman*, III, 365–366; Mary and Logan were Robert Pearsall Smith's daughter and son (see footnotes 1622 and 1641).

1789. See *The Correspondence of Walt Whitman*, III, 366n, and footnote 1152, above.

1790. As Whitman actually made few comments in the *Daybook*, even on the death of Emerson, Robert Pearsall Smith's visit must have moved the poet very much.

1791. Harry Stafford was dissatisfied with his job in Dr Bucke's asylum, but apparently he came back home to Glendale instead of going to Detroit: see *The Correspondence of Walt Whitman*, III, 367n.

1792. These figures have to do with money, including rent money, Whitman gave to Alfred Lay, Tasker Lay's grandfather; the Lay family was living — and continued to do so through September — in the house at 328 Mickle Street, Camden, which Whitman bought: see *The Correspondence of Walt Whitman*, III, 366n, and Gay Wilson Allen, *The Solitary Singer*, pp. 514–518.

1793. This must have been Francis Howard Williams (see footnote 1765).

1794. For George Chainey, publisher of *This World* (Boston), see footnote 1543; Henry Irving was in Camden at the time; and in December Whitman had to decline an invitation to a reception for him (see *The Correspondence of Walt Whitman*, III, 356); the poet met

March 26 – moved to 328 Mickle st.   Camden[1795]

27 – am writing this in my new premises
   in Mickle Street – slept here last night
   – the plumbers are here at work at gas
   & water fixings & the carpenters –
   – Mr and Mrs Lay[1796] – Will Laverty

[Entry in pencil:]

   paid Lou $14 – balance ☞   see   Memorandum
                                      last of this book

April 3, '84 – paid $1750 cash[1798] for the premises 328
   Mickle Street, Camden, to Rebecca Jane Hare,
   & took the deed, which I left at the Registers
   office to be recorded.[1799]

                                                    [250]

Charles Brant, age 26, W J Freight & Express Phil Side[1800]
                lives in 4th st.   April '84

Irving and his young manager Bram Stoker at Thomas Donaldson's house in April 1884 (see Gay Wilson Allen, *The Solitary Singer*, p. 516).

1795.   This was to be Whitman's home for the last eight years of his life.

1796.   Mr and Mrs Lay were renting the house when Whitman bought it, and he agreed to their staying on if they would board him, but the arrangement did not work and they left in January 1885; see footnote 1792.

1797.   This was a final settlement with his sister-in-law Louisa Orr Whitman for his board from June 1873 to March 1884 — see "rough statement" for the 417 weeks he boarded, for which he paid $1501, "ab't $3.60 a week," at the end of the first volume of this *Daybook*.

1798.   Whitman had $1250 from royalties from David McKay, and he borrowed $500 from George W. Childs (see footnote 1764).

1799.   The bill of sale, now in the Walt Whitman House, Camden, is printed in *The Correspondence of Walt Whitman*, III, 368n.

In *Faint Clews & Indirections* (Durham, North Carolina, 1949), p. 18, is the following paragraph from the Trent Collection, Duke University:

                                                    Camden — Phila
   April 8, '84 —
        I have been living here in Camden now for nearly eleven years. Came on from Washington in the summer of '73, after my paralytic-stroke, and the death of my dear mother. Continued for three years in quite a bad way, not strength enough to walk any distance — stomach and head miserable. In '76 began to get better — about that time — went board'g down in the country livg in the open air, as described in the preceding volume. From the fall of '76 to the present writing (April, '84) I have been well enough to go around most of the time, with occasional spells of sickness — one of which, (over two months,) I am just now recover'g from.
(See *Prose Works 1892*, II, 598–600, "Additional Note, 1887, to the English Edition 'Specimen Days,'" the beginning of which is somewhat similar to the above paragraph.)

1800.   As in the case young men in footnotes 1741 and 1766, and on countless other occasions: a name, address, brief note, and that's all.

Rolleston (till end of June) [1801]
Liegan bei die Radeberg – Saxony

Coaches miss the 10 and 40 minutes
    after from Phil: side – after 8 p m only
    take the ½ past boats

Evan Royal
"the Kid" – conductor
Market St cars[1802]

Randolph Lewis
reporter Times

[Three lines in pencil:]
    Mr Patterson, carpenter 529 Mickle[1803]
Vincent S Cook   [on scrap, not in WW's hand:]
    Press   L. B. Harrison[1804]
——————————————————— 108 Queen st
                        Germantown
                        Philada. Pa.

Henry Tyrrell   126 Waverley Place[1805]
                New York
    [two lines in pencil:]
    p o box 3708
    Frank Leslie's Pub House

[251]

April 1884 – now at 328 Mickle street

18 – sent the Centennial Edn two Vols. to Thos. J.
                    [two words in red ink, last word in purple pencil:]
    McKee, 338 Broome st.   N Y City   paid 10   rec'd

1801. Although it is not recorded in the *Daybook*, Whitman received a letter from T. W. H. Rolleston on 17 March 1884 (see Horst Frenz, *Whitman and Rolleston: A Correspondence*, pp. 83–86); and another on 20 April 1884 (see below, that date; and also Frenz, *ibid.*, pp. 87–88).

1802. Evan Royal, Randolph Lewis, and Vincent S. Cook seem to be chance acquaintances Whitman met in Philadelphia.

1803. Patterson, living near Whitman's new location on Mickle Street, was hired on 2–3 June 1884 to work for Whitman; see entry for that date.

1804. L. Birge Harrison wrote to Whitman on 27 June 1884, praising *Specimen Days* (letter in the Library of Congress), and again a few days later (letter in the Feinberg Collection).

1805. Henry Tyrrell, apparently connected with Frank Leslie's Publishing House (as the name written here suggests), wrote to Whitman on 31 May 1884 (letter in the Feinberg Collection), and Whitman thanked him on 2 June 1884 for the "loving note & beautiful little enclosure" — *The Correspondence of Walt Whitman*, III, 372.

20 – rec'd letter from Rolleston, Dresden. He
  has finished the (~~partial~~) translation
  of L of G pieces into German – & now
  seems to be adjusting, polishing, revising
  them into final publication shape
  [two lines in pencil:]
  – sent letter to R. re   suggesting the printing
  of the English text with the German[1806]
  Sent 2^d letter, with endorsement to go in R's preface
  – & recommending that Salut au Monde be included

22 – Cross'd on the boat with Eugene Turner,[1807]
  – walked up together to 3^d street

[Entry, two lines, in pencil:]
24   sent author's Ed'n L of G. to Harry   ⌐paid
                                             │   recd   [word in purple pencil]
     Falkenan, Cornell University, Ithaca   ⌐$3

May 18 – Rec'd letter from Rolleston, Dresden,
  intimates that he will give the English text
  with his German translation – will give Salut
  au Monde[1808]

May 1st [1809] – Paid ($1.44) for Sunday and Daily Press
  – pays up to date

[Seven lines in pencil:]
  Dr Bucke here with Mrs B – staying at R
  P Smith's   Germantown – I go over every after-
  noon – the project for the special ed'n

1806. See footnote 1801, and Whitman's letter in *The Correspondence of Walt Whitman*,
III, 369; another letter is in William Sloane Kennedy's *The Fight of a Book for the World*
(West Yarmouth, Mass., 1926), pp. 249–250, reprinted in Horst Frenz, *Whitman and Rolleston:
A Correspondence*, pp. 89.
  1807. Unidentified.
  1808. See footnotes 1801 and 1806; this letter is in Horst Frenz, *Whitman and Rolleston:
A Correspondence*, pp. 90–91.
  1809. In *Walt Whitman's Diary in Canada* (Boston, 1904), p. 62, is the following paragraph in the section "From Other Journals of Walt Whitman":
    Sunday Morning, early May, '84. As I saunter along I mark the profuse pink-and-
  white of the wild honeysuckle, the creamy blossoming of the dog-wood; everything most
  fragrant, early season; odors of pine and oak and the flowering grape-vines; the difference between shady places and strong sunshine; the holy Sabbath morning; the
  myriad living columns of the temple, the soothing silence, the incense of some moss,
  and the earth fragrance after a rain, strangely touching the soul.

L of G. backed by Mr S. and Dr.   Mr S's per
sudden & peremptory withdrawal from the
project. (Mrs. S "wouldn't allow the book to be
    brought in the house.") [1810]

[252]

[In pencil, on scrap of paper:]
    Mrs Rogers[1811]
    109   6th

[Printed slip:]

            Mrs. Dr. Drake[1812]
                So. Boston,
    35 G. Street.   Mass.

[253]

1884 – June – 328 Mickle Street

newspaper notice of my 65th birthday   May 31 '84 [1813]

Harry Stafford is at Marlton, N. J. – is to be
    married soon[1814]

Critic   May 31 prints a fabulous 'episode' [1815]

June 2 – Evening – met M Altman on the ferry

1810. A few years later Whitman told Horace Traubel, "Mrs. Smith — Hannah — and I never hitched: she is very evangelical: she takes her doctrine, if she don't take her whiskey, very straight: the sort of get under my feet religion which gives hell out to the crowd and saves heaven for the few. Well — I didn't agree very well with Hannah — still, there was no demonstration." (See Horace Traubel, *With Walt Whitman in Camden*, I, 172). This passage in the *Daybook* is as close as we come to a "demonstration," but as seen from the entry below for 2 June 1884, Mrs Smith, with Mary and Alys, gave Whitman "a most kind & serviceable [birthday] present."

1811. This Mrs Rogers may be Susan Stafford's sister, though in 1882 she was living at 431 Linden Street, Camden.

1812. Mrs A. B. Drake, obviously a physician, was sent some article or paper in August 1881 (see entry above); and Whitman visited her on 18 October 1881 when he was in Boston while James R. Osgood & Co. was printing *Leaves of Grass* (see entry above).

1813. According to a transcript of a letter of 29 May 1884 in *The Correspondence of Walt Whitman*, III, 371, Whitman sent a release, "Walt Whitman's Birthday," to be used in the Philadelphia *Times* on 31 May 1884.

1814. In his letter to Harry Stafford, 28 May 1884, Whitman did not mention the marriage — see *The Correspondence of Walt Whitman*, III, 371 — but he does remark on it here, and the wedding is recorded in the *Daybook* on 25 June 1884.

1815. "A Fabulous 'Episode,' " *The Critic*, n.s. I (31 May 1884), 258, in which Whitman (in the third person) repudiated a tale that the first (1855) *Leaves of Grass* was to be dedicated to Longfellow if Whitman would excise some passages: see Whitman's brief letter to Jeannette L. Gilder, 27 May 1884, in *The Correspondence of Walt Whitman*, III, 370.

at his special request
– went with him   to the "beauty show"
(Dime Museum, 9th and Arch) an amusing
                                            hour
rec'd a most kind & serviceable present
from Mary & Alys Smith & Mrs S.   nice
new sheets & pillow and bolster cases
for my bed [1816]

June 2ᵈ, 3ᵈ – Mr Patterson, carpenter, here putting
up the shelving, & cutting the rear window[1817]

                    age
2 Alfred Bennett, 22, spends the evening with
me – one of 6 children – traveling canvasser
for photo: material establishment [1818]

4 Peter Doyle here with me[1819]

6 sent Author's Ed'n L of G to Tom W   [two words in blue pencil:]
                                              recd
                                              ✛ paid

Neal, State Gazette, Dyersburg Tenn

[Two lines in pencil:]
Joshua Killingbeck mason, laying the front
brick pavement, paid him $10.98

11 sent Dr J W Bartlett, Chicopee Falls   Mass
Authors Ed'n L of G. $3 – paid – rec'd [1820]

12 sent $3 ed'n L of G to Chas Aldrich,[1821] Lock Box A
                                [last word in red:]
Webster City   Hamilton County Iowa. $1 due paid

1816. See footnote 1810.
1817. See footnote 1803.
1818. Alfred Bennett does not turn up again, either in the *Daybook* or anywhere in Whitman letters, so this may well be the only time Whitman saw him.
1819. Peter Doyle had previously visited Whitman on 7 December 1883; as far as we know, they had not been corresponding at this time.
1820. See Whitman's letter to Dr J. W. Bartlett in *The Correspondence of Walt Whitman,* III, 372.
1821. Charles Aldrich wrote Whitman on 8 July 1885, asking for an autograph (letter in the Library of Congress).

17   Visit two hours, from Dr Wm A Hawley   Syracuse
N. Y. (bo't Spec Days) spoke of Benton Wilson[1822]

Folger McKinzey comes occasionally[1823]

[254]

[On slip, in pencil, not in WW's hand:]   The Rev. Henry Scott Jefferys,
cor. Post & Powell
San Francisco
California

[in pencil:]
Pete
646 So Broad [1824]
[in pencil:]
Dr J H R Wroth [1825]
13 Cromwell Block
Albuquerque
N M

[Printed slip: G. Davies & Co., booksellers and stationers, Seattle, W. T.]

[255]

June   1884   328 Mickle St
23 – (Monday) visit from George Chainey – 3 hours talk –
very satisfactory – yesterday (Sunday) Mr C delivered
lectures on L of G in N. Y. City, Newark and
Philadelphia – He says " 'T'would have done you
have
good to ∧ seen how responsive the audiences were,
and how enthusiastically they applauded." [1826]

20, 21 &c.   visit from Jeff, Hattie and Jess[1827]

1822. Benton H. Wilson was an ex-soldier whom Whitman met in a War hospital in Washington, and the two corresponded until 1875; Wilson's letters are in the Feinberg and Berg Collections, and Whitman's letters to Wilson, 12 April 1867 and 15 April 1870 are in *The Correspondence of Walt Whitman*, I, 323–324; II, 95–96. Wilson's son was named Walt Whitman Wilson.

1823. Folger McKinsey (1866–1950), described as "a young Philadelphian of literary leanings," wrote to Whitman on 10 June 1884, asking for an autograph (letter in the Feinberg Collection). See Ernest J. Moyne, *Walt Whitman Review*, XXI (December 1975), 135–144.

1824. Peter Doyle's address in Philadelphia?

1825. See footnote 1708.

1826. For George Chainey, see footnote 1543.

1827. Whitman's favorite brother, from St Louis, Missouri, with his two daughters Mannahatta and Jessie.

21, 22, '3 & '4   hot – hot – hot   [line, except '3 & '4 in red ink]

18 – 20 Edward Carpenter here[1828]

25   Sent Author's Ed'n L of G to F H Williams   recd [1829]

24   Spent afternoon & evn'g at Mr & Mrs Williams's
                                     MS
      Germantown — Mr. W's   article ₋o N A Review
         refused [1830]
      in reply – Mr Harrison, artist (his letters to me) [1831]

25   Harry Stafford here – Evn'g at Mayor Bradshaw's[1832]
      H S and Eva Westcott married – (the throat trouble) [1833]

26   a rain, heavy, commenced last night – Cooler

July 6 – sent author's ed'n L of G to Franklin Otis, South
                              rec'd
      Scituate, Mass.   paid   [in blue pencil]

      rec'd   200 from Dr B[1834]

10   sent Specimen Days to Anna M Wilkinson[1835]
      12 Bootham Terrace, York, England.
                          recd   [in red ink]
         for Edward Carpenter   paid   [last word in red ink]

1828. Edward Carpenter (see footnote 20) was here making his second visit to Camden — the first was in 1877 — and was one of the earliest pilgrims to see Whitman at 328 Mickle Street: see Gay Wilson Allen, *The Solitary Singer,* pp. 316–317.

1829. See footnote 1765; the Williamses were one of the families Whitman visited in Philadelphia at this time, as seen in the next entry below.

1830. This MS article is unidentified; Francis Howard Williams's first of several pieces on Whitman did not appear in *The American* (Philadelphia) until 1888.

1831. L. Birge Harrison's letters to Whitman, 27 and 30(?) June 1884, are in the Library of Congress and the Feinberg Collection (see footnote 1804).

1832. Harry Stafford was married to Eva Westcott by Claudius W. Bradshaw, mayor of Camden (see *The Correspondence of Walt Whitman,* III, 371n).

1833. The throat trouble, which Whitman mentions here, was earlier referred to in his letter to Harry Stafford of 28 May 1884: "I am sorry you have that trouble with your throat, but I have no doubt it will go over in time" (*The Correspondence of Walt Whitman,* III, 371; see also III, 3–9, on the Whitman-Stafford relationship).

1834. This $200 which Whitman borrowed from Dr Bucke was probably used to help repair the house on Mickle Street, although the Lays had not yet left the place.

1835. Anna M. Wilkinson wrote Whitman on 21 July 1884 (letter in the Feinberg Collection), acknowledging receipt of the book.

12   D McKay paid me 69.45 for copyright[1836] } $91.41
                      21.96 for overcharge

14   Hatta and Jessie here[1837]

                                rec'd [in red ink]
19   sent L of G to Parker Pillsbury   Concord N H [1838]

30   sent $16 to Mrs. Goodenough for Ed's board [1839]

last of July & first part of Aug.   the sick baby Harry
                                              Lay[1840]

[256]

Talcott Williams   1833 Spruce St   Phila[1841]

[Card of John P. Miller, shirt, collar and cuff manufacturer and dealer in hosiery, etc., 107 S. 8th St., Phila.; printed slip of Cupples, Upham & Co., booksellers and importers, 283 Washington St., Boston.]

[Card of Sierra Grande Mining Co., 330 Walnut St., Phila., with signature, not in WW's hand: Francis Bacon / Secry./; and on card of John K. Randall, attorney, Baltimore:]

_____   dead [1842]

Mercantile Library

T W Rolleston (Jan: 89)[1843]
      Glasshouse   Shinrone King's Co   Ireland
later   ~~Prospect~~, Delganky   Co Wicklow
      Fairview – Delgany.

1836. Whitman wrote the Librarian of Congress on 30 July 1884, renewing his copyright of *Leaves of Grass* for 14 years: see *The Correspondence of Walt Whitman*, III, 373.
    1837. Mannahatta and Jessie Whitman, the poet's nieces from St Louis, made a long visit to Camden the last year, remaining in the East until 1 December 1883: see footnote 1827.
    1838. Parker Pillsbury's letter of 30 July 1884 (in the Library of Congress) acknowledged receipt of *Leaves of Grass*.
    1839. No matter how difficult things became for Whitman financially, he always took care of the board for his feeble-minded brother Edward, who was to outlive Walt by several months (he died 30 November 1892).
    1840. The Lay family, living in Whitman's house at 328 Mickle Street, lost one young son Tasker Lay on 9 March 1884, and the baby Harry Lay died on 7 August 1884 and was buried three days later (see entry below). This page from the *Daybook* is reproduced as illustration no. 10 in *The Correspondence of Walt Whitman*, III, ff. 202.
    1841. See footnote 799; Talcott Williams was editor of the Philadelphia *Press*.
    1842. The end of Whitman's venture in mining stock, given him by Robert Pearsall Smith (see footnote 1715).
    1843. T. W. H. Rolleston, Whitman's Irish correspondent since 1879 (see footnote 50), and "Jan: 89" must refer to Whitman's letter of 22 January 1889, which is now lost.

[257]

Aug: 1884   328 Mickle Street

4   Sent letter to R U Johnson, Century Magazine
     acceding to ~~the~~ his request for Hospital
                         accepted – paid \ [in red ink]
     article for magazine – Sent <u>Father Taylor</u>
     _____$50 [1844]

          [in pencil:] earthquake

                                          funeral
7 – noon — death of the baby, little Harry Lay   10ᵗʰ
                              <u>the earthquake</u>   [last two words in red ink]

_____

8 – sent "What lurks behind Shakspere's
     historical plays?" to <u>Nineteenth Century</u>,
                            returned – sent Sept 1 to N A Review   [four lines in red ink]
     London – 50 – _____
                            sent Sept. 16 to Critic –   returned
                                           published
                                  paid   15 [1845]

_____

9   Saturday Evn'g – dinner at Mr & Mrs: Talcott
     Williams's 1833 Spruce St. Phil [1846]

_____

                              [in purple pencil:]
10   $25 from J H Johnston for portrait   75 due[1847]

_____

"   10th – the baby's funeral [1848] – the earthquake shock – [1849]

_____

13 to 17 – Hannah's sickness – letters from Heyde[1850]

1844. Letter to Robert Underwood Johnson: *The Correspondence of Walt Whitman,*
III, 373–374; Johnson (1853–1937), staff member of *The Century Magazine,* asked Whitman
for a Civil War article, and he sent "Army Hospitals and Cases: Memoranda at the Time,
1863–66," but it did not appear until October 1888, XXXVI, 825–830; "Father Taylor and
Oratory" also took some time to appear in *The Century Magazine,* XXXIII (February 1887),
583–584. Both were included in *November Boughs* (1888), the former with the title "Last
of the War Cases"; see *Prose Works 1892,* II, 549–552, for "Father Taylor (and Oratory),"
and II, 614–626, for "Last of the War Cases: Memorandized at the time, Washington, 1865-'66."
1845. See footnote 1485; "What Lurks Behind Shakspeare's Historical Plays?" *The
Critic,* n.s. II (27 September 1884), 145, reprinted in *Democratic Vistas and Other Papers*
(London, 1888): see *Prose Works 1892,* II, 554–556.
1846. See footnotes 799 and 1841.
1847. See *The Correspondence of Walt Whitman,* III, 368, 374, 382, and 384; and
Horace Traubel, *With Walt Whitman in Camden,* III, 331; when John H. Johnston (of New
York City) visited Whitman in March 1884 he arranged to buy the Hine portrait of Whitman for $200, sending $100 on 25 March and other amounts later.
1848. The baby was Harry Lay: see footnote 1840.
1849. This earthquake shock is not listed among the major quakes.
1850. See *The Correspondence of Walt Whitman,* III, 384n for a brief outline of the

19   to-day one from H.[1851]

19   sent Pliny B Smith, law office, Chicago the
       two Vols – paid $5 –   [in red ink, sideways:]   recd
                                                                 paid [1852]

18, 19, 20, 21.   hot, hot, hot │ sent letter to
                                 │ Rolleston[1853]

21   30 recd – 8th dividend Sierra Grande[1854]

23ᵈ to 28ᵗʰ at R P Smith's – Germantown[1855]

28   sent L of G to Mrs. Annie Bessey, 2
                                 [three words in red ink:]
              West Adams St. Syracuse N Y   recd   paid 3

Sept. 1.   paid newspaper carrier up to date $1.42

     rec'd 'the Booths'   from Edwin B [1855a]

5 – 9ᵗʰ   Sierra Grande dividend   rec'd – 50 [1856]

3ᵈ, 4ᵗʰ 5ᵗʰ 6ᵗʰ 7ᵗʰ &c – hot hot   hot – 9 or 10   days

                                                        [258]

Ruth Stafford married – Wᵐ C Goldy[1857]

relationship between the Heydes and Whitman, especially Hannah's illness and Heyde's asking Whitman for money; for a selection of letters of Charles L. Heyde to Whitman (in the Trent Collection, Duke University) see Clarence Gohdes and Rollo G. Silver, *Faint Clews & Indirections* (Durham, North Carolina, 1949), pp. 213–232, but there are none published from 1884, such as those dated 14 October, 2 and 25 November, and 20 December; Hannah Heyde's letter of 20 (?) October 1884 is in the Library of Congress.

1851.   This letter from Hannah (?) lost.
1852.   Pliny B. Smith's letter, 16 August 1884, ordering the books, is in the Library of Congress.
1853.   Letter: *The Correspondence of Walt Whitman*, III, 375; also in Horst Frenz, *Whitman and Rolleston: A Correspondence* (Bloomington, Indiana, 1951), pp. 92–93, with Rolleston's reply, 9 September 1884, pp. 94–97.
1854.   See footnotes 1715 and 1842.
1855.   This was Whitman's first recorded overnight visit to Robert Pearsall Smith's since January.
1855a.   Edwin Booth (1833–1893) sent Whitman a book on the Booths for a piece which was in the New York *Tribune*, 16 August 1885. See *The Correspondence of Walt Whitman*, III, 376; *Walt Whitman Review*, VI (September 1960), 49–50; and *Prose Works 1892*, II, 591–597.
1856.   This was apparently the final dividend from the mining stock: see footnotes indicated in footnotes 1715 and 1842.
1857.   The wedding was on 19 August 1884; Whitman apparently did not attend.

8 Berkeley Street   [three lines

   Cambridge   not WW's hand]

    Massachusetts.

The Critic [printed]
·743 Broadway
~~28 Astor Place~~ [printed]
New York [printed] [1858]

Folger McKinsey[1858a]

   care H H Yard Monmouth Co:
    Ocean Beach   New Jersey

1716 Vine St
Phil

Mrs Ann E
Farwell [1859]
Nankin p o
Wayne Co
Michigan

Horsman's – hat binding &
  notions – 5th & Cherry

[Two names and addresses not in WW's hand:]
John Addington Symonds[1860]
Am Hof   Davos Platz   Graŭbünden
       Switzerland

Cyril Flower
  Surrey House
   Hyde Park Place
    London   W

[259]

Sept: 1884

1858. On 16 September 1884 (not recorded in the *Daybook*, but see *The Correspondence of Walt Whitman*, III, 377) Whitman sent *The Critic* his piece, "What Lurks Behind Shakspeare's Historical Plays?" (see footnote 1845 and entry above for 8 August 1844).

1858a. See footnote 1823.

1859. Mrs Ann E. Farwell was a member of the family of Reuben Farwell, whom Whitman met in the hospital in Washington (see footnote 174).

1860. See footnote 81; Symonds and Cyril Flower were among the six "friends (or used to be friends) of L. of G. and W. W.," in a list Whitman sent Herbert Gilchrist in a letter of 15 September 1885 — see *The Correspondence of Walt Whitman*, III, 405. For Flower, see footnote 51.

[in purple pencil, four lines on slip pasted to page:]

Mr.

11th   Prof's Tylor, Barrett and ∧ Costello
       call'd – with Mary Smith[1861]
       Talk – (Humphry Ward, London <u>Times</u>) [1862]
       gave "<u>As a Strong Bird</u>" to each[1863]

14   Sunday – jaunt to Cape May, W J. RR
       fine days – ride to Sewell's Point – pleasant
       sail around the little inner bay – boatman
       Richardson – dinner at Mr Duffy's Congress Hall
       – Sea Breeze – Mr Gladding – the champagne[1864]

18   sent L of G   (author's ed'n) to Anna M Wil-
                              paid – recd [1865]
       kinson, 12 Bootham Terrace, York, Eng

19   sent L of G. and S D. to Cupples, Upham
                                    recd
       & Co.   283 Washington St. Boston $5 due   paid [1866]

[in purple pencil, next two entries:]
20   letter from Rolleston – he has returned

1861. Mary Smith was Whitman's favorite member of Robert Pearsall Smith's family (see footnote 1641 and numerous other footnotes and entries above); I cannot identify Professors Tylor and Barrett, but "Mr. Costello" was without doubt Benjamin Francis Conn Costelloe (1854–1899), who was in Montreal in August 1884, came to Harvard shortly afterwards, met Mary Smith there, visited the Smiths in Philadelphia, and came to Camden to see Whitman (see Robert Allerton Parker, *The Transatlantic Smiths*, New York, 1959, pp. 54–55). Mary Smith and Frank Costelloe were married the next year.

1862. Could this be in error for Mrs Humphry Ward (1851–1920), the English author of popular novels at this time?

1863. This was a 68-page publication, *As a Strong Bird on Pinions Free and Other Poems,* which Whitman published in Washington in 1872.

1864. In *Walt Whitman's Diary in Canada* (Boston, 1904), pp. 62–63, is the following paragraph in the section "From Other Journals of Walt Whitman":

Sunday, Sept. 14, '84, Cape May, N. J. I am writing this on the beach at Cape May. Came down this morning on the West Jersey R. R.; had a good ride along the shore, then a sail, beating about in a fine breeze for over an hour; then a capital good dinner (a friend I met insisted on my having some champagne). After dinner I went down alone and have had two soothing hours close by the sea-edge, seated on the sand, to the hoarse music of the surf rolling in.

To this the editor, William Sloane Kennedy, adds in a footnote: "It was on this Jersey shore that, a few months previously, he had composed his wonderful poem 'With Husky-Haughty Lips, O Sea,' of which he sent me a proof-slip (as he often did of other poems) inscribed 'Harper's Monthly, March '84.' " This poem was actually composed, in part, at Ocean Grove, not Cape May (see footnote 1714, above).

1865. See footnote 1835; Anna Wilkinson must have ordered *Leaves of Grass* after reading *Specimen Days.*

1866. The letter ordering the books, 17 September 1884, is in the Feinberg Collection.

to Ireland — he cannot find a publisher
in Dresden for his translation of
  Was added to by Knortz & is to be pub. by Schabeltz   [line in red ink]
L of G – says he will send it here –   ∧ Zurich   [in red ink]
                             Switzerland   [in red ink]
– I wrote a postal card to him[1867]

21 Sunday – James Godfrey here – good day

  sent Centennial Ed'n – 2 Vols – to John K
                      [in red ink:]
Randall, 40 St Paul st   Baltimore   Paid
                      $10 [1868]

Oct 3 – Sent Vols. portrait &c to J. K Randall
            [two words in red ink:]
    Baltimore $5 due   recd – paid –

13 the two boxes arrived from Wash'n by express
                $7.10

                    [in red ink:]
17 sent "Blithe Throat" to Harpers – 30 ask'd acct'd [1869]
                      paid

  sent $20 to Hannah – $3 to Eddy for shoes[1870]

[260]

    left [in red ink]   left [in red ink]
Dick Labar   p o box 274   Ann Arbor   Mich[1871]

1867. Draft letter: *The Correspondence of Walt Whitman*, III, 377; Rolleston's letter, 9 September 1884, is in Horace Traubel, *With Walt Whitman in Camden*, I, 18–21; and Horst Frenz, *Whitman and Rolleston: A Correspondence* (Bloomington, Indiana, 1951), pp. 94–97.

1868. It was on the inside of an envelope from John K. Randall, attorney-at-law, that Whitman wrote his draft of a letter mentioned above in footnote 1867; Whitman added in red ink: "Sent to Rolleston, Ireland, Sept. 20 '84."

1869. Whitman's poem, "Of That Blithe Throat of Thine," was published in *Harper's Monthly*, LXX (January 1885), 264; see *Leaves of Grass*, Comprehensive Reader's Edition, pp. 520–521.

1870. This $20 must have been in response to Charles L. Heyde's letter of 14 October 1884 about Whitman's sister Hannah's illness (see footnote 1850); Whitman helped his retarded brother Edward in a number of ways, paying his board as well as buying shoes.

1871. Richard Labar was Whitman's friend who had been on the staff of the Philadelphia *Public Ledger* (see entries above for 10 November 1881 and others).

```
B H Hinds
134 So: 2ᵈ Special Ag't
cor Gold and Dock
Phila
```

```
Mr. Edward Clifford. [printed] ¹⁸⁷⁴
52 Wigmore Street, W.   [printed]
London
```

```
Smith Caswell ¹⁸⁷⁵
Roxbury
Delaware Co. N Y
```

```
Edward Carpenter¹⁸⁷²
Millthorpe
near Chesterfield
Eng:
```

```
John Burroughs¹⁸⁷⁶
West Park
Ulster Co:  N Y
```

```
Francis H Williams¹⁸⁷³
Return to Room 1 [printed]
No.209 So.Third St., Philadelphia, Pa.
```

```
Gabriel Harrison, [printed]
44 Court St., Brooklyn, N.Y.
[printed] ¹⁸⁷⁷
```

[261]

October   1884

23 – sent L of G. & S D. two Vols. to W M Rossetti¹⁸⁷⁸

recd [in pencil]

5 Endsleigh Gardens, Euston Road, London N W

1872. Edward Carpenter (see footnote 20) was Whitman's English admirer who had visited Whitman recently for the second time.
1873. See footnote 1765.
1874. Edward Clifford, an English portrait painter for whom Whitman sat (see entries below for 3 and 8, 9, 10 October 1884) when he visited Robert Pearsall Smith in Germantown, Philadelphia (see *The Correspondence of Walt Whitman,* III, 380, 381); they talked of Whitman's friends in England.
1875. Whitman must have got Smith Caswell's address from John Burroughs, for whom Caswell worked at Esopus, New York, when Burroughs visited Whitman on 4 and 5 December 1884.
1876. Had Burroughs moved from Esopus, or was this a temporary address?
1877. Gabriel Harrison's letter, 10 March 1885, acknowledging receipt of a book, is in the Feinberg Collection.
1878. William Michael Rossetti (see footnote 14) does not appear in the *Daybook* for several months, and in June 1882 John Burroughs had reported that Whitman's great champion in England called *Leaves of Grass* "nasty" (see *The Correspondence of Walt Whitman,* III, 301n); nevertheless, Rossetti's letter to Whitman, 1 January 1885, acknowledging *Leaves* and *Specimen Days* (see Horace Traubel, *With Walt Whitman in Camden,* I, 436–437), is all praise and affection.
1879. In *Walt Whitman's Diary in Canada* (Boston, 1904), p. 73, is the following paragraph in the section "From Other Journals of Walt Whitman":
PRESIDENTIAL ELECTION. *Oct.* 31, '84. The political parties are trying — but mostly in vain — to get up some fervor of excitement on the pending Presidential election. It comes off next Tuesday. There is no question at issue of any importance. I cannot "enthuse" at all. I think of the elections of '30 and '20. Then there *was* something to arouse a fellow. But I like well the *fact* of all these national elections — have written a little poem about it (to order), — published in a Philadelphia daily, of 26th instant. [The candidates in '84 were Blaine and Cleveland; the issues tariff and Chinese exclusion.

26 "If I should need to name, O Western World"
                    [in pencil:]
    in Phil Press   paid   10 [1879]

Nov 3 – sent two L of G. to Fitzgerald Lee   High-
                                    recd [two words, in red ink]
       lands, St Savior's, Jersey, Chanal Isles – paid [1880]

       Sent check $16 for Ed's board to Mrs Goodenough[1881]

       Edward Clifford here from England – he draws
       my portrait for Addington Symonds.
             two sittings — [1882]

       sent $16 to Mrs. Goodenough for Ed's board

6th & 7th The contested Presidential election,
       Cleveland or Blaine – the excitement
       increasing – more the last two days
       than any time during the election itself [1883]

11 – paid 1:38 to newspaper carrier

8, 9, 10 – visit to R P S's   Germantown
         – Edward Clifford [1884]

13 – Sent $20 to C L Heyde   Burlington, Vt[1885]

Blaine was defeated, owing to [Roscoe] Conkling's defection.]
To this the editor, William Sloane Kennedy, adds in a footnote: " 'If I Should Need to Name,
O Western World.' *Press,* October 26 (styled now 'Election Day, 1884.' It is only poetic prose.
Compare it with Whittier's nervy lyric 'After Election.')"
    "Election Day, November, 1884" was included in *Sands at Seventy* (1888-9): see *Leaves
of Grass,* Comprehensive Reader's Edition, p. 517. Talcott Williams was editor of the
Philadelphia *Press* at this time: see Whitman's four letters to him in *The Correspondence of
Walt Whitman,* III, 378-380.
    1880. See footnote 1424; Lee wanted to translate *Leaves of Grass* into Russian, but
nothing came of the project.
    1881. Whitman twice wrote here in the *Daybook* (see below) that he was paying as
usual for his feeble-minded brother's board.
    1882. See footnote 1874.
    1883. See footnote 1879.
    1884. See footnote 1874; Edward Clifford was visiting his friend Robert Pearsall Smith.
    1885. See footnotes 1850 and 1870; Heyde wrote Whitman on 2 and 25 November
and 20 December 1884 (letters in the Trent Collection, Duke University).

17 – rec'd $25 from J H J for Portrait – ($50 $\overset{\text{due}}{\text{now}}$) [1886]

27 – over to Germantown to the Smiths to dinner[1887]

29   sent L of G. ($3) to Will W Christman

[two words in red ink:]

recd

Quaker st.   Schenectady Co N Y   paid

Dec. 2, 3, 4.   Dr Bucke here – we dine at
    Continental – Phil. every day[1888]

4th & 5th – John Burroughs here – he & Dr B
    & self all at R P S's   Germantown – the ride
    in the morning – they two go to N. Y. afternoon[1889]

[262]

Wm Ramsay , 14 Adams Ex. (Ferry   Phila)   [in pencil]
[On slip:]   Wm M Rossetti[1890]

London
5 Endsleigh Gardens   N W
Euston Square.

[263]

Dec. 1884 _____

10 – rec'd $71.63 from David McKay for royalties[1891]

Dec 19, 20 –   Extremely cold
    gloomy news from dear sister Hannah[1892]
    letter worse than ever from the wretched

1886. See footnote 1847.
1887. Whitman had written the recently married Harry and Eva Stafford, 18 November 1884, that he could not spend Thanksgiving with them in Marlton, New Jersey; instead, as seen here, he was with Robert Pearsall Smith and his family.
1888. Dr Bucke had last visited Whitman in May (see above).
1889. For a long quotation from John Burroughs's journal, 4 December 1884, see Clara Barrus, *Whitman and Burroughs: Comrades* (Boston and New York, 1931), pp. 250–251.
1890. See footnote 1878.
1891. In comparison with 1882 and even as poor a year as 1883 for royalties, 1884 was not financially a good time for Whitman (see footnote 1754): from McKay all that Whitman recorded was $91.41 of 12 July 1884 for copyright and overcharge and this $71.63 for royalties; other earnings and book sales were negligible. Furthermore, he bought the house on Mickle Street, had to repair it, and later to furnish it, borrowing $500 from George W. Childs and $200 from Dr Bucke to help pay for these expenses.
1892. See footnotes 1850, 1870, and 1885 and letters in the Trent Collection.

cur, C L H – 21 – 24 snow, & very cold

22   sent D M Evans, Mapleton Depot, Huntingdon

                                                          [in red ink:]
          co. Pa.   the $3 ed'n L of G.   paid   recd

                                                          [in red ink:]
23 – sent $10 to Hannah – $10 to Mary   both rec'd [1893]

      recd Dowden's "English Criticisms on Walt

            Whitman" from Wilson & McCormick [1894]

      rec'd $50 from J H Johnston, for portrait
                          now paid in full, $200 [1895]

1885 –
Jan 5 – Sent L of G.   S D. Dr B's book & John
      Burroughs's Notes to Mrs. Dr A B Drake
                                                Paid [in red ink:]
      35 G Street South, Boston, Mass $10 recd [1896]

                      [in red ink:]   recd
      Sent L of G. to Gabriel Harrison, by J H J [1897]

      Evn'g Jan 6 – Oyster and champagne supper at
            Bart Bonsall's – good time[1898]

[in red ink,   7   Sent E M Abdy-Williams,[1899] care of Messrs.
sideways:]   Sonnenschein, Time Monthly office, White Hart
                      St. Paternoster Square, London, Eng. the two
a second   Vols. L of G and S D – paid – miscarried
set sent   another set sent   rec'd
rec'd

1893. Despite hard times, Whitman sent Christmas money to his two sisters.
1894. Edward Dowden's "English Critics on Walt Whitman" was included as a supplement to the English edition of Dr Richard Maurice Bucke's *Walt Whitman* (Glasgow: Wilson & McCormick, 1884), pp. 237-255; second edition, 1888.
1895. See footnote 1847, entries for 10 August and 17 November 1884, and *The Correspondence of Walt Whitman*, III, 384.
1896. Whitman's *Leaves of Grass* and *Specimen Days,* Dr R. M. Bucke's *Walt Whitman,* and John Burroughs's *Notes on Walt Whitman as Poet and Person* — all sent to Mrs A. B. Drake, whom Whitman had known for several years and whom he visited in Boston on 18 October 1881 (see entry above). She had as full a Whitman collection as was possible at this time and must have had other copies of these books.
1897. See footnote 1877; Harrison, who lived in Brooklyn, must have been a friend of John H. Johnston, the jewelry merchant.
1898. Bartram Bonsall, a long-time Whitman friend, was coeditor with his father, Henry Lummis Bonsall, of the Camden *Daily Post.*
1899. Letter: *The Correspondence of Walt Whitman*, III, 385.

11   fine dinner, & jolly three hours at

[five words in red ink:]

T B Harned's, Federal St   sent Mrs. H
                           copper kettle[1900]

---

abt   7th or before – visit from Edmund Gosse[1901]

1900.   Thomas B. Harned, a Camden lawyer and brother-in-law of Horace L. Traubel, who was to become, with Traubel and Dr R. M. Bucke, Whitman's literary executor, met the poet about this time; Whitman, as seen from entries below, spent numerous Sundays at the Harned home, and became better acquainted there with Traubel; of course the mention of Harned's name in Traubel's *With Walt Whitman in Camden* runs into the hundreds, and Harned not only wrote pieces on Whitman in *The Conservator,* but edited (with Dr Bucke and Traubel) *In Re Walt Whitman* (Philadelphia, 1893) and *The Complete Writings of Walt Whitman* (1902), containing three Harned essays, "Walt Whitman and His *Second* Boston Publishers," "Whitman and Physique," and "Whitman and Oratory."

The *Daybook* mentions only this visit to the Harned's; but in *Walt Whitman's Diary in Canada* (Boston, 1904), pp. 63–65, is the following material in the section "From Other Journals of Walt Whitman":

Jan. 11, '85. At J. M. S[covel]'s Hinds' army reminiscences as he told them by the wood fire in S.'s parlor. The scenes of May, '64, as witnessed at Fredericksburg; that whole town glutted, filled, probably 15 to 20,000 wounded, broken, dead, dying soldiers, sent northward from Grant's forces on their terrific promenade from the Rapidan down to Petersburg, fighting the way, not only day by day, but mile by mile — sent up from the battles of "the Wilderness"; groups, crowds, or ones or twos, lying in every house, in every church, uncared for; the hundreds and hundreds dying; the other hundreds of corpses of the dead; the fearful heat of the weather; the many undressed wounds filled with maggots (actually more than one thousand, and more than two thousand, such cases).

[The following four items marked in red ink "Specimen Days." There are many such in his MSS. evidently intended for a possible new edition.]

Grisi and Mario arrived in N. Y. Aug. 19, 1854; I heard them that winter and in 1855.

The cholera in N. Y. in 1855.

Kossuth in America in 1851; I saw him make his entrée in N. Y. latter part of 1851, riding up Broadway.

N. Y. Exposition (Crystal Palace), 6th Ave., 40th to 42d St.; opened July 14, 1853 (I go for a year); the great heat August that year — 400 deaths in three or four days in N. Y. [For more about this Crystal Palace, see Dr. R. M. Bucke's *Walt Whitman,* p. 25.]

[Among Whitman's MSS. I find the following clipping from the Brooklyn *Daily Times,* Jan. 20, '85.]

I recollect (doubtless I am now going to be egotistical about it), the question of the new Water Works (magnificently outlined by McAlpine and duly carried out and improved by Kirkwood, first-class engineers, both), was still pending, and the works, though well under way, continued to be strongly opposed by many. With the consent of the proprietor, I bent the whole weight of the paper steadily in favor of the McAlpine plan as against a flimsy, cheap and temporary series of works that would have long since broken down and disgraced the city.

This, with my course on another matter, the securing to public use of Washington Park (old Fort Greene), stoutly championed by me some thirty-five years ago against heavy odds during an editorship of the Brooklyn *Eagle,* are "feathers in my wings" that I would wish to preserve.

WALT WHITMAN.

Whitman's letter, sending this to the *Brooklyn Daily Times: The Correspondence of Walt Whitman,* III, 385–386.

1901.   See footnote 49; this visit by Edmund Gosse on 3 January 1885 has occasioned considerable comment, primarily because Gosse's account in his *Critical Kit-Kats* (London, 1896), p. 100, does not square with the facts as shown in Gosse's letter to Whitman of 29 December 1884 (Horace Traubel, *With Walt Whitman in Camden,* I, 40) and Gosse's diary:

12   sent "After the Supper" to Harpers $30 asked
                    [in red ink:]   returned [1902]

---

13   call at G W Childs – recd 50 – [1903]
        saw Mr. Chambers, of N Y. Herald[1904]

[264]

Lougheed, plumber
        411 Vine Street

        Charlotte Townsend   Dosoris
Mrs ⋀ Townsend, East Island, ⋀ Glen Cove

William Towner (Chas Towner's son
        Washington) call'd – June 14 '85 [1905]

[three lines in pencil:]
Richard Ȿ Fetters[1906]
        Salem   New Jersey
the father John – the son (RR) also John

---

[265]

1885 – Rec'd W J RR pass from Gen. Sewell [1907]

Jan 18 – Camden City RR pass from Mr Hood
            and Mr Wilson[1908]

---

see William White, "Sir Edmund Gosse on Walt Whitman," *Victorian Studies,* I (December 1957), 180–182; and Robert L. Peters, "Edmund Gosse's Two *Whitmans,*" *Walt Whitman Review,* XI (March 1965), 19–21. See also Gay Wilson Allen, *The Solitary Singer,* pp. 520–521, which relies heavily on the Gosse version; and the Philadelphia *Press,* 6 January 1885. Whitman's letter to Gosse, 31 December 1885, on the time the Englishman should call, is in *The Correspondence of Walt Whitman,* III, 384.

1902. See H. M. Alden's letter of rejection in Horace Traubel's *With Walt Whitman in Camden,* II, 211; "After the Supper and Talk" was published in *Lippincott's Magazine,* XL (November 1887), 722–723; see *Leaves of Grass,* Comprehensive Reader's Edition, p. 536.

1903. This $50 from George W. Childs may well have been a Christmas gift, as Childs had given the same amount to Whitman at Christmas 1883.

1904. Julius Chambers was to become managing editor of the New York *Tribune,* and in 1887 he made Whitman "poet laureate" of the paper, which published his short poems at about two a week during the first half of 1888.

1905. Charles Towner was a clerk in the Treasury Department when Whitman was in Washington; at one time Whitman wanted to lodge there with the Towners—*The Correspondence of Walt Whitman,* II, 233, 243, 245, 260.

1906. Whitman listed John A. Fetters's name in the *Daybook* as early as October 1880, and sent papers to Richard on 3, 9 and 17 December 1880, to John on 24 March 1881, and to Richard on 18 December 1881.

1907. General William J. Sewell gave Whitman an annual pass on the West Jersey Rail Road every year.

1908. This was apparently a new annual pass for Whitman; Hood and Wilson were undoubtedly officials of the railway.

20   Sent two Vols. 1876 ed'n to Geo. Smith
                    [in red ink:]   paid $5
     3 Mystic av.   East Somerville Mass.

"   the Lays move out from 328 Mickle
             to Berkeley   3 doors above West[1909]

     Ruth Stafford Gouldy, starts for Topeka,
     Kansas – met her at& Mont, at ferry[1910]

---

     gifts
23. pay∧ Mrs. Lay, (1 – $5) – $6 – $2 = $2 = $2 = $2 = $2 = 2 [1911]

---

25   Sunday, visit from Harry Wright[1912]

     take my breakfast this week at
     Mary Davis's   412 West st.[1913]

[Nine lines in pencil:]
Feb. 2 – sent Mary Smith portrait &c

     "   Logan   Jan   Magazines[1914]
     "   bundle (books &c) to   Mechanics Institute
                                Milville   N J

1909. The arrangements for the Lay family living in the house had not worked out (see footnotes 1792 and 1796).

1910. Ruth Stafford, Harry's sister, had married William C. Goldy on 19 August 1884, and her husband must have gone to Kansas ahead of her; Montgomery Stafford was her brother (although there was an uncle named Montgomery Stafford).

1911. The Lays paid Whitman $2 a week from 5 April to 27 September 1884, but it is difficult, if not impossible, to know what these figures here mean, and Whitman's adding the word "gifts" confuses the issue; in addition, the Lays boarded Whitman, so this is money he may have paid them.

1912. Unidentified.

1913. Mrs Mary Oakes Davis, a widow whom Whitman met in 1884 and who mended his clothes, here begins to prepare his meals; as she was a sympathetic woman who took care of elderly people and lived near Whitman, and as he needed a housekeeper, it was only natural that, sooner or later, she would devote her full time to his needs and move into 328 Mickle Street, which occurred on 24 February 1885 (see below). A summary account of the satisfactory relationship is in Gay Wilson Allen, *The Solitary Singer,* pp. 518–520, 533, 593; for a full record, see Elizabeth Leavitt Keller, *Walt Whitman in Mickle Street* (New York, 1921). After Whitman's death, Mrs Davis unfortunately had to sue the Whitman estate for time and expenses, and she was awarded compensation.

1914. Mary Smith, Whitman's "bright particular star," and Logan Pearsall Smith, were the daughter and son of Robert Pearsall Smith of Germantown; it is difficult to identify "Jan Magazines" — the only Whitman appearance was the poem "Of That Blithe Throat of Time" in the January *Harper's Monthly* (see footnote 1869 above).

sent Mrs G $16 for Ed's board [1915]

---

3   paid $2.12 for Press[1916]

Charley Somers often visits me[1917]

2ᵈ   Debby Browning gives birth to a
        little girl [1918]

---

7   Sent Wm C Skinner, box 1245, Bangor, Maine
                     [in pencil:]   [in purple pencil:]
      Cent Ed. L of G.   paid $3   rec'd[1919]

                      ⎧[three lines in red ink:]
8th to 13ᵗʰ – very cold   ⎪I am here alone
                      ⎨in the house on Mickle
13   visit from Mary Smith ⎩street two weeks[1920]

9th   visit from Alma Johnston & Mr Loag[1921]

[266]

Send MSS –	Butterfly	George Chainey[1923]
Charles Aldrich,[1922]	picture	310 Shawmut av
Webster City,	[Name, address	Boston Mass
Hamilton Co. Iowa	not WW's hand]	167 East 10th st
		East Oakland
		Cal.

1915. This is the usual monthly amount to Mrs Goodenough for the keep of Whitman's institutionalized brother.
1916. For a month's subscription to the Philadelphia *Press*.
1917. How important are Charley Somers — or Harry Wright (see entry for 25 January 1885) or James Godfrey (see entry for 21 September 1884)? Their names do not recur (except when Somers died on 21 August 1886), and apparently Whitman did not correspond with them.
1918. Debby Browning was Deborah Stafford, Harry's sister, who married Joseph Browning on 13 June 1878 (see entry of that date, above).
1919. William C. Skinner's letter, 5(?) February 1885, paying for the book, is in the Library of Congress.
1920. The Lays had gone, Whitman was taking his breakfast at Mrs Davis's, and she did not move into his house as housekeeper until 24 February 1885.
1921. Mrs John H. Johnston, of New York City, and Samuel Loag, a Philadelphia printer and a friend of the family, had made previous visits to Whitman.
1922. Charles Aldrich visited Whitman on 18 February 1885 (see entry that date); Whitman had sent him *Leaves of Grass* on 12 June 1884; Aldrich's letter, 8 July 1885, asking for an autograph, is in the Library of Congress; see also William Michael Rossetti's letter to Aldrich in Clarence Gohdes and Paull Franklin Baum, editors, *Letters of William Michael Rossetti Concerning Whitman, Blake, and Shelley to Anne Gilchrist and Herbert Gilchrist* (Durham, North Carolina, 1934), pp. 185–192.
1923. See footnote 1543 and entry above for 23 June 1884 on his visit with Whitman.

Dr Knortz 540 East 155th St New York

MS went Oct. 10, '85, from N. Y.[1924]

says J Schabelitz Zurich, Switzerland

I rec'd printed books

"will <u>undoubtedly</u> publish the Volume" Feb. 25 '89

J H & Alma Johnston[1925]
   482 Mott av. N Y City

?
.
Fred B. Vaughan?   [Card:] Mr Henry Norman [printed]
Franklin Hotel   National Liberal Club, [not WW's hand]
Harrisburg Pa   Trafalgar Square, London. [not WW's hand]

Harry and Will Black   312 So 2^d st

James Pennington May, driver, 26, has
  been in U S Navy as marine, 6 years,
  is Ocean County, N. J. born – married.

?Enger
Isaac Lee ~~Eniss~~, boy 13, in Post[1926]

---

[267]

–20 – 21 – 22
1885 – Feb. 7th to 18th – storms – winds – snow – very cold

18th Feb: visit from Mr Aldrich, Iowa[1927]

[Two lines in pencil:]
20 "Ah not this granite dead and cold" paid
    Phil Press – Feb 22 [1928]

1924. Whitman wrote Karl Knortz on 27 April 1885, asking about the translation he and T. W. H. Rolleston were making: see *The Correspondence of Walt Whitman*, III, 389–390 (see also III, 404); and Horace Traubel, *With Walt Whitman in Camden*, III, 85–86, 487–489; and Horst Frenz, *Whitman and Rolleston: A Correspondence* (Bloomington, Indiana, 1951), pp. 99–103, and also pp. 10–12. The translation *Grashalme* (Zurich, 1889), with the names of Rolleston and Knortz on the title page, was not a complete *Leaves of Grass*, but the German text of 29 short and long selections.

1925. See Whitman's letter to the Johnstons, 4 March 1885, in *The Correspondence of Walt Whitman*, III, 388.

1926. Fred B. Vaughan was a New York friend, a collector of Whitman books, and business man (letters in the Feinberg Collection). Harry and Will Black, James Pennington May, and Isaac Lee Enger appear to be one more instance of Whitman's compulsion to write names and addresses of young men and boys he met.

1927. See footnote 1922.

1928. Whitman's poem, "Ah, Not This Granite, Dead and Cold," Philadelphia *Press,*

[rule in red ink]

[Line in red ink:]
24th   Mary Davis moves in to 328 Mickle[1929]

[Three lines in pencil:]
March 4. sent Boyle O'Reilly, two copies L of G.   paid   recd [1930]

"   sent Jeff L of G. for Chaffee – rec'd [1931]

8th   dinner at Ed. E Read's[1932] – evn'g at T Harned's

14th   Prof. Corson, of Cornell University, calls[1933]

     Lou here[1934]

[Three lines in pencil:]
20, 21, 22.   Visits from F D Bailey, from N Y

14 to 20 – cold spell – cold as any

J M S gone to New Orleans[1935]

26   sent L of G, Two Riv & Spe Days   3 vols
     to Temple B Robinson, Paris,
                              [in blue pencil:]   [in red ink:]
     Monroe Co. Missouri   paid $10 –   rec'd

22 February 1885, was included in "Sands at Seventy" in *November Boughs* (1888) as "Washington's Monument, February, 1885": see *Leaves of Grass,* Comprehensive Reader's Edition, p. 520.
     1929. See footnote 1913.
     1930. For John Boyle O'Reilly, see footnote 1.
     1931. Jeff of course is Thomas Jefferson Whitman, the poet's favorite brother in St Louis, but who is Chaffee?
     1932. Whitman said to Traubel in 1889, "Do you know Ed Reed? — the lawyer? — the young man down Federal Street? He has fine bindings: some very fine, rare: I have seen them: he has shown them to me" (Horace Traubel, *With Walt Whitman in Camden,* III, 507); although the name is spelled differently, this may be Ed. E Read. Thomas Harned's home (see footnote 1900, above) was also on Federal Street, Camden.
     1933. Whitman said of Professor Hiram Corson that he "seems to have signal abilities — accepts me in a general way, without vehemence"; and Corson wrote Whitman in 1886 that he had long been pondering certain points — "one especially, that of language-shaping, and the tendency towards impassioned prose, which I feel will be the poetic form of the future, and of which, I think, your Leaves of Grass is the most marked prophecy." See Horace Traubel, *With Walt Whitman in Camden,* I, 286–288.
     1934. Whitman's sister-in-law Louisa Orr Whitman, with whom Whitman lived before buying the Mickle Street house, was now living in Burlington, New Jersey.
     1935. James Matlack Scovel must have gone to New Orleans on a visit, as Whitman asked his Camden friend to come around and see him on 7 April 1885 about an article Scovel was preparing for the Springfield *Republican,* "Walt Whitman," which appeared on 16 June 1885: see *The Correspondence of Walt Whitman,* III, 389.

sent Photos, &c.   10 altogether to Boyle O'Reilly[1936]

two copies L of G. to Thos. Donaldson[1937]
    for Messrs Irving and Stoker[1938]

Paid Water Bill $5[1939]

31   sent L of G and S D (two Vols) to E. M Abdy
                        office Time monthly
    Williams, care W Swann Sonnenschein & Co. ∧   [in red ink, sideways:]
                                [in red ink:]   recd
    Paternoster Square   London E C England   paid [1940]   recd

                                [in red ink:]
    sent L of G to Dr G W Melotte   Ithaca N Y – paid

                        Mrs H N Martin
    sent two pictures to 221 St Paul st Baltimore

                                                [268]

Graphic, 39 & 41 Park Place   New York[1941]
    Andrew E Murphy was the attaché who
        wrote to me   May '85

James R Newhall   Walnut st.   Lynn   Mass
[In red ink:]   sent slips &c

1936. John Boyle O'Reilly had bought two copies of *Leaves of Grass* on 4 March 1885 (see entry above, that date, and footnote 1).
1937. See footnote 1573.
1938. Henry Irving, the great English actor, and Bram Stoker, his young manager, met Whitman in Thomas Donaldson's home in Philadelphia in April 1884 (see Bram Stoker, *Reminiscences of Henry Irving* [New York, 1906], II, 92; and Gay Wilson Allen, *The Solitary Singer*, pp. 515–516); both became "staunch" friends of Whitman — the term is Whitman's in Horace Traubel's *With Walt Whitman in Camden*, I, 325 (see also I, 5, 302; II, 145; IV, 179–185; V, 271, 274).
1939. Now that Whitman had become a house-owner he was to pay a number of such bills, keep records of them, and even copies of the bills themselves.
1940. Ellen M. Abdy-Williams had been sent the two books on 7 January 1885 (see *The Correspondence of Walt Whitman*, III, 385), which were never received; new copies are here sent.
1941. Letter to the New York *Daily Graphic*, 21 May 1885: *The Correspondence of Walt Whitman*, III, 390. Whitman asked for the address, perhaps Andrew E. Murphy (named here); the *Graphic* — both the Daily and the Weekly issues — had printed poetry and prose by Whitman in 1873, and in the *Daily Graphic* of 31 May 1885 published a birthday tribute, two portraits, and sketches of Mickle Street and the poet's birthplace.

Sam'l McCandless, W J RR Camden side
    belongs to church – boards with parents

[Five lines in pencil:]
new night bridge-man – Phil side – George Walker

George Chainey   ~~167 East 10th street~~
        ~~East~~ Oakland   California

Harry Spiegle, boy ab't 17, helps me on the
    car (Stanton's)   June '85 [1942]

[On slip:] W H Ballou[1943]
                120 Broadway
                N. Y.

[Clipped ad about Gallery, 298 Fulton St., G. Frank E. Pearsall,[1944] and another about Gabriel Harrison's School of Art and Elocution, Hamilton Building, 44 Court Street, Brooklyn, N. Y.] [1945]

[269]

1885 – April – 2 – sent "As one by one withdraw
    the lofty actors" to Harpers' Weekly (by request
            [three words in blue pencil:]
of editor) – accepted $30 paid – pub: May 16 [1946]

[Eight lines in pencil:]
8 – visit from Robert Buchanan & his
        neice Miss Harriett Jay[1947]

1942. For George Chainey, see footnote 1923 and relevant entries; the names of Samuel McCandless, George Walker, and Harry Spiegle seem to have been casual acquaintances at the ferry and the horsecar.
1943. W. H. Ballou called on the poet on 20 June 1885, and his interview from the *Cleveland Leader and Herald* was reprinted in the Camden *Daily Post* on 28 June 1885, which dealt in part with Whitman's financial situation: see *The Correspondence of Walt Whitman*, III, 398n. (See footnote 2176, below.)
1944. G. F. E. Pearsall, as long ago as June 1876, took Whitman's photograph and sent him the negative for printing: see *The Correspondence of Walt Whitman*, III, 49–50.
1945. See footnotes 1877 and 1897.
1946. "As One by One Withdraw the Lofty Actors," *Harper's Weekly*, 16 May 1885, was reprinted in *The Critic*, on 15 August 1885, but with "Grant" as its title, for the General had died 23 July 1885; the second stanza was changed and the title became "Death of General Grant" before it was included in *November Boughs* (1888); see *Leaves of Grass*, Comprehensive Reader's Edition, p. 519.
1947. Robert Buchanan was an English admirer (see footnote 77) who had praised Whitman as early as 1867.

~~pay water bill for 1885 $5~~

[in ink:]
11 – Lougheed's plumbing bill, 18.95 – paid

supposed [in ink]
Gen. Grant's ∧ death – sickness
the long suspense and many
[four words in red ink:]
fluctuations – he gets up again[1948]

18th   Saturday afternoon – delightful jaunt
down the river to Gloucester – hospi-
tality of Wᵐ Thompson at his hotel
— baked shad, asparagus, & champagne
galore – J M Scovel, Messrs. Hugg
and Fitzgerald, and Judge Gaunt [1949]

22 – 22 – warm weather

[Line in pencil, except June 8, which is in red ink]
28ᵗʰ April to June 8   left foot sprain'd

May 3, sent $10 to Mrs. Goodenough
for Ed: [1950]

6   rec'd $10 from <u>Press</u> for Wash'n Monument poem[1951]

returned   [sideways]
11 sent Fancies at Navesink to Harpers[1952]

1948. When U. S. Grant did die on 23 July 1885, Whitman changed the title of a poem (see footnote 1946) to "Grant" before reprinting it, and changed it again to "Death of Grant" on its third printing; Whitman thought highly of Grant, writing in 1879, "What a man he is! what a history! what an illustration — his life — of the capacities of that American individuality common to us all." ("The Silent General," in *Specimen Days: Prose Works 1892,* I, 226).

1949. For a paper in 1887, Whitman had written some pages which he showed to Horace Traubel: an entry for 28 April 1887 reads, "To Wm. Thompson's Gloucester, N. J., to a noble dinner of baked shad and good champagne galore" (*With Walt Whitman in Camden,* IV, 513). Except that Thomas B. Harned was there instead of James Matlack Scovel, this reads almost word for word like the 1885 entry in the *Daybook*; I cannot identify Hugg and Fitzgerald; Judge Gaunt also unidentified.

1950. For the board of Whitman's feeble-minded brother Edward.

1951. See footnote 1928.

1952. Whitman's group of eight poems, "Fancies at Navesink," was published in *Nine-*

paid paper carrier $~~280~~ 208 [1953]

[270]

[On card:]   Geo   M   Gould
        [Three lines in red:]
        Sent me the synopsis (in type writ
            of Rolleston's   Roxbury, Mass.
            lecture &c [1954]   35 Sherman St.,
                            April 15, 1885. [3 lines typed]

            ans'd Aug 19 [1955]

[First part of letter to Whitman:]

                    32 School St.
                Boston, August 17, 1885
        Dear Walt:
                I am informed by a legal
        friend in New York that Messrs Arnoux,
        Ritch & Woodford of 18 Wall St make
        a specialty of copyright cases. I would
        advise you to write them giving full
        particulars of Worthington's infringements,
        and let me manage the matter for you. [Letter clipped off here.] [1956]

[271]

May 1885 – 22 Col. S's art: to Sp. Republican
                    sent on[1957]

23 – Pete Doyle – his
        mother is dying – $10 – died May 24 [1958]

Sent Fancies at Navesink to James

teenth Century (London), XVIII (August 1885), 234–237, then in November Boughs (1888)
— see Leaves of Grass, Comprehensive Reader's Edition, pp. 513–516.
    1953. $2.08, possibly for the Philadelphia Press.
    1954. For details on Rolleston's lecture, see footnote 1718.
    1955. Letter lost.
    1956. The matter of Richard Worthington's infringements, although he continued to
send money to Whitman, was never settled during Whitman's lifetime (see footnote 1042
above, and The Correspondence of Walt Whitman, III, 196–198).
    1957. For the article by James Matlack Scovel on Whitman, see footnote 1935, above,
and The Correspondence of Walt Whitman, III, 388n.
    1958. Because of the closeness of the relationship between Whitman and his Washing-
ton horsecar conductor friend Peter Doyle, Doyle must have written the poet, who certainly
wrote Doyle when he sent $10 (for flowers?); but both letters are lost.

Knowles, Queen Anne's Lodge, St
accepted – paid
James's Park S W, London, 150 asked –

_____ paid [1959] [in red ink]

George Harding[1960] here – is at
  Eagle Bridge, N. Y.   [in red ink:]

                                                          recd

28 Sent	Wm. C. Bryant,[1961] [printed card]	the two Vols. $5 due
	Attorney & Counselor at Law,	[in red ink:]
	438 Main Street,	(wrote a second time) paid
	over	June 9
	Western Savings Bank, Buffalo N. Y.	

" visit from Mrs. Bigelow of Boston[1962]
  introduced by Boyle O'Reilly[1963]

29 letters to Hannah and Mary $5 to each recd both[1964]

                                                    [in red ink,   paid
June 4 – Pete Doyle here – 15 – (25 altogether) [1965] sideways:]   back
                                                                        all .

1st – shad & champagne at Gloster – Mr Perry[1966]

  burial of Victor Hugo[1967]   X

1959. See footnote 1952.
1960. Unidentified, as were a few other visitors (see footnote 1917).
1961. Not to be confused with William Cullen Bryant the poet, who died in 1878; for William C. Bryant (1830–1898), lawyer and Buffalo Historical Society president, see *The Correspondence of Walt Whitman*, III, 380.
1962. Mrs Bigelow could be the wife of the well-known Boston physician, Dr Jacob Bigelow, but more likely she is Mrs S. A. Bigelow, who contributed to the "Boston Cottage Fund" for Whitman in October 1887: see Horace Traubel, *With Walt Whitman in Camden*, II, 299.
1963. See footnote 1.
1964. Both letters to Whitman's sisters Hannah Heyde and Mary Van Nostrand are lost.
1965. These figures must refer to money which Whitman lent to Peter Doyle, $10 on 23 May 1855 and $15, here, which — as Whitman recorded — Doyle repaid.
1966. This reads as if it were similar to the dinner at William Thompson's of Gloucester on 18 April 1885 (see entry above, that date, and footnote 1949); Mr Perry most likely was F. W. Perry of the Fruit Jar factory, Philadelphia, to whom Whitman sent *Leaves of Grass* on 11 June 1885 (see below).
1967. Victor Hugo (1802–1885) is often mentioned by Whitman in his letters and more than a dozen times in *Prose Works 1892*, where he writes, II, 759: "Victor Hugo, for instance, runs off into the craziest, and sometimes (in his novels) most ridiculous and flatulent, literary

Thos Donaldson here[1968]   [in red ink]

7 – Sunday – sent "the Voice of the Rain" to Harpers

               [in red ink:]
        25   returned [1969]
        [two words in red ink:]

9th   sent the "Voice" to Outing ($12) accepted – paid

11   sent L of G and S D two Vols. to Mrs Agnes
                  M D
      Fletcher care Prof. W. B. Fletcher Indi-
      also sent G G P and Woman's,
      anapolis, Indiana   estimate[1970] paid $10 [three lines in red ink]
                         by C O'B. Bryant

    sent L of G to F W Perry office Fruit Jar
                  [in red ink:]
    factory   cor Gaul & Adams sts Phil rec'd [1971]

                                           [272]

[Line in pencil:]
Sent Spr. Rep. June 16, '85 [1972] *S S   Navesink[1973] O
    [Line in red ink:]
    Post article WW & the Tennyson[1974] 1 set x Booth[1975] B

blotches and excesses, and by almost entire want of prudence allows them to stand. In his poems, his fire and fine instincts carry the day, even against such faults; and his plays, though sensational, are best of all."

    1968. See footnote 1573.

    1969. As seen in the next entry below, Whitman's poem, "The Voice of the Rain," was accepted by *Outing,* edited by Sylvester Baxter, and published in VI (August 1885), 570; see *The Correspondence of Walt Whitman,* III, 391–392; and *Leaves of Grass,* Comprehensive Reader's Edition, p. 528.

    1970. G G P is William Douglas O'Connor's *The Good Gray Poet* (1866), reprinted in Dr Bucke's *Walt Whitman* (1883), pp. 99–130, but the original may well have been sent; Woman's estimate was Anne Gilchrist's "An Englishwoman's Estimate of Walt Whitman," *The Radical,* May 1870, perhaps here an off-print.

    1971. Undoubtedly the Mr Perry whom Whitman met at Glouchester on 1 June 1885 (see entry above).

    1972. James M. Scovel's "Walt Whitman," *The Springfield Republican,* 16 June 1885: see footnote 1935, above.

    1973. Whitman's group of poems, "Francies at Navesink," *Nineteenth Century,* August 1885: see footnote 1952, above.

    1974. Whitman's article, "A Word About Tennyson," *The Critic,* n.s. VII (1 January 1887), 1–2.

    1975. "Booth and 'The Old Bowery,'" *New York Tribune,* 16 August 1885, entitled "The Old Bowery" in *November Boughs* (1888): see *Prose Works 1892,* II, 591–597.

¶ sent "My Book & I" [1976]

¶ Syl: Baxter   x   ¶ Spr: Rep:

¶ 5 Mrs Costelloe[1977]   ¶ 5 Ernest Rhys[1978]

¶ 5 x Dr Knortz, 540 East 155th st   N Y City

[names in pencil:]   ¶ World newspaper   [in ink]

– 5 x * * O Hannah   188 Dundas St L   O

– 5 x * * O Mary   x Will Saunders

– ¶ x B * O Dr Bucke   x x Josiah Child 57 Ludgate

5 x B ** O Jeff   Hill

¶ B * * O Burroughs   x Frederick Locker –

– ¶ 5 x * * O'Connor   O x Mrs Elisa Scholan Leggett

B x * Mrs. Gilchrist   160 E Elizabeth St

5 x ** J A Symonds   Detroit

¶ 5 x * * E Carpenter   ¶ E C Stedman [in ink]

¶ 5 x * * W M Rossetti   Archie Bremner

¶ x * H B Forman   Adv   London

¶ 5 x * * Rolleston   out

* * Geo Chainey   Benj R Tucker po box 3366 Boston [in ink]

* Geo M Gould [1979]   x James and Priscilla Young [?]

¶ 5 x B O * * W S Kennedy   92 Bank st

¶ 5 x * * Dowden   H Ballou 265 Broadway[1980]   [in ink]

Farringford {Wilson &   W T Harris[1981]
            {McCormick   Concord Mass

Freshwater   ¶O*x Mrs Ella H Bigelow Mattapose

                            x Roden Noel[1983]   Mass[1982]

                          Maybury Woking Station

                              Surrey Eng

1976. "My Book and I," *Lippincott's Magazine,* XLIII (January 1887), 121–127, which became, with "How I Made a Book" from the Philadelphia *Press,* 11 July 1886, "A Backward Glance O'er Travel'd Roads": see *Prose Works 1892,* II, 711–732.

1977. In this long list of 46 addressees, to whom Whitman sent one or more of the five items — which he identified by various symbols — most are members of his family, close friends, American and foreign correspondents who had received previous mailings or have been previously identified in footnotes in the *Daybook,* and a few not well known, or who need comment.

1978. Ernest Rhys (1859–1946), English author, in a long letter to Whitman, 7 July 1885 (in Horace Traubel, *With Walt Whitman in Camden,* I, 451–453), proposed a selection from Whitman in The Canterbury Poets. It was published with Rhys's introduction by Walter Scott, London, 1886, 318 pp. See also Traubel, *ibid.,* III, 162–164, for another ardent letter and the proposed volume, of which Whitman wrote in ink on the envelope, "Third letter from Ernest Rhys — the little English selection from L. of G. is out since, and the whole edition (10,000) sold." For Whitman's letter to Rhys, 9 November 1885, see *The Correspondence of Walt Whitman,* III, 407.

1979. George M. Gould, of Roxbury, Mass., sent Whitman a typed synopsis of T. W. H. Rolleston's lecture on Whitman on 15 April 1885 (see above).

¶ x * Alfred Tennyson 80 Eaton Square

London SW or elsewhere   [in ink]

Isle of Wight   S E Gross, s e cor Dearborn & Randolph

x Fitzgerald Molloy[1986]   sts. Chicago Ill [1984]

34 Woburn Place   x W J Linton

x F B Sanborn   p o box 489

Tavistock Square   New Haven

London W C   Mrs F R Ritter[1985]

London S W   ¶ Critic [in ink]

x * Whittier

x Rudolf Schmidt Baggesen's Gade 3 [in ink]

Copenhagen

D

* * H J Bathgate[1987]   Oakenholt Hall near Flint

Helen E Price   Wooside Queens Co

x Rome brothers printers

W J Linton   * Moncure Conway

Rugby[1988]

* * G C Macaulay

[273]

June – '85 – 14th, 15th & 16th – hot, hot, hot [in pencil, except June – '85]

[Three lines in pencil:]
17th refreshingly cool – copious rain last night

Mrs Gilchrists grand essay in June "To-Day" [1989]

---

much better acc'ts from dear sister Hannah[1990]

1980. For W. H. Ballou, see footnote 1943.
1981. For William Torrey Harris, see footnote 771.
1982. This may be the Mrs Bigelow who called on Whitman on 28 May 1885 (see footnote 1962).
1983. See footnote 563.
1984. S. E. Gross, a Chicago real estate man, wrote to Whitman (letter in the Feinberg Collection) after hearing him praised while on a steamship from England.
1985. For Mrs Frédéric Louis Ritter, see footnote 139.
1986. For Fitzgerald Molloy, see footnote 1575.
1987. For Herbert J. Bathgate, see footnote 797.
1988. For G. C. Macaulay, see footnote 1625.
1989. Anne Gilchrist, "A Confession of Faith," To-day, III (June 1885), 269–284, reprinted in Herbert Gilchrist, Anne Gilchrist: Her Life and Writings (London, 1887), pp. 331–362; and Thomas B. Harned, The Letters of Anne Gilchrist and Walt Whitman (London, 1914), pp. 23–55.
1990. See footnotes 1850 and 1885.

16   article in the Springfield Republican[1991]

20   (Saturday) calls from Mary Smith   Mr Ballou[1992]
     of N. Y. (newspaper syndicate) & Harry White

[In pencil:]   25 Chesham st   Belgrave Sq: London S W

24   the Smiths sail in the Eider for England [1993]
         [in red ink:]   arrived July 3

July 14 – Sent six copies ($18) authors Ed'n
                               Oakland
     L of G. to George Chainey   [in blue pencil:]
     ─────────────────────────╲   Cal   recd
                                ╲ $5 [1994]   [in blue pencil]
15 to 26 to Aug 6 – hot – hot – ╲────────

19   Watch, dishes, knives, &c from J H J [1995]

20 – to 23 – the bad vertigo fits – bad fall – [1996]

24 – Talcott Williams here – Lou here – G W C sent [1997]

29 Sent Charles Parsons Photos – Harpers[1998]

31 paid Mrs Goodenough $16 for Ed for July[1999]

1991. See footnotes 1935 and 1972.
1992. For W. H. Ballou, see footnote 1943; he apparently knew Mary Smith, daughter of Robert Pearsall Smith and a Whitman favorite, who brought him to Mickle Street; Harry White is unidentified, except that he is English.
1993. Mary Smith most likely was the instigator of the plan that the Smiths return to England after ten years in America as she had fallen in love with B. F. C. Costelloe, whom she was to marry in Oxford that summer; her sister Alys and her father Robert Pearsall Smith returned then to Germantown. See Robert Allerton Parker, *The Transatlantic Smiths* (New York, 1959), pp. 55–57.
1994. George Chainey (see footnote 1543) had moved to California.
1995. John H. Johnston, New York manufacturing jeweler, was one of Whitman's most constant benefactors; since the Lays had moved out, the poet's home needed many things: see *The Correspondence of Walt Whitman*, III, 398.
1996. Whitman wrote John H. Johnston, 31 July 1885, that he was not really serious: see *The Correspondence of Walt Whitman*, III, 398.
1997. Talcott Williams (see footnote 277) was on the Philadelphia *Press*; Lou of course is Louisa Orr Whitman, the poet's sister-in-law, now living in Burlington, New Jersey; and G W C is George W. Childs, co-owner of the Philadelphia *Public Ledger*.
1998. Harpers.
1999. As usual, for the board of Whitman's feeble-minded brother Edward.

cts

recd $22.06   from David McKay as

my two Vols

my royalties for Leaves of Grass

and Specimen Days for last six

months[2000]

Aug 1 – letters from Herbert and Mrs Gilchrist

– wrote,[2001] accepting (cashed the check at C

& H Bories $239 83 83 [2002]   [last figure in red]

---

4   wrote to Edward Carpenter & to Bessie
    & Isabella Ford acknowledging – [2003]

---

3   cyclone in Camden[2004]

[274]

N. A. Review 30 Lafayette Place
            3 East 14th Street[2005]
Benj: F. C. Costelloe, 33 Chancery Lane   [address in pencil]
            London   W C [2006]
Harry Lanco, electric light man Len's chum
Mrs. Wm Allen, Macomb, Ill:

2000.   See Whitman's letter to Herbert Gilchrist, 1 August 1885, in *The Correspondence of Walt Whitman*, III, 398–399 (see also III, 409n): Whitman's income for 1885 was this $22.06, plus $20.71 in royalties in December, and $350.20 for poems and articles.

2001.   See footnote 2000; Anne Gilchrist's letter, 20 July 1885, apparently her last one — she died on 29 November 1885 — is in Thomas B. Harned, *The Letters of Anne Gilchrist and Walt Whitman* (London, 1914), pp. 233–235.

2002.   For the "free will offering," see *The Correspondence of Walt Whitman*, III, 398n.

2003.   Letters: *The Correspondence of Walt Whitman*, III, 399–400.

2004.   The cyclone was "brief but terrible" but did not touch 328 Mickle Street, though it "came very near," Whitman wrote Mary Whitall Smith (*The Correspondence of Walt Whitman*, III, 401).

2005.   James Redpath, editor of *The North American Review*, wrote Whitman on 30 June 1885, asking for a memorial article on Abraham Lincoln and one on Whitman's experiences in Civil War hospitals; Redpath also wrote on 16 July and 11 August 1885: see Horace Traubel, *With Walt Whitman in Camden*, II, 73–76. The Lincoln piece appeared in *Reminiscences of Abraham Lincoln*, edited by Allan Thorndike Rice (New York, 1886), 469–475; and *The North American Review* was to publish "Slang in America," CXLI (November 1885), 431–435; "Robert Burns as Poet and Person," CXLIII (November 1886), 427–435, revised from *The Critic*, II (16 December 1882), 337; and "Some War Memorandum," CXLIV (January 1887), 55–60 — all four in *Prose Works 1892*, II, 601–604, 572–577, 558–568, and 584–589.

2006.   The Anglo-Irish barrister who married Mary Smith (see footnote 1993).

Westmont

Wm H. Duckett:[2007]   [not in WW's hand]

near

334 Mickle St.   [not in WW's hand]

Haddonfield

Camden   [not in WW's hand]

N J

Came to 328 Mickle – May 1 '86)
Call'd in Mickle St:
Dec: 27 '88

Frank Jess	Josiah Garrison
C C Savage	Livery Stable Mickle
Dow's Stores Brooklyn N Y	& 4th[2008]

F. McKinsey, Elkton Md.   [pencil, not in WW's hand] [2009]

Joseph Paul Hotel, Woodbury
——————————— N J.

[Two lines in pencil:]
Wm Sherman Brown   young man
        trimmed the tree

Seymour I. Hudgens   [not in WW's hand]
Nov 15th 1885   Boston Mass   [not WW's hand]

[275]

Aug: '85 – from July 20 to Sept 3   unwell [2010]

2007. William H. Duckett was a teen-age boy in September 1885, whose mother had recently died and who boarded with Mrs Davis, Whitman's housekeeper; he accompanied Whitman on his drives after the poet got his horse and buggy from Thomas Donaldson on 15 September 1885 (see entry below that date), and assisted with the lines. Unfortunately, although Whitman liked the boy and enjoyed his company for four years, he was dishonest and Mrs Davis had to sue him for the board money, the boy testifying that Whitman had invited him to stay at Mickle Street, which was not true, and Mrs Davis won the judgment. See Horace Traubel, *With Walt Whitman in Camden,* IV, 64–66; Gay Wilson Allen, *The Solitary Singer,* pp. 523, 533; and William White, "Billy Duckett: Whitman Rogue," *American Book Collector,* XXI (February 1971), 20–23.

2008. The stable where Whitman undoubtedly kept his horse and buggy, presented to him by Thomas Donaldson and friends in September 1885 (see Gay Wilson Allen, *The Solitary Singer,* p. 523, and entry below for 15 September 1885).

2009. See footnote 1823; Folger McKinsey often visited Whitman after he moved into 328 Mickle Street.

5 – C W Eldridge here[2011]

7 sent Spec. Days   Dr B's WW – JB's "Notes"
   and good photo to Chaffee – [2012]

sen   answer to Leon & Bro: New York[2013]

6 paid Mr Twoes $12 for pants & vest Frank Twoes[2014]

pleasanter weather begins – less hot

7 George stopt inquired of me ab't health &c
   & invited strongly to come out to B [2015]

8th (Saturday) great funeral pageant for
   Gen. Grant in New York City[2016]

9th quiet comfortable Sunday
   x pleasant visit from Tom Harned [2017]

receive letters from Mary Smith in
England – the "Toynbee Hall" letter – the
visit to Tennyson[2018] – wrote to M S [2019]

2010. Whitman, conscious of his health during these years, first mentioned this illness on 20 July 1885 (see above), mentioned a sun-stroke in letters to various friends — see *The Correspondence of Walt Whitman*, III, 298, 399, 400, 401 — but does not seem to have been too seriously ill. .

2011. Charles W. Eldridge, an old friend and Whitman's former publisher (see footnotes 116, 1621, 1684, and 1721), was in Boston and was to go to California in 1887; he visited Whitman again on 2 October 1885 (see entry below).

2012. *Specimen Days* (1882), Dr Richard Maurice Bucke's *Walt Whitman* (1883), and John Burroughs's *Notes on Walt Whitman as Poet and Person* (2nd edition, 1871) are more easily identifiable than Chaffee.

2013. Letter lost.

2014. H. B. Twoes (see footnote 145) was Whitman's long-time tailor in Camden; Frank Twoes was obviously a member of the family.

2015. George was Whitman's brother, with whom he lived on Stevens street before buying the Mickle Street house; he now had a home in Burlington, New Jersey; Louisa Orr Whitman, his wife, had visited Walt on 24 July 1885 (see above) and must have reported on the poet's illness.

2016. Former President U. S. Grant died on 23 July 1885: see footnotes 1946 and 1948.

2017. Thomas B. Harned was becoming one of Whitman's closest friends (see footnote 1900).

2018. Letter: Thomas Donaldson, *Walt Whitman the Man* (New York, 1896), pp. 234–236.

2019. Letter to Mary Smith: *The Correspondence of Walt Whitman*, III, 401.

sold
15 article <u>Booth & the "Old Bowery"</u> ⋀ to the
    syndicate (A T Rice, N Y) $60 paid.[2020]

<u>Fancies at Navesink</u> in Aug: <u>Nineteenth
           Century</u> \ £30 $145 paid [2021]

19 Winfield S Cox, Camden boy (17 or 18)
    and David Walters, (same age) called

Johnny Sloan here Evn'g to supper[2022]

W<u>m</u> O'Connor at Dr Bucke's Canada[2023]

death of little Leon Kelly[2024]

23 Wm O'Connor with Dr Bucke at
    London   Canada[2025]

[276]

[Two lines in pencil:]
Jeff's St Louis house
    2437 Second Cardondelet av.[2026]

[277]

     rec'd $145.20
1885 – Aug 29 – Pay (30£) from <u>Nineteenth Century</u>
           $145.20
     for "Fancies at Navesink" [2027]

The "Texas Siftings" article – D B Knox[2028]

2020. Whitman's article, "Booth and 'The Old Bowery,'" was in the New York *Tribune*, 16 August 1885 (see footnote 1975 and *The Correspondence of Walt Whitman*, III, 403).
2021. See footnote 1952.
2022. Now that Whitman had a home of his own, and Mrs Davis had moved in and become his housekeeper, he could entertain at dinner, making life much more pleasant for him.
2023. See *The Correspondence of Walt Whitman*, III, 404n.
2024. Most likely the son of a now unidentifiable neighbor.
2025. Why repeated?
2026. This may be a new address for Whitman's brother Jeff, who lived at 2511 Second Carondelet Avenue, St Louis, Missouri in December 1883.
2027. See footnote 1952 and also entry above for 15 August 1885.
2028. D. B. Knox unidentified further.

Rob't Buchanan's poem "Socrates in Camden &

a look around" in London Academy Aug:[2029]

&c

sent photos   to Rev. S A Barnett [2030]   [in red ink:]

Sept. 6)   St Jude's Vicarage, Whitechapel   rec'd

London, E.   for Toynbee Hall

Sept —————————————————————————————

4 – Visit from Mr Thayer – he has been for

some time on the Eve. Telegraph – he

goes on to Boston[2031]

My letter to Herbert Gilchrist is

printed in N Y Times, copied from

London Athenæum[2032]

sent Cent. Edn. 2 Vols to   John

6   K. Randall, Mercantile Library,

[two words in blue pencil:]

Baltimore, Md. $10 due paid   recd [2033]

"   sent 2 copies Burroughs's Notes to

[two words in blue pencil:]

J H Johnston $2 due   paid   recd [2034]

2029.   Robert Buchanan, "Socrates in Camden, with a Look Around," *The Academy* (London), 15 August 1885, was reprinted in his *A Look at Literature* (London, 1887).

2030.   The Rev. S. A. Barnett, as seen here, was connected with Toynbee Hall, a London settlement house named for Arnold Toynbee, a friend of B. F. C. Costelloe, Mary Smith's first husband (see entry above for 9 August 1885). The group of Oxford fellows who founded it felt that Whitman was their "great exemplar" (see *The Correspondence of Walt Whitman*, III, 396n).

2031.   William Roscoe Thayer (1859–1923), editor, biographer, author of "Personal Recollections of Walt Whitman," *Scribner's Monthly*, LXV (1919), 674–687, wrote to Whitman on 26 June 1883, asking about a Sidney Lanier letter (Thayer's letter in the Feinberg Collection); wrote again on 12 October 1885 (letter in the Feinberg Collection); see Whitman's letter to him, 25 November 1885, in *The Correspondence of Walt Whitman*, III, 408.

2032.   This facsimile of Whitman's letter to Herbert Gilchrist, 1 August 1885, about the poet's attitude toward the "free will offering," appeared in *The Athenaeum*, 22 August 1885, and in the New York *Times*, 4 September 1885, from the London periodical. See *The Correspondence of Walt Whitman*, III, 398–399.

2033.   John K. Randall was a Baltimore attorney on whose envelope Whitman happened to write, in September 1884, the draft of a letter to T. W. H. Rolleston (see footnote 1868).

2034.   Others were buying John Burroughs's book, *Notes on Walt Whitman as Poet and Person* (2nd edition, 1871) from Whitman (see footnote 2012, above).

£22.ˢ2.ᵈ6 from Rossetti first instalment "offering" [2035]

8 rec'd $5 from Geo. Chainey for books[2036]

15 wrote Herbert Gilchrist[2037]

"   the horse & wagon presented to me
         (Thomas Donaldson & friends) [2038]

17 ride down to Glendale, to the Staffords[2039]

18 $105 – from T. Donaldson, from friends[2040]
10 more for horse-keep – $10 from Lawrence Bar[r]ett [2041]

[278]

Mᴿˢ B. F. C. Costelloe[2042]
                Westminster
    40 Grosvenor Road ∧ S W
      the embankment [in red ink]
33 Chancery Lane   W. C.
     London   [address not in WW's hand]
     England

[In pencil:]
R U Johnson – Century[2043]

2035. See Whitman's letter of thanks to William Michael Rossetti, 30 November 1885, in *The Correspondence of Walt Whitman,* III, 409; Rossetti's letter, 28 August 1885, is in the Hanley Collection, University of Texas; Rossetti's letters, 4 and 6 October and 13 November 1885 are in the Feinberg Collection (see Horace Traubel, *With Walt Whitman in Camden,* IV, 209; III, 65–66; and II, 330–331, for these last three); Whitman's letters of 8 September and 20 October 1885 are lost.

2036. George Chainey (see footnotes 1543 and 1994) was spreading Whitman's gospel in California: he was sent six copies of *Leaves of Grass* on 14 July 1885, and was now ordering more books.

2037. Letter: *The Correspondence of Walt Whitman,* III, 404–405.

2038. See footnotes 2007 and 2008, also *The Correspondence of Walt Whitman,* III, 405, 406, 407, and the letters from the 28 donors in Thomas Donaldson, *Walt Whitman the Man* (New York, 1896), pp. 173–182.

2039. Whitman had not visited George and Susan Stafford at Kirkwood for some time.

2040. See footnotes 2007, 2008, and 2038.

2041. See Whitman's letter of thanks to Thomas Donaldson, mentioning also the money from Lawrence Barrett, the actor (see footnote 1776 and entry for 30 January 1884), whom Whitman visited backstage after seeing "Francesca da Rimini" in Philadelphia. (*The Correspondence of Walt Whitman,* III, 407.)

2042. Mary Smith's married name (see footnote 1993).

2043. Robert Underwood Johnson (see footnote 1844), who asked Whitman for a piece for *Century,* but it did not appear until October 1888.

Alfred Tennyson, Farringford, Freshwater
　　Isle of Wight [2044]

[Card of Scovel & Costa, Attorneys-at-law, 130 S. 6th St., Phila.: James M. Scovel, George S. Costa.] [2045]

Harriet Hugg Swallow
　　at Dr Neal's Dental Depot
　　314 Mickle Street

Richard E Labar[2046]
　　box 484 Waukesha Wisconsin

Ernest Rhys[2047]
　59 Cheyne Walk
　　Chelsea
　London   SW

W R Thayer[2048]
　68 Mt Auburn st Cambridge Mass

[279]

Sept. and October 1885

recd

Sept 22 – Sent   "Slang in America" to Redpath, N. Y. $50 (paid [2049]

23, 24   bad spell – lost eyesight – lost equilibrium[2050]

24 – Lou here – George here

Wm O Connor here – two days

Oct
　1 – John Burroughs here – 2ᵈ   Eldridge here[2051]

8   went down to see Ed. at J J
　Goodenough's near Mt Laurel beyond

2044. The Smiths visited Tennyson with Whitman's letter of introduction: see *The Correspondence of Walt Whitman,* III, 401n.
2045. James M. Scovel was Whitman's frequent Sunday-evening dinner host.
2046. Richard Labar (see footnote 1871), formerly on the Philadelphia *Public Ledger,* then in Ann Arbor, Michigan, now in Wisconsin.
2047. See footnote 1978.
2048. See footnote 2031.
2049. See footnote 2005.
2050. Recovered from one illness, earlier in the month, Whitman seems to have had another, this one serious enough for his brother George and sister-in-law Louisa Orr Whitman, in addition to William Douglas O'Connor (see next two entries) to visit the poet, although O'Connor may have come without knowing the poet was ill. See also entry below for 19 October 1885.
2051. See footnote 2011.

Moorestown, (14 miles from here) [2052]
Found Ed quite well and hearty –
Staid three or four hours – had dinner –
– cold, dark, half: rainy day –

---

13 – sent autograph L of G. to J Schabelitz
    publisher, Zurich, Switzerland

" went down & spent the evn'g Dr C H
   Shivers, Haddonfield – good time – good supper

---

14 – paid carrier <u>Press</u> & <u>S</u> <u>Press</u> – $2.10 [2053]

---

19 Went over to Phila: to see ab't my eyes
    to Prof. Norris 1530 Locust st. (accom-
    panied by Dr Osler,[2054] 131 So 15th st)
    – Satisfactory visit & examination.
    – I had feared I was becoming blind.
    Dr N. decidedly discountenanced the idea

---

20 recd 37 pounds, 12 sh. from W M Rossetti
    from "free will offering" to me, from English
    friends – ($183.11) [2055]

---

24 saw Alma Johnston May, Mr Ingram
    & little Calder, on the ferry.[2056]

2052. Whitman had been paying for his brother Edward's keep, but he did not see him too often.

2053. As previously recorded, these subscriptions (by carrier) were for the Philadelphia *Press* and the *Sunday Press*.

2054. Dr (later Sir) William Osler (1849–1919), Canadian physician, historian, and literary essayist, then Professor of Medicine at the University of Pennsylvania, became one of Whitman's regular doctors from early in 1886 (at the instigation of Dr R. M. Bucke) until Osler went to Johns Hopkins in Baltimore in May 1889; he is mentioned more than sixty times in the five Traubel volumes, and Osler's own unpublished reminiscences of Whitman are in William White, "Walt Whitman and Sir William Osler," *American Literature,* XI (March 1939), 73–77; see also William White, "Walt Whitman on Osler: 'He Is a Great Man,'" *Bulletin of the History of Medicine,* XV (January 1944), 79–90; and "Walt Whitman and Osler: Three Unpublished Letters," *Journal of the History of Medicine,* XI (July 1956), 348–349.

2055. See footnotes 2002, 2032, 2035.

2056. Alma Johnston was the wife of Whitman's New York jeweler friend and benefactor, John H. Johnston; May was John H. Johnston's daughter by his first wife; Calder was Alma and John H. Johnston's young son; and Mr Ingram may well have been William Ingram, a philanthropic tea store proprietor in Philadelphia (see footnote 894).

2057. Boys who carried the Philadelphia *Press*?

2058. Edmund C. Stedman (see footnote 948) was among the 15 to whom Whitman

[280]

[Four lines in purple pencil:]
John Goldthorpe
        new carrier
        Harry Gamble – temporary – Oct 1 [2057]

'86

Thos: G Gentry
        1912 Christian st
son – Alan F Gentry
        Benj: F Lacy
visit Dec. 30 '85

E C Stedman
        45 East 30th St   N Y [2058]

[281]

1885 – – Oct: & Nov:

Nov. 1 (Sunday) went down to the
    Staffords, at Glendale (5th visit) [2059]
    and evening to Mr & Mrs. T.
    B. Harned's to splendid cham-
    pagne supper – enjoyed all

paid Bennett $18 for horse bill

paid Mrs. Goodenough $16 for Ed. for Oct.

[Newspaper clipping, 17
lines, of "October's Weather
Record".]

[On card of Earl Russell, Balliol College:]
Nov.
    5th & 6th   (Called

from R Worthington $24:
        through J M S [2061]

[On card of Mr. Graham Balfour,[2060] Wimbledon, England:]
(called

asked William Sloane Kennedy, on 2 December 1885, to send copies of Kennedy's *The Poet as Craftsman* (Philadelphia, 1886).

2059. Whitman did not record all the visits in the *Daybook*, nor was he citing the letters he wrote and received, as he had been in earlier years.

2060. Whitman's visitors on 5 or 6 November 1885 were Earl Russell, John Francis Stanley (1865–1931), brother of Bertrand Russell and contributor to William Michael Rossetti's "offering" (see Horace Traubel, *With Walt Whitman in Camden*, IV, 209); and Sir Graham Balfour (1858–1929), cousin and biographer of Robert Louis Stevenson.

2061. See footnotes 1042 and 1956; unscrupulous as he was, Worthington did pay Whit-

£   s
9th   cashed   the   10:10 – sent by Walter Scott,
    London, Eng. (through Ernest Rhys) & sent him
    a rec't – W. S. is to publish a volume
    of selections from my   poems in his
    "Canterbury Poets," but is not to send or
    sell the Volume in United States[2062]

---

9 – Ferry pass for horse & buggy recd through T D [2063]

---

go out in wagon every afternoon – Wᵐ Duckett
                                                drives[2064]

---

11   Sent article "Diary Notes at Random" to O S
                                        [Two words in red ink:]
    Baldwin, Brooklyn, N Y. $10 due   recd
                                        paid [2065]

---

14   fine wolf-skin lap robe recd from Lou[2066]

---

15   down to the Staffords' – Glendale[2067]

                                        [Three words in red ink:]
    Sent "Abraham Lincoln" article to Redpath   recd
                                        paid $33 [2068]

Have been a second time to Dr Shivers' [2069] } good
    "   "   to Harry's and Eva's – Marlton[2070] } times
to Debby & Jo Browning's Thanksgiving 26ᵗʰ [2071]

man, through the poet's lawyer-friend James M. Scovel, some money for unauthorized copies of *Leaves of Grass* he sold.
    2062.   See footnote 1978.
    2063.   Thomas Donaldson (see footnote 1573) was an official of the Pennsylvania Railroad, which owned the ferry from Camden to Philadelphia.
    2064.   See footnote 2007.
    2065.   Whitman's "Some Diary Notes at Random" was published in *Baldwin's Monthly* (Brooklyn), XXXI (December 1885), 8: see *Prose Works 1892*, II, 580–584.
    2066.   Louisa Orr Whitman was always kindly disposed toward her brother-in-law.
    2067.   George and particularly Susan Stafford continued to be the best of friends to Whitman, and their home in Kirkwood a place where he greatly enjoyed visiting in all seasons.
    2068.   See footnote 2005.
    2069.   Dr C. H. Shivers lived in nearby Haddonfield, New Jersey, and the first time Whitman was there was 13 October 1885 (see entry above, that date).
    2070.   Eva and Harry Stafford, whose wedding on 25 June 1885 Whitman attended, were living in Marlton, New Jersey.
    2071.   Deborah Stafford, Harry's sister, had married Joseph L. Browning on 13 June 1878; their daughter Ruth lived only from 2 February until 26 July 1885.

[282]

English "free will offering" [2072]
rec'd from Rossetti – 1885

                        £   s   d
Sept 8ᵗʰ (ab't   1ˢᵗ   22 . 2 . 6 $107. 54
          Sept 8)

Oct 20ᵗʰ rec'd   2ᵈ   37 . 12 . —   183.11
Nov 28 third   31 . 19 . —   155.53
          instalmt
Jan: 25.'86-fourth   33 . 16 .6 –   164.93
          up to March 15 '86 – recd: $611.11
        dated
letter ∧ May 17, 1886 fifth 29. 18. 3.   145.58
                        altogether $ 756.68
⌐   ⌐
| in addition rec'd | $10 more   766
| £   s   └ [Clipping:] Press / Jan 2 '86
| July 3ᵈ '87 – 2 . 2
| from Wᵐ M Rossetti)
└

MONEY FOR WALT WHITMAN.
Distinguished Foreigners Raise a Fund
for the Good, Gray Poet.

LONDON, Jan. 1. — The Walt Whitman Fund amounts to £115. Among the
subscribers are Mr. Rossetti, Louis Stevenson, Francis Darwin, Mr. Dryden
and Henry James.

Edward Carpenter's and the
Misses Ford's check
[four words in red ink:] $239.83
3ᵈch:July 1887 July 1885–

£20   2ᵈd check   [in red ink]
          June '86 £45 – ($216.75) [2073]   [in red ink]

      Royalties rec'd for "Leaves of Grass"
and "Specimen Days" for 1885, from David
McKay, publisher

      June 1 '85 for last six months
              for both Vols. 22.06
      Dec 1 '85 " " " "   20.71

      Both Volumes Total $42.77 cts [2074]
      for ~~the year~~ —

              for the year

2072. As many have stated, Whitman never solicited gifts, and certainly not money, but
when they were given by admirers in good faith, he likewise did not turn them down and kept
careful records of them in the *Daybook's* left-hand pages, this page going three years beyond its
opposite right-hand page.

Dec. 19 } McKay here – paid me 120.21 for the
  1886 }   year ending Dec. 1, 1886

Jan. 3, '87 – Rec'd from <u>Pall Mall</u> <u>Gazette</u>
  (Henry Norman.) £81.6.6 – $393.61

McKay here Sept. 22, '87 – pays me $76.91
                          for royalties   611.11

McKay here night of Feb. 29, '88 & paid
      me $113.95 for royalties   446.18

[283]

  1885 – Nov.   Dec
_____

Nov { [First 3 lines not in WW's hand:]
24 {   Gopàl Vinàyak Joshee, a native of
    {   Sangamner, Bombay <u>India</u>
       1400 North 21$^{\underline{st}}$ street, Philadelphia, Pa.

                                      £   s
28 – rec'd the <u>third</u> instalment from Rossetti   31:19 [2075]

"   gloomy news from Mrs. Gilchrist – the cancer[2076]

"   down to Atlantic City – Chalkley Gasprill

---

29 (Sunday) down again to Glendale[2077]

Dec. piece "Some Diary – Notes at random" in
1
    "Baldwin's Monthly," sent to friends &c[2078]

2073. See *The Correspondence of Walt Whitman*, III, 399.
2074. This was financially a low point for royalties, but Whitman also received $350.20 for contributions to magazines in 1885. Royalties, however, for 1886, 1887, and 1888 improved slightly, but still not a "living wage."
2075. See opposite page for full accounting, and *The Correspondence of Walt Whitman*, III, 409, for Whitman's letter of thanks.
2076. Anne Gilchrist died on 29 November 1885 — see entry below, 15 December 1885, and Whitman's letters to Herbert Gilchrist, 30 November 1885, and to Anne Gilchrist, 8 December 1885 (Whitman did not know she had died), in *The Correspondence of Walt Whitman*, III, 408–409, and 411.
2077. Whitman had visited the Staffords on the 1st and 15th of November.
2078. See footnote 2065.

2 – paid Mr Bennett $18 for horse for Nov[2079]

   had the nag shoed fore: feet.

   W S Kennedy's pamphlet "the Poet as a Crafts-
                                     man" [2080]

   sent Arnold Wyman, Stanton, Marion
                          [In red ink:]
      County, Florida $3 ed L of G. paid $3 rec'd

3   visit from H R & Mrs. Harvey & Miss Bennett

4   rec'd $33 from A T Rice for "Abm Lincoln" [2081]

    went to p. o. to cash Rossetti's money orders
    $155.53 – & to bank to deposit [2082]

5   call from Ed: Reed – (two bottles wine)
                          sm: one whisky[2083]

12 Will Duckett moves to Westmont [2084]

15 – death of Mrs: Gilchrist – news rec'd to-day
      she must have been buried Dec 1 [2085]

   Lou here – Harry Stafford here yesterday[2086]

   half-annual "Statement" from D McKay
      $20.71^{cts} for 6 mo's preceding Dec 1, '85 (royalty both
                                 vols) [2087]

2079. This $18 (also paid 1 November 1885) was the monthly amount to stable and feed the horse Whitman had received on 15 September 1885 from Thomas Donaldson and friends.
2080. David McKay published this 20-page pamphlet by William Sloane Kennedy: see Whitman's letter to Kennedy in *The Correspondence of Walt Whitman*, III, 410.
2081. See footnote 2005.
2082. This was the third instalment of the British "offering" received on 28 November 1885 (see entry that date, and Whitman's letter to Herbert Gilchrist, 4 December 1885, in *The Correspondence of Walt Whitman*, III, 411).
2083. See footnote 1932.
2084. See footnote 2007.
2085. See footnote 2076.
2086. Louisa Orr Whitman had been to Mickle Street on 24 September and sent Walt a robe on 14 November 1885 (see entries above); and the poet had spent Thanksgiving, 26 November 1885, with Harry Stafford and his wife in their home.
2087. See footnote 2074 and its entry above.

[284]

Express, RR & Ticket office
        324 Federal St.   Camden

John W Alexander
    "The Chelsea" 22 West 23ᵈ St   N Y ²⁰⁸⁸

B H Hinds U S Public Stores – N Y City

Harlowe Curtis (College,)
        Newark, Delaware²⁰⁸⁹

[Card:]   R. W. Kerswell, [printed in script]
            S.E. Cor 3ʳᵈ & Berkley [not WW's hand]
            Press [not WW's hand]
The Philadelphia ~~Times~~. [printed]

Mrs Townsend   572 Washington st

Harry M   Fritzinger²⁰⁹⁰
            on board ~~the Otago~~
Coast Seaman's Union
                Phil:
    Care ~~of Joseph~~   Cohen
518½ East St
513½   48 Stewart Street
        San Francisco,   Cal

---

[285]

    1885 – 1886 –

                        [Two words in red ink:]
Dec: 22 – Sent sister Hannah and Mary $10 each²⁰⁹¹   rec'd
                                                both
    nice two hours visit from Mr and Mrs: Ingram²⁰⁹²

2088. See *The Correspondence of Walt Whitman,* III, 391n.
2089. Harlowe Curtis saw Whitman on 7 February 1886 (see entry below).
2090. Henry M. (Harry) Fritzinger was the son of Captain Fritzinger, a seaman whom Mrs Mary Davis was taking care of when she secretly married another seaman Captain Davis (who shortly afterwards died). Harry Fritzinger and his brother Warren (who was to become Whitman's male nurse) were both at sea themselves when their father died; when they returned to Camden Mrs Davis was Whitman's housekeeper. See Gay Wilson Allen, *The Solitary Singer,* p. 519, and Elizabeth Leavitt Keller, *Walt Whitman in Mickle Street* (New York, 1921), pp. 119–120, 163–164, 190–194. (Harry named his son Walt Whitman Fritzinger.)
2091. The poet's usual Christmas gifts to his sisters Hannah Heyde and Mary Van Nostrand.
2092. Mr and Mrs William Ingram? (see footnote 894).

1886 – Jan 1. – 50 from G W C [2093]

Jan 2 – letter from Mary Smith – she has been
     very sick – (Mrs xxxxxxage) is in London[2094]
         Westminster
     40 Grosvenor Road, ∧   S W – visit to Russia

6 – paid $2.00 for <u>Press</u>   paid Bennet
                          horse – bill $18 [2095]
                          for December

8 – 9 – 10 – to – 25 cold, cold, & snow 10^{in} deep

12 – gas –bill paid, $3.42 – up to Jan. 1

10 – Harry and Eva S's little girl born (Dora) [2096]

Annual pass from W J – RR &c recd
   "   "   "   Camden Horse RR " [2097]

21   visit from Mr Aldrich (of Iowa) on his
     return from England [2098] – Mr Clark

                         £   s   d
25 – fourth instalment from Rossetti   33 16 6 [2099]

rec'd horse & buggy ferry pass

2093. On 13 January 1885 Whitman received a similar amount from George W. Childs; see *The Correspondence of Walt Whitman*, IV, 15, for a transcript of Whitman's thank-you note, and the editor's note on the poet in such money matters.

2094. Mary Smith, Robert Pearsall Smith's daughter, had married Frank Costelloe in the previous June; her letter to Whitman is presumably lost. See footnote 1993, and Robert Allerton Parker, *The Transatlantic Smiths* (New York, 1959), pp. 59–63, but no mention is made of a trip to Russia.

2095. Whitman refers to his horse in a letter to Susan Stafford, 24 February 1886; see *The Correspondence of Walt Whitman*, IV, 20.

2096. Although Whitman wrote to Harry Stafford, one of the best of his young friends, during these years, there are far more letters in *The Correspondence* to Harry's mother Mrs. Susan Stafford, in which he sends his love to Harry, his wife Eva, and their daughter Dora.

2097. See footnotes 1907 and 1908 about these annual passes on the West Jersey Rail Road and the Camden Horse Rail Road.

2098. This is Charles Aldrich, mentioned in Whitman's letter to Dr. Bucke,.1 November 1888; see *The Correspondence of Walt Whitman*, IV, 230; and Horace Traubel, *With Walt Whitman in Camden*, III, 1–2; Mr Clark is unidentifiable.

2099. Whitman refers to this "English 'offering'" in a letter to William D. O'Connor, saying it will amount to over $500, "on which I am really living this winter," as his semi-annual royalty was down to $20.71. (See *The Correspondence of Walt Whitman*, IV, 18.)

2^d Feb: went down to Elkton, Maryland,
    delivered the lecture, "Death of Abraham
    Lincoln" in the evening – the pleasant Evn'g
    banquet of the "Pythian Club"   Evening[2100]
  – returned next day Feb 3 – snow storm
  – was paid $30 – Mrs. & Mr. Reese – Folger McKinsey[2101]
    – Billy Duckett – [2102]

2^d, 3^d (bad snow storm) 4th 5th – 6th cold, cold,
           bitter cold nights

---

7   visit from Harlowe Curtis[2103]

                                      [286]

rec'd horse & wagon from Thos: Donaldson[2104]
          Sept. 15, 1885
      paid for horse = keep, &c,

to Joe Franklin from Sept 15 to 31 –	$ 9.
October '85 – to Bennett —	18.
November " "	18.
December " "	18.
other expenses, shoeing, whip, &c, &c –	6
Jan. '86	18
Feb: "	18
March, 18 – April 20 –	38

[Line in purple pencil:]
May, June, July, Aug. $18   each Sept. ^{18}
                $10 add'n $100

2100. See *The Correspondence of Walt Whitman*, IV, 19n, for more about this lecture and Folger McKinsey, who arranged it and called it "a failure."

2101. McKinsey (see footnotes 1823 and 2009, above) arranged for this Lincoln lecture; a railway clerk in Philadelphia, he became, in 1885, editor of the *Cecil Democrat* in Elkton, where the talk was given on 2 February 1886; and later edited the Baltimore *Sun*.

2102. William H. Duckett (see footnote 2007), who became Whitman's buggy driver in 1885, when he was 17 years old, moved to Westmount in December of that year and then boarded at 328 Mickle street in May and June 1886; see *The Correspondence of Walt Whitman*, IV, 35n, 278, especially the latter and other mention of Duckett in various Whitman letters, some written to help Duckett get jobs (*ibid.*, IV, 91–92). He got into difficulty with Mrs Davis, Whitman's housekeeper, who sued him and was awarded $190 (see *ibid.*, IV, 280) in February 1889, yet on 20 December 1889 he wrote Whitman for a loan (letter in the Feinberg Collection). See also Gay Wilson Allen, *A Solitary Singer*, p. 533; and Horace Traubel, *With Walt Whitman in Camden*, IV, 64–66.

2103. Harlowe Curtis lived in Newark, Delaware (see Whitman's notation above, opposite entries for December 1885).

2104. See entry above for 15 September 1885 and footnotes 2009 and 2038, above; see also *The Correspondence of Walt Whitman*, III, 405; among the donors were Whittier, Mark Twain, Holmes, and Edwin Booth. For Donaldson, see footnote 1573. The notations here in the *Daybook* are for expenses in keeping the horse, some going to October 1887.

Oct. Nov. Dec. $18 each – $10 additional   68
1887 from Jan. to July inclusive 140

[Clipping from The Post, Washington, headed 'A Remarkable Career. /
Death of Louis Fitzgerald / Tasistro. / ....', dated May 5, 1886, with marginal notation:]

died Sunday
May 2 – 1886 [2105]

[Another clipping, headed 'End of a Living Death', about Egbert A. Driggs
of Amityville, L. I., born at Dix Hills, town of Huntington, L. I. in July, 1827,
who died at the age of 58 – crippled by disease at 14, bed-ridden at 21, blind
last 30 years, and completely helpless for 20 years, cared for and nursed by his
mother, now 89. Notation:]

N Y Herald
Feb 5, '86 [2106]

[287]

Feb: 1886

10   sent – Jessie Crossfield, 1 Byng Ter-
                        C
     race, Gordon Sq: London, W. E.   Eng.
                    paid   [last word in red ink]
     the two Vols: 1^{pd}: 2^{sh} due   – rec'd [last word in red ink]

___

11 sent Keningale Cook,   Arnewood Rise[2107]
    Lymington, Hants, Eng. the two Vols.
                    pd sh recd – paid   [two words in red ink]
                    1 – 2 – due

2105. Louis Fitzgerald Tasistro (1808–1886), who came to America from Ireland, edited
a newspaper, became an actor, wrote a few books, and was a translator for the State Department
in Washington, where Whitman met him in the 1870s. The poet helped to raise money for
him when he became ill, destitute, and dying; when Whitman went to Camden in 1873 he
often asked in his letters to Peter Doyle about Tatistro (see *The Correspondence of Walt
Whitman*, II, 173, 178, 228, 233, 236, 296, 311, 335). As Whitman stopped asking Doyle on 6
August 1875 (see *ibid.*, II, 338), Professor Miller assumed that Tasistro had died: see also his
article in the *Walt Whitman Review*, VII (March 1961), 14–16. As we can see, however, in this
clipping Whitman placed in his *Daybook*, with an annotation, Tasistro did not die until eleven
years later on 2 May 1886.
    2106. Egbert A. Driggs, born in Whitman's home town of Huntington, eight years younger
than the poet, must have enlisted Whitman's sympathy with his "living death."
    2107. Whitman wrote to Kenningdale Cook on this same date (see *The Correspondence
of Walt Whitman*, IV, 19–20); he also ordered books on 29 February 1876, and on 23 April
1877 asked permission to quote Whitman in *Dublin University Magazine* — see Traubel, *With
Walt Whitman in Camden*, II, 219. Whitman may have written to Jessie Crossfield, but the
letter is not extant.

12 – paid Mrs: G. $16 for Ed: also 4 for the Doctor[2108]
    sent receipt to Lou[2109]

[Four lines in pencil:]
12 – visit from D McKay ab't the Wor-
    thington plates – subscription to purchase[2110]

13 – recd 12 "Spec: Days" from McKay

Sunday
14 –   Col. Scovel here to breakfast [2111]

22, 23, 24.   J W Alexander here, painting
    the portrait – (three sunny days) – [2112]

26   sent A H Evans, (prin: R schools) Reeds-
                      recd   [in red ink]
    ville, Mifflin Co: Penn. L of G, $3 ed.   Paid   [last word in red ink]

March 1 – Lecture "death of Ab'm Lincoln"
    at Morgans Hall, Camden – sent papers[2113]
    [in red ink:]   rec'd paid $25

March 7, (Sunday) down to Glendale – went alone[2114]

2108. "Mrs G." is Mrs J. J. Goodenough, of Mt Laurel, New Jersey, who was caring for the poet's brother Edward (see entry above for 8 October 1885).

2109. "Lou" of course is Louisa Orr Whitman, the poet's brother George's wife.

2110. This matter of the plates bought by Richard Worthington came up again and again: see footnotes 732, 949, 1042, and 1308; *The Correspondence of Walt Whitman,* III, 196n–197n, and IV, 160n–161n; not until after Whitman's death did Worthington stop using the plates to issue his own copies of *Leaves of Grass.*

2111. James Matlack Scovel and Mrs Scovel, one of Whitman's most constant friends, had the poet to dinner on Sunday, 3 January 1886.

2112. For Whitman's brief letter to John White Alexander (1856–1915), about the poet sitting for his portrait, see *The Correspondence of Walt Whitman,* IV, 20; the painting went to the Metropolitan Museum of Art, but Burroughs said it was an "emasculated Whitman," and the author himself was unimpressed. Whitman wrote Mrs Susan Stafford (*ibid.,* IV, 20) that Alexander, of *Century* magazine, was "a first rate young fellow, a good talker, and has already travelled a good deal over the world." See *ibid.,* IV, opp. p. 279 for a reproduction of the painting.

2113. This was the second time this spring Whitman made his Lincoln lecture — the first was on 2 February at Elkton, Maryland — and he made it a third time on 15 April in Philadelphia, and a fourth time in Haddonfield, New Jersey, on 18 May.

2114. Whitman planned to visit the Staffords in Kirkwood (Glendale) early in February, but this was the first time in 1886 that he made it.

2115. Whitman told Burroughs on 18 March (*The Correspondence of Walt Whitman,* IV, 21–22) that he "Had a violent spell of illness ab't a week ago — remained in bed all last

12th (Friday) bad spell sickness – stomach & head
in bed all day — (better & up next day) [2115]

16   sent $3 edition to Frederick L Manning,[2116]

                        recd   [in red ink]
     Counsellor at Law, Waterloo N. Y.   paid   [last word in red ink]

                  [In red ink:]   3 copies recd
18   rec'd Ernest Rhys's little Vol.   Poems of Walt
                      s d
     Whitman (selections), (1ˢ – 1.6 &c) Walter Scott
     24 Warwick Lane, Paternoster Row, London, Eng.[2117]

                                                          [288]

[On slip, not in WW's hand:]

                              [Six lines in red ink:]
     from Ernest Rhys   address now (March '87)
       59 Cheyne Walk   care Walter Scott Co.
         Chelsea,   publishers
           London   24   24 Warwick Lane
                             ₴X Warwick Lane
                             London   E C

[Clipping from a magazine or pamphlet, with a large picture of a railroad train at a station:]

women must have a chaperone, or go with father, mother, brother, or party, to the seaside or mountains. But in these days of independence and "personally conducted tours" they can go alone. Why not travel — and see and learn something new? why not get a radical change — of air, scene, and surroundings — and thereby come home recreated and refreshed? / Here are three ladies determined to see their own country. They are bound for Colorado, and are going to get health, pleasure, and information. They will come home with something worth talking about. They have got as far as Chicago, and have put themselves in

Friday — am up since, & go out a little, but dont feel even as half-well as usual," and on 26 March he wrote O'Connor (ibid., IV, 23), "Had a bad spell two weeks ago, but am now around after my sort, nearly the same (a letting down a little peg, if no more, every time)."
    2116. No letters from or to Frederick L. Manning are known.
    2117. See Whitman's letter to Rhys on 20 March 1886, The Correspondence of Walt Whitman, IV, 22, in which he hopes the Scott volume will "reach the working men, & guilds of the British Islands — especially the young fellows." Rhys told the poet that 8,000 copies were sold by 22 May, and a second edition was expected (ibid., IV, 23n).

March   1886

16, 17, 18. the nag Frank seems to me p̲l̲a̲y̲e̲d̲ o̲u̲t̲ [2118]

" " "   partially sick – head & stomach – 12 – 20ᵗʰ – 23ᵈ

Billy Duckett here in Camden – working
at notion store 257 Market St. Phila [2119]

---

20   went out to Mr & Mrs McIlvaine's, 58th st   " [2120]

---

23 – Wm & Ruth Goldy, & their little one Amy [2121]
start for Topeka, Kansas – Debby & Jo here [2122]

---

24 – J H & Alma Johnston off for Europe
[Six words in red ink:]
in the E̲m̲s̲ – rec'd letter – they were at Berlin – [2123]

---

28 – (Sunday) Bo't the new horse of Edwin
down
Stafford – price $152.50 – $100 paid
him – 52.½ the next
Sunday [2124]

---

visit from E H Woodruff, Cornell Uni: Ithaca
N Y [2125]

March 4, (Sunday)   Went down to Glendale [2126]

2118. Whitman wrote Burroughs (see footnote 2115) that "my old horse has quite given out" and, as seen below on 28 March, he bought a new one from Edwin Stafford for $152.50.
2119. William H. Duckett changed jobs frequently; see footnotes 2007 and 2102.
2120. Charles McIlvaine (?) whose two letters to Whitman of November 1890 and of an unknown date are in the Feinberg Collection.
2121. Ruth Goldy was Susan Stafford's daughter; she and William Goldy were married on 19 August 1884 (see entry above on that date, and footnote 1857). They are mentioned in a letter to Edward Carpenter, 29 May 1886 (*The Correspondence of Walt Whitman,* IV, 30).
2122. "Debbie" is another Stafford daughter who married Joseph Browning ("Jo").
2123. This letter from Whitman's New York friends, whom he often visited there, is apparently lost.
2124. This mare, "Nettie," was a replacement for "Frank" (see entry above for 16, 17, 18 March); Edwin Stafford was one of Susan's sons.
2125. Edwin H. Woodruff (1862–1941), a member of the library staff at Cornell, sent Whitman a poem on 4 June 1882, was introduced by letter to the poet on 26 March 1886 from Hiram Corson (see Traubel, *With Walt Whitman in Camden,* I, 286–287), and now visits him. See *The Correspondence of Walt Whitman,* IV, 59n, and Whitman's brief letter to Woodruff of 21 December 1886.
2126. Whitman's second visit so far in 1886 to the Stafford's; the horse is mentioned immediately above.

? April
- paid Ed Stafford, $52:50 making $152:50
  p'd to him for the mare "Nettie" –

April 14, 15 – Dr Bucke sails for
  Europe in "Grecian Monarch" [2127]

15 – read "Death of Abraham Lincoln"
  in Chestnut St Opera House – Phila[2128]

$13 more

evn'g 15th   370 from T D – (155 cash, 215 checks)
              394 "   Talcott Williams $687: altogether
                          $687

wrote cards of
thanks to TD and TW [2129]

24 (Saturday)   planked shad & champagne
  dinner at Billy Thompson's[2130]

28   sent the two Vols. L of G & S D
  to James Wylie, Yspitty Works,   [Two words in red ink:]
                                    paid
  Loughor, R S O, S   Wales   rec'd

my old horse "Frank" dead and buried [2131]

[290]

F. W. Fisher [not WW's hand]   (Fred) [2132]
290 Chestnut St.   Camden. [not WW's hand]
and at The Philadelphia Press. [not in WW's hand]

2127. Whitman referred to Dr R. M. Bucke's two-month visit to Europe in letters to O'Connor, W. S. Kennedy, Burroughs, and Mary Smith Costelloe (*The Correspondence of Walt Whitman*, IV, 24–28); Bucke was back in July, and visited Whitman on 18 July (see entry below on that date).

2128. The third Lincoln lecture Whitman made thus far in 1886; for his reaction, and for some details see *The Correspondence of Walt Whitman*, IV, 24–25; see 18 May, below for the fourth lecture.

2129. For Whitman's cards of thanks to Thomas Donaldson and Talcott Williams, see *The Correspondence of Walt Whitman*, IV, 27–28.

2130. Billy Thompson was a friend of Whitman's who apparently operated a restaurant at Gloucester, New Jersey, on the Delaware River edge: this is suggested by Whitman putting it in quotes, "Billy Thompson's," in a letter to William Sloane Kennedy on 29 April 1887. See *The Correspondence of Walt Whitman*, IV, 27, 89, 165, 166.

2131. Whitman said the horse was "played out" on 16–18 May (above), and he must have taken care of him, or had someone do it, until his death on 28 April.

2132. Fred W. Fisher appears to be someone who worked on *The Philadelphia Press*, a casual acquaintance? His name does not turn up elsewhere in Whitman material; although Whitman did write to the *Press* on 22 June 1886 in behalf of William H. Duckett (whose name appears here just below), so Fisher may have been the man who saw Duckett or got the letter.

[Printed slip:] McKinley & Horn,   W H D left early in June[2133]
              Notions & Woolen Goods
257 Market Street,   Philadelphia.

885 words in solid two Col. page. Century
                    solid
546   " 650   ∧page Lippincotts' (new)
440   " in N. A. Review page[2134]   [Clipping from newspaper paragraph
        solid minion   on number of words in columns of
1755 in ordinary ∧news col Press   newspaper type]

Sylvester Baxter[2135]
   Herald office 255   xxxxx
                    Boston

Roden Noel   46 Marlborough Hill
   5̶7̶ ̶A̶n̶d̶s̶l̶e̶y̶ ̶P̶a̶r̶k̶ ̶S̶ ̶E̶   London
       St John's Wood   London N W [2136]

Wm Bushell   [Clipping from envelope of E. & J. Baker, ship chandlers,
   25   State St.[2137] 138 N. Delaware Ave., Phila.]

[291]

May, 1886 – 1ˢᵗ – 2ᵈ – 3ᵈ – Sent $16 to Mrs: Goodenough
    for Ėd's board – [2138]

2133. W H D is William H. Duckett (see footnotes 2007 and 2102), whom Whitman was at this time trying to help in finding a job, certainly on the *Press* (see *The Correspondence of Walt Whitman*, IV, 35), perhaps with McKinley & Horn. By "left" Whitman means that he moved out of 328 Mickle Street.

2134. This word-per-page figuring has to do with a piece, "How I Made a Book — or Tried to," which Whitman sent to James Redpath of *The North American Reiew*, 3300 words, for which he asked $80 (see *The Correspondence of Walt Whitman*, IV, 36). It was not published there, but did appear in the Philadelphia *Press* on 11 July 1886 as "How I Made a Book." With other articles it became "A Backward Glance O'er Travel'd Roads" in *November Boughs* (1888).

2135. For Baxter, see footnotes 1102 and 1307; Whitman wrote the Boston newspaperman at least seven times during 1886–1889 (see *The Correspondence of Walt Whitman*, IV, 56, 93, 102, 110, 114, 125, 262), mainly about funds Baxter was raising for the poet or pieces Baxter wrote about him in the Boston *Herald*; he is also mentioned dozens of times in various letters.

2136. For Noel, see footnote 563; among his pieces on Whitman are "Mr. Swinburne on Walt Whitman," *Time: A Monthly Magazine*, December 1887; and "A Study of Walt Whitman," *The Dark Blue*, October–November 1871, reprinted in his *Essays on Poetry and Poets* (London, 1886), pp. 304–341. His letter to Whitman of 30 March 1886 is in the Feinberg Collection and is printed in Traubel, *With Walt Whitman in Camden*, I, 432–433; another, 16 May 1886, is in Traubel, I, 394 (also in the Feinberg Collection); but Whitman's letter to Noel is lost.

2137. Bushell bought 20 sets of the 1876 Centennial Edition of *Leaves of Grass* and *Two Rivulets* on 5 June 1886 (see that date, below) and also a MS page for $5 on 19 April (see *The Correspondence of Walt Whitman*, IV, 25).

2138. Another payment for the poet's brother (see footnote 2108, above).

Billy came to 328 to board [2139]

---

go out driving with Nettie, every day

---

5 – visit from John Burroughs, en route for Kentucky[2140]

May 28
10 – sent ∧ Cent: Ed'n – two Vols – to Beatrice
Taylor, Aston Rowant House, Tetsworth,
[Two words in red ink:]
Oxon. – England –   rec'd   paid

Walter Stoy, of Collingswood, here. I promised to go down to Haddonfield, Tuesday
evn'g, May 18, & deliver "the Death of Lincoln"
lecture, without pay, for the benefit of
a new Church, building fund, at Collingswood [2141]

---

sent T & E. ed'n to Mrs Charles Fairchild,
rec'd [in red ink]
191 Commonwealth av. Boston, $5 due   paid [2142] [last word in red
ink]

18th   went to Haddonfield & read the lecture[2143]

23d   went down (2nd time) to see Walter Borton
[Four words in red ink:]
went down 3d time June   at Clementon – went down
4   16th June[2144]

2139. This refers to William H. Duckett, who left early in June (see footnote 2133, above), but at this time was serving as Whitman's driver.
2140. See *The Correspondence of Walt Whitman,* IV, 28.
2141. See footnote 2113, above; *The Correspondence of Walt Whitman,* IV, 24n; and Roy S. Azarnoff, "Walt Whitman's Lecture on Lincoln in Haddonfield," *Walt Whitman Review,* IX (September 1963), 65–66.
2142. Mrs Fairchild (see footnote 8, above) was interested in forming, with Sylvester Baxter, a "Whitman Society" which "petered out" (see *The Correspondence,* IV, 136n); she also helped him in fund raising for the poet; and she is frequently mentioned by Whitman in his letters to William Sloane Kennedy. Her 1888 note to Whitman, now lost, brought this comment from him: "I had a note from Mrs. Fairchild acknowledging the book. It is a good note. She speaks of the book being 'sumptuous.' Sumptuous? sumptuous? that's scarcely the word. . . . Nor do I think so: sumptuous means parchment, vellum, gilt bindings: that is scarcely the word." (Horace Traubel, *With Walt Whitman in Camden,* III, 404.)
2143. For a full account of the Lincoln addresses, see *Walt Whitman's Memorandum During the War* [&] *Death of Abraham Lincoln,* reproduced in facsimile, edited with an introduction by Roy P. Basler (Bloomington: Indiana University Press, 1962); the Haddondale talk is on pp. 38–40.
2144. All we know about Borton is what is here and in a letter of 16 June 1866 to Talcott Williams: "just going to drive down 12 miles to visit a poor young fellow, Walter Borton, very low with consumption." (*The Correspondence of Walt Whitman,* IV, 32.)

[Line in red ink:]

Mr B took the other 10 (20 sets altogether) & paid 35 $80

altogether

28 – sold Mr. Bushell, 20 copies, (10 sets)

Centennial Ed'n – L of G. & T R – he

paid $45 – is to have 10 more sets, & pay $35 [2145]

–from W M Rossetti – £29.18.3 $145.58 [2146]

29 – from E Carpenter –   45 . . . . . $216.75 [2147]

31   sent the two Vols, L of G & S D   by

also Dr Bucke's book, three Vols. altogether

∧ express to James Gaunt, 55 Grand

[Three words in red ink:]

st.   New York –   paid $18   rec'd [2148]

[292]

[In red ink:]

3 East 14ᵗʰ Street

3 East   14th   Street[2149]

N A Review,   ~~30 Lafayette Place~~

J. O.

Mr ∧ Bentley,   812 Arch st [2150]   New York

[293]

June 1886

5ᵗʰ – Sold Mr Bushell, 20 sets, (40 Vols.) Centennial

Edition L of G. and T R. $80 – paid [2151]

11 – Alice Smith call'd

12   Alice Smith sails for Europe[2152]

2145. See footnote 2137.

2146. A few more details are in Whitman's letter to Rossetti, 30 May 1886: *The Correspondence of Walt Whitman,* IV, 30. Rossetti's letter, 17 May, is in the Feinberg Collection.

2147. Whitman acknowledged this birthday gift from Edward Carpenter, of Millthorpe, Chesterfield, England, on 29 May 1886: *The Correspondence of Walt Whitman,* IV, 29–30. Carpenter's letter, 17 May, is in the Feinberg Collection.

2148. James Gaunt is unidentified, other than his address here. It would be interesting to know about all those who bought Whitman's books from him, but this is obviously impossible.

2149. *The North American Review* address is here because Whitman sent the magazine an article on 29 June 1886 (see footnote 2134, above).

2150. Except that he is from Philadelphia, J. O. Bentley is unidentified.

2151. See entry above for 28 May and footnotes 2137.

2152. Alys Smith was the daughter of Whitman's wealthy Germantown, Philadelphia,

[Three lines in red ink:]
16th   went down to Clementon to see Walter
      Borton — he is dying — consumption[2153]

    Nettie, the mare, lame, hind foot [2154]

28th – W R Thayer call'd – he is to sail for
      Europe next Saturday – to be
      gone a year, or more – goes to
      Germany and Italy – has a book
      on the stocks ab't the Unifi-
              culminating
      cation of Italy as ∧ at present[2155]

27th – down at Glendale – a good ride – good visit
      Nettie all right – travels first rate[2156]

24th   30 to $35 – taken out of my pocket book
'5th
or'6th   by some one unknown – stolen from me

29 – sent "How I made a book – or tried to"

             [Five words in red ink:]
             recd
to James Redpath $80 – & 100 slip-sets   paid $80
————————————————————— July 10 [2157]
"   sent L of G, author's ed'n to A J Bromfield
        [In red ink:]
      N A Rev. office   rec'd

---

friend, Robert Pearsall Smith; her family was living in England. She became the first wife of Bertrand Russell in 1894: see Robert Allerton Parker, "Alys and Bertie (1894–1921)," *The Transatlantic Smiths,* pp. 113–134. Although Mary seemed Whitman's favorite of the Smith children, Alys often came to see the poet, and he frequently spoke of her in his letters — more than fifty times between 1884 and 1891.

2153. See entry above for 23 May 1886 and footnote 2144.

2154. Whitman faithfully reported in the *Daybook* about the health of the horses who drew his carriage: see the comments on Frank in the entries above for 16 March and 28 May 1886. Because of the mare's sprain, Whitman was unable to visit the Stafford farm at Glendale on 20 June: see his letter to Susan Stafford in *The Correspondence of Walt Whitman,* IV, 34.

2155. For Thayer, see footnote 2031, above, and *The Correspondence of Walt Whitman,* IV, 15n. Though reluctant to visit Whitman in 1885, he seems to have come this time without anyone's urging.

2156. See footnote 2154, above.

2157. See footnote 2134, above, and Whitman's letter to Redpath, 10 July 1886, *The Correspondence of Walt Whitman,* IV, 37. The money was for the article's use by a newspaper syndicate, not *The North American Review.*

[In red ink:]
"   sent $5 to Hannah   rec'd [2158]

[In red ink:]
30 – down to Glendale[2159]

"   paid back taxes 1884 $23.43

–   water rent tax   1886   8.

July   gas bill up to July 1 "   3.08
 2

[294]

Mrs: Ella H Bigelow
care of Brown, Shipley & Co.   London Eng
                                   ~~the~~ a
went in the "Cephalonia" June '86 for   "summer
                                        trip" [2160]

Dr ~~Osll~~ Osler, 131 S 15th st.   Phila[2161]

[Calling card of:]   Frederic R. Guernsey [printed]
            address care of [WW's hand]
                   ~~Editor,~~
        "The Mexican Financier," [printed]
        and Resident Correspondent
           "Boston Herald,"
           City of Mexico. [printed]
                      Mexico [WW's hand] [2162]

Jos: G. Hyer, 209 Walworth st
                   Brooklyn[2163]

2158.   This letter to Hannah Heyde, Whitman's sister, is lost.
2159.   He has just visited the Stafford family a few days before, on 27 May 1886; from the *Daybook* record, he went once more with Dr Bucke on 18 July but did not get to Glendale again until 21 November.
2160.   Mrs Bigelow; see footnote 1962.
2161.   For William Osler, professor at the University of Pennsylvania medical school and one of Whitman's physicians at this time, see footnote 2054. His address may be given here in the *Daybook* because Whitman sent Osler's address to Harry Stafford in September 1886.
2162.   Guernsey was on the staff of the Boston *Herald*, apparently on a visit to *The Mexican Financier*; Kennedy sent Whitman Guernsey's pamphlet on Thackeray in 1888 (see *The Correspondence of Walt Whitman*, IV, 223n).
2163.   Joe Hyer was an old Brooklyn friend of Whitman's, mentioned in a letter from Samuel G. Stanley, 13 July 1886: see William White, "Some New Whitman Items," *Prairie Schooner*, XLIV (Spring 1970), 51 and 52.

C Oscar Gridley[2164]
   9 Duke street   London Bridge
     London S E Eng:

                                                     [295]

            July 1886   [Two words in red ink:]
                                  rec'd [2165]

2^d – sent "Specimen Days" to Al Johnston   paid

paid Mrs. Goodenough $16 for Ed's board [2166]
   in full up to July 1, 1886

[Three lines in red ink:]
My next payment should be 1st Nov.
   as I have got a month ahead as above
   my proper turn to pay being July

3^d   went down to Sea Isle City, on
4th   Jersey Coast, 64 miles from Camden,
5th   – the "Minerva House" – Mr. Bentley –
&
       Mr & Mrs Fenton, Irving Latham
6th
       Mr Walsh – the beach & surf – the inlet [2167]

sent Burroughs's "Notes" to Gertrude   (paid [in red ink]
Van Dusen, Cq University, Ithaca N Y [2168]

9   sent Mr Bentley, the two Vols, L of G. & S D [2169]

10 rec'd $80 from A T Rice, (James Redpath)
     for "How I Made a Book" [2170]

2164. Gridley, secretary of the Carlyle Society, visited Whitman in April 1884: see entry of that date, above and footnotes 827 and 1782.

2165. Al[bert] Johnston was the son of John H. Johnston, the New York jeweler.

2166. Hardly affluent, Whitman nevertheless kept up paying for the upkeep of his younger and more or less helpless brother.

2167. These people most likely are those Whitman met at Minerva House; he mentioned his jaunt there, without comment, to Kennedy (*The Correspondence of Walt Whitman,* IV, 36).

2168. Gertrude Van Dusen, Cornell University, ordered John Burroughs's *Notes on Walt Whitman as Poet and Person* (New York, 1867, 1871) on 5 July 1886 (letter in the Feinberg Collection).

2169. Bentley may have met Whitman at Sea Isle City, New Jersey (see above).

2170. See footnotes 2134 and 2157; Charles Allen Thorndike Rice (see footnote 1093) was head of the syndicate that took Whitman's article — see entry immediately below also.

11   "How I Made a Book" appears in the
                                      pub: in newspaper syndicate
        Syndicate (Sunday) papers   Sundays
_____

18   Dr Bucke return'd from England -- we
        go down to Glendale[2171]
_____

      W H D on the RR train – "news agent" [2172]
_____

[Line in red ink:]
   Jan. '87 goes in ~~De~~Jan No ~~'86~~ '87

                                         accepted   [in red ink]
22 – sent "My Book and I" to Mr Walsh, Lippincott
                          $50 and 50 proofs   paid [2173]
                          [last word in red ink]
_____

      sent $3 by Wm Brown to get Panama hat
          & parrot [2174]

                                                            [296]

photos: J. P. Silver
formerly Potter & Co: 57 North 8th st
_____Phila:[2175]

   W H Ballou
         265   Broadway   New York[2176]
_____

Critic   743 Broadway[2177]
_____

      2171. See footnotes 2127 and 2159.
      2172. Billy Duckett again: see footnotes 2007 and 2102, and *The Correspondence of Walt Whitman,* IV, 34n.
      2173. "My Book and I," another part of the essay that became "A Backward Glance O'er Travel'd Roads," was sent to William S. Walsh, of *Lippincott's Monthly Magazine,* where it was published in January 1887 (XLIII, 121–127).
      2174. Perhaps a young man whom Whitman befriended.
      2175. In the unpublished *Whitman Portraits,* with notes, compiled by Henry S. Saunders (now in the Feinberg Collection), Portrait No. 83 is by Potter & Co., taken in Philadelphia in 1882; a photograph of the poet by J. P. Silver is not known.
      2176. William Hosen Ballou wrote Whitman on 18 June 1886 concerning Whitman's pension (the letter is in the Feinberg Collection); his interview with Whitman in the *Cleveland Leader and Herald,* reprinted in the Camden *Daily Post,* 28 June 1885, is quoted in *The Correspondence of Walt Whitman,* III, 398n: "My income [said Whitman] is just sufficient to keep my head above water — and what more can a poet ask?" (See footnote 1943, above.)
      2177. *The Critic,* edited by Jeannette L. Gilder, printed 28 pieces by Whitman between 1881 and 1891; on 14 August 1886 (n.s. VI, 73) "A Thought on Shakspeare" was published, and "A Word About Tennyson" on 1 January 1887 (n.s., VII, 1–2). See *The Correspondence of Walt Whitman,* IV, 33; and *Prose Works 1892* (New York, 1964), II, 556–558, 568–572.

July   1886 – July

23 – sent L of G to Sig: Adolfo de Bosis[2178]
       [in red ink:]   paid   85 cts
   Villa d'Este, Tivoli, Rome, Italy

         [In red ink:]   accepted [2179]
26 – sent Hospital article to "Century"   paid   [in red ink]
                     – 150

   In sending pieces – as "My Book & I"
to <u>Lippincott</u>'s – or "Army Hospitals & Cases"
to <u>Century</u> – I always specifically "<u>reserve</u>
<u>the right to</u> <u>print in future book</u>." [2180]

         [In red ink:]   pub'd – paid
27   sent <u>Critic</u> "a Thought on Shakspere" – 10 – [2181]

---

28 – went down on W J RR to Millville & back[2182]

---

29 – rec'd 10¼ yds Halifax tweed from Dr Bucke

         [In red ink:]   paid
"   sent Dr Bucke "Two Rivulets" –
   making $10 or 12 – to pay for the cloth

---

30 – 28th, 29th, 30th 31st   hot, hot, hot.

30th $2.75 to George Stafford, Jr – ($1 paid)

"   Ed Stafford here Sunday[2183]

2178.   See the brief letter to Agnes Margaret Alden, 23 July 1886, in *The Correspondence of Walt Whitman,* IV, 38.

2179.   This article, "Army Hospitals and Cases," was published in *The Century Magazine,* October 1888 (XXXVI, 825–830), and reprinted in *November Boughs* (1888); see Walt Whitman, *Prose Works 1892* (New York, 1964), II, 614–626; and *The Correspondence of Walt Whitman,* IV, 38.

2180.   Whitman did print both of these pieces in *November Boughs* in 1888, with different titles and revised.

2181.   See footnote 2177.

2182.   Whitman was using of course the annual pass he got for the West Jersey Railroad (see footnote 1079).

2183.   Ed Stafford was Harry's brother and both were sons of George and Susan Stafford, whose farm at Glendale Whitman visited from time to time.

Aug: 1 – pocket picked of $1 – (two half dollars) [2184]

[In red ink:]
3–5   sent Hannah $5 in letter   rec'd [2185]

"   cool and pleasant – 6 or 7 days –

[In red ink:]   accepted – is to go in Nov. number N A Rev:
6   sent "Burns as Poet and Person" to Redpath   paid   [in red ink]
                                                    $70 [2186]

10th letter from J R

7   recd pay for Hosp: Art: from Century
                                          150

8   sent Copy & Rec't to Century rec'd [2187]

11   sent Tom Donaldson (at his request) a full report
                      [in red ink:]   recd
     of the Death of Lincoln lecture, for Bram Stoker[2188]
          hot weather

                      [In red ink:]   rec'd
13   sent back W S Kennedy's MS book by Adams
                         Express[2189]
[In red ink:]   hot to 14th inclusive

2184. Where was Whitman when this happened?
2185. He had sent $5 on 29 June (see entry above); the letter of 5(?) August 1886 is lost.
2186. This article, "Robert Burns as Poet and Person," was published in the *North American Review* in November 1886 (CXLIII), 427–435, expanded from *The Critic*, 16 December 1882 (II, 337); it was included in *November Boughs* (1888); the letter sending the MS to James Redpath is lost. See *Prose Works 1892* (New York, 1964), II, 558–568.
2187. Letter, sending "Army Hospitals and Cases," to the magazine is in *The Correspondence of Walt Whitman*, IV, 40–41. Sent in August, the article appeared in October. See footnote 2179.
2188. See the letter to Donaldson, *The Correspondence of Walt Whitman*, IV, 41; Bram Stoker (1847–1912), author of *Dracula*, visited Whitman in April 1884, and on 22 December 1887, and was in correspondence with him from February 1876 (see *The Correspondence*, III, 28, and Gay Wilson Allen, *The Solitary Singer*, p. 516).
2189. In *Faint Clews & Indirections: Manuscripts of Walt Whitman and His Family*, edited by Clarence Gohdes and Rollo G. Silver (Durham, North Carolina, 1949), pp. 63–66, is the following material under "Notes for Kennedy" from the Trent Collection, Duke University (originally in a scrapbook compiled by William Sloan Kennedy). The first two items were written by Whitman in 1881, the rest in 1886; in connection with the latter, one should see the nine short letters from Whitman to Kennedy, 30 July–19 August 1886, in *The Correspondence of Walt Whitman*, IV, 39–44, which deal with Whitman looking over Kennedy's

article, "Walt Whitman, the Poet of Humanity," and his two books, *Reminiscences of Walt Whitman* (Paisley, Scotland, 1896) and *The Fight of a Book for the World* (West Yarmouth, Mass., 1926). Whitman's remarks:

I

Among my special   young men *littérateur* friends are W S Kennedy 7 Waterhouse street Cambridge, Mass: A young college chap — — Greek, Latin &c — —accepts L of G. —yet bolts at the sexual part — — *but I consider Kennedy as a real & ardent friend both of* self & book

II

Jo Swinton 21 Pk Row,

C. O. B. Bryant.
      Lafayette Hotel

Edwd Howland
      Hammondton N. Jersey

Wm M. Singerly Ed Record

H. H. Furness 7th & Locust

Geo H Boker 1720 Walnut

Geo. W. Childs. 2128 Walnut

Horace H Traubel 140 S. 8th

John Swinton. 21 Park Row

Knortz 540 E 155 st.

Wesley Stafford
      Kirkwood
            N. J

Geo Stafford,

[These names were probably sent to Kennedy for a mailing list of subscription blanks for his proposed book; such a blank is in the Trent Collection.]

III

doubtful ab't the "Dedicated to," & on p 1 — probably *better leave* it out

IV

for *motto — Don't like Ruskin's lines* — they are not fitting at all — the other line beginn'g "Allons!" is all right

V

I suggest inquiringly whether it wouldn't be well to put this — adding perhaps what is also marked with red ink on MS page 31 — what I have mark'd on the edge of the sheet with red ink — on the very first page of the text, or introduction — or even on a page by itself at the beginning? — sort of motto

VI

pages 26 '7 '8 '9 &c please & satisfy me well
[In Kennedy's hand: "Refers to my book (where I defend the sex poems, imaging an inhabitant of Mars looking over American poetry that has drifted to that planet or been shot there in a projectile &c)." See Kennedy's defense of the sex poems, *Reminiscences of Walt Whitman* (Paisley, Scotland, 1896), pp. 124–125.]

[298]

Wm Davis, black, farmer's truck
— at John Hutchinson's, ?White Horse pike[2190]

Edward F Gladwin
    366 Henry St., Brooklyn N Y
young man (24) that sent the pict. to be signed [2191]

[Clipped from end of letter, not in WW's hand:]
        yours truly   Nancy Whitman[2192]
        5 Siegle St   Brooklyn   E D

[299]

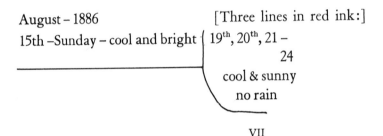

August – 1886   [Three lines in red ink:]
15th –Sunday – cool and bright { 19th, 20th, 21 –
                                        24
                                  cool & sunny
                                     no rain

VII

page 45 MS
R W Gilder, the now editor of "Century" is a warm admirer of L of G. & personally markedly friendly to W W — The "Century of Sept. '86 is to contain a short article "Father Taylor (& Oratory)" by W W — Furthermore the "Century" has just taken & handsomely paid for "Army Hospitals & Cases," by W.W. & will publish it in due time. see p. 237 your MS. [See "Father Taylor and Oratory," *Century Magazine*, XXXIII (February 1887), 583–584; and "Army Hospitals and Cases," *Century Magazine*, XXXVI (October 1888), 825–830; both now in *Prose Works 1892* (New York, 1964), II, 549–552, and 614–626, the latter entitled "Last of the War Cases."]

I have my doubts ab't pages 50 and 51 — I *would leave them out*

VIII

Seems to me this letter of Scovel's is better than Ballou's [see Kennedy's *Reminiscences of Walt Whitman,* pp. 11–13, 16–17; and 13–15] the one in the Book commenc'g p. 248 — reads better, & gives more desirable information. If you should think so too, substitute it in place of the one Ballou's now in the Book (the MS) — I dont like the latter pages 248 and 255 in Book at all —

2190. One wonders why Whitman recorded the name of a black whom he saw or met at a farm on White Horse Pike, just as he recorded other boys' and men's names in the *Daybook.*
2191. Letter now lost from Edward F. Gladwin, as well as Whitman's, if there was a letter.
2192. Nancy Whitman, wife of Walt's brother Andrew, she was widowed in 1863 and became a whore and an alcoholic; see the numerous references to her in letters from Mrs Walter Whitman, *Faint Clews & Indirections,* edited by Clarence Gohdes and Rollo G. Silver (Durham, North Carolina, 1949), pp. 183–205. See also *The Correspondence of Walt Whitman,* I (a dozen references to Nancy); II, 49n; III, 432, 444 (Walt's letter to Nancy, 22 January 1879, is lost; hers is in the Feinberg Collection); with nothing in IV and V. Gay Wilson Allen, *The Solitary Singer,* tells Nancy's distressing tale in half a dozen references (see especially pp. 395 and 398). This current letter, if it is to Walt Whitman and is of the 1886 period, indicates he was still in touch with her; unfortunately all we have is this signature and address.

19 sent $5 to Charley Somers, also 5 to Emma Lay[2193]

21 death of Charley Somers – afternoon –

24 – Sent card – & John Burroughs's book
to Rich'd W Colles, 122 Tritonville
Road, Sandymount, Dublin, Ireland.[2194]

"   lent Col. Scovel $50 [2195] – (rec'd £2 from Dowden thro' H Gilchrist [2196]

"   funeral Charley Somers

25 sent "Lafayette in Brooklyn" to Baldwin[2197]
returned   10

dry & parched & dusty – no rain for 12 days

wrote to Edward Dowden[2198]

25, '6 '7 '8, '9, 30, hottish spell again – putrifying smells

[In red ink:] pub in Nov '86 No – paid $70
31 sent "Robert Burns" proof back to N A Review[2199]

Sept 1 – paid $1.42 for "Press" [2200]

2193. Charley Somers, who died on 21 August 1886 and was buried on the 24th, most likely was a Camden neighbor (see footnote 1917, above); Emma Lay is, I believe, a member of the family that rented Whitman's house on Mickle Street in 1884 when he bought it: see Gay Wilson Allen, *The Solitary Singer*, pp. 516-518; *The Correspondence of Walt Whitman*, III, 366–368; and footnote 1792, above.

2194. Richard W. Colles, a student or friend of Edward Dowden's: see Whitman's letters to him, *The Correspondence of Walt Whitman*, IV, 44–45, 54, and 145; and Colles's letter in Horace Traubel, *With Walt Whitman in Camden*, IV, 141–142. Whitman sent *Leaves of Grass* and *Specimen Days* to him on 18 September, and Mrs Gilchrist's essays on 18 October (see entries for those dates, below).

2195. James M. Scovel was Whitman's Camden lawyer friend: why did he borrow $50 from the poet?

2196. Herbert Gilchrist's letter: *The Correspondence of Walt Whitman*, IV, 44.

2197. This essay, "Lafayette in Brooklyn," rejected by *Baldwin's Monthly*, is most likely the one that was not published until John Burroughs edited it after Whitman's Death, *Lafayette in Brooklyn* (New York: George D. Smith, 1905).

2198. Letter: *The Correspondence of Walt Whitman*, IV, 46 (but here the date is "Aug: 26 '86."

2199. See footnote 2186.

2200. For Whitman's subscription to the Philadelphia *Press*.

W H D laid off from RR – after two months
work[2201]
[in red ink:]   went on again soon

---

cool, bright day – after a hot spell

---

death of dear neice Hattie at St Louis buried
Sept 6 [2202]

---

14   sent $5 to C L Heyde in letter to H.[2203]

---

15   sent "War Reminiscences" to Harpers – 70 (rejected [2204]

⟨ 18 – sent L of G and S D two vols.
   to Richard W. Colles, 122 Tritonville Road, Sandymount, Dublin[2205]
   [first word in red ink:]   rec'd   paid £1.2ˢ

[300]

Dr Norris, Oculist – 1530 Locust st
Phila:[2206]

---

go to Fleischner's 310 north 8th & get a wire broiler
   & special salt cellar for B [2207]

---

straw hats – Gershon's – 42 north 8th st

2201. William H. (Billy) Duckett (see footnotes 2007, 2102, and 2133) was hired on 18 July 1886 as a "news agent."

2202. Whitman wrote six letters to his brother Jeff on the death of Mannahatta on 3 September 1886: they are dated 6, 7, 8, 11, 13, and 15 September (see *The Correspondence of Walt Whitman,* IV, 46–51).

2203. This letter is missing, but the entry here shows that, although Whitman did not always think well of Charles L. Heyde, husband of Walt's sister Hannah, he did help in a small way to support him when his painting paid little.

2204. This article, which Whitman called a "pot-boiler" in a letter to Jeff (*The Correspondence of Walt Whitman,* IV, 48), was "Some War Memorandum. Jotted Down at the Time"; after its rejection by *Harper's Magazine,* it was sent to James Redpath (see first entry in October, below) and appeared in *The North American Review,* CXLIV (January 1887), 55–60, later in *November Boughs* (1888) — see *Prose Works 1892* (New York, 1964), 584–589. See Horace Traubel, *With Walt Whitman in Camden,* II, 226, for H. M. Alden's rejection letter (*Harper's*) and Redpath's acceptance (both in the Feinberg Collection).

2205. See footnote 2194, above.

2206. Whitman had gone to see Dr Norris about his eyes on 19 October 1885 (see entry that date, above).

2207. Who is "B"? John Burroughs? Dr Bucke?

32 mo	4 inches wide	5½ inches high [2208]
18 "	4½ " "	6 " "
16 "	5 "	7 "
12 "	5½ "	7½ "
crown 8vo.	5½ "	8 "
8 vo	6 "	9 "
royal 8vo	7½ "	10 "
4[to]	10 "	12½
folio	13 "	15 "

Richard W Colles,   26 Oxford Road
    Randagh   Dublin   Irland [2209]

[Printed slip: Brass Bedsteads, Wm Wiler, 223 S. Fifth St., Phila.:]   also
Dunn & South
6 & 8
North 6th

[Printed slip: P.J. O'Shea, attorney & counselor, 163 Randolph St., Chicago.]
743   743
Critic 743   Broadway [2210]
743

[301]

Sept. and October, 1886   [In red ink:]
(arrived safe – letter from him [2211]
22 – afternoon – visit from Mr Hartmann, my

2208. These book page sizes may be here because Whitman was looking ahead to a new printing of *Leaves of Grass,* though the next one was not printed until 1889.
2209. This is a new address for Colles: the previous page in the *Daybook* gives it as 122 Tritonville Road.
2210. Why all these "743" figures for the address of *The Critic,* the same address as written three pages previously? (See footnote 2177.)
2211. C. Sadakichi Hartmann (1869–1944), son of a Japanese mother and a German father, is here mentioned for the first time in the *Daybook,* although he tells of his first meeting Whitman in November 1884 (the *Daybook* for that date is silent about the visit); however, on 22 September 1886, the poet calls Hartmann "my Japanese friend." In 1887 Hartmann tried to form a Whitman Society, made himself director and appointed officers without consulting them, but it seems to have petered out no matter what Whitman thought of it or how Boston admirers of the poet felt about the club; and in the *New York Herald* of 14 April 1889 he published "Walt Whitman. Notes of a Conversation with the Good Gray Poet by a German Poet and Traveller," not wholly accurate and certainly disturbing to some living personages, such as E. C. Stedman (who was called "a sophisticated dancing master"). After Whitman's death, Hartmann published, from the *Herald* piece, *Conversations with Walt Whitman* (New York, 1895). For the relationship between Whitman and this fascinating and highly individual "Japanee" (as Whitman called him), see George Hendrick, "Walt Whitman and Sadakichi Hartmann," *Walt Whitman Birthplace Bulletin,* III (October 1959), 15–19; *The Correspondence of Walt Whitman,* IV, 61, 108, 110, 136, 192, 208, 213n, 224n, 322, 325, 331, 340, and 368; V, 61, 68; Horace Traubel, *With Walt Whitman in Camden,* II, 37, 281, 305, 321, 379, 394, 507; V, 37, 38, 44, 62, 66, 94, 95, 106, 107, 116, 166, 169, 187, 243; William Sloane Kennedy, *The*

Japanee friend – He has been to New York &
seen Dr Knortz, Ned House and Stoddard – [2212]
has been to Boston – Sailed for Antwerp

Oct 9 '86

21 – 22   Cool weather, especially evenings

[Clipping from newspaper about a physician
saying that "a great deal of what passes
for heart disease is only mild dyspepsia;
that nervousness commonly is bad temper..."]

[Five lines in red ink:]
"Too often we are weak
because it never enters
into our thoughts that
we might be strong
if we would."

28th hot
26, 27, (Sunday and Monday)   warm & sultry

here
Logan Smith ∧ yesterday (26th) – I did not see him[2213]

27 – paid tax – bill on 328 for '86 – $25.82

Oct.   sent War Memoranda to Jas
[two words in red ink:]
Redpath   60   accepted   paid [2214]

8 –   Horse – board &c, $19.76 – paid

6th   paid gas bill – $1 54 ⎧ fine October
                           ⎨ weather – two weeks
                           ⎩   of it

9   Mr Smith and Alys[2215] here – bo't 4 Vols.   11

Fight of a Book for the World, pp. 87–88; and George Knox, "The Whitman-Hartmann Controversy," *Sadakichi Hartmann Newsletter,* I (Spring 1970), 2–3, I (Fall 1970), 5–7; I (Winter 1970), 7–9; II (Fall 1971), 8–12; III (Winter 1972), 3–8; and William White, "Whitman on Hartmann's 'Society': An Unpublished(?) Walt Whitman Piece," III (Fall 1972), 8. Hartmann's "Conversations with Walt Whitman" is reprinted in *The Long-Islander,* 30 May 1963, Sec. 2, pp. 8, 10.

2212. For Karl Knortz, see footnote 1580, above; for Charles Warren Stoddard, see footnote 919, above; Ned House is unidentified.

2213. Logan Pearsall Smith (see footnote 1622) is mentioned at least 20 times in *The Correspondence of Walt Whitman,* IV, with two letters from the poet to him, pp. 104–105, and 116.

2214. See footnote 2204, above.

2215. Robert Pearsall Smith and his daughter Alys (see footnote 1622): they are men-

[In red ink:]   proof sent

12 – gave Mr Powell a sketch ∧ (life) for   History
                                             Camden[2216]

13 – wrote to Ernest Rhys, giving permission
     to publish (through Walter Scott) Specimen
     Days – I to have 10 copies & whatever
     W. S. feels to pay me[2217]

18   sent R W Colles   Dublin   Mrs G's   Essays[2218]
           & papers – letter Spr. Rep.

                    indeed 8 or 9
21 – Drouth the last five ∧ weeks

                                                    [302]

[Clipping: recipe for coffee cake.]

[Clipping from newspaper on number
of stars one can see in the sky.]

Chatto & Windus, publishers
        Piccadilly, London[2219]

[Written name and address on slip, not
in WW's hand:] Geo. R. Prowell
                  54 North Sixth st
                  Philadelphia

[Printed on card:]
   L. J. Richards & Co.,
          Publishers,
52 & 54 N. Sixth St., Philadelphia, Pa.

James Harding, 214 Senate st

     Mrs Costelloe
  40 Grosvenor Road
Westminster   London[2220]
  the Embankment ∧ S W

tioned as back in America, from England, in Whitman's letter to Mary Smith Costelloe, *The Correspondence of Walt Whitman*, IV, 51–52.

2216. Mr Powell is a misspelling of George R. Prowell, who was writing *The History of Camden County, New Jersey* for L. J. Richards & Co., Philadelphia, publishers (see next page of the *Daybook*); Prowell (1849–1928) published the Camden history in 1886 and wrote several local histories.

2217. Letter: *The Correspondence of Walt Whitman*, IV, 52. Rhys wrote on 19 January 1887 that Scott would pay ten guineas for *Specimen Days* (letter in the Feinberg Collection).

2218. See footnote 2194, above.

2219. This is the English publishing house Whitman wrote to on 18 November (see entry below, that date) about exchanging a Centennial Edition of *Leaves of Grass* for copies of Rossetti's second edition of *Poems by Walt Whitman*, which they had just published; on 13 December he received six copies (see below). Letter: *The Correspondence of Walt Whitman*, IV, 53.

2220. Mary Smith Costelloe (see footnotes 1622 and 2215), to whom Whitman wrote on

S E Gross   s e cor: Dearborn & Randolph st
100 Nov. 30, '86   Chicago   Ill

[303]

Oct.   1886 – Oct.   and Nov.

23 – Good drive to Merchantville Driving Park
    & timing Nettie – (3.49 a mile) – finest weather

[In red ink:] 2.20 p m
Nov. 1 –   Sent back proof "My book & I" to Mr Walsh
                                        Lippincotts[2221]

5 – paid Mrs Goodenough $16 for Ed. for Oct[2222]
    (I pay next early in Jan:)

16th   perfect day – ride alone 2½ hours midday
                                              [Two words in red ink:]
                              with letter   rec'd – paid
18   sent R W Colles, Dublin the two Vols. ∧   Cent. Ed'n – $10 due[2223]

sent to Chatto & Windus to exchange[2224]

21 – went down to Glendale[2225]

22   sent green card to Thomas T Greg, 15 Clifford's
    inn
    Inn, London, Eng:[2226]

23 November (*The Correspondence of Walt Whitman,* IV, 55), not recorded below. Whitman, by no means, listed in the *Daybook* all the letters he sent or received.
    2221. See footnote 2173.
    2222. The usual payment for the keep of Whitman's feeble-minded brother.
    2223. See footnote 2194.
    2224. See footnote 2219.
    2225. One of Whitman's many trips to visit the Stafford family at Timber Creek, both for his health and because he enjoyed the company of Mrs Susan Stafford; however, he had not been there for four months.
    2226. If Whitman wrote anything on the "green card" — Whitman's small printed advertisement for *Leaves of Grass* ($3, with autograph) and *Specimen Days* ($2) — it is not known: this card is not extant; Greg wrote to Whitman on 16 December 1888, and though that letter is now lost, Traubel printed it in *With Walt Whitman in Camden,* III, 432–433. Greg also sent a copy of pamphlet, *Walt Whitman: Man and Poet,* a speech he made at the Warrington (Lancashire) Literary and Philosophical Society, 16 October 1888; among other things, Greg says in his letter that Whitman "infused into my life and into the lives of many others, a fresher, healthier happiness than we knew of."

[In red ink:]   paid
24   sent Cent. Ed'n – 2 Vols. – to Dr Bucke
[in red ink:]
"   back the MS pages &c   rec'd [2227]

Dec. 6.   Visit from Harry C Jewett,   Phil:
                                       N American[2228]

"   5th   cold, bitter cold – commenced 4th Dec. &
                                                        ⟶ to 19th
snow-storm, Sunday mn'g – 5th Dec, 6th, 7th, & 8th ∧ cold

9th   paid Bennett, 19.75, for horse-board for Nov.
         & the horseshoer's bill –

Tennyson is 77 – & Whittier is 79 – [2229]

---

13   rec'd six copies their book from Chatto & Windus[2230]

[In red ink]
18   sent Chatto & Windus Vol. to Dr Bucke   rec'd [2231]

---

19.   sent 2 Centennial Vols. to Mrs. Maxwell
            [in red ink:]   paid   rec'd [2232]
         Lichfield House, Richmond   S W London

David McKay here – he paid   120.21
   for royalties for 1886 (both Vols:) [2233]

2227. MS pages?
2228. Harry C. Jewett? *Philadelphia North American*?
2229. Why are these ages mentioned here? Tennyson's birthday was 6 August 1809; and Whittier's 17 December 1807 (he wasn't yet 79); both barely outlived Whitman, Whittier dying on 7 September 1892 and Tennyson on 6 October 1892.
2230. The book Whitman received was Chatto and Windus's (London) publication of *Poems by Walt Whitman,* second edited by William Michael Rossetti, 1886 (see footnote 2219, above).
2231. If Whitman wrote Dr Bucke at this time, the letter has not survived.
2232. Gerald Maxwell, a young admirer, wrote to Whitman on 17 December 1886 (the letter is in the Feinberg Collection); and on 19 December — as noted here — Whitman sent *Leaves of Grass* and *Two Rivulets* (1876) to his mother.
2233. For a few details of Whitman's relationship with his publisher McKay, see *The Correspondence of Walt Whitman,* III, 310n, 314, 371n, 414; for 1885 the poet got only $42.77 for *Leaves of Grass* and *Specimen Days* royalties, plus at least $350.20 for poems and articles; so $120.21 in royalties for 1886 is an increase, though hardly a princely sum. *The Correspond-*

Out, first time in two weeks – raw, wet fog

sent the two Cent'l Vols. to Chatto & Windus[2234]

[304]

Mrs R Brisbane
83 Boul'd St Michel   Paris   France[2235]

R. J. Hinton[2236]
78 E 11th St
N. Y.

Sporting Goods
J D Shibe & Co
223 North 8th st
Phila

Capt. R A Rayner[2237]
Doylestown
Bucks co.   Penn

[305]

Dec '86 – & – 1887

[Two words in red ink:]
both

Dec
22   Sent $10 each to Hannah and Mary   rec'd [2238]

all sent   [two words in red ink:]
sent L of G. 82 Ed'n to Dr Bucke   now   rec'd   paid

Kind letters, mostly from England, often
with money enclosures – some from U. S. too – [2239]

ence, IV, 61n, cites Mr Miller's tabulation: Whitman received, for lectures, royalties, articles, poems, and gifts in that year, at least $2,289.06. (For earlier years, see footnote 1891, above.)

2234. See footnote 2219. (See Whitman's thank-you letter, *The Correspondence of Walt Whitman*, IV, 59.)

2235. R. Brisbane apparently wrote to Whitman about a French translation of *Leaves of Grass* (the letter is now lost), and a letter about the matter, dated 1 February 1887, is in Horace Traubel, *With Walt Whitman in Camden*, IV, 266–267. Whitman gave his permission, but this translation in book length does not seem to have been made. Jules Laforge, the translator named in the letter, did translate 34 poems of Whitman into French — in *La Vogue*, June, July, August 1886.

2236. For Colonel Richard J. Hinton, see footnote 249, above. Not much in evidence from 1876 to 1888, he visited Whitman early in January 1889 and wrote about it in "Walt Whitman at Home," New York *World*, 14 April 1889, the same day as Sadikichi Hartmann's "Conversation." Whitman did not care for Hinton's piece ("three crowded columns of gush"), though Hinton was his friend. See *The Correspondence of Walt Whitman*, IV, 322n.

2237. Captain R. A. Rayner unidentified.

2238. These are typical Christmas gifts to Whitman's sisters, Hannah Heyde and Mary Van Nostrand.

Kind visits from R P Smith – liberal & kind
                                      gifts

                    [In red ink:]   paid   rec'd
sent $3 L of G. to Dr H H Morrison, Greencastle, Ind

Jan 2

   Sent L of G & S. D. to Mrs. Noble T Biddle
      San José California – paid 5 – [2240]   rec'd   [last three words
   ————————————————————————————————   in red ink]

Jan. 3 – Rec'd letter from Henry Norman, <u>Pall Mall</u>
      <u>Gazette</u>, London,   £81.6.6 $393.61 [2241]

"   paid Bennett's bill for horse for Dec $18 — [2242]   [in purple pencil]

---

   very cold – 8 days   [in purple pencil,
                           except figure 8, which is in red ink]

---

5 – rec'd from Mrs Emily Pfeiffer, London 24
      thro A J Kenealy, N. Y. Herald [2243]

---

   paid 1.36 to <u>Press</u> collector

---

   sent L of G. to Mrs. Sophia B. Robinson
                              [Two words in red ink:]
                              paid
      Franklin Falls, New Hampshire   rec'd

2239. See Whitman's letter to Mary Smith Costelloe, 3 January 1887, about these and
other related matters, *The Correspondence of Walt Whitman,* IV, 62; her father, Robert Pearsall
Smith, who was then in America, visited Whitman (see next entry in the *Daybook*) on 22
December 1886 and 24 February 1887.

2240. Although Whitman wrote to Mrs Biddle on sending the books (*The Correspondence of Walt Whitman,* IV, 62), if he did write to Dr Morrison (above) the letter is now
lost, as are the letters from Mrs Biddle and Dr Morrison to Whitman, ordering *Leaves of
Grass* and *Specimen Days.*

2241. See Whitman's letter of thanks to Henry Norman, *The Correspondence of Walt
Whitman,* IV, 63; and also to William T. Stead, IV, 116; Norman was acting for the editor of
the *Pall Mall Gazette,* and the money was a gift from English donors, a citation of which
caused a little difficulty (see *The Correspondence,* IV, 63n).

2242. This $18 was for taking care of Whitman's mare "Nettie," which he bought in
the fall from Edwin Stafford.

2243. I cannot find any additional information than is given here about Mrs Emily
Pfeiffer of London and A. J. Kenealy of the New York *Herald*; but apparently she sent a gift
of $24 (£5?) to Whitman through Kenealy. Whitman certainly must have thanked someone,
though no letters are extant.

          freight paid
8   sent by Express∧ two copies L of G. and [two words in red ink:]
                               paid
   two copies, Spec. D. to Edward Maher
                                   rec'd
   law office, 122 La Salle street, Chicago[2244]

---

   cash'd p o orders –   37.94

---

   paid gas bill   6.12

---

10 Mrs. Watson died at 5 this morning[2245]

                            "War
11 – rec'd pay   60. from N A Rev. for ∧Memoranda" [2246]

---

   call from Albert Edmunds England – [2247]

---

   cash'd <u>Pall Mall Gazette</u> order, 81.6.6 ($393.61) [2248]
      at Brown Bro. & Co.
   deposited money in bank

                                              [306]

[Blank.]

                                            [307]

Jan.   1887
12 – Cold – ground all cover'd with snow – good sleighing
     all ab't here – went out a couple of hours midday,
     yesterday, with horse & wagon – went to Brown Bros,
                    Phila:
     bankers, Chestnut st ∧ to cash the order the New Year's
             (£81.6.6)
     present, $393.61,∧ sent over to me by <u>Pall Mall Gazette</u>
     people – went to bank to deposit money & checks.

    2244. Nothing known of Mrs Sophia B. Robinson or Edward Maher other than that they
bought copies of *Leaves of Grass* and *Specimen Days*.
    2245. Mrs Watson, a neighbor on Mickle Street.
    2246. For "Some War Memorandum. Jotted Down at the Time," see footnote 2204.
    2247. Albert Edmunds is unidentified.
    2248. See footnote 2241 and entry above for 3 January 1887.

– Am very feeble, especially in walking power – don't
go out doors at all – pretty fair appetite – sit up here
in the little front room 328 Mickle street well bundled
up, this weather – read & write rather aimlessly – How
considerate, gentle and generous, my British friends are! [2249]

[In red ink:]   rec'd
14   sent L of G & S D to Dr Bucke – 4 due paid [2250]   [last word in red ink]

12 L of G & 12 S D. recd from McKay – $28

16   sent article (25) to N O Picayune
                [In red ink:]   paid [2251]
     to appear 25th Jan. (Tuesday) – printed –

19 – very cold – yesterday's papers' Congressional
     Proceedings say Mr Lovering, of Mass: introduced
     a bill in H of R to pension W W $25 a month
     – (a month or so ago I wrote Sylvester Baxter
     a friend of Loverings, positively declining to apply
     for such a pension, & that I did not deserve it) [2252]

                [In red ink]
22 – sent Dr Bucke L of G.   paid   milder
                   Lou here

23 – drive to Glendale [2253] – weight 205

24 – Sent L of G & S D – two Vols, to Thomas Locke
     Laurel Walk, Gosforth Newcastle on Tyne   paid

2249.   See previous entry and that of 3 January 1887.

2250.   Dr Bucke also got copies on 22 December 1886 (see above).

2251.   See Whitman's letter to the editor, New Orleans *Picayune,* 17 January 1887, *The Correspondence of Walt Whitman,* IV, 64. The article, "New Orleans in 1884: Walt Whitman Gossips of His Sojourn Here Years Ago as a Newspaper Writer: Notes of His Trip Up the Mississippi and to New York," appeared in the *Picayune* on 25 January 1887; it was reprinted in *November Boughs* (1888). See *Prose Works 1892* (New York, 1964), II, 604–773. The piece was reprinted in the New Orleans *Picayune* 25 January 1937.

2252.   See Whitman's letter to Baxter, 8 December 1886, *The Correspondence of Walt Whitman,* IV, 56; and to William Sloane Kennedy, 26 January 1887, ibid., IV, 65–66; also Gay Wilson Allen, *The Solitary Singer,* pp. 524–525. Because Whitman did not wish to receive a pension, the bill, which would have passed the House of Representatives, was quietly dropped.

2253.   Though Whitman invited Mrs Stafford to visit him in Camden on 18 January, he apparently went to visit the Staffords on the 23rd: see his letter to her, *The Correspondence of Walt Whitman,* IV, 64–65. Lou in the previous entry here is George Whitman's wife Louisa.

25   rec'd box of Florida oranges from Arthur Price[2254]

---

29   xxxxxx   changeable weather – cold – bad roads

---

30   (Sunday) visit from Clayton Wesley Pierson[2255]

---

31   sent G P Wiksell, 40 Boylston st paid   [in purple pencil]
                                      recd [2256]   [in red ink]
        Boston, L of G –

---

[308]

Clayton W Peirson
at Greene's Printing House, 27 South 5th St. Phila[2257]

O'Connor   care of Dr W F Channing[2258]   ret'd
                                           to Wash
        Pasadena, Los Angeles Co.   Cal.   July 1
                                             '87

J B Marvin   1121 J street Wash:[2259]

Mr Bacon, Photo: 40 N 8th St – Phila

    Albert Edmunds

Geo Herbert Kersley   [name and address
     Nevill House   not in WW's hand]
        Brimpton   [In red ink,
           N^r Reading   sideways in WW's hand:]
England   Berks   Wilson Barrett's Company[2260]
                             March 1887

2254. See Whitman's letter of thanks to Arthur Price, of Woodside, Queens County, New York, the son of Whitman's old friend, Mrs Abby H. Price, *The Correspondence of Walt Whitman*, IV, 65. (See footnote 287, above.)

2255. Clayton Wesley Peirson (see *The Correspondence of Walt Whitman*, IV, 269) was connected with Greene's Printing House of Philadelphia (see address next page, below).

2256. Dr Gustav Percival Wiksell, a Boston dentist, who became an intimate friend of Horace Traubel's. Dr Wiksell read a paper, "Self-Primacy in Whitman," at the 31 May 1897 meeting of the Walt Whitman Fellowship: International (published in the *Fellowship Papers* for 1898, pp. 41–42); and he also served as president of the Fellowship. For *The Conservator*, which Horace Traubel edited from 1890 to 1918, when he died, Dr Wiksell wrote 14 pieces, several of them dealing with Whitman. He later retired to California.

2257. See footnote 2255.

2258. Dr William F. Channing, William Douglas O'Connor's brother-in-law (Mrs. Channing and Nellie O'Connor were sisters). One of the reasons O'Connor went to California was for his health. (See *The Correspondence of Walt Whitman*, IV, 73.)

2259. Joseph B. Marvin (see footnote 81) was an old Washington friend of Whitman's, often mentioned in his letters.

2260. In three letters of 6 March 1887 (*The Correspondence of Walt Whitman*, IV, 72–73)

Silvanus Dauncey   [not in WW's hand
  c/o W. S. Jones   five lines]
    Winslow
      Buckinghamshire
       England

[309]

Feb: 1887

                          4th – sent card
                                      again
Feb. 2 – sent Spec. Days (copy) to Ernest Rhys – 3^d – sent
                                  postal card [2261]

    "   also letter

3   sent Mrs. Goodenough $16 for Ed's board
                  4th Mrs. G here[2262]

4   paid Mrs. M. for the 4 shirts – 1.50 [2263]

"   the Pension matter in abeyance – letter from
      Mr Lovering to me – my letter to him
    the H of R Pension Committee reported favorably on the bill [2264]

    paid Mr Bennett $18 for Nettie's board, Jan 1 [2265]

11 – very moderate – thawing – roads muddy – was
      out driving yesterday

                                 Sunday
14 – very cold – sunny – was out driving yesterday ∧

Whitman mentions the actor Wilson Barrett, whose company was acting in "Clito," at the Chestnut Street Opera House, Philadelphia; two actors came over to see Whitman and took him and Mrs Davis to a performance — they were undoubtedly George Herbert Kersley and Silvanus Dauncey, who wrote their names and addresses in Whitman's *Daybook* (see entry below for 5 March 1887).

    2261.   Whitman's letter to Rhys, 4 February 1887, *The Correspondence of Walt Whitman,* IV, 66–67, gives permission to issue *Specimen Days & Collect*; but see Ernest Rhys's reply of 15 February, *ibid.,* IV, 66n.

    2262.   Mrs G is Mrs Goodenough, who took care of Whitman's feeble-minded brother Edward, who did not die until November 1892.

    2263.   Mrs M. was Mrs Miller, who made shirts for Whitman — at 4 for $1.50! and made shirts — 4 for $1.50!

    2264.   The bill was quietly dropped: see footnote 2252.

    2265.   Nettie was Whitman's mare, and Mr Bennett was owner of the stable where the horse was kept.

16 – visit from Mr & Mrs.   Johnston of N Y [2266]

[Next seven entries, 17 lines, written on a sheet pasted on page:]
22 – went over to the "Contemporary Club" Phila. $20
   – read the "Word by the Sea," "Mystic Trumpeter" &c

   – Horace Traubel, Dr Brinton (& Marcus L Ward Elder the driver) [2267]

---

brain like
24th – R P Smith & his cousin [2268] – pretty sick to-day – a lump of
heavy dough
25th — Mr Lay call'd — $1 — I feel better [2269]

Wm O'Connor at Pasadena, Los Angeles Co.
California (with C W Eldridge) – in a bad way [2270]
                                          I send letters
   – my thoughts (gloomy enough) turning to him – & papers often

---

   – Kennedy's letter to me ab't Trowbridge – my letter to K [2271]

2266. John H. Johnston, Whitman's long-time jeweler friend, and his wife Amelia were often Whitman's host when he visited in New York.

2267. In a letter to Mary Smith Costelloe, 11 February 1887, 11 days before his talk in Philadelphia, Whitman said he was going there, and that's about all; the event was reported in the Philadelphia *Press* of 23 February — see *The Correspondence of Walt Whitman,* IV, 67n. See Traubel's comments on the reading in *In Re Walt Whitman* (Philadelphia, 1893), pp. 130–131; it was not until more than a year later that Traubel began visiting Whitman daily, often more than that, and took notes for *With Walt Whitman in Camden,* which starts 28 March 1888. Dr Daniel Garrison Brinton was a professor at the University of Pennsylvania, an archeologist, whom Whitman admired and who was pleased that Brinton, as a scientist, liked *Leaves of Grass* ("Brinton is a brick," the poet told Traubel: see *With Walt Whitman in Camden,* I, 324, *et passim,* with numerous references to Brinton); Brinton was to speak at Whitman's funeral. Brinton wrote to Whitman on 28 February 1887 (letter in the Feinberg Collection) thanking him on behalf of the Contemporary Club for the poet's talk. It is interesting to note that, in addition to mentioning Traubel and the eminent archeologist Dr Brinton, Whitman also refers by name to the driver of the carriage, Marcus L. Ward, who was as important in his mind to the others.

2268. In his letter to Mary Smith Costelloe in London, 6 March 1887 (*The Correspondence of Walt Whitman,* IV, 73), Whitman does not even mention this visit by her father.

2269. See footnote 2193 on Emma Lay: she and her husband lived at 328 Mickle Street when Whitman bought the house.

2270. See footnote 2258 and the entry, above, to it in the *Daybook*: O'Connor returned to Washington on 1 July 1887 and did not die until 9 May 1889. Charles W. Eldridge (see footnote 116), an old friend and publisher of the 1860 *Leaves,* wrote Whitman on 11 February 1887 about O'Connor: see Clara Barrus, *Whitman and Burroughs — Comrades* (Boston, 1931), pp. 262–263. It's not clear what Whitman means by "I send letter & papers often," for there are no letters extant to O'Connor between 19 November 1886 and 28 October 1887; but Whitman did write to Eldridge in Los Angeles on 5 April 1887, 21 April 1887, 6 May 1887, and 21 June 1887 — at least these letters are in *The Correspondence of Walt Whitman,* IV, 79, 87, 91, 103–104; the letters, if any, to O'Connor may be lost.

2271. William Sloane Kennedy's letter is apparently lost, but Whitman's very interesting letter to Kennedy on this date is in *The Correspondence of Walt Whitman,* IV, 69–70: in it,

am collating "Elias Hicks" these days[2272]

Clayton Peirson was here Sunday last, &
    took my "Day Book" to be re-bound – (is
                                return'd the old one
    to make me a new one also) handsomely re-bound
                            this is it[2273]

    half sick (or more than half) most of this month –
    bad, sulky weather, cold – O'Connor's illness &
    journey to Southern California, (a gloomy affair[2274]

[310]

[Several long clippings from newspapers about Whitman. (WW's annotation in red ink): N. Y. Tribune. April 15, '87. Headlines: "Hearty Cheers for Whitman. / He Speaks on Abraham Lincoln. / Many Well-Known Writers Present — A Recep- / tion in the Evening." WW's annotation on another, "March '87" on "Walt Whitman. / An Eminent Englishman's Opinion / of an Eminent American." /, giving Robert Buchanan's interview.]

[On a slip paper, in WW's hand:]
John Newton Johnson
    Mid p o
    Marshall Co:
        Alabama

[311]

<u>Feb: & March   1887</u> [2275]

[Two entries, 10 lines, written on a slip pasted on page:]

he begins "It is of no importance whether I had read Emerson before starting L. of G. or not. The fact happens to be positively that I had *not*," and he continues about his poetry; however, Kennedy records in *Reminiscences of Walt Whitman* (Paisley, Scotland, 1896), pp. 79–83, that John T. Trowbridge said that Emerson inspired the first poems of Whitman, who told him (Trowbridge) that "My ideas . . . were simmering and simmering, and Emerson brought them to a boil."
    2272. The Elias Hicks essay was not published until Whitman issued *November Boughs* in 1888: see *Prose Works 1892* (New York, 1964), II, 626–653.
    2273. See footnote 2255; the *Daybook* entries from 22 February 1887 to here are written on a sheet and placed in the book.
    2274. Whitman makes a few additional comments on his health in his letters of 25 February 1887 ("the worst is my enforced house-imprisonment") and 2 March 1887, *The Correspondence of Walt Whitman,* IV, 70–71 and 72; on O'Connor's illness, see footnotes 2258 and 2270 and their accompanying entries.
    2275. The *Daybook* entries for this date, 25 February 1887 and its verso page (pp. 311–312) are written on a large sheet, placed in the book.

Feb.

25th   afternoon – Am I not having a "happy hour," or
      as near an approximation to it, (the suspicion of it)
      – as is allowed? – (See p. 92 – Specimen Days) – (Is it
            really
      not largely a∧ good condition of the stomach, liver & ex-
      cretory apparatus?) – I was quite ill all yesterday
                  – (how quickly the thermometer slides
                        up or down!)[2276]

      25th – Clayton Peirson[2277] here to-night – brings me a
      fine lot of paper & envelopes – & the rebound
      Day book – (this book) – welcome & useful to me – all

---

      26   Snow storm   – (fearful earthquake on the northern
                  Mediterrannean coast) – 3 days ago[2278]

---

      27 – A quiet Sunday – cold, sunny, some wind blowing

---

      28 – Cold – sharp cold – last night cold

      March 1 – W D still at Sewell practising (6) (1)[2279]

      The last closing days of Congress – great hubbub
      & confusion – not the least probability of my pension
      bill passing[2280] – hazy – not quite so cold

---

      2 – Paid "Press" carrier $1.36 [2281]

2276. Edwin H. Miller has commented on the candor of this remark: see *The Correspond-ence of Walt Whitman*, IV, 70n. For "happy hour" (Whitman refers to p. 92 of *Specimen Days*), see *Prose Works 1892* (New York, 1964), I, 133–134.

2277. See footnotes 2255 and 2273. Could Whitman's comments on the *Daybook* itself suggest that it was important to him, or that it might be used by future biographers or editors?

2278. The earthquake, which Whitman calls "fearful," killed about 400 people on the Italian Riviera; however, it is not listed among the world's major quakes.

2279. "W D" could be William Duckett (see footnotes 2007, 2102, 2119, 2133, 2139, 2172, and 2201), but he was with Whitman on 2 March 1887 (see Whitman's letter of that date, *The Correspondence of Walt Whitman*, IV, 72); so "still at Sewell practising" is not clear. "W D" could not be William Douglas O'Connor, as he was in California. Dr W. B. Drinkard is an outside possibility for "W D," but he was Whitman's physician in Washington in 1873, 14 years before this entry in the *Daybook*.

2280. See entry for 19 January 1887 and footnote 2252. Despite Whitman's seemingly strong statement ("positively declining to apply for such a pension, & that I did not deserve it"), the present words, "not the least probability of my pension bill passing," suggest that he might well have enjoyed the honor of such a pension and may even have accepted the money but did not wish to appear a pauper or one who was begging for support from Congress or anyone.

2281. For Whitman's subscription to the Philadelphia *Press*.

4 – rec'd 5 shillings from Newcastle-upon-Tyne[2282]
    acknowledged

5 Saturday afternoon – went over to Phila:
  to see "Clito" – Wilson Barrett and Miss Eastlake
  – young Kersley and Jones (Dauncey) came for me
  in a carriage at 1¼ and bro't me back at 5¼
  – enjoy'd the ride, the performance & everything
  Mary Davis went with me – a good 4 hours[2283]

6 Sunday – a cloudy, sulky day – drizzling – ground
        just covered by snow

7 Paid Mr Bennett $18 for the mare Nettie for Feb[2284]

8 sent MS. preface to English Ed'n Spec. Days
                              [in red ink:]
    to Ernest Rhys, (two pages print)   rec'd [2285]
    – H W Beecher died to-day[2286]

[312]

[Two names and addresses in blue pencil:]
Moncure D. Conway
  230 West 59th St   New York[2287]

2282. This is probably from Thomas Locke, who was sent *Leaves of Grass* and *Specimen Days* on 24 January 1887: see entry for that date, above.

2283. See footnote 2260 and the names and addresses, above, of Kersley and Dauncey, who wrote in Whitman's *Daybook* when they came to pick up Whitman.

2284. As the *Daybook* also served as sort of an account book, Whitman added up these payments to Bennett for the upkeep of his horse on p. [286] (see above).

2285. This edition, called *Specimen Days in America*, was in The Camelot Classics, edited by Ernest Rhys, "Newly revised by the Author, with fresh Preface and additional Note," published in London by Walter Scott, 1887. The "Preface to the Reader in the British Isles" closes: "In [this] volume, as below any page of mine, anywhere, ever remains, for seen or unseen basis-phrase, Good-Will Between The Common People of All Nations."

2286. Henry Ward Beecher (see footnote 1412) was the subject of one of Whitman's "Paragraph Sketches of Brooklynites" in the Brooklyn *Daily Advertizer* (25 May 1850), reprinted in Emory Holloway, *The Uncollected Poetry and Prose of Walt Whitman* (Garden City, N. Y., 1921), I, 234–235 ("his written compositions are models of nervous beauty and classical proportion — being equal to many of our standard English authors"); and Whitman was less flattering in "Beecherolatry," *The* Brooklyn *Daily Times,* 4 May 1859, reprinted in Emory Holloway and Vernolian Schwarz, *I Sit and Look Out* (New York, 1932), pp. 84–85. See also Horace Traubel, *With Walt Whitman in Camden,* I, 137–138 and II, 471–472; and Gay Wilson Allen, *The Solitary Singer,* pp. 214–215. Whitman knew and respected Beecher, who is said to have admired the *Leaves* ("a friend of the Leaves from the first — even applied himself to it," Whitman said to Traubel), but the poet later commented that Beecher "stole most terrifically from it . . . what infernal plagiarists the big fellows are — big lawyers, big preachers, big writers" (Traubel, II, 471–472).

2287. For Moncure D. Conway, see footnote 36. He visited Whitman on 20 March 1887 (see entry, below); Whitman's letter to him, saying that he would be home, is in *The Correspondence of Walt Whitman,* IV, 76.

Walter Scott & Co: Publishers
24 Warwick Lane   London E C [2288]

Charles Rowley   [not in WW's hand]
     New Cross
Manchester England[2289]

Return to   C. W. Eldridge [on slip not in
P. O. Box 1705   WW's hand]
                LOS ANGELES, Cal., [printed]

M. H Traubel   [not in
          WW's hand] If not delivered within 10 days.[1290]
   509 Arch Str
                                  U S Revenue
      Camden[2291]
                                    agent

(Horace also) [written by WW]

                        San Francisco Cal:

[Four clippings, "A Vigorous Old Man", "Relic of the Chesapeake and Shannon", obituary of Mrs Anne Penelope Hoare, and obituary of "The Great Napoleon's Sledge Driver"; the first one with WW's notation that it is from the Boston *Transcript*.]

[313]

March 1887

8 – rec'd   by letter signed Saml Hales, Liverpool, Eng.[2292]
   £2.12.6 – acknowledged – also to Newcastle-on-Tyne
                                     Chronicle

2288. See footnote 2285: Walter Scott was to publish the British edition of Whitman's *Specimen Days in America*, for which Whitman received ten guineas from Scott and sent "additional Notes" to Ernest Rhys on 14 and 15 March 1887 (see entries, below).

2289. Charles Rowley ("introduction from Wm M Rossetti") visited Whitman on 6 April 1887 (see entry, below), and the poet had him write his name and address in the *Daybook*; and Whitman wrote Herbert Gilchrist, "had a good visit from Chas Rowley of Manchester yesterday" (*The Correspondence of Walt Whitman*, IV, 80).

2290. This return address was undoubtedly taken from an envelope containing Eldridge's letter to Whitman some time before 5 April 1887: Whitman's reply is in *The Correspondence of Walt Whitman*, IV, 79 (Feinberg Collection; Eldridge MS lost).

2291. M[aurice] H[enry] Traubel was Horace Traubel's father. "Horace" on the next line obviously refers to the son, now becoming important in the Whitman household. Maurice Traubel, who emigrated from Germany, was an excellent lithographer, artist (he made a crayon sketch of Whitman), and reader of Goethe, Heine, Schiller, and other Germans. See Gay Wilson Allen, *The Solitary Singer*, p. 532. Maurice Traubel may have written in the *Daybook* at this time (March 1887); and Whitman does say that the older Traubel was at a dinner at Thomas B. Harned's in December 1887 and visited the poet in August 1888, but they met long before that, despite no mention in the *Daybook* — which was not a complete record of Whitman's comings, goings, correspondence, or visits.

2292. Samuel Hales's letter to Whitman, as well as Whitman's acknowledgment, are both now lost; Newcastle-on-Tyne *Chronicle* also lost (?) — see footnote 2282, above.

10 sent two sets, Cent: Ed'n to John Hay, 800

30

Sixteenth st. Lafayette Sq: Wash'n – paid[2293] [in red ink]
22 rec'd [last word in red ink]

---

paid horse-shoer's bill 1.50   Mr Williams
11th and 12th freezing cold – but sunny

---

12 Lou here[2294]

---

14 10 guineas ($£10.10$) from Walter Scott, (D.
Gordon) pub'r, London for "Spec. Days" pub'n[2295]

---

15 – Sent "Additional Note" for Spec. Days to

Ernest Rhys, London – rec'd [in red ink]
(also Rec't for 10 guineas)[2296]

---

20 – M D Conway here[2297] – a cold spell
20 to 25

---

21 – cash'd London   p o orders $14. 01 [2298] – a ride out

Harry Stafford at Hospital [2299]
25 My visit there – the sick ward – Dr Westcott

28'9 – Harry S – here – through the throat – April trouble[2300]

2293. John Hay (see footnote 65) had just published, with John G. Nicolay, the first two instalments of his life of Lincoln in the *Century*, November and December 1886; see also *The Correspondence of Walt Whitman*, IV, 75.

2294. Lou is of course the poet's brother George's wife Louisa, with whom Whitman boarded before he bought the Mickle Street house.

2295. See footnotes 2285 and 2288.

2296. See footnotes 2288; the "Additional Note, 1887, to English Edition 'Specimen Days'" appeared in *November Boughs* (1888), except for a concluding paragraph; it is also in *Prose Works 1892* (New York, 1964), II, 598–600, as is "Preface to the Reader in the British Isles."

2297. See footnote 2287.

2298. This was the money from Samuel Hales of Liverpool (see entry of 8 March 1887, above).

2299. Harry Stafford, Susan's son and Whitman's most intimate friend from 1876 to 1885 (Harry was married in 1884), was living at the Stafford farm in Glendale, where Whitman of course saw him; but he had not visited the poet in Camden for some time. See Edwin H. Miller on the Whitman-Harry Stafford relationship, *The Correspondence of Walt Whitman*, III, 3–9, and (about the current situation, brief though it is), *ibid.*, IV, 78 — Whitman's letters to the young man's mother, 29 and 31 March 1887. See also *ibid.*, IV, 80.

2300. Harry Stafford's throat trouble was a long-time affliction, often mentioned in the *Daybook*.

correspondence ab't the N Y lecture
    & getting ready for it[2301]

_____

April 5 "Death of A. L." at Unity Church – Camden

_____

April 6 – visit from Chas Rowley, (introduc-
    tion from Wm M Rossetti) of Manchester
    _____ England [2302]

5th rec'd the book "Anne Gilchrist" – wrote to Herbert[2303]

_____

    W D at Stockton (left Sewell)[2304]

_____

8   paid Mr Bennett $18 for Nettie's board March

_____

[In red ink:] 10th, 11, 12   warm
12   sent Spec. Days to C A Spofford   rooms 1 & 2
                                [In red ink:]
        Mills Building   New York City   paid   rec'd [2305]

                                                            [314]

[Clipping, long one, from *The New-York Times*, Friday, April 15, 1887, head-

2301. Whitman refers briefly to the 5 April 1887 Lincoln lecture before the Unitarians in Camden in letters to William Sloane Kennedy and Charles W. Eldridge (*The Correspondence of Walt Whitman*, IV, 75, 78, 79); but it was the New York lecture on the same subject — arranged by John H. Johnston — that was a tremendous success. Whitman devotes more space to it, and the reception afterwards, than almost anything else in the *Daybook* (see entry for 13 April 1887, below); also attached to this book are three clippings, about the address, from *The New-York Times, The Evening Sun* (New York), and *The Boston Transcript*. Andrew Carnegie, whom Whitman records as giving $350 toward expenses for the lecture, wrote to Johnston: "When the *Pall Mall Gazette* raised a subscription for Mr. Whitman, I felt triumphant democracy disgraced. Whitman is the great poet of America so far." (Carnegie was the author of a book, *Triumphant Democracy*, in 1886.) Gay Wilson Allen, in *A Solitary Singer*, p. 525, mentions that Mark Twain and James Russell Lowell also heard the Lincoln lecture, and so did José Marti, the Cuban journalist in exile, whose eulogistic account went far to spread Whitman's frame in Latin America.
    2302. See footnote 2289.
    2303. Letter to Herbert Gilchrist, 7 April 1887: *The Correspondence of Walt Whitman*, IV, 79–80. The book, edited by Herbert Gilchrist, *Anne Gilchrist: Her Life and Writings* (London, 1887) was reviewed in the Boston *Sunday Herald*, 17 April 1887; in his letter to Whitman, 31 March 1887 (Feinberg Collection), Gilchrist wrote of the book's success in England, and he spoke of his coming visit to America (he arrived on 3 June 1887, according to Whitman's entry of that date, below). "Wonderfully well done," Whitman said of the Gilchrist book.
    2304. As in the case of footnote 2279, "W D" can only be William Duckett, who is here making another of his several changes of jobs.
    2305. C. A. Spofford had written on 12 February 1887 (letter in the Library of Congress) about *Leaves of Grass*; if Whitman replied, as he most likely did, the letter is now lost.

lined "A Tribute from a Poet / Walt Whitman Tells of Lincoln's Death. / Two Notable Assemblages Pay Honor to the Day and the Words of the Gray-haired Orator"; and another clipping, and Whitman's notation on it: "Bost: Trans. May 18 '87".] [2306]

[315]
[Three words in red ink:]

1887– April – & May   New York
                                    lecture

April

13th   Went on to New York – R P Smith was
          my convoyer & host – went to Westminster
          Hotel, Irving Place. – Stedman, Johnston, Gilder
          & John Burroughs Evn'g – next afternoon, Ap. 14th
          my "Death of Lincoln" piece at Madison Sq: Theatre[2307]
          – good audience – next day, 15th – sat to C C
          Cox, photographer, 12th and Broadway – also to

2306.   The long piece in *The New-York Times* of Friday, 15 April 1887, which Whitman inserted here, begins, "Yesterday was the anniversary of the death of this country's greatest President. There was no public evidence of the fact, however. The majority of men in the pressure of personal affairs forgot it entirely. But a poet, an old man bent with years and tottering through the sunset of life to the twilight and the dark, came feebly forth from his retirement to lay his wreath upon the grave of his friend. The Poet was Walt Whitman and the President was Abraham Lincoln." After a paragraph on some of the notables in the audience, the news report has three paragraphs of summary, then six long quotations from the lecture, which vary slightly from the text in Roy P. Basler's facsimile edition of *Walt Whitman's Memorandum During the War* [&] *Death of Abraham Lincoln* (Bloomington: Indiana University Press, 1962). The account, which totals more than 26 column inches in the *Times*, ends with a section subheaded "The Poet Greets His Friends," on the reception in the Westminster Hotel. The smaller clipping in the *Daybook*, which Whitman notes is from the Boston *Transcript*, is on an entirely different subject; without a heading, it reads: "A new edition — the seventh in four years — of 'Voice, Song and Speech,' the joint work of Lennox Browne, aural surgeon of the Royal Society of Musicians, and Emil Behnke, lecturer on vocal physiology, has just been published by G. P. Putnam's Sons. It is a work absolutely necessary for the student of music and elocution, as it is explanatory of the first principles of both arts. The methods of sound production are carefully described, with the aid of plates, and the student is instructed in the minutiae of training the vocal organs, dressing and caring for the throat, dieting, etc. There is no other work on the subject comparable with it for thoroughness and reliability. [Clarke & Carruth.]"

2307.   See footnote 2301. For Whitman's reaction to his lecture, see his brief comments in letters to William Sloane Kennedy, John H. Johnston, Major James B. Bond, and especially Charles W. Eldridge in *The Correspondence of Walt Whitman*, IV, 83–87. Edmund C. Stedman (see footnote 948), whom Whitman mentions here in his *Daybook*, with John H. Johnston, Richard Watson Gilder, and John Burroughs, gave him a copy of his (Stedman's) *Poets of America* (Boston, 1885), which contains a long essay on Whitman, pp. 349–395, reprinted from *Scribner's*, XXI (November 1880), 47–64. Stedman inscribed Whitman's copy: "to Walt Whitman with the love and sincere admiration of Edmund C. Stedman. New York April 14th 1887. Dies memoriae et lachrymarum." (Incidentally, Whitman left the book at his hotel in New York and wrote the proprietor to send it to John H. Johnston's for him.) Whitman told Traubel that the book "interested him." "But it is not convincing . . . . it still lacks root — still misses a saving earthiness." (Horace Traubel, *With Walt Whitman in Camden*, I, 70.)

Miss Wheeler, portrait painter – good time – [2308]
felt pretty well – rather overwhelm'd with friends,
& pulling, & talk – R P Smith very kind, faith-
ful, & liberal – Wm Duckett with me – A
        Thursday Evn'g
grand ovation ∧ – reception, two or more hundred –
at Westminster Hotel Parlors, to me, Thursday
       returned to Camden April 16th
Evn'g, April 14 ∧ – (If I had staid longer, I sh'd
have been kill'd with kindness   & compliments) [2309]
rec'd $~~250~~ $600   Andrew Carnegie $350 [2310]

19 – sent L of G. (author's ed'n) to Mr Chandler
Christian Union, Lafayette Place, N. Y.
                [Two words in red ink:]
          ~~$3 due~~ rec'd   paid [2311]

[In pencil on a lined piece of paper pasted on page:]

    April 22 '87 – I write this [2312]
at 1307 Arch St. Phila:
at R P Smith's, where I slept
last night – Saw Miss Carey Thomas [2313]
of Bryn Mar Girls' College last night
– am most hospitably used here –
– W D. [2314] drove me over yesterday
afternoon – am sitting here in

2308. On the Cox photograph and Dora Wheeler's portrait, see Clara Barrus, *Whitman and Burroughs — Comrades* (Boston, 1931), pp. 264–265.

2309. He made almost exactly the same comment, "if I had stayed long, I sh'd have been killed with kindness & attention," in a letter to Kennedy on 19 April 1887: *The Correspondence of Walt Whitman*, IV, 85.

2310. In three letters, as well as here, Whitman recorded that he had got $250 for the lecture; then on 20 April 1887 he got $350 from Andrew Carnegie (through Richard Watson Gilder), which so impressed him that he mentioned it in six letters: *The Correspondence of Walt Whitman*, IV, 84–88.

2311. This man, Arthur D. Chandler, most likely a friend of John H. Johnston of New York, for Whitman wrote the diamond merchant that he had sent Chandler *Leaves of Grass: The Correspondence of Walt Whitman*, IV, 86.

2312. As Whitman often did when he left Camden for overnight, he wrote a notation on a slip — which he did here — and pasted it in the *Daybook* on his return.

2313. Although Whitman here mentions Martha Carey Thomas (1857–1935), professor of English at Bryn Mawr College, in his letter of 21 April 1887, he wrote that he was going to Robert Pearsall Smith's "to be sculp'd by St. Gaudens," which apparently was not so: *The Correspondence of Walt Whitman*, IV, 87.

2314. William H. Duckett (see footnote 2279) often referred to during this period in the *Daybook*, was back in Camden, went with Whitman to New York for the Lincoln lecture, and here drove the poet to Philadelphia.

Edwd Carpenter Commonwealth Café   [316]
   Scotland st: Sheffield, Eng. letters
                        recd May 3
[Clipping from *The Evening Sun,* New York, Friday, April 15, 1887, head-
lined: "An Old Poet's Reception. / How the Majestic Walt Whitman Received
His Friends. / The Scene at the Westminster Hotel Last Evening — Poets,
Artists, Men with Horse Sense, and Lovely Women in Line." With Whitman's
notation at the top:]

                        New York
                     April 15 '87 [2315]
[On calling card, not in WW's hand, in pencil:]
        James Hunter
           Vienna, Fairfax Co.,
   _____   Va.

Bothwellaugh
_____

   2315. The account in *The Evening Sun* (New York), 15 April 1887, with a notation
in Whitman's hand at the top, "New York April 15 '87," was inserted here. Occupying more
than 38 column inches in *The Evening Sun,* it reads:

                AN OLD POET'S RECEPTION.

        HOW THE MAJESTIC WALT WHITMAN RECEIVED HIS FRIENDS.

           The Scene at the Westminster Hotel Last
           Evening — Poets, Artists, Men with Horse
              Sense, and Lovely Women in Line.

   Last evening at 8 o'clock Walt Whitman, the poet, received his friends at his apartments
in the Westminster Hotel. Three cosy parlors had been set apart for the reception. A portrait
of Dickens had been put in a prominent place. "The dear old man," as his friends call him,
had lectured in the afternoon at the Madison Square Theatre on Lincoln, but he appeared
little fatigued. Indeed he had reason to feel in good spirits, for the lecture was as successful in
a financial as in a literary sense. J. H. Johnston, a wide awake merchant, with Dundreary
whiskers and a face aglow with good nature had agreed to hold himself responsible for the
expense of the lecture, which amounted to $450, but the proceeds paid all that, and a profit
of $190 beside. Mr. Johnston feels as proud of the venture as he does of the fact that he was
one of the first advertisers in the first number of THE EVENING SUN.
   The first caller to greet the poet was an EVENING SUN reporter. The old man sat en-
throned in a great armchair, cushioned with dark red plush. He wore trousers and waistcoat
of dark gray stuff, gray woollen stockings, such as our grandmothers used to knit for us, low-
cut, comfortable shoes, and a coat of some dark material.
   The striking feature of his toilet, however, was his shirt. Its wide collar, loose at the
throat, and its cuffs, which turned over the ends of his coat sleeves, were trimmed with narrow
lace of a pretty pattern. He held in his hand an old cane like a shepherd's crook, from which
the polish had been worn. His long white hair and full white beard and mustache, which
entirely shaded his lips, and his heavy white eyebrows, characteristic of a man of magnetism,
set off his massive face and gave him a look of quiet grandeur which led Mr. Laurence Hutton
to remark, "He looks like a god."
   Indeed, he does look like a painting of Jove. Although his eyes are small, they have a
merry twinkle as he talks. The rich red blood of a manly man, who feels intensely and likes
to live and love, gives his face a ruddy glow. His voice is steady and gentle, but at times in
conversation he hesitates to select the most fitting word.
   On account of his lameness he remained sitting all the evening. A young man who bore

the double burden of receiving the cards of the callers and having the toothache had come over from Camden with Mr. Whitman as his attendant. He is William Duckett. In an hour Mr. Duckett had a very full hand of the cards of distinguished men and the crowd became so great that he gave up trying to announce each newcomer.

Early in the evening he arranged about the room some of the flowers that had been presented to the poet at the lecture. There was a great laurel wreath from Wilson Barrett, tied with rich satin ribbon of many colors. On one ribbon Mr. Barrett had written:

How like a winter hath thy absence been!

and on another:

Return, forgetful muse, and straight redeem in mighty numbers time so wisely spent.

Still another ribbon was inscribed:

So long! Walt Whitman.

WILSON BARRETT.

There were offerings from E. C. Stedman, the poet, and others, but the one which the old man most prized was a bunch of lilacs, which a little girl wandered out on the stage and gave to him at the lecture, with the words suggestive of his own poem:

I've brought you some lilacs that in our door yard bloomed.

A young man who wears his hair like Wm. Walter Phelps, and who fairly worships the poet, entered, shook him warmly by the hand, and called him "Walt," as did nearly every one.

"You are the man who has been sending me the paper," said the poet.

The young man, who is Henry Tyrrell of *Frank Leslie's,* admitted that he had, and shook hands with the poet again.

A rather tall young man with sandy hair and beard and a face alive with good nature entered. The poet greeted him with "Ah, Joe, glad to see you!"

It was courteous Joseph Gilder, editor of the *Critic.* Later he assisted in presenting the many who called to pay homage to the old man.

A little group gathered about the poet, who began talking about the time when he used to drive stage.

"It used to be the delight of my life to ride on a stage coach," said he. "I knew many of the old drivers. They were hale fellows, chewed tobacco or smoked if they chose and each had a nickname. There was Yellow and Dressmaker, who won his sobriquet by being greatly mashed on a pretty dressmaker. There was Gold Dollar Bill and a big fellow they called Elephant. His brother, a little man, came to work on the line, and they called him Little Elephant. There was my friend Jack Finley. He stayed on the line till the last, and I presume it seemed hard to him when the old stages were abolished."

THE EVENING SUN reporter, by way of a little literary gossip, asked the poet, "How do you divide your time? Do you write daily?"

"Well, I get up at 7; eat a hearty breakfast, and then write some, or at least go through the motions; then — "

"Ah, Judge! How are you?" said the poet, as Judge Harnett of Camden, a very young man for a judge, entered.

Then a gentleman of medium stature, with full beard tinged with gray, and a face of calm repose entered and was warmly greeted. He was plainly dressed and looked like a well-to-do farmer. He is John Burroughs, who paints nature in books as few men are able to do. He was flushed with success at having just come from making 250 pounds of maple sugar in a bush in Delaware county, and he has promised to write up his experience. The reporter ventured to ask him: "Do they still catch the sap in whitewood troughs?"

Alas, the age of progress has invaded the sugar bush! Mr. Burroughs reluctantly admitted that the old whitewood trough has been supplanted by a new-fangled tin pail, and the old elder spile through which the sap flowed from the tree has been driven out by a patent iron arrangement.

A young enthusiast entered and presented Walt two numbers of *La Vogue,* a French magazine, one number of which contained selections from the poet's "Leaves of Grass," and the other a French translation of his fervid production, "A Woman Waits for Me."

"Just like the French to pick out that poem," said Walt with a smile.

"Let me see," said the poet to THE EVENING SUN reporter, "Where was I? Oh, yes, I was answering your question as to how I spent my time. Well, it is very monotonous. I breakfast at 7, then — "

Then a gentleman with long black hair and full beard came in, and Walt greeted him with fraternal warmth. He is Joel Benton, the philosopher. Mrs. Morton of Boston, who proudly declared that she was by birth a Whitman, was presented next. A young man of medium stature and wearing a full tawny beard, a suit of the same complexion and thick eye-glasses, was Mr. Johnson, one of the editors of the *Century.* Mr. Metcalf of the *Forum,* who wears a heavy gray mustache and a studious look, was introduced, and he and Mr. Johnson stepped behind the poet's throne and engaged in conversation while newcomers were being presented.

Mr. Learned of the *Evening Post,* who loves nature about as well as John Burroughs, sat at the poet's left and talked awhile with him, when the conversation was interrupted by the coming of a lady of the intense, poetry-reading school, and her pale, willowy daughter. A kindly, plain woman who looked as if she could make good doughnuts, said she had just come from a many years' residence in the Sandwich Islands to greet the poet. A tall, gaunt man, who wore a gray flannel shirt, was Dr. Holbrook of the *Herald of Health.* He looked as consumptive as writers on health topics usually do.

The poet again tried to resume answering the reporter's question, but had got no farther than "after breakfast," when a tall man, looking aggressively and solemnly in earnest, came up and presented Walt a tract, which he first dodged, and then generously took and secreted somewhere about his capacious coat. Then came another very intense lady. She said: "I wrote you a love letter once, Mr. Whitman."

His merry eyes twinkled, as he asked: "Did I answer it?"

"No," she answered, whereat Walt's eyes twinkled the more, and the lady uttered a pretty little compliment about being so thankful that the good poet had lived. He murmured something about feeling thankful on his own account, and then reached out his hand to grasp that of a plump little gentleman with Burnsides and a dress suit. No one would have picked him out as the editor of a religious weekly, but he is Editor Mabie of the *Christian Union.*

A big man with black mustache and imperial, and wearing glasses divided in the centres, as if his keen eyes had shattered them, came next. He is Major Pond, who was business manager of Mr. Whitman's lecture. A gentleman with gray side whiskers, a bald head and the fine face of a typical English lord was Pearsall Smith of Philadelphia, who is a friend of Gladstone's and who enjoyed the acquaintance of Carlyle.

Walt made another effort to finish answering the reporter's question, but had scarcely taken up the thread of conversation when the floor shook beneath the tread of a massive man, whose smooth-shaven face denoted force of character.

"How air ye?" he asked with a Scotch inflection as he shook the poet's hand.

It was Robert Collyer. As the poet and preacher sat side by side, the big head of each crowned with long white hair, an enthusiastic beholder said aside: "See the two grand old men."

Mr. Collyer soon withdrew, but he paused to ask Mr. Johnston how much the receipts of the lecture were. When told that the profits were $190, he said: "Put me down for enough to make it $200."

A young lady of striking appearance, tall and resolute, entered. She wore a plain hat, of dark material, with no nonsense about its trimming, and a jacket something like a man's coat. She had a large leather hand bag attached to the side of her dress. She is Miss Jennie Gilder of the *Critic.* She was accompanied by a lady in plain black, with a beautiful complexion and a winsome face, who needed no introduction to the poet. This was Mrs. R. W. Gilder, wife of the editor of the *Century.*

An elderly gentleman, spare featured and gray whiskered, accompanied by his daughter, a decided brunette, who wore a dress of black satin, was presented as Moncure D. Conway. Miss Conway timidly asked the poet to give her his autograph, and he took out a very plain brass-mounted pencil and wrote his name on a card, using THE EVENING SUN reporter's note book as a rest.

"Please let your pencil wander over on a page of that book with another autograph," asked the reporter, and the poet smilingly granted the request.

These were the only attacks of autograph hunters during the evening. A not very literary looking young man with thin whiskers was presented as Sidney Luska. He has written some successful books, and started out in literature while he was writing in the Surrogate's office. His story bore the appropriate title "As It Was Written."

A very attractive, slender lady in black was the next comer. Her bright eyes danced as she greeted the host. She is Mrs. Gen. Custer. Mrs. Ward, a lovely lady of social prominence, was the next comer. E. S. Nadal, about the handsomest man in the party, who was formerly Secretary of Legation at London, had just been introduced, when a slender, beardless young man in evening dress, whose shirt front was plentifully pleated, was introduced as Wolcott

Balestier. He is the editor of *Tid Bits,* and an author of more than ordinary success.

The saddest, thinnest man of the assemblage, who wore side whiskers and looked anything but a poet, is J. H. Bonner, late of North Carolina, whose poems have elicited some kind words from E. C. Stedman. He has just settled in New York and is trying to find a place where he can breathe.

No one needed to be told that the next comer was an artist. His pointed beard and picturesque appearance betrayed that fact. He is Wyatt Eaton. Miss Collins, a plump young lady, who wore glasses and a black flat-brimmed hat, accompanied him. She paints. A solidly-built man, with a broad face and the appearance of a well-to-do merchant, was introduced as Frank Carpenter. He doesn't look it, but he, too, is an artist, and once painted a portrait of Lincoln.

A tall, slender young man, with a full blonde beard and pompadour hair and the keenest of eyes is J. W. Alexander, whose portraits of prominent men adorn the magazines. He is still very young. He is going to make a portrait of Mr. Whitman, who will probably give a sitting to-day.

A little dark-featured man, very spare and unliterary in appearance, enters. His black hair and mustache are streaked with gray, and, he has hard work to keep a frown from his brow. He is Frank R. Stockton, who is just now in the zenith of his popularity as a story writer. The plain, practical looking lady who accompanies him is his wife.

Then comes E. C. Stedman, a small man with square-trimmed gray beard and close-fitting cutaway coat. He looks a typical broker. His son, who wears a black mustache and speaks in a voice as soft as a woman's, says that at Mr. Whitman's lecture on Lincoln in the afternoon there were present Frank Carpenter, who painted Lincoln's portrait; Lowell, who wrote the national ode, and John Hay, who wrote the life of Lincoln.

The next comer was an African, his slender figure clad in evening dress, a low cut collar encircling his neck, and his hair parted near the middle and combed back high above his ears. He is the Chevalier de Salas, and the red button of his order gleams in his lapel. He carried a brindle fiddle under his arm. It looked like an ordinary affair, but it was a Ruggeri, worth a small fortune. He spoke no English, and told Walt so in French and German, which the poet doesn't understand. He went over to the piano, which Prof. Toledo stroked a few times, while the Chevalier tucked his fiddle under his chin. Then the way the Chevalier made that fiddle talk was a caution. It raved like a cyclone and then relapsed into the soft murmur of a zephyr through the leaves. It wailed with anguish till the tears gathered in sympathetic Mrs. Custer's eyes, and again it sang with joy like the birds, and everybody felt glad. Everyone felt sorry, too, when the African finished his tune. It was for making a fiddle behave as sweetly as he does that he was made a Chevalier. He was born in Havana, where his father used to play the fiddle for home amusement. The lad began playing when he was but little taller than his father's fiddle. He went to Berlin and to Paris, and was trained to a degree of perfection that would astonish his old father. Walt was mightily pleased with the music, and the Chevalier played some more.

Meantime, W. H. Bishop, a young man, with a firm, good natured face and a genial look, entered with his wife, a beautiful lady in dark evening dress. Mr. Bishop doesn't look a day older than 25, but he has written several successful stories, one of which was "The House of a Merchant Prince."

A young man, smooth shaven and with close cut red hair, doesn't look old enough to be an editor, but he is, and a good one, too. He is Henry Walsh, editor of the *Catholic World.*

Miss Breese, a wealthy society lady, who is a stockholder in an opera house, is another comer.

Prof. Hjalmar Hjorth Boyesen of Norway greets the poet, and a tall young man, with sandy mustache, who has left a sick bed to meet the poet, is introduced as Mr. White. He is an architect and the son of Richard Grant White.

Then Mr. Lawrence Hutton, who looks like a very prosperous young banker, and who writes mighty entertaining literary notes for *Harper's Magazine,* comes forward with his wife to bid Mr. Whitman good night. Miss Gilder and her sister-in-law bid the poet adieu until morning, when he is to meet them with some friends at a breakfast party.

R. R. Bowker, editor of the *Publishers' Weekly,* arrives, and Walt talks with him about the curious effect that Lincoln's death had on the army. Previous to the event the soldiers had had their cries, that went from division to division in great choruses, but a hush fell on the army when the news came of the great man's assassination, and the cries were heard no more.

John Fiske, a sturdy, deep-chested man, is one of the latest comers. He is a philosophical writer, and Darwin thought no one could expound Darwinism better than Fiske.

A young man, who has brought his opinions along with him, asks Walt if he doesn't dislike the Howells-James school of literature, but the poet declares that the very fact that a

[317]

1887 – April – May

April 22 [2316]

∧ [In pencil, except last line, on lined piece of paper pasted on page, nine
lines:]
the back room, feeling a little
heavy and inert physically, but
in good spirits.   Have had a capital breakfast – nice coffee.
– found a Vol. of Walter Scott's poems[2317]
& have been reading – especially the
Notes – a good part of the forenoon
– bright, mild   sunny forenoon

Camden

April 22 – drove home   ∧   5 p m

---

26 – sent L of G. to Edgar R Tratts, 21 Philsborough
Road Dublin   paid rec'd [2318]

---

28 – To W$^{\underline{m}}$ Thompson's, Gloucester N J. to-day
to a noble dinner of baked shad and
champagne galore.   T. B Harned, Col. Scovel
Judge Hugg, and W$^{\underline{m}}$ Duckett – good time – [2319]
– drove down & back with Nettie –

---

school or religion exists is proof that the people are ready for it. The young man talks with warmth about democracy, and Walt says that Carlyle was after all expounding the essence of true democracy when he was preaching what many interpreted as the antithesis of it.

Prof Ritter, who makes music and musicians at Vassar College, and is a well known composer, bids the poet adieu and one after another of the many guests, not half of whom have been named above, drop away. Never has the spectacle of so many eminent persons paying homage to a poor, plain old man been witnessed in New York. Walt has taken all their compliments with the pleasant "O-h!" that he utters when pleased. When the excitement has somewhat subsided he turns to the reporter and says. "Oh, yes; I was answering your question. Will I get up at 7 and — "

Then a new detachment of guests call to bid the poet adieu, and having got no farther than 9 o'clock in his account as to his method of spending his days, he gives up trying to answer the question.

2316.   The entry that begins here on the right-hand page is a continuation of the comments on the pasted-in slip.

2317.   The issue of *Harper's Weekly* for 23 April 1887, which Whitman asked John H. Johnston to see (*The Correspondence of Walt Whitman*, IV, 86), has a column that refers to Whitman's preference for Scott's poetry, "The only poetry that had nourished him."

2318.   For a man who had just received, the week before, $600 for a lecture, it seems strange that he should write, in a letter to Harry Stafford (*The Correspondence of Walt Whitman*, IV, 88), "Sold one of my books to-day, which helps along." The book he sold must have been *Leaves of Grass* to Edgar R. Tratts.

2319.   See footnote 2130; Whitman wrote Kennedy about this dinner and how much he enjoyed it: *The Correspondence of Walt Whitman*, IV, 89. Duckett was still driving Whitman's mare Nettie.

paid Mrs. Goodenough $16 for Ed's board [2320]

May 2 – Sent "November Boughs" to James Knowles
    Editor <u>Nineteenth</u> Century 1 Paternoster Row
    London, Eng: £22 – (returned) [2231]

3 paid Mr Williams' horse – shoeing bill $1.40

4 visit from Talcott Williams & Mr [2332]

6 paid Mr Bennett $18 for nag Nettie for April

10 Evng Mrs Hooper to supper

11 paid 1.38 for <u>Press</u>

                              [In red ink:]
" sent L of G to Rev: Robt Colyer N Y. /paid/ rec'd [2333]

" warm, growing weather – almost hot –

2320. Ed was obviously Whitman's incapacitated brother Edward.
2321. This "November Boughs" is not to be confused with the book of the same name, containing prose and some poems and published by David McKay, Philadelphia, in 1888 and Paisley, Scotland, in 1889. "November Boughs" here consists of the poems, "You Lingering Sparse Leaves of Me," "Going Somewhere," "After the Supper and Talk," and "Not Meagre, Latent Boughs Alone," all later incorporated in "Sands at Seventy," in *November Boughs* (1888) and then in the 1889 *Leaves of Grass*. See the texts of the four poems in *Leaves of Grass*, Comprehensive Reader's Edition, edited by Harold W. Blodgett and Sculley Bradley (New York, 1965), pp. 532, 525, 536, and 532–533. The poems, rejected by *Nineteenth Century* (see Knowles's letter, now in the Feinberg Collection, in Horace Traubel, *With Walt Whitman in Camden*, I, 28), were sent to William S. Walsh, *Lippincott's Magazine*, on 31 May 1887 (letter lost, but see entry of that date, below); they were accepted, Whitman was paid $50, and they were published in November 1887 (XL, 722–723). See also *Daybrook* entries for 1 and 2 September 1887, below.
2322–2331. Footnotes cancelled.
2332. Talcott Williams (see footnotes 277 and 799), a staffer on the Philadelphia *Press*, and his wife were old friends of Whitman's; he visited them, for example, in Philadelphia on 10 April 1887; and there are seven letters from the poet to Williams in *The Correspondence of Walt Whitman*, IV: 27–28, 32, 66, 96–97, 115, 135, and 155.
2333. This is the man of whom Horace Traubel writes in *With Walt Whitman in Camden*, I, 120: "W[hitman] recalled a Robert Collyer incident. W. had said to him of preaching what he has so often said to us — that the day of the preacher is past. 'Collyer turned the statement back upon the poets: "Why write poetry any more? All the songs were long ago sung." It quite embarrassed me on the instant — was an unexpected shot: I had no answer ready for it: indeed, I don't know that there is an answer. Collyer's not deep but he's damned cute — for the preacher class very damned cute: for, as you know, I don't as a rule expect anything of preachers. Occasionally one of them surprises me with a bit of well-borrowed wisdom. Collyer is a kind of reduced Beecher — a Beecher with much of the grace lopped off.'"

"   building, hammering, digging, next door
                         Mickle Street

[318]

[Top of letterhead pasted in: Chas. E. Merrill *President* / Joseph B. Gilder *Treasurer* / Edwin C. Merrill *Secretary* / The Critic Company / 743 Broadway New York May 12 1887 /.] [2334]

[319]

May   1887 – May – <u>June</u>
13 – Visit from Canon and Mrs. Wilberforce of Eng:[2335]

_____   _____

18   19, 20. – Sidney Morse here, sculping figure[2336]
                                              to
         sitting in chair   warm spell   23

_____

                         I
"   John Newton Johnson here   –   sent cloth to WWJ. [?] [2337]

_____   _____

2334. Although *The Critic* printed but three articles by Whitman in 1887 — "A Word About Tennyson," 1 January (X, 1–2); "Five Thousand Poems," 16 April (X, 187); and "Walt Whitman on Lincoln," 23 April (X, 206) — and none in 1888; the Gilders's magazine did print a poem, "Yonnondio" on 26 November; Jeannette L. Gilder got proofs for him of the Cox photographs (see *The Correspondence of Walt Whitman*, IV, 88); *The Critic* of 26 March 1887 printed a brief unsigned paragraph Whitman wrote of Tennyson (see *The Correspondence of Walt Whitman*, IV, 76); and the magazine on 28 May published Elizabeth Porter Gould's "Walt Whitman Among the Soldiers" (see *ibid.,* IV, 96); later Whitman corrected her excerpts, according to the *Daybook,* 22 September 1887. If a letter from *The Critic* of 12 May 1887 was to Whitman, it is now lost.

2335. Canon Wilberforce may be Ernest Roland Wilberforce (1840–1897), who retained his canonry when he became Bishop of Durham in 1882.

2336. Sidney Morse sent Whitman on 16 February 1879 an earlier head he had sculped in 1876 (see entry for that date, above, and see footnote 421). A magazine editor, he was a self-taught sculptor, and some time after the earlier sculpture of Whitman — which the poet called "wretchedly bad" — Morse began making a new bust. See his "My Summer with Walt Whitman" in *In Re Walt Whitman* (Philadelphia, 1893), pp. 367–391, which deals with this 18–23 May 1887 and on into June and November. Gay Wilson Allen describes the summer also (*The Solitary Singer,* pp. 525–526), first the messiness of Morse's clay, then Herbert Gilchrist's painting of Whitman in June and July (see the numerous entries in the *Daybook,* below); in the fall J. W. Alexander came to paint Whitman, and finally Thomas Eakins in December to do the best known portrait of them all (entry for 22 December 1887, below). Whitman's opinion of these paintings is in Horace Traubel's *With Walt Whitman in Camden,* I, 131–132: "Of all portraits of me made by artists I like Eakins' best: it is not perfect but it comes nearest being me. I find I often like the photographs better than the oils — they are perhaps mechanical, but they are honest." For a full account of all of this, see Gay Wilson Allen, "The Iconography of Walt Whitman," in *The Artistic Legacy of Walt Whitman: A Tribute to Gay Wilson Allen,* edited by Edwin Haviland Miller (New York, 1970), pp. 127–152.

2337. John Newton Johnson (see footnotes 9a and 1600) first wrote to Whitman in 1874; he visited Camden in May 1887, and the poet wrote of him to Susan Stafford: "He is the queerest, wildest 'cutest mortal you ever saw — has a boy 12 y'rs old named Walt Whit-

I go out driving an hour or more almost
every evening at and after sunset – sometimes
alone – sometimes one of the neighboring boy with
me – sometimes Mrs. D –[2338]

---

the little boy Woodford Hopple Thomas comes to see me[2339]

(not accepted)
22 – sent "Poet's 68th year" to C.   10 – &
10 C's and 25 slips[2340]
sent to Phil Press 24th   50   [?]

sent back   papers

23   anniversary of dear mother's death – 1873[2341]

"   rec'd £25 from Edward Carpenter[2342]

---

26 "summer cottage" project from Kennedy
and Baxter – Boston – Mrs. Fairchild –[2343]

man —'" (*The Correspondence of Walt Whitman*, IV, 94–95). But by 9 July, Whitman was writing, "J N J is certainly crazy — a cross between Zdenko (in *Consuelo*) & something more intellectual & infernal" (*ibid.*, IV, 107). For more on Newton, see *ibid.*, III, 324n–325n; Camden *Courier*, 19 May 1887; William Sloane Kennedy, *Reminiscences of Walt Whitman* (Paisley, Scotland, 1896), pp. 18–21; *In Re Walt Whitman* (Philadelphia, 1893), pp. 376–378. The cloth Whitman sent to W W J most likely was for Johnson's son.

2338. This refers to Mrs Mary O. Davis, Whitman's housekeeper.

2339. There are numerous references to Whitman and children, and they too responded to him and liked to visit him.

2340. Apparently this piece, "A Poet's 68th Year," sent back from *The Critic* and the Philadelphia *Press* (both letters by Whitman, sending the MS, have been lost), was never published; the letter of Talcott Williams, in *The Correspondence of Walt Whitman*, IV, 96–97, asks him to return the piece to him, so Whitman may have sent it to one of the Camden newspapers.

2341. Although nowhere else in the *Daybook* does Whitman mention his mother's death, the fact that he can recall the day 14 years later is another reminder of the strong bond between them.

2342. Whitman had written his youthful admirer in England on 3 May 1887 — but Whitman does not record it in the *Daybook*: see *The Correspondence of Walt Whitman*, IV, 89–90. Carpenter's letter of 20 April 1887 is in the Feinberg Collection.

2343. Whitman's Boston friends, Sylvester Baxter, William Sloane Kennedy, and Mrs Charles Fairchild (the wife of Colonel Fairchild, president of a paper company), decided to raise money for what Kennedy called "The Timber Creek Cottage Project" (see his *Reminiscences of Walt Whitman* [Paisley, Scotland, 1896], pp. 10–11); Whitman wrote Baxter that he would "most gratefully accept & most intensely enjoy a little spot of my own to live in 6 or 8 months of the 12 in country air, so pined for by me. . . . I want a cheap ¼ or ½ acre & 4-or-5-room house, spot & design selected by myself" (*The Correspondence of Walt Whitman*, IV, 93). There are numerous letters from Whitman to Baxter and Kennedy about this Boston Cottage Fund, the final one of 7 October 1887 (*ibid.*, IV, 125) about the $800 that was collected; and Horace Traubel, *With Walt Whitman in Camden*, II, 298–300, gives Baxter's list on contributors, which includes William Dean Howells, Samuel Clemens, Charles Eliot Norton, Edwin Booth, John Boyle O'Reilly (the New York *Times* of 11 June 1887

28 – letter from Dr John Johnston & J W Wallace
    of Bolton, England – £10 ($48.70) – ans'd [2344]

————————————————————————————

                              accepted – paid [2345]
31 – sent "Nov: Boughs" to Mr Walsh – Lippincotts ∧
———————————————————————— $50 – and 20 copies

June 1 – Wednesday – To day I begin my 69th
    Year – almost altogether disabled in walking
    power & bodily movement – writing & compo-
    sition power fair – hand-writing power pretty good –
    – appetite fair – sleep fair to middling not
    markedly bad, & not really good – weight 200 over
    – am still at 328 Mickle street, Camden, as for
    the last three (3) years, Mrs. Davis housekeeping for me,
    as for last two (2) years – I sit in the big arm
    chair nearly all the time – read & (partially) write
    much or rather most of the time – Sidney Morse
    here sculping the full length sitting figure in rocking
    chair from life – Seems to me I like it well – O'Connor
    in So. California, sick – frequent visitors & some dear friends
                    call to see me – [2346]

said he was treasurer of the fund), and Frank Sanborn, among 46 in all. Mark Twain was reported in the Boston *Herald* (24 May 1887) as saying: "What we want to do is to make the splendid old soul comfortable" (see Bliss Perry, *Walt Whitman* [Boston, 1906], p. 253, and Clara Barrus, *Whitman and Burroughs — Comrades* [Boston, 1931], p. 268). Whitman called it an honor list to be proud of and "a chapter in my personal history that must not be lost sight of" (Traubel, *op. cit.,* II, 300); and he got the money but apparently the cottage was never built. (See footnote 2361, below.)

2344. Dr John Johnston and James W. Wallace, ardent English admirers of the poet, here first wrote to Whitman (a typescript of their letter is in the Bolton, England, Public Libraries), sending £10, along with congratulations and love on his birthday; for Dr Johnston, Whitman's books were "his constant companions, his spiritual nourishment, his continual study and delight" (see *The Correspondence of Walt Whitman,* IV, 95n); Whitman replied on 29 May 1887 (*ibid.,* IV, 95). As Edwin H. Miller says in his introduction to Vol. V of the *Correspondence,* p. 3, Whitman became a father figure to Dr Johnston and a mother to Wallace; they became his most partisan advocates in England, visited him in Camden, and wrote dozens of letters to him — 7 joint letters, 106 from Wallace, 94 from Dr Johnston — Whitman's letters to Johnston total 73 and to Wallace 29. They formed, with several friends in England, the humorously called "Bolton College" to read and discuss Whitman's writings, and as a result of their trip to America wrote one of the most interesting early books on the poet's life, *Visits to Walt Whitman in 1890–1891 by Two Lancashire Friends* (London, 1917, revised 1918). See also Gay Wilson Allen, *The Solitary Singer,* p. 537.

2345. See footnote 2321.

2346. Rather a rare outburst of prose for the *Daybook;* in 1885 and 1886 he said nothing about himself on his birthday or the day after, but here in 1887 he sums up his condition. For a photograph of the Morse plaster model of Whitman in a rocking chair, referred to above, see the frontispiece to Traubel's *With Walt Whitman in Camden,* Vol. III; and *Camden's Compliment* (1889). See also *Walt Whitman Review,* XV (September 1969), 197–198.

[320]

Benj R Tucker box 3366
                    Boston p o .[2347]
Thomas Spear – Camden[2348]
Wᵐ M Rossetti   5 Endsleigh Gardens London   n w [2349]
[Clipping of The Thistle, a small sailboat]

[321]

June   1887 –   June
1 – Young Upton Jeffries (reporter Courier) call'd

                                                    both[2350]
    Piece in "Courier" June 1 – Piece in "Critic" May 28 – good
            U. Jeffries   E P Gould

3   Herbert Gilchrist arrived afternoon[2351]
            6th at R P Smith's   Phila
    went down to Glendale 5th[2352]

5ᵗʰ6ᵗʰ&7ᵗʰ – plenty of rain – a bad heavy spell
                                    unhealthy [?]

8th Sidney Morse, Herbert G. & J. N. Johnson[2353]
                            here

        T B Harned comes to see me quite frequently

2347. Benjamin R. Tucker (see footnote 1562), editor of the magazine *Liberty,* was to publish a "memoriam" to William Douglas O'Connor, written by Horace Traubel, in the 7 September 1889 issue.

2348. Thomas Spear, unidentified, apparently signed his name in the *Daybook* two pages below.

2349. On 3 July 1887 (see entry, below), Rossetti's £2.2 was received by Whitman, who had not written him since 30 May 1886 and had not heard from Rossetti since 16 November. Of course other letters may be now lost.

2350. Elizabeth Porter Gould's piece was "Walt Whitman Among the Soldiers" (see footnote 2334, above). The piece in the Camden *Courier.*

2351. Herbert Gilchrist, now a fairly well-known painter and a member of the Royal Academy, was in Camden — in part, at least — to draw a portrait of Whitman; he was to remain until 20–21 September. At the same time Sidney Morse was making a sculpture of the poet (see footnote 2336, above).

2352. Whitman wrote Susan Stafford on 3 June 1887 about driving down to Kirkwood with Gilchrist (*The Correspondence of Walt Whitman,* IV, 98), and he must have invited them down — Gilchrist knew the Stafford family very well. (Mrs Stafford's letter is now lost.) Robert Pearsall Smith, Whitman's great Philadelphia friend, sailed for England on the steamship Eider on 10 June 1887.

2353. For Sidney Morse and Herbert Gilchrist, see footnotes 2336 and 2351; for John Newton Johnson, see footnote 2337.

– & I go there, (often to dinner or supper) –
– both he & Mrs. H. very hospitable[2354]

sent letter & photo. to Mrs. Walter Bowne
Woodside, Queens Co N Y. for Elizabeth
Burroughs[2355]

10 – the big head in plaster – Sidney Morse's work – good [2356]

12   went down to Glendale[2357]

13: sent L of G to Nelson Sizer 775 Broadway
N Y $2 – rec'd – paid [2358]

17 rec'd the books "Specimen Days in America"

from Walter Scott – 56 and 5 – 61 copies
altogether

$5.45 freight
bill & duties[2359]

18, 19, 20, 21.   hot, hot, hot, hot
H Gilchrist, Sidney Morse, J N Johnson, T B H.[2360]
the portrait – the sculpturing

20 letter from Sylvester Baxter, Boston, abt the

2354. For Thomas B. Harned, Camden lawyer, see footnote 1900, above.
2355. This letter to Mrs Walter Bowne is lost; neither she nor Elizabeth Burroughs identifiable.
2356. In his letter to Mary Smith Costelloe, 13 June 1887, Whitman said, "Sidney Morse has modelled a large (colossal I suppose) head of me — I think the best thing yet": *The Correspondence of Walt Whitman,* IV, 99. (See footnote 2336.)
2357. Whitman did not stay long with the Stafford family this time, for he was back in Camden on 13 June.
2358. It is obviously not possible to identify everyone who bought a copy of *Leaves of Grass,* nor necessary or of any importance — as interesting as it might be to speculate or generalize on the kind of purchaser or reader attracted to Whitman in these early days when his poetry did not have the reputation it has in 1970.
2359. See footnotes 2285, 2288, and 2296.
2360. It must have been one mad household at 328 Mickle Street, with Whitman posing for his portrait in the parlor for Herbert Gilchrist, Sidney Morse working on his clay model in the back yard and making frequent trips back and forth through the house to look at his subject, while all the time the wild philosopher from Alabama, John Newton Johnson, was acting "crazy" (Whitman's own phrase); and what was Whitman himself doing? Perhaps writing, which he says in his letters he was doing, and 1887 was one of his busiest and best of the late years. T B H refers to Thomas B. Harned (see entry for 8 June, above), Camden lawyer and Whitman's hospitable friend, who seems a little out of place in all this madness.

Cottage Scheme – he has $300 – (says will be $800)[2361]

---

21   sent L of G to Dr Channing California[2362]

"   Spec Days (Eng ed'n) to Dr Bucke[2363]

---

22   rec'd 373 from Sylvester Baxter, Boston[2364]
        Herbert G. painting the portrait – good [2365]
    sharp thunder & rain last night

[322]

Thos Spear
            316 P   [?]St   [not in WW's hand][2366]
        125 West Chester Park Boston[2367]
C S Hartman, ̶1̶1̶0̶ ̶P̶o̶p̶l̶a̶r̶ ̶S̶t̶   ̶P̶h̶i̶l̶a̶:
Miss Peddrick, 227 Vine st.   Camden

2361. For the Cottage Scheme, see footnote 2343. The $800 was to be used as Whitman saw fit, but he never made any accounting of it; and when Hamlin Garland wrote to Horace Traubel in July 1889 about what had become of the cottage money and Traubel asked the poet, "W. was equally quick to retort — 'That was all fixed — understood — fully settled — long and long ago — it is a closed book — it is a question not again to be re-opened.'" (*With Walt Whitman in Camden*, V, 355; see also *The Correspondence of Walt Whitman*, IV, 158n.) The letter from Baxter, 18 June 1887, is in the Library of Congress; Whitman's letter, same date, in *The Correspondence of Walt Whitman*, IV, 102, strongly suggests he wanted "a conveniently plann'd & built house, & garden, of my own (cheap & democratic) either in the woods, or in sight of the sea, where I can haul in & breathe a sane atmosphere, & be secure like, either for the summers, or all the time yet vouchsafed to me."

2362. Whitman wrote Charles W. Eldridge, also in California, that he was sending *Leaves of Grass* to Dr William F. Channing, with whom William Douglas O'Connor was staying: see *The Correspondence of Walt Whitman*, IV, 103–104.

2363. Whitman kept Dr Richard Maurice Bucke up to date on his writings, also sending him, through William Sloane Kennedy, a copy of Walter Lewin's review of *Specimen Days in America* (London: Walter Scott, 1887) in *The Academy*, 4 June 1887. See *The Correspondence of Walt Whitman*, IV, 103; and Horace Traubel, *With Walt Whitman in Camden*, I, 445.

2364. The $373 was the first part of the "cottage fund" to be sent to Whitman (see footnotes 2343 and 2361); for Baxter's letter, now in the Feinberg Collection, see Horace Traubel, *With Walt Whitman in Camden*, II, 305.

2365. Whitman referred in several letters to Herbert Gilchrist's sketch — which he was making to take to England, where he was to make an oil painting of Whitman; John Burroughs did not think so well of it: "Herbert tried to paint Walt, but it was a failure. It gave none of Walt's power" (Clara Barrus, *Whitman and Burroughs — Comrades* [Boston, 1931], p. 265). For Gilchrist's pen and ink sketch of Whitman, see *Walt Whitman Review*, XI (September 1965), 106.

2366. See footnote 2348.

2367. For C. Sadakichi Hartmann, see footnote 2211. In the *Daybook*, other than recording these two Hartmann addresses, Whitman did not here say anything about his Japanese-German "promoter"; but in his letter to Sylvester Baxter, 13 July 1887, he says Hartmann has been in Philadelphia, and on 21 July 1887 (*The Correspondence of Walt Whitman*, IV, 108, 110), Whitman asked, "What have you to say ab't the W W 'society' project? & ab't Ch: Hartman?" Baxter didn't think much of the project and Hartmann's methods of selecting the officers ("We all had to sit down on him," Baxter said — see Horace Traubel,

W^m D O'Connor, 1015 O st Wash'n N W
          Care Dr Kinnear, Wall's Cottage, Bar Harbor, Maine[2368]
Sidney H Morse   (paid $70 Aug: 27 '87 $10 Oct
                                          22 [2369]

Editor of Cosmopolitan 29 Park Row N Y [2370]

[323]

June   1887 – June and July

23^d sent "the Dying Veteran" to S S McClure $25
                              accepted   paid [2371]

25   Saturday – fine day – just right
        a good drive 1½ to 4½

July
2   W H D   goes to Haddonfield to work as
        night operator   R R Station[2372]

With Walt Whitman in Camden, II, 379, for Baxter's letter of 2 August 1887); for Whitman's opinion of Hartmann and the "Walt Whitman Club" at that time, see *ibid.,* V, 38–39, and though Whitman told Traubel, "It was at that time I wrote to Kennedy and Baxter, in whom I most confided there, to squelch it," in none of Whitman's extant letters to them does he even suggest squelching anything. As late as 7 December 1887, Whitman merely queried Kennedy (*ibid.,* IV, 136): "Have Hartmann & the 'Society' completely fizzled?" One might conclude that Whitman was more flattered and amused by Hartmann and the Whitman society than annoyed, no matter what he told Traubel a year or two later.

2368. William Douglas O'Connor had left Pasadena, California, and Dr William F. Channing informed Whitman on 29 July 1887 that he had accompanied O'Connor as far as Pittsburgh (letter in the Library of Congress; see *The Correspondence of Walt Whitman,* IV, 106n); and Whitman assumed he was on his way to Washington (*ibid.,* IV, 109), but Ellen M. O'Connor wrote on 2 August (Feinberg Collection) that he had secretly gone to Maine to try Dr Kinnear's method (*ibid.,* IV, 115). That's why Dr Kinnear's address is here. O'Connor was in Camden on 17 October (see entry, below).

2369. On the Morse bust, see footnotes 2336 and 2356. The $70 was for ten cast heads of Whitman (see entry for 27 August, below).

2370. Whitman sent *The Cosmopolitan* a six-line poem, "Shakspere-Bacon's Cipher," on 13 September 1887 (after its rejection by S. S. McClure on 3 September, and by *Harper's New Monthly Magazine* on 6 September); and *Cosmopolitan* published it in its October issue. See entry for 13 September, below. The poem was included in *Good-bye My Fancy* (1891) and in the final *Leaves of Grass;* see the Comprehensive Reader's Edition (New York, 1965), p. 544. A proof (for private distribution) is in Horace Traubel, *With Walt Whitman in Camden,* I, opp. 180.

2371. Whitman's poem, "The Dying Veteran," was published in *McClure's Magazine,* June 1887; *Pall Mall Gazette* (London), 9 July 1887; Springfield *Daily Republican,* 11 July 1887; in *November Boughs* (1888) as part of "Sands at Seventy," and in the 1888–9 *Leaves of Grass.* See the Comprehensive Reader's Edition (New York, 1965), pp. 529–530. The letters to the McClure Syndicate and S. S. McClure are in *The Correspondence of Walt Whitman,* IV, 102 and 104.

2372. Once more, a new job for William H. Duckett (see footnotes 2279 and 2314). Whitman wrote a letter for him, dated 6 May 1887, to help in finding employment: see *The Correspondence of Walt Whitman,* IV, 91–92.

8
June 29, 30, July 1, 2, 3, 4, 6, 7,   hot, hot, hot
9

2   paid for Press $1.40   I last paid 1.38 May 11 [2373]

4   drive to Merchantville Racing Park
    young Dr Wm Jennings of Haddonfield [2374]

5   Sent L of G (2^d copy sent) to Dr Channing[2375]

    paid gas bill – $1.20   rainy day

3^d rec'd 2. 2   add'l from W^m M Rossetti[2376]

    "Twilight" sent to Century – accep'td – paid 10 [2377]

6   muggy, warm, close – violent thunderstorm this
    morning before daylight.

7   sent Spec. Days   London Ed'n, to Cassius M Clay[2378]

    sent Spec D to Mrs. Morse, Richmond Indiana[2379]

8   Paid Mr Bennet $18 for Nettie for June[2380]

2373. Whitman seemed rather more careful about recording such very minor details as subscriptions to the Philadelphia *Press* than more important things he was doing, or that were happening.

2374. Dr William Jennings of Haddonfield is not otherwise identifiable; Whitman may have met him at the Merchantville Racing Park.

2375. The first copy of *Leaves of Grass* was sent to Dr William F. Channing, Pasadena, California, on 21 June 1887, as recorded above on that date: see Whitman's letter to him, 4 July 1887, in *The Correspondence of Walt Whitman*, IV, 106.

2376. See footnote 2349.

2377. This three-line poem, "Twilight," was published in *Century*, XXXV (December 1887), 264, and came into *Leaves of Grass* (1888–9) as part of "Sands at Seventy": see the Comprehensive Reader's Edition (New York, 1965), p. 532.

2378. Cassius M. Clay acknowledged receipt of this book, *Specimen Days in America* (London: Walter Scott, 1887) — see footnote 2285 — in a letter to Whitman on 9 July 1887, and included an address he delivered at Yale: letter now in the Feinberg Collection.

2379. Mrs Morse was the wife of the sculptor (?), now working on a sculpture of Whitman; at about this time Whitman sent several of his friends copies of the Walter Scott edition of *Specimen Days in America*.

2380. This $18 was for the board and upkeep of Whitman's mare.

9   oppressive hot spell commenced June 29, 30
    continued July 1, 2, 3, 4, (rained 5th) 6, 7, 8, 9 – 10th & 11th fine
    12 to 22 hot to 31 hot – Aug 1, 2, very hot[2381]

10 Sunday – drove down to Glendale   better
                                        weather[2382]

11 better weather – letter from W^{m} O'Connor[2383]

    he returns to Wash'n – Geo: Stafford ill ~~his~~   [?] [2384]
                                            ~~te~~   [?]

    letter from E Carpenter – 20 Bessie & Isa-
    ————————————————————   :bella Ford [2385]

12 W D O'C back in Wash'n – card from Mrs O'C [2386]

23 and 24 (Sunday) showery – thunderstorms day
                                    and night
    the Boston "cottage" scheme (Sylv: Baxter treasurer)
    so far 503 – eventually 788 paid me by S B [2387]

2381. In his letters Whitman also mentioned the hot spell: "O how the sun glares" and "two poor little babies have died from it [long spell of hot weather] in this block the last week" (*The Correspondence of Walt Whitman*, IV, 105).

2382. Whitman wrote Susan Stafford he would drive down to visit them: *The Correspondence of Walt Whitman*, IV, 195.

2383. This letter is now lost. This seems like an assumption by Whitman or a purposely misleading statement that W. D. O'Connor made, for he was not on his way to Washington, going secretly to Maine instead (see footnote 2368).

2384. Whitman wrote Susan Stafford on 15 July that he was feeling poorly and it was too hot for him to come to Glendale (*The Correspondence of Walt Whitman*, IV, 108–109); on 1 August he wrote her he would be down "one of these days" (*ibid.*, IV, 113); and on 4 August Whitman did drive down (see *Daybook* entry of that date, below). Her husband George, according to the *Daybook,* was suffering from "lung hemorhages" but was better on the 4th. Whitman was to drive to the Stafford farm on 14, 18 (with John Burroughs), and 28 August, on 4 September, and again on 11 September 1887 with Dr R. M. Bucke. George Stafford recovered from this illness and lived until February 1892.

2385. Letter from Edward Carpenter is not extant; in a letter to William Sloane Kennedy and Richard Maurice Bucke, 11 July 1887, Whitman mentions the £20 from Bessie and Isabella Ford, two wealthy English girls (see footnote 1689, above): *The Correspondence of Walt Whitman*, IV, 107.

2386. This card from Ellen M. (Mrs William Douglas) O'Connor is lost; either W. D. O'Connor, her husband, was actually back in Washington — as Whitman says here and below in his long entry for 24 July 1887 — or he was secretly in Maine (see footnote 2368); of course O'Connor could have come from California to Washington, D. C., and then gone to Bar Harbor.

2387. For the Boston "cottage" scheme, see footnotes 2343 and 2361; also Baxter's letter, 3 August 1887, from Whitman, *The Correspondence of Walt Whitman*, IV, 114.

[324]

[Blank]

[325]

July   1887 – July and August – Camden

24 (Sunday) – I write this at noon – a heavy shower –
                    to eleven

have had seven ∧ weeks of very hot weather – few
intermissions – heat &c. has affected me badly – yet I
have kept up & am sitting here feeling pretty comfortable
– Wᵐ O'C is very ill in Wash'n – (ret'd from So: California)
– Geo: Stafford ill (lung hemorhages) – W H D at Haddonfield
in R R office – Sidney Morse here – H Gilchrist here painting
portrait – Pearsall Smith, Alys, &c. in London – A quiet
day, but violently raining outside as I write[2388]

Aug. 2   visit from T Donaldson – also Aug. 10 [2389]

Aug 3 – letter from Sylvanus Baxter   285
                              788 altogether [2389a]

Wᵐ O'Connor goes to Bar Harbor, Maine[2390]

W H D left Haddonfield[2391] –⟩Talcott Williams here
          is at Ancora[2392]   ⟩

4   Drove down to Glendale – G S better[2393]

2388. This unusual (for this *Daybook*) summary of Whitman's health, the weather, and his friends is somewhat similar to his entry of 1 June 1887. Of those mentioned here, for William Douglas O'Connor, see footnote 2368 and 2386; for George Stafford, see footnote 2384; for William H. Duckett, see footnotes 2279, 2314, and 2372; Sidney Morse and Herbert Gilchrist and their activities are mentioned in footnotes 2360 and 2365 (there is no mention of the wild "philosopher" John Newton Johnson); and Robert Pearsall Smith, his daughter Alys, see footnotes 1622, 2152, and 2215, but there are so many letters to and about them in the *Correspondence,* one cannot contain them in a footnote or two.

2389. Thomas Donaldson (see footnote 1573), a Philadelphia lawyer, was an important man in Whitman's circle — see letters to him in *The Correspondence of Walt Whitman,* III, 356, 406, 407; IV, 23, 27, 41, 50, 53, 268–269, 348; V, 53–54, 278 — even though William Sloane Kennedy was uncertain about him as a friend or idolator of the poet (*ibid.,* IV, 41n), and he was not as much to Whitman in his later years as Dr Bucke, Horace Traubel, Harned, O'Connor, and one or two others.

2389a. See *With Walt Whitman in Camden,* II, 378–379, for $285 Baxter sent.

2390. See footnote 2386.

2391. William H. Duckett — again and again — changes, or loses, his job: see footnotes 2279, 2314, and 2372.

2392. For Talcott Williams, see footnote 2332.

2393. On George Stafford's illness and Whitman's visits, see footnote 2384.

5 – Hot day – went to bank   deposited   432

Paid Mrs. Goodenough $16 for Ed. for July[2394]

Lou here – Warren and Amy[2395]

6 (Saturday) – afternoon cooler –

7th, 8, 9, 10, 11, 12, 13   pleasant weather (on to 20

                                    — much less hot)

                                                (reporter
11 Sylvester Baxter here – Sanborn   Record)[2396]

the Swinburne piece Eng: Fortnightly Aug:[2397]

14   Drove down to Glendale afternoon[2398]

15   paid 24ᶜ P̲o̲st̲ and C̲o̲urier̲[2399] – cloudy & cooler

2394. The usual monthly bill for Whitman's brother Edward's upkeep.
2395. Lou was George Whitman's wife and the poet's sister-in-law; Amy and Warren Dowe were the children of her sister Emma of Norwich, Conn. For Amy H. Dowe's recollections of this visit and others, see her "A Child's Memories of the Whitmans," in Edwin Haviland Miller's "Amy H. Dowe and Walt Whitman," *Walt Whitman Review*, XIII (September 1967), 73–79.
2396. Sylvester Baxter came down from Boston, where he was on the staff of the Boston *Herald* (he had written on 2 August — Horace Traubel, *With Walt Whitman in Camden*, II, 378–379 — to say he would be in New York and run over to Philadelphia), and may well have brought (?) Sanborn of the Philadelphia *Record* to Camden to see Whitman.
2397. This article by Algernon Charles Swinburne, "Whitmania," *Fortnightly Review*, XLII (August 1887), 170–176, was an about-face in the English writer's attitude toward Whitman; in it he praised some laudable and valuable qualities but then attacked him as a thinker, as a prosodist, and said his Eve was "a drunken apple-woman" and his Venus "a Hottentot wench." As evident here, Whitman said little about it; "Aint he [Swinburne] the damnest *simulacrum!*" he told a friend (Clara Barrus, *Whitman and Burroughs — Comrades* [Boston, 1931], p. 266); but his friends were outraged by the intemperate repudiation. John Addington Symond's "A Note on Whitmania," *Fortnightly Review*, XLII (September 1887), 459–460, William Sloane Kennedy called a "milk and water affair" (Horace Traubel, *With Walt Whitman in Camden*, IV, 124); Kennedy himself comments on Swinburne's "venomous and studied insult" and quotes the *Pall Mall Gazette*, "Never in the whole history of apostasy was anything so treacherous as this brutal kick at a dying old man whom he once hailed as a strong-willed soul in his prime, and from whom he once begged for his inspiration" (*The Fight of the Book for the World*, West Yarmouth, Mass., 1926, pp. 23–24). See a brief summary of it all in Gay Wilson Allen, *The Solitary Singer*, pp. 526–527; see also Harold Blodgett, *Walt Whitman in England* (Ithaca, N. Y., 1934), pp. 112–121; and *The Correspondence of Walt Whitman*, IV, 119, where Whitman writes Kennedy on 7 September 1887: "I return S[ymond]'s letter — All I can say ab't it is I myself like to get views from every quarter — then I go on the tack that seems *to me* rightest," and "the article was not worth answering at all — I have not given it a thought" (*ibid.*, IV, 121).
2398. See footnote 2384.
2399. These were two Camden newspapers.

18, 19 – John Burroughs here – 18 drove to Glendale[2400]

25, '6, '7, 8, 9, 30. cooler – fine & sunny

27   paid S H M $70 to pay to caster for the 10 heads[2401]

28 – afternoon drive to Glendale – Tom with me[2402]

29   Leonard Morgan Brown goes back to Croton-
-on-Hudson – has been here ab't a week[2403]

30 weather pleasant, bright & sufficiently cool &
     rainy ever since the 6th

the Donnelly-Shakespere – Bacon question up[2404]

[326]

Sidney H Morse – 136 north 17th st.   Phila[2405]

665 W Lake st   Chicago

Coxs
     Photos – very good – profile, limited edition[2406]
          "   "   head with hat   No 3

2400. Whitman was making more trips than usual to the Stafford farm because of George Stafford's illness (see footnote 2384), and had even been there just four days before. He had not seen his friend Burroughs since 13 April 1877 when Whitman made his Lincoln address in New York City. He refers to this visit to Glendale in his letter to Ernest Rhys: *The Correspondence of Walt Whitman*, IV, 117.

2401. For more on Sidney H. Morse and the head he was sculpting of Whitman, see footnotes 2336 and 2356; it is mentioned numerous times in letters of this period and in the *Daybook*.

2402. On this trip to the Stafford farm (see footnote 2384), Whitman was accompanied by Thomas Donaldson (see footnote 2389).

2403. Leonard Morgan Brown was an English teacher and friend of Herbert Gilchrist who contributed £5 to funds Gilchrist sent Whitman in December 1886; in March 1887 Gilchrist praised Brown to Whitman as "uncommonly good . . . earnest . . . full of solid worth" (letter in the Feinberg Collection, quoted in *The Correspondence of Walt Whitman*, IV, 132n); and in May 1887 Brown came to America. After his week's visit to Camden, he returned to Croton-on-Hudson, New York; in November 1887 he sent Whitman a gift of $25, and a similar amount in February 1890 (his two letters are now lost, but Whitman's letters of thanks are in *The Correspondence of Walt Whitman*, IV, 132–133; V, 25). Another letter from Brown to Whitman, 9 May 1891, is in the Feinberg Collection: he regretted that he could not send his annual gift.

2404. On 30 August 1887, Whitman wrote Kennedy, Burroughs, and Dr Bucke (*The Correspondence of Walt Whitman*, IV, 118) if they had read "the Bacon-Shakspere résumé in the last Sunday's N. Y. World," referring to the first two pages of the 28 August *World*, where there was a full discussion of Ignatius Donnelly's *The Great Cryptogram* by Thomas Davidson. By Whitman's further remark in his letter, "I am tackling it — take less and less stock in it," he undoubtedly meant he was writing his poem, "Shakspere-Bacon's Cipher," at this time; it was published in *The Cosmopolitan* (see footnote 2370, above).

2405. See footnote 2401; the change of address must have been made after Morse ceased working on the bust of Whitman and went to Chicago.

2406. By "Coxs Photos" Whitman referred to those made on 15 April 1887, while he

Thos: B Harned, $\begin{matrix}566\\568\end{matrix}$ Federal St:[2407]

[327]

Sept   – 1887 – Camden – September

1 – sent note to J H Johnston to go to Cox's to see
    ab't the photos[2408] – sent proofs N B to Walsh[2409]

2 –   the three young Connelly boys here to see me[2410]

Morse bro't the heads – four bro't   cast
    by – one head went to Dr Bucke London,   rec'd
              one went to England [2411]

rec'd <u>Nov.</u> <u>Boughs</u> poems proof – from Walsh
                        from Lippincotts[2412]

3   the little boys – gamins – at the window
    Jacob –   and Geo: Edward   — [2413]

Johnston went to see Cox, photographer –
    J thinks "it is all right" [2414]

4   drive to Glendale alone – weigh 201½ lbs[2415]
                    good weather 4th, 5th 6th   (dry)

was in New York for his Lincoln lecture (see entry for 13 April, above): both the profile and the "head with hat" are in *The Correspondence of Walt Whitman,* IV, following p. 278. See letter: *ibid.,* IV, 101: also letters to Jeannette L. Gilder, IV, 88; and to John H. Johnston, IV, 118, in which Whitman was needlessly upset over Cox selling photographs of the poet with a forged signature. As seen in Whitman's entries below for 1 and 3 September ("it is all right") and in his letter to Johnston (*The Correspondence of Walt Whitman,* IV, 118–119), plus Edwin H. Miller's summary (*ibid.,* IV, 118n), Whitman made money on the project — 3 October, 2 November, and 2 December *Daybook* entries record $74 for him.

2407.   See entry above for 8 June 1887 and footnote 1900.

2408.   See footnote 2406.

2409.   See footnote 2321 for details about the poems, "November Boughs," and William S. Walsh, editor of *Lippincott's Magazine.*

2410.   The three young Connelly boys unidentified; they may be Camden neighbors.

2411.   For the sculptures of Whitman by Sidney Morse, see footnotes 2336, 2356, and 2360. For a reproduction of the bust, see *The Correspondence of Walt Whitman,* IV, following p. 278. In his letter to Robert Pearsall, 12 September 1887, Whitman says he has sent him in London a large plaster head by Morse, to be donated to the Royal Academy (*ibid.,* IV, 120) or — in a later letter (*ibid.,* IV, 121) — to the Kensington Museum; he refers to the head he gave Dr R. M. Bucke in a letter to Mary Smith Costelloe (*ibid.,* IV, 121: Bucke, Whitman said, "is quite enthusiastic ab't it").

2412.   For "November Boughs" (poems) and William S. Walsh, see footnote 2321.

2413.   Running through the *Daybook,* especially in the earlier years' entries, are the names of young boys which Whitman recorded here, and they rarely if ever appear again.

2414.   For the photographs by G. C. Cox, the New York photographer, see footnote 2406.

2415.   Whitman had been making almost weekly trips to see the Stafford family at

sent "Shakspere – Bacon Cipher" to McClure

refused [2416]

paid $2 to Mr Williams for horse shoeing

6   sent "Shakspere – Bacon's Cipher" to Alden $25

returned [2417]

8   sent L of G, $2 ed'n, to Amy Jessy Pratt

~~Marly~~, Marley, near Shottermill

[in blue pencil:]

Haslemere Eng   paid   15ˢ   rec'd [2418]

11   went to Glendale with Dr Bucke [2419]

12   paid 1.52   for Press [2420]

?48

13   Cox's photos came – I signed them &

sent them back to N Y – retained four [2421]   [One word

in blue pencil:]

printed   paid [2422]

sent "Shakspere — Bacon" to Cosmopolitan   20

Dr Bucke here (with Mr Pardee) [2423]   cloudy & rain

two days

this time, perhaps because George Stafford was still recovering from his illness (see footnote 2384); a week later he went there with Dr Bucke.

2416. For this poem, "Shakspere-Bacon's Cipher," see footnote 2370 and the entries below for 6 and 13 September and 12 October 1887. Whitman's letter to S. S. McClure: *The Correspondence of Walt Whitman*, IV, 119.

2417. See footnotes 2370 and 2416. Henry M. Alden edited *Harper's Monthly*.

2418. Even though David McKay was, in a way, Whitman's publisher, the poet himself continued to sell his own books, *Leaves of Grass* in this case to an English purchaser. Also, in this case, both the letter from Amy Jessy Pratt and Whitman's to her — he often wrote acknowledgments to those who ordered copies — are lost.

2419. See footnote 2415.

2420. For Whitman's two months' subscription to the Philadelphia *Press*.

2421. See footnote 2406, and letter to G. C. Cox, *The Correspondence of Walt Whitman*, IV, 123.

2422. See footnote 2370.

2423. In his letter to Mary Smith Costelloe, 14 September 1887, Whitman wrote, "Dr Bucke has been here for five or six days — leaves to-night — he is well — hearty as ever & 'much the same" (*The Correspondence of Walt Whitman*, IV, 121); Timothy Blair Pardee, Commissioner of Crown Lands, was Whitman's host when he was in Sarnia, Canada West (Ontario), 20 June 1880, and on this 1887 trip he apparently joined Dr Bucke in Camden. In 1888 Dr Bucke accompanied Pardee on a trip to Florida — they stopped over to see Whitman again — but this time Pardee was ill ("an invalid friend" is Whitman's description of him in a letter to William Sloane Kennedy, *ibid.*, IV, 146); Pardee died in July 1889.

14   Harry S. here – Herbert here – Dr B leaves to-night[2424]

16   sent L of G (1876 Ed'n) to Rob't Shiells, National
      Bank, Neenah, Wisconsin – Paid [2425]

More Photos from Cox, N Y [2426]

Phil. Constitutional Centennial [2427]

[328]

[Clipping of classified announcement of opening day of School for Feeble-minded, Home for Aged, Millville, N. J., 25 October 1887, and a one-paragraph news story of the same event.] [2428]

Money paid S H M [2429]	Rec'd from Wm Carey[2430]
$70 –	for photo sale
10 –	Oct. 3 $42
30 –	Nov. 2 16.50
10 –	Dec.2 for Nov. 15.50
10 –	
3	

[329]

Sept.   1887 – Camden – September
17   – drew 50 from bank – cash'd p o orders

2424.   Harry S. is Susan and George Stafford's son (see footnote 2299); Herbert is the British painter and son of Whitman's great friend Anne Gilchrist, who was putting final touches on his oil painting of Whitman (see footnotes 2351 and 2365), leaving for England 21 September 1887; and Dr B is Dr Richard Maurice Bucke (see footnote 2423).
2425.   In his letter to John H. Johnston of New York City, 29 September 1887 (*The Correspondence of Walt Whitman*, IV, 124), Whitman wrote, "I sent Shiell's the book 16th Sept," so Shiells must be a friend or acquaintance of the New York diamond merchant.
2426.   On the Cox portraits, see footnote 2406; Whitman wrote to Cox on 15 September 1887 and to William Carey, 15 and 28 September about the matter (*The Correspondence of Walt Whitman*, IV, 122, 123, and 124); see also Whitman's letter to John H. Johnston, 29 September (*ibid.*, IV, 124).
2427.   Whitman wrote William Sloane Kennedy on 14 September 1887: "Phil: is all alive with the Centennial U S Constitutional commemoration, & will be thro' the week — I have been pressingly invited, but cannot go — (A crowd & hubbub are no place for me" (*The Correspondence of Walt Whitman*, IV, 122); and on 3 August Whitman had been asked by the Centennial Commission to write and read a "patriotic poem commemorative of the triumph of popular institutions" (*ibid.*, IV, 122n, letter in the Feinberg Collection), but no such poem seems to have been written. None was published, and there is no such MS.
2428.   Whitman, in clipping this article, may have had his brother Edward in mind.
2429.   S H M was Sidney H. Morse the sculptor, and the $133 was paid him for heads he had made and Whitman had sent to various friends (see footnotes 2336, 2356, 2369, 2411, and the entries in the *Daybook* for 27 August and 2 September 1887).
2430.   This $74 from William Carey was for the sales of G. C. Cox photographs autographed by Whitman: see footnotes 2406 and 2426.

Signed Cox's Photos & sent them back – several
packages came[2431]

20–21 – Herbert Gilchrist returns to England
on the "Germanic" from N Y. came here June 1
been here nearly 6
months[2432]

22 – David McKay here – brings statement
pays me $76:91 for royalties[2433]

My letter in Pall Mall Gazette, April 30 '87 [2434]

MS of Elizabeth Porter Gould's excerpts – I consent[2435]

29 – paid tax bill 1887, ($25:37)[2436] – cloudy   rainy

sent Eng. ed'n Spec. Days to Kennedy[2437]

Sunday afternoon – drove to Glendale[2438]

Oct: 3 -- rec'd $42 from Wᵐ Carey for Cox's Photos[2439]

2431. There is no Whitman letter to Cox of this date; he may not have written as he did on 15 September (see footnote 2426).
2432. For Herbert Gilchrist, see footnote 2424 and two letters of 14 September 1887, *The Correspondence of Walt Whitman*, IV, 121–122.
2433. Whitman refers to the royalties (for the past eight months from his publisher) in a letter to John H. Johnston of 29 September 1887 (*The Correspondence of Walt Whitman*, IV, 124).
2434. In his summary of Walt Whitman's pieces in the 1887 *Pall Mall Gazette*, Edwin H. Miller (*The Correspondence of Walt Whitman*, IV, 63n) does not list this letter of 30 April 1887; it is in no Whitman bibliography, nor in *Prose Works 1892* (New York, 1964).
2435. For Elizabeth Porter Gould, see footnote 2334: these excerpts, made by her from Whitman's works, were not published until 1889, when David McKay issued *Gems from Walt Whitman* in 58 pages: see his letter to McKay, 27 December 1888 (*The Correspondence of Walt Whitman*, IV, 257; and Horace Traubel, *With Walt Whitman in Camden*, III, 395), in which he says he neither objects nor approves; he also told Traubel these gems and extracts yield "nothing to the seeker for sensations" (*ibid.*, III, 396), and he also "dreads such volumes," Traubel said (*ibid.*, III, 405). See other comments of his on Miss Gould and the book in *The Correspondence of Walt Whitman*, IV, 302, 382); she wrote to him on 30 December 1889, regretting that her verses were not in *Camden's Compliment to Walt Whitman*, which Traubel edited (Philadelphia, 1889): letter in the Feinberg Collection.
2436. These taxes were paid to the City of Camden for his house at 328 Mickle Street.
2437. For *Specimen Days in America*, see footnotes 2285, 2288, 2296, and 2379. Whitman told William Sloane Kennedy on 4 October 1887 that he liked "the little English Spec. Days, too — you keep y'r copy" (*The Correspondence of Walt Whitman*, IV, 125).
2438. Once more, to visit the Staffords, but the first time since 11 September.
2439. See footnote 2430.

12 Sent "Shakspere Bacon's Cipher" to Spr: Republican
     Wash'n Star, Sylvester Baxter, Phil: Press & Athenaeum[2440]

Jessie[2441] here – Coolish weather

13 sent slips November Boughs to Pall Mall G [2442]

                                    two   [In blue pencil:]
15 sent W͞m Carey, MS of "Captain" & ~~to~~   photos[2443] rec'd

17 Wᵐ OConnor returns to Washington
     – seems to be somewhat better – the trouble
     has settled into paralysis – he uses crutches

18 O'C here afternoon & evn'g – went on to W.
     in the midnight train[2444]

21 sent Nov. Lippincott to Dr B., Kennedy, O'C., Mary,
     Hannah, Jessie, Johnston N Y., T B Har[2445]

     Mr W H Shoemaker here[2446]

2440. See footnotes 2370 and 2416. The letters accompanying this poem are all lost; Whitman sent, not the poem in MS, but either a proof (or reprint), or a copy of it from the October 1887 *Cosmopolitan*.

2441. Jessie Louisa Whitman was Jeff's daughter from St. Louis, Missouri, who was 26 years old at this time (her sister Hattie had died a year previously).

2442. If Whitman sent a letter to the *Pall Mall Gazette* (London) with these slips (off-prints) of the poems, "November Boughs," *Lippincott's Magazine,* 13 May 1887 (see footnote 2331, above), the letter is now lost.

2443. Letter, if any, now lost; for William Carey, see footnotes 2406 and 2426; he was selling those autographed photographs and also presumably this MS of "O Captain! My Captain!"

2444. Whitman wrote William Sloane Kennedy, 20 October 1887, that he had written Dr R. M. Bucke an account of William Douglas O'Connor's meeting with the poet at this time, but the letter is now lost.

2445. The November 1887 *Lippincott's Magazine* contains the poems, "November Boughs" (see footnote 2331, above); copies were sent to Dr Richard Maurice Bucke, William Sloane Kennedy, William Douglas O'Connor, Mary Van Nostrand and Hannah Heyde (Whitman's sisters), Jessie Whitman (his niece in St. Louis), John H. Johnston (the New York jeweler), and Thomas B. Harned.

2446. W H Shoemaker may be W. L. Shoemaker, an admirer, who wrote Whitman on 7 July 1886 (letter in the Feinberg Collection). Under the date of 17 October 1888, Horace Traubel, *With Walt Whitman in Camden,* II, 494, reported: "W. called my attention to a copy of the Yonkers Gazette containing two sonnets (marked with blue pencil) by W. L. Shoemaker: September Sonnets: The Valley Pathway Blue. W. spoke of S.: 'He was here a week ago [not mentioned however in the *Daybook* at that time]: came up: I liked him: an old man — rather past the age of vigor — but discreet, quiet, not obtrusive.' Then added: 'Take the paper: give the sonnets more careful reading: they are not bad — good, rather: I was attracted. He sent me the paper after he had gone home.' "

23   drive to Glendale[2447]

24   sent the Gilchrist book to Dr Knortz[2448]

[330]

[On a pasted slip, part of an envelope, in WW's hand, in pencil:]

Moncure D. Conway
230 West 59 Street
New York[2449]

[On a pasted slip, not in WW's hand:]

Dear Cousin
Walter Whitman
M. L. Avery[2450]
185 Sterling Place

[Clipping, with WW's annotation, "Century Magazine / Nov: 1887," of a young man's head, with headline College Composite, and cutlines: "Fifty-seven members of the Class of '87 at Williams College. About 35 per cent. from New England; 45 per cent. from the Middle States. (From negatives by Lovell.)".]

[331]

Nov: 1887 – Camden – Oct: and November

2 – 30 & 10 – $40 to Sidney Morse[2451]
" J H Johnston & T B H here[2452]

$16 from Wm Carey, on acc't of photos[2453]

2447. To see the Stafford family, first time in three weeks.
2448. As early as 14 June 1887 he wrote Dr Karl Knortz (see footnote 1580) that he (Whitman) would lend him Herbert Gilchrist's *Anne Gilchrist: Her Life and Writings* (see footnote 2303, above), "to read at your leisure — Will send it on in a day or two" (*The Correspondence of Walt Whitman*, IV, 101) — the "day or two" became four months.
2449. For Conway, see footnotes 36 and 2287. On 12 November 1887, Conway came to see Whitman (see entry below for that date).
2450. Margaret[t]a L. Avery (and William Avery) were evidently cousins of Whitman's mother; they visited Whitman in Camden on 19 October 1876 (see *Daybook* entry and footnote 115). Her letter to Whitman, 25 February 1889, is in the Library of Congress.
2451. This $40 to the sculptor for Whitman heads which Morse had cast for the poet is in addition to the $133 already paid him and listed above (see footnote 2429).
2452. Visits between Whitman and Thomas B. Harned were frequent and not all are recorded in the *Daybook*, which is not hit-and-miss on the poet's activities but is also certainly not complete. For example, Whitman had supper with Harned and his wife at their home in Camden on 29 October (see *The Correspondence of Walt Whitman*, IV, 129) and again on 7 November (*ibid.*, IV, 130) — neither is recorded in the *Daybook*. John H. Johnston, the New York diamond merchant, did not come to Camden that often and most likely visited Whitman now because he was in Philadelphia on business.

3 – sent $16 to Mrs. Goodenough for Ed's board [2454]

[On a scrap from an envelope, in purple pencil (first two words), ink (next two words) and pencil (two bottom lines):]

8   Paid $1.40 for Press
             from Sep^t 1st
          to Nov   1st[2455]

12 – visit from Moncure D Conway with Car-
     riage, to take me over to R P Smith's
     for a few days.   (I do not go)[2456]

[In blue pencil:]
the 1st head goes to Dr Bucke   rec'd [2457]

Sidney Morse here, working at the full length
– figure in arm-chair[2458]

[One word "paid" in red ink:]
15   sent "Yonnondio" to "Critic"   paid   printed
                                  $8 Nov. 26[2459]

rec'd 10 from J H Johnston – (wh – I paid to M)[2460]

2453. This payment is listed above for Whitman's photo and autograph (see footnote 2430, above, and letter to Carey, *The Correspondence of Walt Whitman,* IV, 130).

2454. The usual monthly payment for Whitman's brother Edward. While his sisters Mary and Hannah could not be expected to support their weak-minded brother George and Jeff — both of whom had jobs and were presumably better off financially than a poet might ever expect to be — apparently let Walt carry far more than his share of the burden.

2455. Obviously subscription for the Philadelphia *Press*; Whitman also read Camden newspapers — all of this evidence that he kept up with what was going on locally and nationally.

2456. See footnote 2449 for references to Conway; as for Robert Pearsall Smith, he and his son Logan and daughter Alys were back in this country (they saw Whitman in Camden on 30 October 1887); Whitman wrote Mary Smith Costelloe in London on 1 November — see *The Correspondence of Walt Whitman,* IV, 129–130).

2457. On 2 September 1887, just after Sidney Morse delivered four heads he had had cast of Whitman (see entry above), one was sent to Dr R. M. Bucke, who now received it in London, Ontario, which seems rather a long time for it to go from Camden.

2458. A reproduction of a plaster model of this cast of Whitman in a rocking chair is the frontispiece of Vol. III of Horace Traubel's *With Walt Whitman in Camden.*

2459. For Whitman's brief note, sending this poem to *The Critic,* see *The Correspondence of Walt Whitman,* IV, 131; the poem was published in *The Critic,* VII (26 November 1887), 267, included in "Sands at Seventy" of *November Boughs* (1888), then in *Leaves of Grass* (1888–9), and for the text, see Comprehensive Reader's Edition (New York, 1965), p. 524.

2460. This $10 from Whitman's New York "patron" (certainly not Whitman's term for the jeweler and diamond merchant) must have been for one of Sidney Morse's heads of the poet ("M" is most likely, in this context, to refer to Morse). Johnston's letter of this date is lost. Shortly after this same date Whitman received a letter from Alfred Lord Tennyson

16   sent head to Kennedy   (by Ex: to care of

Baxter, Herald off: Boston) both rec'd [in pencil]
∧also photo[2461]

---

19   letter from Leonard M Brown Croton
                        Landing 25 [2462]

Dec:7 – sent Mr Munyon the Whittier birth –

place lines – $10 paid by him pub: Jan. '88 [2463]

S H Morse takes a room temporarily in· Post
Building, Federal st. to work

Dec. 3. Rec'd 15.50 from W$^{\underline{m}}$ Carey for photos: [2464]

---

10   paid Mr Bennett $18 for Nettie's keep – pays
      up to Nov. 30 '87 in full [2465]

Harry Stafford here 7th – Joe Browning here 8th [2466]

[332]

[Label pasted on page: From the New York Herald, / Philadelphia Office,
/ No. 112 South Sixth St./.] [2467]

(now lost) in reply to Whitman's sending a Cox photo to the English poet, yet neither one of these letters is recorded in the *Daybook*. Tennyson's letter was·published in the New York *Tribune* on 22 November 1887: see the text of Whitman's letter, *The Correspondence of Walt Whitman*, IV, 131.

2461. This was another of Sidney Morse's heads of the poet: see *The Correspondence of Walt Whitman*, IV, 131; and IV 132 (where Whitman explains to William Sloane Kennedy that this is a second head, different from the one Morse made earlier and which the poet sent to several friends, including Kennedy and Dr Bucke — this explains also the question of dates in footnote 2457). The photographs Whitman sent were those by G. C. Cox called "the laughing philosopher": see a reproduction in *ibid.,* IV, foll. p. 278.

2462. For Leonard M. Brown, see footnote 2403; Whitman's thank-you letter for the $25 is in *The Correspondence of Walt Whitman,* IV, 132–133.

2463. Letter to *Munyon's Illustrated World,* sending "As the Greek's Signal Flame," is lost. The poem in honor of Whittier's 80th birthday appeared in the New York *Herald* on 15 December (see entry for 14 December, below) and in the Boston *Advertiser* on 17 December before its publication in Munyon's magazine. Included in "Sands at Seventy" in *November Boughs* (1888) and *Leaves of Grass* (1888–9): see Comprehensive Reader's Edition (New York, 1965), p. 533. See *The Correspondence of Walt Whitman,* IV, 136, 136n, and 137n.

2464. This $15.50 from Carey brought the total to $188.50 Whitman had received so far for the Cox photos (see footnote 2430.

2465. Nettie was Whitman's mare.

2466. Harry Stafford, still undoubtedly bothered by throat trouble, saw Whitman last on 14 September (see footnote 2299); Joseph Browning, married to Debbie Stafford on 13 June 1878 and thus Harry's brother-in-law, last saw Whitman on 29 March 1887.

2467. The New York *Herald* address is pasted here because Whitman sent the news-

[333]

Dec: Dec. '87 and Jan. '88 – Camden
10 – in Mickle street in the old shanty – a dark rainy
      day – somewhat more unwell than usual these days.

                          pub Dec 15 '87 – paid $25 [2468]
14 sent "As the Greek's Signal Flame" to N Y Her. ∧$20

    $10 to S H M [2469]

19 sent Cent'l ed'n, 2 vols. to P J Loftus, Pough-
      keepsie, paid $5 [2470]

           [In red ink:]   both rec'd
22 $10 to Hannah – $10 to Mary   p o orders[2471]

"   Sitting here alone 9 o'c evn'g, at 328 Mickle
      st. writing this.   S H M, who has been here
      the last seven or eight months, started this
      evn'g by Western RR, for Richmond, Indi-
                                    small
      ana.[2472]   (The big sculptured heads and the ∧ full
      figure in chair – very fine both, I think –
      & the medallion profile head, & the little
      oil paintings – Dr Bucke has the two
                        replica
      heads, 1st. and 2d – one ∧ is in London, Eng. —
      one is in Boston – & one in Academy School
      in Philadelphia. Morse has sold 3 or 4 or 5
      I have now three here)[2473]

paper a poem on Whittier on 14 December — see entry below for that date, and *The Correspondence of Walt Whitman,* IV, 136.
    2468. See footnote 2463.
    2469. Another payment to the sculptor Sidney H. Morse undoubtedly for another head
of the poet.
    2470. Whitman wrote Loftus, an instructor at Riverview Academy, Poughkeepsie, New
York (*The Correspondence of Walt Whitman,* IV, 137) that he was sending *Leaves of Grass*
and *Two Rivulets,* 1876 editions.
    2471. Although he did not send large sums, Whitman always remembered his two
sisters, Hannah Heyde and Mary Van Nostrand at Christmas time.
    2472. Sidney H. Morse the sculptor went to Richmond, Indiana, to spend Christmas
with Mrs Morse.
    2473. This is the fullest summary of the heads and figures of Whitman made in 1887
for the poet by Morse (see various footnotes above, 2336, 2356, 2360, and 2411, and *Daybook*
entries).

Ernest Rhys is here from England [2474]
My eyes palpably giving out – knees also.
Thos. Eakins is here painting my portrait
– it seems strong (I don't know but powerful)
& realistic – very different from Herbert's)
It is pretty well advanced & I think I like
it – but we will see – [2475]

[334]

[Blank]

[335]

Dec.   Camden – Dec. '87   and Jan. 1888
22 – Thos. Donelson and Bram Stoker here – I gave
    them pictures & the little green bound "Strong
    Bird" (for Irving and Miss Terry also) [2476]

_____

[Three words in red ink:]
paid back
24 – lent E E Harned, $15 (by Will)   26th [2477]

_____

25th   (Sunday, Christmas) good dinner & good four
    hours at T B and Mrs. Harned's – Mr & Mrs Traubel
    Horace, Aggie, Ernest Rhys, H Bonsall [2478]

_____

2474. Ernest Rhys was, with Rossetti, Whitman's great British champion and promoter in England; he was in the firm of Walter Scott Publisher, under whose imprint Whitman's books appeared in London, such as *Specimen Days in America,* 1887 (see footnote 1978, above, and the ten letters to Rhys from the poet, 1886–1889, *The Correspondence of Walt Whitman,* IV, *passim,* and the last letter, 22 January 1890, *ibid.,* V, 22). Rhys is mentioned more than 80 times in the five volumes of Horace Traubel's *With Walt Whitman in Camden* (see I, 161–163, for example); in 1887 Rhys had Christmas dinner at the Thomas Harned's with Whitman and the Traubels.

2475. Although this is the first mention here of Thomas Eakins, he actually began painting Whitman's portrait late in November: see *The Correspondence of Walt Whitman,* IV, 133, 134, 135 ("comes off & on painting my portrait — it is going to be realistic & severe I think," the poet wrote Dr R. M. Bucke). Eakins worked at the painting in January and February, finishing it early in March (see *ibid.,* IV, 143, 147, 154, 160, 163); and Whitman liked the result ("it is like sharp cold cutting true sea brine"). A reproduction of an oil study of Whitman by Eakins, probably made in 1887, serves as a frontispiece to Vol. IV of *The Correspondence of Walt Whitman.*

2476. See entry above for 11 August 1886, and footnote 2188 for Donaldson (also footnotes 1573 and 2389) and Bram Stoker; both of them, as well as Henry Irving and Ellen Terry, are referred to in *The Correspondence of Walt Whitman,* IV, 41n.

2477. E. E. Harned was the brother of T. B. Harned; Will is possibly Billy Duckett.

2478. For Thomas B. and Mrs Harned, see footnote 1900 and 2452; for Maurice Henry Traubel, see footnote 2291; their son Horace is beginning to be mentioned here in the *Day-book,* and his *With Walt Whitman in Camden* was to commence on 28 March 1888; Aggie is his sister Agnes; for Ernest Rhys, see footnote 2474; H Bonsall is Harry Bonsall, the

Ernest Rhys here daily – his talks &c.
ab't English matters & people[2479]

Jessie is here, at George & Lou's, Burlington[2480]

1888

Jan. 1 Sunday – Supper at T B & Mrs. Harneds[2481]

2 – paid Mr Bennett $18 for Nettie, for Dec.
    pays up in full to Dec. 31 '87 [2482]

                    42 Bradford st   both rec'd   [purple pencil]
5 sent Fred Ryman ∧ Boston Spec Days ∧ paid   [line in purple pencil]
        also "Good Gray" Jan 11.   paid [2483]

" paid gas bills to Jan 1 '88   [line in purple pencil]

   pleasant sunny forenoon   [line in purple pencil]

11 – sunny & fine – cold – headache

14 Evn'g – sent off letters, or cards, to O'Connor,
    Dr B,   Morse, Courtland + Palmer.[2484]

young son of Henry Lummis Bonsall, editor and politician, or Henry the father (see *The Correspondence of Walt Whitman*, III, 215n).

2479. See footnote 2474.

2480. These are Walt Whitman's closest relatives: Jessie is the daughter of his St Louis brother Jeff, George is his brother, and Lou is George's wife. The poet lived with them in Camden until he bought his house in Camden, and this move came about, in part, because he did not want to move with them to their new home in Burlington, where they had a room for him.

2481. The friendliness of Thomas B. and Mrs Harned for Whitman is indicated by his just having had Christmas dinner at their home.

2482. Again, this $18 is for the upkeep of Whitman's horse Nettie.

2483. F. S. Ryman's birthday greetings to Whitman, 31 May 1888, is in the Feinberg Collection. At this time in January Ryman purchased Whitman's *Specimen Days* (Philadelphia: Rees Welsh, 1882–'83), a copy of which Whitman may still have had (it is not likely that Whitman was selling the British edition, *Specimen Days in America* [London: Walter Scott, 1887], though it was a more recent publication); by "Good Gray," is undoubtedly meant William Douglas O'Connor's pamphlet *The Good Gray Poet: A Vindication* (1866), but it was reprinted in R. M. Bucke's *Walt Whitman* (Philadelphia, 1883), pp. 99–130. Possibly Whitman had copies on hand of both publications. Letters to or from Ryman of January 1888 are now lost.

2484. Of these 4 letters — to William Douglas O'Connor, Dr Richard Maurice Bucke, Sidney H. Morse, and Courtland [?] Palmer — all but Morse's are in *The Correspondence of Walt Whitman*, IV, 141–142. Palmer invited Whitman to go to Ernest Rhys's lecture before the Century Club, New York City, 7 February 1888, and to say a word at the conclusion, but Whitman wrote that he was "disabled" and could not go.

Saturday Night – Been in the house all the
past week – Unwell – bad weather.
– I am writing this in the little front room, in
my arm chair, alone, ½ past 8 – Eakins was here
forenoon, painting my portrait.[2485]   Lou call'd [2486]

[336]

Fidelity — Ashton A Work
309 Walnut St Phila

[On card:]
          Fidelity
               Jan 20 '88

     Philip   E.   Margerum   [printed in script] [2487]
[Two lines in purple pencil:]
  533 South 2nd St
     Phila

[Clipping:]

WALT WHITMAN BACKING THE PRESIDENT.

[DAILY NEWS TELEGRAM.]

NEW YORK, January 26. — Walt Whitman sends the
following letter to the _Herald_: — "Looking out from
my loophole of retreat, I wish to heartily thank President Cleveland for his Free-trade message and for his
Jubilee gift to the Pope. Though voices and squads
here and there, perhaps hundreds, will object, thou-
sands of America's quiet thinkers everywhere will be
satisfied. I wish he had sent something to Queen Victoria. She was a good friend to the Union in the time
of its greatest need." [2488]

[In WW's hand:]

Edinburgh

Scotland

paper

'88

2485. For Thomas Eakins and the portrait, see footnote 2475, above.
2486. Louisa Whitman ("Lou"), George's wife, had just seen Whitman on Christmas
Day; at this time, in January, Whitman described himself as "pottering along — certainly no
worse in my late physical ailments — rather better possibly" (_The Correspondence of Walt
Whitman_, IV, 143).
2487. Philip G. Margeman was apparently a businessman or salesman connected with
Fidelity.
2488. This brief paragraph about President Grover Cleveland's free-trade message,
clipped from the _Daily News_, Edinburgh, is taken from a larger piece by Whitman headed

[337]

January   1888   Camden
                              23ᵈ, 24 [2489]
17⑨ severe cold spell –16ᵗʰ, 17ᵗʰ, 18ᵗʰ, 19ᵗʰ, 20ᵗʰ, 21ˢᵗ, 22ᵈ ⋀

18ᵗʰ Evn'g – 9 o'c – Sitting here alone – been reading Shelley, (Forman's fine 2 vol. ed'n he
   sent me by Herbert Gilchrist) [2490] and "The
   trial of Queen Caroline" (Harned's books) [2491]
   – cold in the head keeps on – grows worse
   I think – any thing like easy bodily movement
   will soon be impossible – it is very nearly
   so now – trouble in head, kidney botheration
   pretty bad, joints all gone, locomotion &
   movement gone – mentality all right yet
   – & spirits far better than could be expected,
   – appetite fair – sleep, minus to tolerable. [2492]

20ᵗʰ J H Johnston, N Y. here – took Pepys, [2493]
   4 vols. and Shelley, 2 vols – which I am to
                    [Last word in pencil:]
   send him bill for — ($9) paid [2494]

"To the Editor of the Herald: Pleases Walt," in the New York *Herald,* 26 January 1888. About this time Whitman became sort of a "poet laureate" for *The Herald,* through Julius Chambers, the new managing editor, and with the consent of the owner, James Gordon Bennett, the son of the newspaper's founder. (See footnote 235.) Between 27 January and 27 May 1888 Whitman contributed 32 pieces of verse, for which he received $180. They were all collected in the final edition of *Leaves of Grass.* (See *The Correspondence of Walt Whitman,* IV, 144n–145n; and Gay Wilson Allen, *The Solitary Singer,* p. 527.) Prose pieces in *The Herald* include "Walt Whitman's Tribute [to General Sheridan]," 8 August 1888; and "[On Elias Hicks]," 17 September 1888.
    2489. The weather was so cold that Whitman's rich jeweler friend from New York, John H. Johnston, suggested a trip to Havana, but obviously Whitman did not go: *The Correspondence of Walt Whitman,* IV, 143.
    2490. This edition of Shelley's *Works* is now in the Beinecke Rare Book and Manuscript Library of the Yale University Library; it contains no markings or underlinings by Whitman, in contrast to another edition (1847) edition of Shelley, now in the library of Bryn Mawr College. See Roland A. Duerksen, "Markings by Whitman in His Copy of Shelley's *Works,*" *Walt Whitman Review,* XIV (December 1968), 147–151; and Mary K. Sanders, "Shelley's Promethean Shadow on *Leaves of Grass,*" *Walt Whitman Review,* XIV (December 1968), 151–159.
    2491. *The Trial of Queen Caroline.*
    2492. These details on his health are somewhat similar, though a little more in detail, to what he was writing Dr R. M. Bucke and W. D. O'Connor about this time. See *The Correspondence of Walt Whitman,* IV, 143–144.
    2493. This is the edition about which Whitman wrote Johnson on 29 September 1887: "have been amusing myself with *Pepys' Diary* (McKay sent it to me, good edn. 4 vols.)" — *The Correspondence of Walt Whitman,* IV, 124.
    2494. For the Shelley, see footnote 2490. Johnson paid the $9 in April: see Whitman thank-you letter, *The Correspondence of Walt Whitman,* IV, 165–166.

21☉ Saturday night – have had an <u>unwell</u> week

Cold, bitter cold, 16th 17,18,19,20,21,22,23,24,25,26,27, (28, 29, 30.

24 letter from J G Bennett, N Y. Herald, ask'g
    me to write for "Personal" col   Herald,
    – sent 4 small bits (2 poetic)[2495]

25☉ reading Kennedy's MS (sent me by express)[2496]

27 sent L of G. to R W Colles, 26 Oxford Road,
                                       sent
    Ranelagh, Dublin, Ireland – & ~~promised~~
             March 2
    Spec. Days ~~soon.~~   One pound due – Paid[2497]

29 (Sunday) sent two bits to Herald[2498] – Mr Ingram[2499]

2495. The letter from James Gordon Bennett, Jr, 23 January 1888, is in the Library of Congress. (See footnote 2488.) The two "poetic" ones here mentioned were "To Those Who've Failed," published 27 January 1888, and "Halcyon Days," 29 January; the prose piece on President Cleveland's free trade message appeared on 26 January 1888 (see footnote 2488); the fourth piece, prose, was apparently not published. The poems are in *Leaves of Grass,* Comprehensive Reader's Edition, pp. 508 and 513. (Thirty poems, with present titles, are listed in *The Correspondence of Walt Whitman,* IV, 144n.) See full account, below, of *Herald* printings and payments. On 7 March 1888 Whitman asked Julius Chambers for $40 a month for 10 pieces monthly — see *The Correspondence of Walt Whitman,* IV, 155.

2496. William Sloane Kennedy's MS is the one he told Whitman on 2 January 1888 that Frederick W. Wilson was willing to publish, called "Walt Whitman, Poet of Humanity" (see *The Correspondence of Walt Whitman,* IV, 139n and 150n); and he wrote Kennedy on 26 January, "I have look'd over the MS &c — hardly made any emendations." However, it does not seem to have been published, though later Kennedy did publish *Reminiscences of Walt Whitman* (Paisley, Scotland, 1896) and *The Fight of a Book for the World* (West Yarmouth, Mass., 1926), and of the latter book he says (p. xii) "the first draft [was] made away back in 1886."

2497. See letter to Richard W. Colles, *The Correspondence of Walt Whitman,* IV, 145; and Colles's reply, 12 February 1888, in Horace Traubel, *With Walt Whitman in Camden,* IV, 141–142. See entry for 18 October 1886, above, and footnote 2194.

2498. See footnote 2495 about Whitman writing pieces for the New York *Herald.* The two "bits" here most likely are "After the Dazzle of Day," which appeared on 3 February 1888, and "America," 11 February. (Now in *Leaves of Grass,* Comprehensive Reader's Edition, pp. 512 and 511).

2499. William Ingram, whom Whitman described to Peter Doyle in 1873 as "a good, kind-hearted, rather queer old fellow" who came from Philadelphia, where he kept a tea store, to see Whitman when the poet was ill: "I found him good company, & was glad to see him" — *The Correspondence of Walt Whitman,* II, 231–232. See Whitman's letters to him, *The Correspondence of Walt Whitman,* IV, 120, 158, 209–210, 370–371; V, 319. His gifts and his visits are mentioned in numerous letters, *ibid.,* IV, 154, 200, 210, 228, 333, 337, 371, 407; V, 52, 73–74, 108, 133, 272.

[338]

[Clipped from envelope:]   M H Spielmann[2502]

   Return to ANDREW CARNEGIE,[2500]   Magazine of Art
   No. 6 West 51st St., NEW YORK, N.Y.,   La Belle Sauvage Ludgate Hill
   If not delivered within 10 days.
                           London   Eng
   [Two lines in purple pencil:]   E C

    Talcott Williams[2501]
    1833 Spruce st

[339]

       1888   Camden
Jan 31ˢᵗ (Tuesday) Dr Bucke here on his way to Florida
   with the Pardees — Stay & talk, the afternoon[2503]
   – Dr Osler here – more moderate weather[2504]
   am feeling pretty well afternoon & Evn'g

Feb: 2 – paid Mr Bennett $18 for Net for Jan:[2505]

3.   death of Moses A Walsh, aged 54 at
          – buried 6th –
     Natrona Penn[2506]   Wᵐ Ingram   here[2507]
     unwell two days past

2500. See entry below for 7 February 1888.
2501. Whitman wrote Talcott Williams (see footnote 799), his good friend on the Philadelphia *Press,* on 6 March 1888, about his pieces in the New York *Herald.* See *The Correspondence of Walt Whitman,* IV, 155.
2502. On 30 November 1887 M. H. Spielmann, of the *Pall Mall Gazette* (London), and also editor of the *Magazine of Art,* wrote to Whitman, asking for a poem (letter in Horace Traubel, *With Walt Whitman in Camden,* II, 232–233). Whitman sent him "Twenty Years," which was published in the *Gazette* in July 1888 and the *Magazine of Art* in August, with illustrations by Wal Paget. For the poem, see *Leaves of Grass,* Comprehensive Reader's Edition, p. 531; for Whitman's letters to Spielmann, 7 and 10 February 1888, see *The Correspondence of Walt Whitman,* IV, 147–148 and 148; for Spielmann's letter, 24 July 1888, see *With Walt Whitman in Camden,* II, 104; and II, 134, for Whitman's opinion of Paget's drawing.
2503. Whitman was invited by his jeweler friend J. H. Johnston to go to Havana with Dr R. M. Bucke and Mr and Mrs Timothy Blair Pardee, but he did not go (see footnote 2489).
2504. For Dr William Osler, Dr Bucke's friend and one of Whitman's physicians, to become famous himself, see footnote 2054.
2505. This money is for boarding Whitman's horse Nettie.
2506. I don't know how well Whitman knew Moses A. Walsh, but he wrote to the poet on 9 April 1886 (see the letter in the Feinberg Collection) about the Wesley Water Cure; Whitman was having spells of bad health at this time in 1886, though not much more than usual.
2507. Another of William Ingram's welcome visits (see footnote 2499).

5⊕ Sunday – pleasant weather – in all day –

---

small pieces in N Y. Herald – personal col.[2508]

---

7 Sent L of G to Andrew Carnegie, N Y
        rec'd – letter from A C [2509]

---

8 Ernest Rhys's lecture before the Nineteenth
        Century Club, N Y. & the debate afterward [2510]

9⊕   Cold again – 10th, – Harry S here – 5.[2511]

---

10 sent "Abm Lincoln" to Herald [2512]
    rec'd $20 from Cassell & Co. 104 Fourth av
      N Y for "Twenty Years"   sent rec't[2513]
    paid Mrs. Goodenough, $17 for Ed. for Jan.[2514]

---

11   little pieces in the N Y Herald personal
        column – "America" appears to-day[2515]

2508. See footnotes 2488, 2495, and 2498. The "small pieces" here must be "Halcyon Days," 29 January, and "After the Dazzle of Day," 3 February 1888.

2509. For Whitman's letter to Andrew Carnegie (1835–1919), the famed Scottish-born industrialist, see *The Correspondence of Walt Whitman*, IV, 146; Carnegie donated $350 for Whitman's Lincoln lecture in New York City, 14 April 1887 (for Whitman's reaction to this, see several letters he wrote at this time, *The Correspondence of Walt Whitman*, IV, 83n, 85, 86, 87, 88); Carnegie also donated $50 to a fund in 1889 for a nurse for Whitman (see Carnegie's letter to Traubel, *With Walt Whitman in Camden*, IV, 435).

2510. For Ernest Rhys, see footnotes 1978 and 2474, and see entry above for 25 December 1887. Rhys published "The Portraits of Walt Whitman," *Scottish Art Review*, II (June 1889), 17–24; and "Walt Whitman's Leaves of Grass," *Everyman*, I (28 February and 7 March 1913), 623 and 656–657; the latter contains material used in this lecture at the Contemporary Club, Philadelphia, not New York. Whitman refers briefly to the lecture in his 7 and 16 February 1888 letters to Dr R. M. Bucke: see *The Correspondence of Walt Whitman*, IV, 147, and 151; also 150n–151n.

2511. The "5" is cryptic, but Harry S is not — it is Whitman's very good friend Harry Stafford, who was last mentioned in the *Daybook* on 14 August 1887 (see entry, above, and also footnotes 2299 and 2424). In his letter to Dr R. M. Bucke, 6 January 1888, Whitman said that Harry's "throat trouble is the same as ever" (see *The Correspondence of Walt Whitman*, IV, 139).

2512. "Abm Lincoln" was published in the *New York Herald* 12 February 1888; a two-line poem, it is entitled "Abraham Lincoln, Born Feb. 12, 1809" (see *Leaves of Grass*, Comprehensive Reader's Edition, p. 512). It is not listed among the *Herald* poems in *The Correspondence of Walt Whitman*, IV, 144n, but it is in Whitman's own list below.

2513. The $20 Whitman received was for "Twenty Years," published in the *Pall Mall Gazette* and the *Magazine of Art*: see footnote 2502.

2514. As so often and as usual, this money is for the upkeep of Walt's brother Edward.

2515. "America" was in the *Herald* on 11 February 1888 (see *Leaves of Grass*, Comprehensive Reader's Edition, p. 511), but the plural "pieces" is confusing, for the previous one was

14 Sunny good day – more moderate ⟨MS rec'd⟩

sent back Kennedy's MS by Express pd.[2516]

---

15 visit from David Newport Willow Grove
Pa. – talk ab't Elias Hicks – cold.[2517]

---

17 – Milder weather – E Rhys left for N Y [2518]
Evn'g – sent "Soon will the winter's foil" & "the Dismantled
Ship" to Herald – [2519]

---

18 death of Jesse Lay – buried 21st [2520]

[340]

acc't with N Y Herald [2521]   1888
Commenced ab't 26th or 27th Jan. 1888,

(letter from Jas Gordon Bennett, requesting ⎞ paid $25 for [written
                    me to contribute) ⎠ the Whittier sideways]
                                                    bit[2522]

Pieces pub'd in Herald

From my loop – hole of retreat (prose)[2523]

eight days ago on 3 February, and the Lincoln poem was not until 12 February (so how
could Whitman have seen it on the 11th?).

2516. For William Sloane Kennedy's MS, see footnote 2496, and his letter to Kennedy
in *The Correspondence of Walt Whitman,* IV, 150.

2517. Whitman wrote Ellen M. O'Connor on 16 February 1888, "An old Quaker paid
me a visit to-day (I am yet writing my *Elias Hicks* paper)," which must refer to David Newport. "Elias Hicks," a long essay on a subject which had interested Whitman for some time,
was first published in *November Boughs,* which David McKay (Philadelphia) was to publish in 1888. See *Prose Works 1892,* II, 626–653.

2518. For Ernest Rhys, see footnote 2510.

2519. These two poems, "Soon Shall the Winter's Foil Be Here" and "The Dismantled
Ship," appeared in the New York *Herald* on 21 and 23 February 1888 (see *Leaves of Grass,*
Comprehensive Reader's Edition, pp. 528–529 and 534).

2520. Jesse Lay was apparently a member of the Lay family that lived in Whitman's
house at 328 Mickle Street, Camden, when he bought it in 1884: see footnotes 1792 and 1796.

2521. This is a fairly full bibliographical and financial account of Whitman's publications, both poetry and prose, in the New York *Herald* at this time, but the abbreviations are
difficult at times to make out. They are all — except the little prose — now in *Leaves of
Grass,* Comprehensive Reader's Edition, pp. 507–534, in a section called "Sands at Seventy,"
first published in book form in *November Boughs* (Philadelphia, 1888) after their appearance in the *Herald.* See also footnotes 2488 and 2495. See *The Serif,* XI (Summer 1974), 31–38.

2522. See footnote 2467 and entry, above, for 14 December 1887. By "the Whittier bit"
Whitman means the poem in the 15 December New York *Herald,* "As the Greek's Signal
Flame," which says beneath the title, "For Whittier's eightieth birthday, December 17, 1887";
it was reprinted on that date in the Boston *Advertiser.* (See *Leaves of Grass,* Comprehensive
Reader's Edition, p. 533.)

2523. "From My Loop-hole of Retreat" was Whitman's title for a 26 January 1888 letter

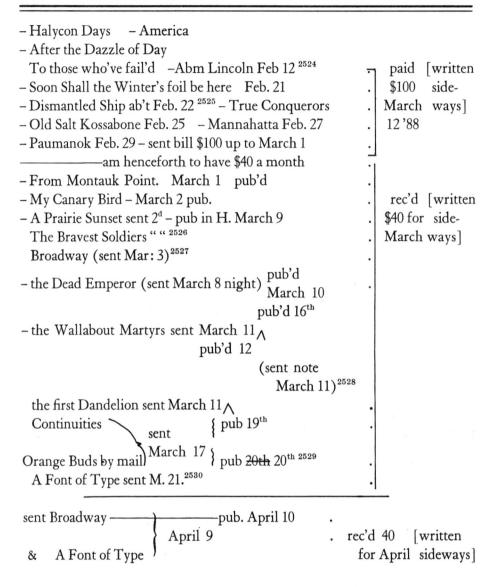

– Halycon Days   – America
– After the Dazzle of Day
   To those who've fail'd   –Abm Lincoln Feb 12 [2524]   paid [written
– Soon Shall the Winter's foil be here   Feb. 21 $100   side-
– Dismantled Ship ab't Feb. 22 [2525] – True Conquerors   March   ways]
– Old Salt Kossabone Feb. 25   – Mannahatta Feb. 27   12 '88
– Paumanok Feb. 29 – sent bill $100 up to March 1
─────────am henceforth to have $40 a month
– From Montauk Point. March 1   pub'd
– My Canary Bird – March 2 pub.   rec'd [written
– A Prairie Sunset sent 2ᵈ – pub in H. March 9 $40 for side-
   The Bravest Soldiers " " [2526]   March ways]
   Broadway (sent Mar: 3) [2527]

– the Dead Emperor (sent March 8 night)   pub'd
                                          March 10
                                          pub'd 16ᵗʰ
– the Wallabout Martyrs sent March 11∧
                      pub'd 12
                               (sent note
                                  March 11) [2528]

   the first Dandelion sent March 11∧
   Continuities ╲   { pub 19ᵗʰ
                  sent
   Orange Buds by mail⟍ March 17 } pub 20th 20ᵗʰ [2529]
   A Font of Type sent M. 21. [2530]

─────────────────────────

sent Broadway ───────────pub. April 10   .
                          April 9   . rec'd 40   [written
   &   A Font of Type   for April sideways]

to the editor of the New York *Herald* (see clipping on p. [336] of the *Daybook* and footnote to 2488).
   2524.   The dates are those of publication. For this poem, see footnote 2512.
   2525.   "The Dismantled Ship" was actually published on 23 February 1888, and "True
Conquerors" on 15 February.
   2526.   "The Bravest Soldiers" was published on 18 March 1888 (see *Leaves of Grass*,
Comprehensive Reader's Edition, p. 509).
   2527.   "Broadway" waited until 10 April 1888 before publication (see *Leaves of Grass*,
Comprehensive Reader's Edition, p. 521).
   2528.   This note to the Editor of the New York *Herald* is missing.
   2529.   Whitman has these dates reversed: "Continuities" was published on 20 February
and "Orange Buds by Mail from Florida" on 19 February 1888 (see *Leaves of Grass*, Comprehensive Reader's Edition, pp. 523–524 and 531–532).
   2530.   "A Font of Type" was in the *Herald* 9 April 1888; it is not in the list in *The
Correspondence of Walt Whitman*, IV, 144n. See entry below in *Daybook*, and *Leaves of
Grass*, Comprehensive Reader's Edition, p. 509.

Ap: [?]

sent Life ∧ – pub'd Sunday April 15   April ~~18~~   •

   & To get the real lilt of Songs – pub. Ap. 16 [2531]   •

a ¶ on Matthew Arnold's death, pub. April 18 – [2532]   •

sent To-day and Thee April 21 pub'd April 23   •

   " To those who've Fail'd [2533] " "   •

                                                •

April   ⎫ Queries to my 70ᵗʰ Year pub May 2   •
  28 sent ⎭   & the Bravest Soldier – pub'd Ap. 30 [2534].

May 6 Sunday sent A to O W. critics pub'd May 8 [2535].

   " 8 sent As I Sit writing Here pub. May 14   •

   "   ⎫ Out of May's Shows Selected, pub May 10.
May 19 ⎬ A carol closing 69, pub'd May 22   •
  sent ⎭ Life and Death . . . pub May 23   •

May 23 [?]   The Calming Tho't of all [2536]   •

   Sent   While not the Past Forgetting [2537]   •

[341]

Feb: 1888   February   Camden

21 – Cent: ed'n   L of G, two vols. to Dick & Fitzgerald [2538]

              paid 24ᵗʰ

   N Y. $6.66 ~~due~~ — mild spring weather

[Two rules and one line in purple pencil:]

22 sent "Old Salt Kossabone" to Herald [2539]

2531. "To Get the Real Lilt of Songs" was not the title used in the *Herald*; there it appeared (on 16 April 1888) as "The Final Lilt of Songs"; in *Leaves of Grass* (see Comprehensive Reader's Edition, pp. 521–522) its title became "To Get the Final Lilt of Songs."

2532. This prose piece is apparently uncollected.

2533. "To Those Who've Failed" was the first poem the *Herald* published, on 27 January 1888.

2534. "The Bravest Soldiers" had appeared on 18 March 1888.

2535. "A to O W. critics" refers to "The United States to Old World Critics," the 5-line poem in the 8 May 1888 *Herald* (see *Leaves of Grass*, Comprehensive Reader's Edition, p. 526).

2536. "The Calming Thought of All" was published on 27 May 1888 (see *Leaves of Grass*, Comprehensive Reader's Edition, p. 527). The other poems listed by Whitman all appeared in the *Herald* on the dates he mentions.

2537. Whitman has a notation, "Publish'd May 30, 1888," after this poem in *November Boughs* (1888) as it is a Decoration Day verse (see *Leaves of Grass*, Comprehensive Reader's Edition, p. 529). Written at this time, it was not published in the *Herald* on that date. "The Calming Thought of All" was the last in that newspaper, except for one 12 August 1888.

2538. Dick & Fitzgerald was a firm at 18 Ann Street, New York City: see a transcript of Whitman's letter to the company, 18 February 1888, in *The Correspondence of Walt Whitman*, IV, 152.

2539. "Old Salt Kossabone," as noted above (and in *Leaves of Grass*, Comprehensive Reader's Edition, p. 522), was published in the *Herald* on 25 February 1888.

24 sent "Mannahatta" and "My Canary Bird" to Herald [2540]

25 – cloudy & rainy –
                26ᵗʰ, 27, 28, 29   cold

29 – David McKay call'd – paid $13.95 [2541]

March 1 – Dr Bucke here returning from Florida
            leaves to-morrow (via N Y) for Canada [2542]

2 – sent bill to Herald, $100 paid [2543]

   "   letter to Harry S: [2544]   cloudy, dark –
                                     moderate temp:

   "   "Prairie Sunset" & "Bravest Soldiers" to H [2545]

3   paid Mr Bennett $18 for Nettie for Feb: [2546]

4 5   Lou here – went to bank for me dep: 194:11 [2547]

5 snow storm all day – visitors – ¾ sick

7 – paid $1.38 for Press Jan: & Feb:
   Mr Browning here ab't bill to Herald &c
   wrote to Herald (Mr Chambers) offering to write
   10 pieces a month for $40 a month
            – offer accepted by letter from Herald
                 March 8 [2548]

2540. These two poems were published on 27 February and 2 March 1888 (see *Leaves of Grass,* Comprehensive Reader's Edition, pp. 507 and 510; on pp. 474–475 is another poem entitled "Mannahatta," first published in the 1860 *Leaves of Grass*).

2541. For royalties?

2542. Dr R. M. Bucke and Mr and Mrs Timothy Blair Pardee went through Camden on the way to Florida on 31 January 1888 (see entry, above), obviously staying about a month. Whitman's seven letters to Dr Bucke, sent to St Augustine, Florida — see *The Correspondence of Walt Whitman,* IV, 146–153 — are not recorded in the *Daybook.*

2543. This is for the material published in January and February: see Whitman's account, above. The money was paid on 12 March; after that, Whitman was to receive $40 a month for 10 contributions.

2544. This letter to Harry Stafford is lost.

2545. These two poems were printed in the *Herald* on 9 and 18 March (see *Leaves of Grass,* Comprehensive Reader's Edition, pp. 530–531 and 509).

2546. For horsekeeping.

2547. This $194.11 deposited by Whitman's sister-in-law Louisa came from McKay, sales of *Leaves of Grass,* "Twenty Years" in the *Pall Mall Gazette,* and other sources (not all recorded in the *Daybook*); but the *Herald* payment had not come yet.

2548. This discussion with C. H. Browning of the New York *Herald,* and the letter

8 Mr Browning here from Herald – wants
    a piece ab't Emp. William's death – piece

                                          sent[2549]

9 – 11th sent "Wallabout Martyrs" & "First Dandelion" [2550]
    to Herald – Dined at T B H's[2551]

12 Storm & gale last night – heavy snow fall
      the blizzard

11, that night
     12, & 13   heavy storm & gale –deep snow – cold
    two days now, (Monday and Tuesday)
    of cold, snowy, biting winter – hard to keep
    comfortable here in the little front room[2552]

[342]

[Tiny tintype of a young woman, 1″ by ¾″, pasted to page, without identification; clipping from an envelope, printed: THOS. J. McKEE, / Law Offices. /

to Julius Chambers have to do with the poems (and a few prose pieces) Whitman had been writing in January and February for the newspaper — see footnotes 2488, 2495, 2498, and Whitman's long entry in the *Daybook*, above, headed *"acc't with N Y Herald."* Whitman's letter to Chambers is in *The Correspondence of Walt Whitman*, IV, 155; the letter from the *Herald* is missing. See *ibid.*, IV, 160.

    2549. What Whitman calls "a piece ab't Emp. William's death" is a poem, "The Dead Emperor," published in the *Herald* on 10 March 1888: see *Leaves of Grass*, Comprehensive Reader's Edition, p. 533. The emperor, Wilhelm I of Germany, had died in Berlin on 9 March 1888 (how could Whitman have written the poem on 8 March?). Benjamin Tucker and many friends of Whitman protested to him about the phrase "a faithful shepherd" in the poem, and he told Horace Traubel (*With Walt Whitman in Camden*, I, 22–23), "too many of the fellows forget that I include emperors, lords, kingdoms, as well as presidents, workmen, republics. . . . There was nothing in this little poem to contradict my earlier philosophy. It all comes to the same thing. I am as radical now as ever — just as radical — but I am not asleep to the fact that among radicals as among the others there are hoggishnesses, narrownesses, inhumanities, which at times almost scare me for the future. . . . [M]y reference was to the Emperor as a person — that my dmeocracy included him: not the William the tyrant, the aristocrat, but the William the man who lived according to his light: I do not see why a democrat may not say such a thing and remain a democrat."

    2550. "The First Dandelion" and "The Wallabout Martyrs" were in the *Herald* on 12 and 16 March 1888: see *Leaves of Grass*, Comprehensive Reader's Edition, pp. 511 and 510–511. The martyrs were the thousands of revolutionary patriots from British prisons and prison ships who were buried between 1776 and 1783 in trenches in Wallabout Bay sands at the bend of the East River, where the Brooklyn Navy Yard now stands.

    2551. Whitman had not recorded a visit to Thomas B. Harned's home in Camden since Christmas Day 1887; on 15 February he had proposed Harned for membership in The Contemporary Club, but this is not mentioned in the *Daybook*. See Whitman's letter in *The Correspondence of Walt Whitman*, IV, 150; also see *ibid*, IV, 156, 157, for mention of the dinner at Harned's.

    2552. Yet this is not quite the same thing as he wrote William Sloane Kennedy on 15 March 1888: "A fearful four-day spell of cold, snow & gale here, but I have not felt it — the sun is shining as I write — " (*The Correspondence of Walt Whitman*, IV, 157).

338 Broome Street, corner Bowery. / Mechanics' & Traders' Bank Building. / New York./] [2553]

[Front of an envelope, not in WW's hand: Harry D Hughes / 3343 North 21st street / Philadelphia / Pa / — Century Banquet — Wednesday / - March 21 /.] [2554]

[343]

March & April   1888   Camden

pass'd

15ᵗʰ less cold – sunny – storm all ∧ over – melting

17ᵗʰ – milder – the snow well gone

sent "Orange Buds by Mail" & "Continuities" to H [2555]

_____

20ᵗʰ – sent letter to Kennedy and Dr B. enc: Mrs. C's [2556]

_____

21ˢᵗ – Her: commenced coming [2557]

_____

23ᵈ – Lent E H H $15 – T Eakins painting
        $15 returned [2558]

_____

2553. Thomas J. McKee was a New York lawyer who was investigating, at the request of Dr R. M. Bucke, J. H. Johnston, as well as Whitman, the poet's claims against Richard Worthington, who was publishing *Leaves of Grass* from plates of the 1860 edition. The whole story is told in Whitman's letter to Richard Watson Gilder, 26 November 1880, and Professor Edwin Haviland Miller's annotations in *The Correspondence of Walt Whitman*, III, 195–198. See brief *Daybook* entries above (and footnotes) for 26 November and 6 and 7 December 1880. The matter was never settled during Whitman's lifetime. McKee's letter to Whitman, 7 April 1888, which the poet sent to Dr R. M. Bucke, is in the Feinberg Collection; Whitman's letter to the lawyer is missing. See *The Correspondence of Walt Whitman*, IV, 160n–161n.

2554. If Whitman wrote to Harry D. Hughes or saw him at this time (21 March 1888), the letter is missing and the visit is unrecorded. The poet did write Hughes on 12 February 1887 — see *The Correspondence of Walt Whitman*, IV, 67 — to thank him for his article, "Walt Whitman's Prose Works," *Leisure Moments,* II (February 1887), 17.

2555. The poems, "Orange Buds by Mail from Florida" and "Continuities," were published in the New York *Herald* on 19 and 20 March 1888: see *Leaves of Grass,* Comprehensive Reader's Edition, pp. 531–532 and 523–524.

2556. This letter to William Sloane Kennedy and Dr R. M. Bucke is in *The Correspondence of Walt Whitman,* IV, 157; in the letter he enclosed a "cheery" one from Mary [Smith] Costelloe (now lost?).

2557. This is merely an indication that Whitman began getting copies of the New York *Herald,* probably a gift subscription from William Ingram (see footnote 2499), whom he wrote on this date, "The Herald has just come — all right —" (that's the entire letter, in *The Correspondence of Walt Whitman,* IV, 158).

2558. The only reason that Whitman records that he lent Ezra H. Heywood $15 (which was repaid) and Thomas Eakins's painting on the same line is that the two events took place on the same day: there's no other connection. For Heywood, see entry for 9 and 12 November 1882 and footnote 1613: he was arrested for printing "To a Common Prostitute" and "A Woman Waits for Me," and now, almost six years later he visits Whitman and makes a loan — see *The Correspondence of Walt Whitman,* IV, 157. Eakins, on the other hand, came on 19 March 1888 to take the painting he had made of Whitman (see entry above for 22 December 1887 and footnote 2475), but brought it back to Camden on 23 March (see

24 – the pulse-pains (heart?) in left breast the
last 20 hours, and during last night

27, 28, part of 29, dull, dark, rainy, not cold

29

April 1 – sent bill $40 to Herald – note to Editor[2559]

3   sent picture (Spieler's photo) to Hollyer, 216
W 22ᵈ St. N Y.[2560]

4   paid gas ($8.55) & water ($8) bills
£
cash'd p o orders (4) – Mrs Stafford here
burial of Mrs: Rogers, April 2 [2561]

6   rec'd letter from Sam'l Hollyer, etcher, 216
West 22ᵈ St.   N Y City – He has rec'd photo.
(Spieler's ¾ face, open neck, the "Lear", – Mary
Costello's favorite –) wh' he admires, & is to
[Line in pencil:] he etched it & sent me copy[2562]
etch, & send me copy (clear, fine day)
– wrote to Harry Staf: & sent papers[2563]
– extra dull & unwell the last 3 days

ibid., IV, 157, 157n, and 160). ·

2559. The $40 was to be paid to Whitman for 10 contributions to the New York *Herald* during March (see footnote 2548 and *The Correspondence of Walt Whitman,* IV, 155 for Julius Chambers's letter from Whitman); but apparently — Whitman wrote William Sloane Kennedy (*ibid.,* IV, 159) — there was "a lull in my *Herald* contributions" and none appeared between 20 March and 10 April, only four poems being published in April. There was a "hitch" in their arrangements (see *ibid.,* IV, 160). The note to the *Herald* editor is missing.

2560. This letter to Samuel Hollyer, sending a photograph to be etched, is missing — see entry below, for 6 April, for more on Hollyer.

2561. Mrs Susan Stafford, Whitman's friend from Timber Creek and Harry's mother, had visited the poet about 12 March 1888 also; Mrs Elizabeth Rogers was Susan Stafford's sister (see *The Correspondence of Walt Whitman,* IV, 163; and, for more on Mrs Rogers, III, 278n).

2562. Horace Traubel, who had begun his long and detailed account on 28 March 1888 of Whitman's day-to-day activities — though Whitman does not say so in his *Daybook* — gives the poet's opinion of Hollyer's etching: "I do not think it good enough to be good — this is especially true of the eyes — they are too glaring: I have a dull not a glaring eye. . . . It is not first class as an etching — far from first class as a portrait. It is taken from the Lear original. Do you know, it was Mary Costelloe who gave that picture its name? — a good name, too, as most of my friends have allowed." (*With Walt Whitman in Camden,* II, 131–132; see also II, 144.)

2563. This is the first mention in some time of Whitman's practice of sending newspapers and magazines, this time to Harry Stafford, often containing material by or about the poet.

7⊙ sent note to Herald ²⁵⁶⁴
   paid Mr Bennett $18 for Nettie for March[2565]

8 – fine Sunday – out to H's to dinner – a ride[2566]

                             accepted – paid
9 sent "Old Age's lambent Peaks" to Century — 16 [2567]
  " "A Carol Closing Sixty Nine" to Lippincotts 18

                           returned [2568]
  " "To get the real Lilt of Songs" to Cosmop. 12 [2569]

10⊙

[344]

[Blank]

[345]

   April & May 1888
16 Elias Hicks' head – Evn'g – Horace Traubel
came in & open'd the box wh' has been here
two weeks – (sent by Sidney Morse from Indiana) – and took out the plaster cast of
head of Elias Hicks. I had it placed in the
back corner of my sitting room, & it is there

2564. Whitman's note to the *Herald* is missing, but James Gordon Bennett wrote on 7 April 1888 (letter in the Feinberg Collection), after getting a bill for $40, that there was an error and he asked for 10 more poems for April. Whitman sent only five, and after an additional seven in May, the arrangement ceased.
    2565. The usual amount for caring for Whitman's horse.
    2566. Whitman had previously dined with Mr and Mrs Thomas Harned on 11 and 25 March 1888 (see entry, above, for former date, and *The Correspondence of Walt Whitman,* IV, 159).
    2567. "Old Age's Lambent Peaks" was published in *The Century Magazine,* XXXVI (September 1888), 735: see *Leaves of Grass,* Comprehensive Reader's Edition, p. 535. Horace Traubel (*With Walt Whitman in Camden,* II, 289) told Whitman that Thomas Harned liked the poem "a whole lot," to which he replied, "So do I, if I may be allowed to say it: to me it is an essential poem — it needed to be made." The "16" refers to the $16 the magazine paid him for it.
    2568. This poem, rejected by *Lippincott's Magazine,* was sent to the New York *Herald,* where it appeared on 21 May 1888 (Whitman's note in *Daybook,* above, gives 22 May as the date). See *Leaves of Grass,* Comprehensive Reader's Edition, pp. 508–509. The "18" is what he asked for the poem from *Lippincott's*; instead of that sum, he got, from the *Herald,* perhaps $40 for all of the poems published in May — though he did not record having received payment for May.
    2569. "To Get the Real Lilt of Songs," for which he asked $12 from *Cosmopolitan,* was rejected by this magazine; it too went to the *Herald,* appearing on April 1888 (see footnote 2531).

now as I write (9½ env'g.) – as far as first
impressions go, I am well pleased with the
head – may turn out that I will think it
                – (some days afterward) – [line in pencil]
grand – we will see –∧ yes I continue
to like it well – [2570]

17° 20° 28°   27, 28, 29, 30   hot days

27 & 28 – warm days – out driving

28 paid Mrs: Goodenough $16 for Ed's board [2571]

29 (Sunday) drove down to Glendale – hot day – evn'g at
        T B & Mrs. Harned's [2572]

May 5 – paid Mr Bennett $18 for Nettie for April
                ? Herald
    "   "   rec'd 40 from H. for April (rec'd $205 altogether) [2573]

❀

9   paid Hartrauft 1.40 for Press March & April [2574]

14° – under the weather badly 10, 11, 12, 13, 14, 16, 17, 18

2570. Traubel's entry for this date in *With Walt Whitman in Camden,* I, 41, quotes Whitman on the Hicks bust (its present location unknown): "Morse has done well, better, almost best. It more than meets my expectations: its serenity, its seriosity — which stops finely short of ministerial goody-goodishness. It impresses me, with regard to the head above the eyes, however, that Morse has given it too much mass — has idealized it. . . . And yet I am pleased. Morse, you have done first rate. A good piece of work I should say. Its points strike you as you stay with it. Morse is getting stronger. He never could have done such work till last summer, when he got in the back yard here, away from the art schools, and slashed and dashed away — and hit it!" See Whitman's comments in his letters of 18 April in *The Correspondence of Walt Whitman,* IV, 163, 164.

2571. A good deal, but not all, of the money Whitman paid for his brother Edward's upkeep was noted at the back of the *Daybook.*

2572. Whitman had not recorded a visit to the Stafford farm in Glendale since 23 October 1887 (he often went in the summer time); this time he did not spend the night. Three weeks ago, on 8 April 1888, he dined at the Harned's in Camden. Traubel, *With Walt Whitman in Camden,* I, 80–83, as might be expected, goes into some detail over the current visit at the Harned's and what was said.

2573. This $205 was for the poem ($25), January and February bits ($100), March contribution ($40), and those for April ($40), even though — as he told Traubel (*With Walt Whitman in Camden,* I, 106) — he did not send a bill to the *Herald* on 1 May 1888.

2574. Whitman continued to mention trifling matters, such as paying board for his horse Nettie (just above), and subscriptions to the Camden *Post* and Camden *Courier* (see

15 Ernest Rhys goes this afternoon to N Y. &
   thence (after visiting Dr B) to England [2575]

"   paid the <u>Post</u> and <u>Courier</u>

17 sent copy of L of G. to   Griffin   15 rue
   de Bourbon, Paris, France

19⁹ 23⁹ rainy – dark — 24ᵗʰ, '5ᵗʰ '6ᵗʰ

[346]

[Written on a slip of paper, not in WW's hand:

                    Ernest Rhys
                    c/o E.C. Stedman,
                    44 East 26ᵗʰ Street
                    New York[2576]

[In WW's hand:]
         was to sail
              June 5
         arrived all right
has written to me
         from Eng:[2577]

Dec: 12⎱ 11 Cowley Street
   '88 ⎰   Westminster S W   London Eng:[2578]

[347]

                    Memᵭ.

'76

below), and to the Philadelphia *Press*. Many more important matters are neglected in the *Daybook*.

2575. Ernest Rhys (see footnote 2510) lectured in Boston on Whitman (he wrote Whitman from there on 3 April 1888 — letter in Horace Traubel's *With Walt Whitman in Camden*, II, 30–31); he was in New York in May (see letter in *ibid.*, II, 31) at E. C. Stedman's, still in Camden on 27 May (see below), and did not sail for England until 7 June (see third letter to Whitman, *ibid.*, II, 33); see also *The Correspondence of Walt Whitman*, IV, 155n, 156n, 160n, 169n, and 172n for brief summaries of Rhys's travels and doings.

2576. See previous footnote.

2577. This letter from Ernest Rhys, 9–10 July 1888, is in the Feinberg Collection; see note on it and Whitman's reply in *The Correspondence of Walt Whitman*, IV, 190, 190n, and 192–193.

2578. A letter of this date, from Ernest Rhys in London, is in the Feinberg Collection.

2579. This cancelled and somewhat out–of–place 1876 entry has to do with the wife of a Vassar College professor: see footnote 139 and *The Correspondence of Walt Whitman*, III, 153n.

Sept 17 – to send a budget of
  slips to Mrs. Fanny R
  Ritter 63 South Hamilton St
  Poughkeepsie N Y

[two lines in
red ink:]
Ships sent
Nov 21   76 [2579]

May   1888   Camden

24 – David McKay call'd – he says if I
      will renew the contract with him for
      my books, giving him the right to publish

      L of G. and Spec. Days for five years
      he will sell me the plates of Spec:
      Days for $150 – he gives consent to
      my using the plates of Spec. Days for
                              or 600
      my complete works edition – 500 ∧ copies [2580]
                              from
26 — Warren Fritzinger here (comes ∧ Montreal) [2581]

[Rest of page, six lines, in pencil:]
27 – Ernest Rhys here – sails June 5 from
                                    N Y [2582]

---

29 – Jeff here – fine summer day⊗ [2583]

---

30 – ("Decoration Day") – sent note to Ferguson
      printer – Tom Harned, Kennedy & Horace

2580. In a letter to Dr R. M. Bucke (*The Correspondence of Walt Whitman*, IV, 172), Whitman merely said that McKay saw him: "nothing particularly new — he wants an extension of the contract five years more to publish L of G. and Spec. D. — I told him I would think it over"; and in Horace Traubel, *With Walt Whitman in Camden*, I, 205–206, there are more details about these negotiations.

2581. Warren Fritzinger, one of the sons of the sea captain whom Mrs Mary Davis, Whitman's housekeeper, had previously served, is pictured with Whitman in *The Correspondence of Walt Whitman*, V, opposite 212. He did not become the poet's male nurse until October 1889, when Edward Wilkins left. From that time until Whitman's death in March 1892 "Warry" remained with Whitman, was devoted to him, and was in turn Whitman's favorite among his nurses. (See Gay Wilson Allen, *The Solitary Singer*, pp. 519, 535; and Elizabeth Leavitt Keller, *Walt Whitman in Mickle Street* [New York, 1921], pp. 119 ff.)

2582. For Ernest Rhys, see footnotes 2510 and 2575.

2583. Horace Traubel reported in *With Walt Whitman in Camden*, I, 227, that Whitman said: "My brother Jeff, from St. Louis — civil engineer there: until nine months ago for some time in the Water Department — has been here today." He then added that none of his "people," even his mother, "ever had any time for Leaves of Grass — thought it more than an ordinary piece of work, if that."

here – the bottle of wine – talk ab't

half rainy

Donnelly's "Cryptogram" lush warm ∧ day[2584]

[348]

[Name and address in pencil, correction in ink:]

Sidney H Morse[2585]

665 W Lake St   Chicago

~~21 Laflin street~~   Ill

R Pearsall Smith

44 Grosvenor Road

Westminster Embankment   S W

London   England [2586]

Geo: Rush, Jr   ⎛ call'd Sept: 2 '89
                  ⎝ his imp't expired

Concordville, Delaware Co:

Pa

County Prison   Untried Department

sent him

Spec:Days in W<u>m</u>   Ingram   call'd Aug: 3 '88

America   Telford

Bucks Co:

Penn[2587]

2584. The note to George Ferguson the printer of the upcoming *November Boughs* is missing; the visit at 328 Mickle Street by Thomas B. Harned, William Sloane Kennedy, and Horace Traubel, and their discussion of Ignatius Donnelly's book, *The Great Cryptogram* (on the authorship of Shakespeare's plays) is discussed in more detail in *With Walt Whitman in Camden,* I, 233–236. It was Whitman's belief "that the Shakespearean plays were written by another hand than Shaksper's," though he did not know whose.

2585. Sidney H. Morse, the sculptor who had been working on a sculpture of Whitman all fall at Mickle Street, had recently (in April, see above) sent a bust of Elias Hicks, and at this time Whitman was thinking of having the Morse plaster bust of Whitman cast in bronze: see a reproduction of the bust and the poet's comments in *With Walt Whitman in Camden,* I, 198–199.

2586. Robert Pearsall Smith, one of the most wealthy friends in Philadelphia, who was quite ill early in May (see *The Correspondence of Walt Whitman,* IV, 169–170), seems to have joined his family in London; he talked at length to Horace Traubel about them on 18 May 1888 (see *With Walt Whitman in Camden,* I, 172–173).

2587. The left-hand pages of Whitman's *Daybook* were apt, on occasion, to get ahead of the right-hand pages. Here, for example, is a visit of 3 August 1888 by William Ingram (see footnote 2499), a visit not recorded below under this date. Whitman gave him a copy of *Specimen Days,* which Ingram sent to George Rush, Jr., of Concordville, Delaware County, Pennsylvania, who was a prisoner in Bucks County, Pennsylvania, jail. On 10 August 1888, Ingram wrote Whitman (letter in the Ohio Wesleyan University Library) about Rush and his thanks for the book; and on 2 September 1889 (see that date in the *Daybook,* below) Rush visited Whitman. See *The Correspondence of Walt Whitman,* IV, 200n.

[349]

June   Camden   1888
4 bad spell – a slight shock (or two or three
   shocks) of paralysis – Dr B says vertigo[2588]

---

5 am having <u>Nov</u>: <u>Boughs</u> put in type
   & electrotyped at Ferguson Bros: foundry
   15 North 7ᵗʰ St. Philadelphia[2589]
                                three
   Dr Bucke here – (linger'd sick over ~~two~~ ∧mo's
                                after this[2590]

---

6 Harry Stafford here – warm weather

---

   were laid up here 328 Mickle Street
                        September
   all thro' June, July, & August ∧ '88
                        imprison'd in the room
   sick in my 2ᵈ story room∧ – very
   weak (bodily) & feeble, week after week
   – hardly out in the 2ᵈ story entry
   am writing this Sept: 5 '88 [2591]
   Herbert Gilchrist has arrived – just rec'd
   note from him Lafayette Hotel – Phila:[2592]
   – Mrs: Davis has just gone to bank for me

2588. It will be noticed that Whitman made no entry for 31 May or 1–3 June 1888, in which he might well have mentioned the reception at Thomas B. Harned for the poet's 69th birthday. See Horace Traubel's *With Walt Whitman in Camden*, I, 238–242, for activities of that day; as for this illness in June, see the letters to William D. O'Connor and William Sloane Kennedy, *The Correspondence of Walt Whitman*, IV, 172–173.

2589. A number of previous entries in the *Daybook* have referred to Whitman and Ferguson Brothers, the printers of *November Boughs,* which was not actually published until about 6 October 1888. One of the reasons for the delay was that Whitman wanted "Army Hospitals and Cases: Memoranda at the Time, 1863–66" to appear first in *The Century Magazine,* which it did in October 1888 (XXXVI, 825–830), before being included in *November Boughs* as "Last of the War Cases" (see *Prose Works 1892,* II, 614–626).

2590. There is no question that Whitman was ill at this time, but though he wrote very little in his *Daybook,* he wrote 17 letters in June and 31 in July, many of them to Dr Richard Maurice Bucke, William D. O'Connor, Mary Smith Costelloe, and William Sloane Kennedy; so we do know what he was doing during this period: see *The Correspondence of Walt Whitman,* IV, 172–195, plus a very detailed account in Horace Traubel's *With Walt Whitman in Camden,* I, 242–468; and II, 1–69 (through July 1888).

2591. This is an unusual procedure for writing in the *Daybook.*

2592. Herbert Gilchrist's arrival was in September, not June 1888: see Whitman's letter to Susan Stafford, 5 September 1888 in *The Correspondence of Walt Whitman,* IV, 205–206. This same letter mentions Mrs Mary Davis's visit to the bank that day: see next line of the *Daybook.*

– The printing &c. (at Ferguson's) goes on well

– Horace Traubel is invaluable to me.[2593]

[350]

[On card, not in WW's hand:]

Oldach and Co

1215 Filbert

Phila.[2594]

[In WW's hand on small bit of a letterhead of Herald Bureau / No. 112 South Sixth Street / Philadelphia, Pa.:] [2595]

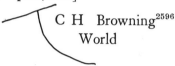

C H Browning[2596]

World

[351]

July   Camden   1888

3 – <u>Paid</u> Ferguson Bros: <u>fifty dollars</u>[2597]

to feel

23 – Am beginning∧ my<u>self</u> a little – eat my

meals quite heartily[2598] – last yesterday fix'd

2593. No one reading *With Walt Whitman in Camden* can doubt this about Traubel.

2594. Frederick Oldach was the binder of *November Boughs*: see Whitman's letter to him, 22 November 1888, in *The Correspondence of Walt Whitman*, IV, 225; the address is given as 1215 Market Street in Whitman's letter of 27 November (*ibid.*, IV, 239) and 1215 Filbert Street on 15 February 1889 (*ibid.*, IV, 290).

2595. Whitman's last poem in the New York *Herald*, under the special arrangement, was "The Calming Thought of All" on 27 May 1888; but on 12 August 1888 (see also 8 August) he did have another poem in the *Herald*, "Over and Through the Burial Chant," now called "Interpolation Sounds," having to do with General Philip Sheridan's burial (see *Leaves of Grass*, Comprehensive Reader's Edition, p. 545).

2596. C. H. Browning was in the Philadelphia office of the New York *Herald*; he wrote Whitman on 15 August 1888 for an opinion on a poem (see the letter in *With Walt Whitman in Camden*, II, 146–147, and Whitman's reaction), and a few days earlier Browning had asked Whitman for something on General Sheridan (see *ibid.*, II, 97, and footnote 2595, above). Whitman described Browning as "a fine, dark-browed, vital, affectionate sort of man — a newspaper man made of the real stuff" (*ibid.*, II, 126). Browning called on Whitman on 3 September 1888 (see *ibid.*, II, 249), which may be when the poet wrote his name here; however, the word "World" written below the name suggests that it was written in 1889 when Browning became the Philadelphia man for the New York *World* and got Whitman to write a poem on the Johnstown flood (see *ibid.*, V, 265–267, and "A Voice from Death," New York *World*, 7 June 1889, in *Leaves of Grass*, Comprehensive Reader's Edition, pp. 551–553).

2597. This is also recorded below in the *Daybook* under "Expenses on the two Books / 'November Boughs' & the big Book" for 1888.

2598. In Whitman's letters and in his talks with Horace Traubel there is a great deal about his illness, though he simply ceased to write anything at all in the *Daybook* for much of June and three weeks in July; then about mid-July in correspondence and *With Walt Whitman in Camden*, I, 464–468, and II, 1 ff., Whitman felt greatly improved.

up the "Elias Hicks" memoranda to make
a paper (such as it is) for the printers
for N<u>ov</u>: <u>Boughs</u>. & sent it off to

N. B's

them, to-day — cut [?] ~~its~~ ∧ last pages.[2599]
– I now make a memorandum
~~for George Fox~~ for same purpose.

with

– Concluding "George <u>Fox</u> (~~&~~∧ <u>Shakspere</u>")" [2600]

29∧ have finished <u>all</u> <u>the</u> <u>copy</u> for N<u>ov</u>:
<u>Boughs</u> ("Last of the War Cases," "Elias
Hicks" and "George Fox (& Shakspere)")

final

and am reading the ~~concluding~~ proofs.[2601]

Wednesday   left the Goodenoughs &
Aug: 1   Ed has ∧ gone to board at
             Blackwoodtown, Camden Co:
             annex of Insane Asylum,
             (Mrs. Nichols) – $3.50 a week –
             (I paid $45:50 3 mo's advance)

who went with him
back

Lou and Jessie ∧ were here ∧ noon day.

(Mr. Bennett drove all.)

to-day – they went   [?]e ∧ with him.
             Ed
             ~~He~~ has a good little bedroom to himself –

2599. As early as 5 April 1887, Whitman said he was writing his paper on Elias Hicks (see *The Correspondence of Walt Whitman*, IV, 79); on 11 July 1888 he wrote Dr R. M. Bucke, "I am trying to get the E H paper presentable — but hard work — but I keep at it obstinately" (*ibid.*, IV, 184; see also IV, 189, 191, 194, 198, 199 ["very hurried & scratchy paper on 'Elias Hicks' — done mostly when I was sickest all"], 201, 205, 206, 210). The New York *Herald* of 17 September 1888 had a piece by Whitman of one paragraph about Hicks from *November Boughs*. Hicks is mentioned more than eighty times in Horace Traubel's *With Walt Whitman in Camden*, especially in the first two volumes, which cover 28 March to 31 October 1888. (See footnote 2517, above.) For *November Boughs*, see footnote 2589.

2600. Whitman's letter of 24 July 1888 to Dr R. M. Bucke reads: "I have put together the *Elias Hicks* fragments last night & sent off the 'paper' to the printer — not knowing how it will look in print — but with some fear & trembling — then three or so pages (all done now) on *George Fox* — evolutionary on the E H piece — & the *Nov. Boughs* will be *done*" (*The Correspondence of Walt Whitman*, IV, 191). "George Fox (and Shakspere)" was published in *November Boughs*, probably intended as a subdivision of "Elias Hicks": see *Prose Works 1892*, II, 649–653.

2601. Yet the book was not published until October (see footnote 2589).

– has good table – washing – bath – &c.
– good care, superintendence, &c.[2602]

[352]

I saw the (then) young Prince of Wales, riding
(debuting   on Broadway, New York, Oct. 11, 1860.[2603]
arriving)

[Written on a slip, four lines in pencil not in WW's hand:]

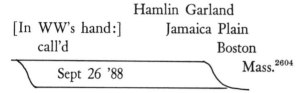

Hamlin Garland
[In WW's hand:]   Jamaica Plain
call'd   Boston
Sept 26 '88   Mass.[2604]

2602. Edward Whitman, the poet's feeble-minded younger brother, was constantly on his mind; as he told Horace Traubel on 29 July 1888: "I have for years done so many things with reference to Eddy — have stinted, spared, saved, put by, cherished, watched — so that I might not slip cable some day with him unprovided for. Eddy is helpless: has been at Moorestown — is shortly to go elsewhere: was a poor, stunted boy almost from the first. He had the convulsions — it was all up with him — the infernal, damnable, fits, that left him not half himself from that time on forever" (*With Walt Whitman in Camden*, II, 56–57). As Whitman writes here in his *Daybook* and as he told Mrs Susan Stafford on 22 August 1888 (*The Correspondence of Walt Whitman*, IV, 201–202), Eddy was moved from Mr and Mrs Goodenough's in Moorestown, New Jersey, by Louisa Whitman and Jessie (Whitman's niece from St. Louis) to the Insane Asylum in Blackwoodtown, New Jersey; the poet continued to pay all of Eddy's expenses. Below, under the date of 4 September, Whitman reports that Mrs Mary Davis and Warren Fritzinger (his housekeeper and male nurse) visited Edward and found him "to be all right & as happy as is to be expected." Eddy outlived his brother Walt by just eight months, dying on 30 November 1892 at the age of 57.

2603. One is curious to know why this sentence is here about seeing the Prince of Wales in 1860. The only other reference to the Prince is in *Specimen Days* under "Broadway Sights," where Whitman writes that on Broadway he saw "during those times ['50 to '60], Andrew Jackson, Webster, Clay, Seward, Martin Van Buren, filibuster Walker, Kossuth, Fitz Greene Halleck, Bryant, the Prince of Wales, Charles Dickens, the first Japanese ambassadors, and lots of other celebrities of the time" (*Prose Works 1892*, I, 17).

2604. Hamlin Garland (1860–1940), Wisconsin-born novelist of the Middle Border, first wrote to Whitman on 19 April 1888 when he was giving a series of lectures in Boston on "Literature of Democracy," analyzing life here "in accordance with the principles you [Whitman] have taught." He told Whitman he found many friends, sympathizers and converts to his doctrines; they "find your poems mainly irresistible in effect" and acknowledge "their power and beauty" (the letter, from the Feinberg Collection, is quoted in part in *The Correspondence of Walt Whitman*, IV, 167n). Garland was among the three who visited Whitman on 26 September 1888 (see entry below of that date), and the poet talked about him with Traubel: "I am more than favorably impressed with Garland. He has a good voice — is almost Emersonee — has belly — some would say, guts . . . the good kind; has voice, power, manliness — has chest-tones in his talk which attract me: I am very sensitive to certain things like those in a man. Garland seemed to be enthusiastic about Leaves of Grass" (*With Walt Whitman in Camden*, II, 384). In October 1888 Garland began a series of twelve lectures in Waltham on "Walt Whitman's Message," and wrote the poet, "At the earliest possible moment I intend to get that article into shape concerning your work as a landscapist" (*ibid.*, II, 509), on which Whitman commented to Traubel, "Garland seems to be getting actively on our side: he seems to swallow the lump without gagging over it" (*ibid.*, II, 510). Garland also appears to have influenced William Dean Howells to have a more mellow attitude toward Whitman's poetry: Garland wrote Whitman on 24 October 1888 that Howells "spoke of you again with a good deal of feeling" (*ibid.*, II, 530), but of Howells's review of No-

Speaks
of Joseph E Chamberlain on the Transcript[2605]
Carlyle died Feb: 5, 1881, 85 years old
Emerson died April 27, 1882, aged 79 [2606]

[353]

August   Camden   1888
3 here sitting up in big chair – have now been
  sick here seven weeks – now partially better[2607]
  – the copy for printers for <u>Nov: Boughs</u>
  has all given out – finish'd – I am reading
  the last proofs – will make 140 pages.[2608]

pretty hot weather, 1st 2d, 3d, 4, 5 [2609]
    was
  (been pretty moderate – even cool – most all
  July) — the etching from S Hollyer[2610]
  rec'd – I rather like it – Miss Elizabeth
  Porter Goulds "Death Poetry of W W" in
                              paper[2611]

vember Boughs in the February 1889 Harper's Monthly, Whitman said it was "so-so" and
"friendly" but (according to Traubel) "didn't in the least warm up over it" (With Walt
Whitman in Camden, IV, 17). Garland himself wrote about November Boughs in the Boston
Transcript on 15 November 1888 (see his letters to Whitman in With Walt Whitman in
Camden, III, 67 and 114), a "notice" which he called "simply a good word which will allay
if possible some of the antagonism which still exists toward your work." Garland is mentioned
more than fifty times in Traubel's volumes and more than fifteen times in Whitman letters;
and the poet's three brief letters to the young novelist are in The Correspondence of Walt
Whitman, IV, 226, 234–235, and 268.
    2605. Chamberlain, of the Boston Evening Transcript, wrote "My dear Poet" on 5
March 1889 about a reading of Whitman poems by women and men and a discussion, and
the sentence that struck Whitman in his letter was "Neither you nor the Leaves of Grass are
on trial any more" (With Walt Whitman in Camden, IV, 320–321).
    2606. Carlyle and Emerson are mentioned here because at this time Whitman had been
reading James Anthony Froude's two volumes on Carlyle (1882 and 1884) and James Elliot
Cabot's A Memoir of Ralph Waldo Emerson (1887): see The Correspondence of Walt Whitman, IV, 208; and With Walt Whitman in Camden, II, 251–252.
    2607. Whitman said just about the same thing to Dr R. M. Bucke: see The Correspond-
ence of Walt Whitman, IV, 195–197.
    2608. As previous entries and several footnotes above indicate, Whitman was fussing a
good deal over November Boughs, two months before publication.
    2609. Letters to Mary Smith Costelloe, Dr R. M. Bucke, and William D. O'Connor seem
to be almost entirely on the weather and the heat: see The Correspondence of Walt Whitman,
IV, 196–197.
    2610. This etching by Samuel Hollyer (from a photo Mary Smith Costelloe called
the Lear, reproduced in The Correspondence of Walt Whitman, IV, foll. p. 278) is mentioned
in the Daybook entry for 6 April 1888; see also footnote 2562.
    2611. Elizabeth Porter Gould's "Walt Whitman Among the Soldiers" was published
in The Critic, 28 May 1887; it was reprinted in Gems from Walt Whitman (Philadelphia:
David McKay, 1889), pp. 53–58, which she edited. She was also the author of "Anne Gilchrist

– young Dr Mitchell comes – [2612]

5

Sunday, 5th – hot – a frantic little thunder & light-
ning storm last night, (10, 11) – thunder near[2613]

19th Sunday – Aunt Mary died 6 a m[2614]
sent "Antiquary" to Hannah[2615]

21 David McKay here[2616]

Still remain in the sick room

23[d] Thursday – old Aunt Mary buried [2617]

cool temperature

Sept 4 – Mrs Davis and Warren went down to
Blackwoodtown to see Ed – he seems to

and Walt Whitman," *Current Literature,* December 1900, published as a book (Philadelphia: David McKay, 1900); the paper in which she published "Death Poetry of Walt Whitman" is not identified. Whitman told Horace Traubel he was indifferent about Miss Gould's *Gems:* "while I don't interfere I have no vehement desire to see the project furthered." He later added: "These gems, extracts, specimens, tid-bits, brilliants, sparkles, chippings — oh, they are all wearisome: they might go with some books: yes, they fit with some books — some books fit with them: but Leaves of Grass is different — yields nothing to the seeker for sensations" (*With Walt Whitman in Camden,* III, 395–396; see also III, 405, and Whitman's letter to David McKay, *The Correspondence of Walt Whitman,* IV, 257).

2612. "Young Dr Mitchell" is Dr J. K. Mitchell, the son of Dr S. Weir Mitchell, who attended Whitman during Dr William Osler's absence beginning of 8 July 1888; Whitman told Traubel: "The young man Mitchell did not take me by storm — he did not impress me . . . I know J. K.'s father somewhat — Weir: he is of the intellectual type — a scholar, writer, and all that: very good — an adept: very important in his sphere — a little bitter I should say — a little bitter — touched just a touch by the frosts of culture, society, worldliness — as how few are not!" (*With Walt Whitman in Camden,* I, 433, 454–455).

2613. Everyone, even great poets, talks of the weather, as is obvious to the reader of Whitman's *Daybook* or his *Correspondence.*

2614. "Aunt Mary" was not really Whitman's aunt but an old woman who often came to 328 Mickle Street to help Mrs Mary Davis, Whitman's housekeeper. On 17 August 1888 she had a stroke in Whitman's kitchen, and she was taken home; Traubel said that Whitman was "concerned but not worried," and when she died the poet remarked, "Poverty, old age, trouble, the severe heat — and then the finish! The extreme poor suffer extra burdens of life — carry an unfair load. Some day we will get all that fixed right in the world — some day after many days" — *With Walt Whitman in Camden,* II, 152, 157, 164, 168, 188. The old lady was buried on 23 August (see entry below).

2615. I cannot identify this issue of the "Antiquary" which Whitman sent to his sister, Hannah Heyde; if a letter accompanied it, it too is missing.

2616. Whitman's publisher David McKay talked to him about "the little book," *November Boughs,* which he was to publish a few weeks hence: see Gay Wilson Allen, *The Solitary Singer,* pp. 529–531, for a summary, but see Horace Traubel, *With Walt Whitman in Camden,* II, 174–176, about that day's visit. Traubel did not feel that Whitman was particularly sick, merely says, "W. got up not feeling extra well" (*ibid.,* II, 172).

2617. For "Aunt Mary," see footnote 2614.

be all right & as happy as is to be expected.[2618]

Sept: 5 – Mrs Davis has drawn $50 for me from the
    bank (see back two leaves) – & has now gone
    to the City Hall to pay my taxes[2619]
paid Big tax bill 1888 $24:47 – paid – (folio 145–3ᵈ)
    also old culvert tax 9.62 paid

Jessie here[2620]   I paid $240.10

                              for paper[2621]

Sept 6 – cold wave

[354]

[On a calling card, not in WW's hand:]
                    5 to 6 P. M.
                    1708 Chestnut

[The card is printed: Herbert Harlakenden Gilchrist. / 12 Well Road, /
Hempstead / The Arts Club, 17, Hanover Square /.[2622] Clipped from a
newspaper: Charles T. Dillingham, / 718 and 720 Broadway, N. Y. /.[2623]
Another card printed: J. H. Johnston, / Diamond Merchant, / 17 Union
Square, (West),/ Cor. Broadway and Fifteenth Street./.]
[In WW's hand:]

John H Johnston   ⎫   305 East 17ᵗʰ St
Alma Calder Johnston   ⎬   New York City
                       ⎭   (Sept. '88)[2624]

2618. For this visit to Whitman's brother, see footnote 2602.

2619. In the back of the *Daybook* Whitman used the pages for an account book for 1888 and 1889: "*Bills, Moneys, &c: &c: paid out*". But some of his data goes back to 1873.

2620. Jessie Whitman, daughter of Jeff (Whitman's brother in St. Louis), was staying with Louisa and George, another brother of the poet; she and Louisa took Eddy to Blackwoodtown on 1 August 1888 (see entry, above, and footnote 2602).

2621. This is also recorded as paid to Alexander Balfour of Philadelphia, for the paper to be used in *November Boughs,* being printed at this time.

2622. Herbert Gilchrist, painter and son of Anne Gilchrist, "has arrived all right," Whitman wrote Mrs Susan Stafford on 5 September 1888; he was staying in Philadelphia, had paid Whitman a short visit, and planned to be painting "here for a year to come" (*The Correspondence of Walt Whitman,* IV, 205–206). Gilchrist actually stayed much longer, settling in Long Island in the 1890's and attempting to support himself, unsuccessfully, as an artist. His relationship with Whitman waned, their correspondence dwindled, and, says Harrison S. Morris in *Walt Whitman: A Brief Biography with Reminiscences* (Cambridge: Harvard University Press, 1929), pp. 83–84, "In the end he snuffed out his career, like a comedian who hides his grief under a courageous smile." Incidentally, there are more than a hundred references to Herbert Gilchrist in Traubel's five volumes.

2623. Charles T. Dillingham was a wholesale bookseller who ordered a copy of *Leaves of Grass* from Whitman on 5 September 1879 (see entry of that date, above).

2624. John H. Johnston and his wife Alma were dear New York friends of Whitman's whom he stayed with in New York; Johnston was preparing a piece on "Walt Whitman and

[Clipped from a newspaper: McKay's Old Book Store / 23 South Ninth Street. /. Another clipping is an ad of William Wiler, manufacturer of stair-rods, step-plates, brass bedsteads, and cribs, in Philadelphia.][2625]
[Three addresses in WW's hand:]
Horace Traubel
    509 Arch st
       Camden[2626]

E C Stedman
44 East 26ᵗʰ St
  N Y City

                    T W Mather
         Sheffield S S   Yale College
                    New Haven Conn

W L Shoemaker
    3116 P street
       Georgetown
          D C

[355]

September   1888   Camden ⟨ short literary
6 sent "Elias Hicks" to Herald   notice in Herald
                                  Sept 17 '88 [2627]

still staying altogether in my sick room – 2ᵈ story[2628]

7 sold Nettie & the Phaeton to Mr Corning $130 [2629]
      cold weather – 8, 9, moderate

His Friends" and had asked Dr R. M. Bucke for a portrait of himself: see *The Correspondence of Walt Whitman,* IV, 215 and 222n, and *With Walt Whitman in Camden,* II, 423. Whitman expected to see Alma Johnston 21 or 22 September 1888.

2625. These seem to be simply companies from which Whitman wanted to buy what they sold. Connection between McKay's bookshop and David McKay?

2626. Horace Traubel and Whitman were so closely in touch at this time, one wonders why he bothered to write his address here; Edmund C. Stedman (whose address is written below) had sent Traubel, on 8 September 1888, proofsheets of the passages from Whitman's poetry he had selected for his *Library of American Literature:* see the letter in *With Walt Whitman in Camden,* II, 301, and the poet's brief comment to Dr R. M. Bucke in *The Correspondence of Walt Whitman,* IV, 210. The third address here in the *Daybook,* W. L. Shoemaker's, is of a man who had sent Whitman the *Yonkers Gazette* with two of his sonnets (see footnote 2446). The fourth address on this page, T. W. Mather's, has to do with a wood engraving Whitman wanted to use in his *Complete Poetry & Prose,* which David McKay was publishing soon: see *With Walt Whitman in Camden,* II, 465; and *The Correspondence of Walt Whitman,* IV, 210.

2627. This "short literary notice" was a paragraph about Hicks in the New York *Herald* in a piece about *November Boughs* (see footnote 2599, above). The letter to the *Herald* is in *The Correspondence of Walt Whitman,* IV, 206.

2628. Whitman may have been in his "sick room" but Horace Traubel said nothing whatever about Whitman being ill on this day's entry in *With Walt Whitman in Camden,* II, 267–273.

2629. For Whitman's remarks on selling his horse and buggy to the Rev. J. Leonard

10 sent Cent: Ed'n Two Vols: by Express to
            Jacob Klein, lawyer, rooms 5, 6 & 7
                                    rec'd
        506 Olive st.   St Louis Mo. ∧ paid $10 [2630]

Horace bro't me the printed sheets complete
        "November Boughs" 140 pp.   look good [2631]

11 sent to Librarian Congress for Copyright
        for Nov: Boughs ..... rec'd 22ᵈ Sept

        Paid $1.47 for "Press" [2632]
12 paid Ferguson $246:98 by check[2633]

13ᵗʰ paid W W Bennet $22:20 in   [in pencil]
        full [2634]   [in pencil]

16ᵗʰ, 17ᵗʰ & 18ᵗʰ – bad days – depression low

19 – Still kept closely in my sick room
        2ᵈ story 328 Mickle
    – easier a little[2635]

21 short visit from John Burroughs
    – (bright weather)
            he left this morning[2636] – bad day
                            in my health

Corning, see *With Walt Whitman in Camden,* II, 273–274; and *The Correspondence of Walt Whitman,* IV, 204, 206.

2630. For Whitman's letters to Jacob Klein, see *The Correspondence of Walt Whitman,* IV, 207 and 211; in *With Walt Whitman in Camden,* II, 337, Whitman mentions "a spurious edition of the Leaves," Klein had somehow got.

2631. Whitman's phrase here, "look good," is somewhat in contrast to Horace Traubel's report of the poet's "undisguised exhilaration" with *November Boughs:* "Horace — the deed is done! My blood, your blood, went to the making of this book! Some men go to the North Pole to do things — some go to wars — some trade and swindle: we just stay where we were and make a book!" And he continued in this vein at some length: see *With Walt Whitman in Camden,* II, 294.

2632. For his subscription to the Philadelphia *Press.*

2633. For printing *November Boughs.*

2634. For the monthly care of Whitman's horse Nettie, which had just been sold (see footnote 2629).

2635. Horace Traubel writes of these "bad days," "quite indisposed," "feeling bum," and 17 September "one of his [Whitman's] very worst days," and "not improved" on the 18th; on 19 September Whitman was "bright though somewhat fagged" (*With Walt Whitman in Camden,* II, 317, 322, 328, 334, 339, 344).

2636. John Burroughs had actually visited Whitman on 19 September 1888 (he was staying with Thomas B. Harned); on the 20th Whitman was feeling so bad that he did not see Burroughs or anyone else (except Traubel and Mary Davis, who were taking care of

piece in N Y Sunday Herald Sept 23
    "Walt Whitman's Words" [2637]

26 – Cooler weather – sunny to-day
    Mr Summers   Hamlin Garland   Dr Osler[2638]
    English MP   Boston

[356]

[Addresses in WW's hand on left; clipping on right of "List of Dates and Events of the Earlier / Settlers of Long Island."]

saw the Prince of Wales
    Broadway N Y. 1860 [2639]

W A Musgrove[2640]

Fred S Ryman[2641]
    42 Bradford st
    Boston Mass:

him); and on the 21st Burroughs started off for Sea Bright: *With Walt Whitman in Camden*, II, 344, 350, 356. Whitman wrote to Dr R. M. Bucke 22 September that Burroughs had been to see him, "the good hearty affectionate nature-scented fellow, very welcome — he left yesterday en route to visit Johnson (Century staff) at Sea Girt, on the N J sea coast . . ." (*The Correspondence of Walt Whitman*, IV, 214); and Burroughs wrote in his journal that he and Whitman kissed and parted, "probably for the last time. I think he has in his own mind given up the fight, and awaits the end" (*ibid.*, IV, 214n).

2637. "Walt Whitman's Words," New York *Sunday Herald*, 23 September 1888: for Whitman's reaction to this unsigned column, see *With Walt Whitman in Camden*, II, 385.

2638. William Summers, the British Member of Parliament, is mentioned in Whitman's letter to Dr R. M. Bucke in *The Correspondence of Walt Whitman*, IV, 215–216, and in Horace Traubel, *With Walt Whitman in Camden*, II, 384–385, 390–391: "Summers hit me hard. He made a grand show-up — had fine ways — was young, strong, optimistic," and they talked about Gladstone and Ireland. For Hamlin Garland, the second visitor that day, see *With Walt Whitman in Camden*, II, 383–384, and footnote 2604, above. Dr William Osler, now back in Philadelphia, is mentioned in the same pages of Traubel and in footnotes 2054 and 2161.

2639. This is the second time within a few pages that Whitman mentions seeing the Prince of Wales on Broadway in 1860 (see footnote 2603).

2640. W. A. Musgrove was Whitman's nurse from 15 July until 5 November 1888; Whitman found him "kind active & considerate all through" (see *The Correspondence of Walt Whitman*, IV, 230–231), but Horace Traubel did not like him; he was replaced by a younger man, Edward Wilkins, largely because Thomas B. Harned and Dr R. M. Bucke wanted a change: "I do not hear good accounts of your present nurse," Dr Bucke wrote Whitman on 24 October 1888 (*With Walt Whitman in Camden*, II, 536). Musgrave was "sort o' *vexed* ab't it all," said Whitman (*The Correspondence of Walt Whitman*, IV, 231), who did not want to hurt Musgrave's though the poet was "not indisposed to a change" (*With Walt Whitman in Camdem*, II, 537). Nevertheless, Musgrave felt no ill will toward Whitman and visited him on 8 May 1889: "I have a friendly feeling toward him," Whitman told Dr Bucke (*The Correspondence of Walt Whitman*, IV, 333).

2641. Fred S. Ryman sent Whitman birthday greetings on 31 May 1888 (letter in the Feinberg Collection), and he commented on it to Traubel: "I got a card from Ryman, of Boston, containing photographs and a bit of four-leaved clover" (*With Walt Whitman in Camden*, I, 249).

Miss E P Gould
   131 ~~Chelsea~~
      Chestnut street
         Chelsea Mass:[2642]

---

ample Book-store &c – new
   W H Lowdermilk & Co:
     1424 F street
Dec: '88   Washington D C [2643]

Louis W$^{\underline{m}}$ Ingram[2644]
   Middleton
      Washington Co:
        Oregon
[Three lines in red ink:]
Motalla
  Corner
Clackamas Co:

S Morris Waln
     Attorney &c
530 Locust st
    Phila[2645]

[357]

Sept: and October – 1888   Camden
  28– the new stove in my 2^{d} story front room
     pain in my breast, diaphragm & abdomen[2646]

Oct: 1 – the Century prints "Army Hospitals & Cases" [2647]

    2642. For Miss Elizabeth Porter Gould, see footnote 2611.
    2643. Lowdermilk's bookstore in Washington was still in business in 1968, but ceased operation the next year.
    2644. Louis William Ingram may well be a son or related to William Ingram (see footnote 2499), who visited the poet often and was well liked by Whitman — "the best salt of the earth: he is the finest sample of the democrat" (*With Walt Whitman in Camden*, II, 320).
    2645. S. Morris Waln was Mrs Mary Davis's lawyer in her suit against William H. Duckett for a large unpaid boarding bill (see footnote 2687, below).
    2646. This is just about what Whitman wrote Dr R. M. Bucke on 1 October 1888, referring to his pains and to the new stove: "better & larger, for wood, the same style as the old one, but an improvement — I like it —" (*The Correspondence of Walt Whitman*, IV, 217).
    2647. This piece in the *Century Illustrated Monthly Review*, XXXVI (October 1888), 825–830, was the one Whitman was waiting to see published so he could include "Last of

Lou here – the proposition for Ed: in the
Media institution[2648]

I feel easier to-day than for a week

" 7 still in the sick room – Mickle street[2649]
        November Boughs   out[2650]

I send copies to
 Dr Bucke 2 copies
Wm O'Connor
W S Kennedy
T B Harned   3 copies
Sister Lou
Wm Ingram

(Mr Corning
 Jerome Buck, lawyer
    (Mr Harned's copies)
Mrs H L Heyde
 Mrs. Davis
Mrs Wetherbee   bo't
W D Howells
Mrs Costelloe
Anna Montgomerie
            by Horace
 Mr Aldrich   bot
Dr Bringham, Burl'ton
Mrs. Leach   "
Harry Stafford   [in pencil]
Tom Donaldson 10 copies
Dr McAlister

bo't Dr Gubbins   [in pencil]
 "   Ed Lindell
   Sidney Morse
   J V Blake
   E C Stedman
   John Burroughs
   Williamson N Y
   Frank Williams
   Dr Conner (bo't)
Hamlin Garland
Talcott Williams
Mrs Mary E Van Nostrand
Mrs. Brotherton   bot
      553 N 16th st Phila
Herbert Gilchrist
Edw Carpenter   [in pencil]
Dr Osler   [in pencil]
Dr Wharton   [in pencil]
Dr Walsh
Ed Stafford (bot)
J H Johnston
R J Hinton

---

the War Cases" (his new title for it) in *November Boughs*: see footnote 2859, above; *The Correspondence of Walt Whitman*, IV, 216, 217; and Horace Traubel, *With Walt Whitman in Camden*, II, 411 ("I was in honor bound to keep back November Boughs until the magazine was out").

2648. This has to do with Whitman's sister-in-law Louisa and the care for his brother Eddy: see footnote 2602.

2649. In Traubel's *With Walt Whitman in Camden*, II, 443; in his letters in *The Correspondence of Walt Whitman*, IV, 220; and here in the *Daybook*, the story is similar: his health is the same, no worse, but not much better. However, he was to live for about three and a half more years.

2650. *November Boughs* was actually ready for Whitman on 4 October 1888, when Horace Traubel said he brought in 25 copies to Mickle Street (*With Walt Whitman in Camden*, II, 427); and Whitman inscribed one to Dr R. M. Bucke and spoke of David McKay publishing it. Of the 40 people Whitman has listed here, to whom he sent copies of the

[358]

[Blank]

[359]

October   1888   Camden
                   say
8   – Jessie here to ∧ good bye – she leaves
      Wednesday night for St Louis[2651]

_____

9 David McKay calls & pays me $106.13
—————————————————— for royalty[2652]

book, most can be easily identified: his two sisters, Mrs Hannah Heyde and Mrs Mary Van Nostrand; his sister-in-law, Louisa Whitman; his very closest friends, Dr R. M. Bucke, William Douglas O'Connor, William Sloane Kennedy, Thomas B. Harned, young Harry Stafford, Mrs Mary Smith Costelloe, Thomas Donaldson (why 10 copies?), Sidney Morse (the sculptor, whom he had come to admire), John Burroughs, Talcott Williams, the artist Herbert Gilchrist, and John H. Johnston; William Imgram and the Rev. J. Leonard Corning both visited Whitman often during this period; Mrs Mary Davis was Whitman's housekeeper; Mrs Wetherby, who bought a copy, cannot be identified; of the six others who bought copies, Mr Aldrich is most likely the author Thomas Bailey Aldrich (1836–1907), editor of the *Atlantic Monthly* at this time (1881–1890), who was to buy *Complete Poems & Prose* in March 1889 for $25 (see *The Correspondence of Walt Whitman*, IV, 309), Dr Gubbins and Dr Conner are not identifiable, Ed Lindell is the Captain Respegius Edward Lindell of the Camden ferries who also played the viola (see footnote 76) and was a long-time friend, Ed. Stafford is Edwin, Harry's brother from whom Whitman bought his horse Nettie on 28 March 1886, and Mrs Brotherton is a Quaker lady who came to see Whitman on 30 November 1888 because she was attracted by his piece on Elias Hicks (see *With Walt Whitman in Camden*, III, 209); William Dean Howells (see footnote 2604) was to review *November Boughs* in *Harper's Monthly*, February 1889; Anne Montgomerie on 28 May 1891 was to marry Horace Traubel; Dr Bringham and Mrs Leach were from Burlington, where Whitman's brother George and his wife Louisa lived, so one may presume they were friends of the Whitmans; Dr Alexander McAlister, Dr William Osler, Dr Wharton, and Dr Walsh are all physicians who were looking in on Whitman at this time; Jerome Buck was a lawyer friend of Thomas B. Harned (see his enthusiastic letter of praise, 16 October 1888, in *With Walt Whitman in Camden*, II, 501); Edmund Clarence Stedman, Hamlin Garland, and Edward Carpenter need little comment to readers of this *Daybook*; the Rev. James Vila Blake was a Unitarian minister in Chicago and a friend of Sidney Morse, who hoped Blake would review *November Boughs* in *Unity* (see *With Walt Whitman in Camden*, II, 104, 272, 404, 422, 484, 487, 510); Blake visited Whitman on 28 March 1889; Francis Howard (Frank) Williams (see footnote 1765) wrote "The Poetry of Walt Whitman: A Rejoinder" in *The American*, about which the poet commented to Horace Traubel on 17 September 1888 (see *With Walt Whitman in Camden*, II, 336); and the final name on this list, that of Colonel Richard J. Hinton (see footnote 249), whose relationship with Whitman goes back to his days in Washington hospitals, though his name had been missing from the *Daybook* for some time lately; on 28 September 1888 Whitman said of him: "Dick's an anarchist — something like that — wants to upset society — send it to the devil or some other — knock things all helter-skelter: but he's a good fellow — and they were always very kind to me — Dick and his wife, both" (*With Walt Whitman in Camden*, II, 396; see also V, 40–42). See this same book, II, 483–484; Traubel reported on Whitman's notations as he sent copies of *November Boughs* to various people.

   2651.   Whitman's niece was returning to her father's home (Jeff Whitman) after visiting George and Louisa Whitman in Burlington, New Jersey.

   2652.   Both *With Walt Whitman in Camden*, II, 456, and *The Correspondence of Walt Whitman*, IV, 221 (Whitman to Dr R. M. Bucke) mention David McKay's visit and the royalty payment.

10   writing the autograph W W names for
    the big book[2653]

24   sent L of G. to A A J Züllig

    care of M L Mülilemann   paid
                                  $5
    13 Waverly Place New York City
            paid $5
    ordered by Dr Hawley 52 Warren st
        Syracuse N Y – sent word to him[2654]

Hannah seriously ill at Burlington[2655]
           (jaundice)
recovers during the month & November

Nov. 5.   sent L of G. to Theron R Woodward [2656]
    500 Rialto Building   Lanward   [?] Publishing
    Co: Chicago Ill paid   rec'd.

" 5   Edward Wilkins arrived & began
        nursing & caring for me[2657]

2653. Whitman told Horace Traubel that he autographed a hundred sheets — see *With Walt Whitman in Camden*, II, 456 — of what he called "the big book," a one-volume edition of *Complete Poems & Prose,* printed by Ferguson Brothers & Co., Philadelphia, which David McKay issued in November 1888. Now generally considered the eighth edition of *Leaves of Grass,* this book contains the 1881 edition, *Specimen Days & Collect* (1882), and *November Boughs* (1888); each of these sections is separately paged, having been printed from the original plates, their title pages now becoming half-titles. The only new material is "A Note at the Beginning" and a "Note at the End." About 600 copies were published, most of them signed by Whitman.

2654. This letter to Dr W. A. Hawley, telling him that Whitman had sent *Leaves of Grass* to A. A. J. Züllig in New York City, is now lost.

2655. Hannah Heyde, Whitman's sister, lived in Burlington, Vermont (not New Jersey, where George and Louisa Whitman lived); the poet still had no use for Charles L. Heyde, calling him "her viper husband" (*With Walt Whitman in Camden*, II 493). Of Hannah he said on 31 October 1883: "The news is good news — thank God for that! It is from my sister — I have been worried about her. She has never been here: she is frail, delicate — gets about but little" (*ibid*, II, 559).

2656. Not otherwise identified.

2657. Edward Wilkins (1865–1936) was the young man, sent from Canada by Dr R. M. Bucke, to replace W. A. Musgrove as Whitman's nurse (see footnote 2640). Wilkins had been described by Dr Bucke as "a real good, nice looking young fellow [who] is as good as he looks" (*With Walt Whitman in Camden*, II, 537), and Whitman found him satisfactory, pleasant, and cheerful during the year he stayed at 328 Mickle Street; Traubel's Vol. II has more than a hundred references to him, and there are almost as many in *The Correspondence of Walt Whitman,* Vol. II. He left because he wanted to go to the Ontario Veterinary School in Toronto, from which he graduated in 1893 and came to Alexandria, Indiana to practice, staying the rest of his life. See Bert A. Thompson, "Edward Wilkins: Male Nurse to Walt Whitman," *Walt Whitman Review,* XV (September 1969), 194–195. See also *The Correspondence of Walt Whitman,* IV, 227n, 232, 233 *et passim.*

6 – Better to-day & for two days past –
    continue so a week

8th – Josiah Child   Trübner's London
            me
        sent $14.43 due me on books sent him
                    long ago[2658]

[360]

Wᵐ H Blauvelt
            Richfield Springs New York
sent me the good partridges   Nov. 26 '88 [2659]

    Edward Wilkins
Nilestown, Middlesex
        Ontario   Canada[2660]

[On clipped slip, printed: Now, Sept. 1889
    Charles W. Eldridge   28 No Spring St   U S Revenue Agent
    Lawyer   San Francisco   Cal
    Los Angeles, Cal.
    PO Box 1705]
        Gabriel Sarrazin
            10 Rue Troyon
                Paris   France
wrote the criticism in La Nouvelle Revue
———————————————— May 1888 [2661]

2658.   This money had been sent for 99 copies of *Democratic Vistas* on 20 October 1888, which Whitman acknowledged on 20 November — *The Correspondence of Walt Whitman*, IV, 235.

2659.   William H. Blauvelt was an illustrator who asked on 31 October 1888 (see *With Walt Whitman in Camden*, III, 8) about the portrait of him in the 1885 *Leaves of Grass*, saying that he wanted it for Edmund Clarence Stedman's *Poets of America*; the other references to him (*ibid.*, III, 13, 28, 55, 71; and 182, 189) have to do with this portrait, or the engraving used in *Leaves*; or Whitman's letter of thanks for the partridges, which he enjoyed for breakfast (the letter is now missing).

2660.   For Edward Wilkins, whose home address this is, see footnote 2657.

2661.   Charles Aldrich, an Iowan, told Whitman about a review of *Leaves of Grass* in a French journal (see *With Walt Whitman in Camden*, III, 1–2; and *The Correspondence of Walt Whitman*, IV, 230), which was Gabriel Sarrazin's "Poètes modernes de l'Amérique: Walt Whitman," *La Nouvelle Revue*, LII (1 May 1888), 164–184 (reprinted in *In Re Walt Whitman*, edited by Horace Traubel, 1893). Thus began a long relationship, by letter, between Whitman and the young French critic, who is mentioned many, many times in Horace Traubel's volumes III, IV, and V, and in the *Correspondence*, IV and V. See Roger Asselineau, "Walt Whitman to Gabriel Sarrazin: Four Unpublished Pieces," *Walt Whitman Review*, V (March 1959), 8–11, and *The Correspondence of Walt Whitman*, IV, 330–331; V, 80, 141, 220 (Whitman's letter to Sarrazin), *et passim*. For Charles W. Eldridge, see footnote 116, also *The Correspondence*, IV, 290–291.

T W Rolleston
Fairview
Delgany
Co: Wicklow   Ireland
he
sent last proofs German trans:
last of Dec: '88 [2662]

the German book "Grashalme"
(18 copies) rec'd 25ᵗʰ Feb: '89

[361]

1888

Wesley R Stafford, Dixie, Polk county
Oregon, Rickreal p o
Feb. & March '78, sent papers &c – rec'd letter[2663]
J W Whelply, U S Treasurer's Office
Washington D C [2664]
T J Whitman   Office Board of Water
Commissioners   City Hall St Louis[2665]

Nov: Nov: & December   1888   Camden
26 – Monday – looks wintry indeed,
snow, sleet & rain – cloudy – cold

27   the big book – "Complete Works" – bound
up in one Vol. paper covers – & I
am looking over it – satisfactory[2666]

2662. For T. W. H. Rolleston, see footnote 50; for Whitman on the German translation of *Leaves of Grass,* entitled *Grashalme,* which he did with Dr Karl Knortz (Zurich: Schabelitz, 1889, 180 pp.), see *The Correspondence of Walt Whitman,* IV, 220, 265, 270, 287, 293, 295n, 319n, 401n; and Horace Traubel, *With Walt Whitman in Camden,* III, 253, 487–489; IV, 111–112, and especially 381–386. Whitman mentioned receiving his copies of *Grashalme* both here (below) and in the later entry for 25 February 1889, below.

2663. Wesley R. Stafford (see footnote 253), niece of Mrs Susan Stafford, was known well enough by the poet for Whitman to mention his marrying Lizzie Hider in February 1881 (see *The Correspondence of Walt Whitman,* III, 210); they apparently moved to Oregon. This letter has been lost.

2664. J. W. Whelply: otherwise unidentified.

2665. Thomas Jefferson (Jeff) Whitman, Walt's favorite brother, had written him on 14 July 1888; his daughter had been in Camden and seen the poet recently; and Jeff visited the poet on 20 February 1889 ("he is not well, stomach & throat botheration," he told Dr R. M. Bucke, *The Correspondence of Walt Whitman,* IV, 293). See also *With Walt Whitman in Camden,* IV, 192–193. Jeff died on 25 November 1890.

2666. Although Whitman referred here and a few lines below to the "big book" as "Com-

Nov: and Dec: '88 – still sick
  – the bladder   malady – pains –
    the gastric   "   –

---

the big book "Complete Works" bound
  up in cheap binding   150 copies[2667]
  – Dr B. likes it well – I like it[2668]

---

rec'd

20th sent Mary and Hannah $10 each[2669]
  Ed Wilkins here with me[2670]

---

24 sent "To the Year 1889" to <u>Critic</u> $6
      pub'd Jan: 5 '89 – paid $6 [2671]

[362]

<u>Sent the big book</u> – Dec. '88 & '89 [2672]
          rec'd

Chas Shepard, Long Islander		Dr Walsh
Ed: Wilkins		Thos Donaldson
Horace Traubel 2		T W Rolleston (rec'd)
	rec'd	Fairview Delgany
Dr Bucke, 4 copies		Co: Wicklow Ireland
Kennedy	rec'd	Sarrazin Paris (rec'd)
Mrs. Fairchild rec'd		T B Harned calf bd'g
Baxter rec'd.		Jeff
Sanborn	rec'd	Lou
H Garland rec'd		

plete Works," the title actually is *Complete Poems & Prose* (see footnote 2653, above).

2667. See Whitman's letter to Frederick Oldach, *The Correspondence of Walt Whitman,* IV, 242, about binding details.

2668. Dr Richard Maurice Bucke's letters to Whitman are in the Feinberg Collection; in his letter to Dr Bucke of 20 December 1888, Whitman wrote: "so the books arrived at last — & you are contented & pleas'd — & the trilogy [*Leaves of Grass, Specimen Days & Collect,* and *November Boughs*] hold together & fuses, tho' various & paradoxical & rapidly twittering, (probably like Dante's filmy ghosts, rushing by with mere gibberish) — yes it is mainly all *autobiographic* environ'd with my time & deeply incarnated & tinged with it, & the moral begetting of it (I hope)" — *The Correspondence of Walt Whitman,* IV, 250–251.

2669. This money was Christmas presents to Whitman's sisters, Hannah Heyde and Mary Van Nostrand (both letters are now lost).

2670. Edward Wilkins had been with Whitman since 5 November 1888 (see footnote 2657).

2671. This poem, "To the Year 1889," *Critic,* 5 January 1889, was included in *Good-bye My Fancy* (1891) with the title "To the Pending Year" and then in the 1891–92 *Leaves of Grass*: see the Comprehensive Reader's Edition, pp. 543–544.

2672. The big book, *Complete Poems & Prose,* was sent at this time to only 16 people, in contrast to 40 who received *November Boughs* two months previously. Of these 16, seven

[363]

Dec: Christmas, 1888 —— 1889

22, 23 & 24 – Easier & less uncomfortable[2673]

1889

Jan: 2 – paid the Gas bill. (Oct., Nov. & Dec.
'88, $9.76   5 p c ded:) $9.27

" 4 – sent "Spec: Days & Collect" and "Nov:
Boughs" to Nathan Greeley, Times
newspaper, Kansas City, Mo: paid $5   rec'd [2674]

Ship
sent "Old Age's ∧& Crafty Death's" to Century $12
accepted & paid [2675]

5 – Sylvester Baxter's splendid notice of
the big book   Boston Herald, Jan: 3 '89 [2676]

8   David McKay here paid me for November

had also got *November Boughs* (see footnote 2650) — Dr R. M. Bucke, William Sloane Kennedy, Hamlin Garland, Dr Walsh, Thomas Donaldson, Thomas B. Harned, and Louisa Whitman — and two others were in the house, so to speak, and need not have been "sent" the book, Horace Traubel and Edward Wilkins; Gabriel Sarrazin (see footnote 2661) had just come on the Whitman "scene"; Jefferson Whitman, for some strange reason, was not sent *November Boughs,* though his other close relatives were; four other recipients were old friends of the poet's, Mrs Charles (Elizabeth) Fairchild (see *The Correspondence of Walt Whitman,* III, 354n), Sylvester Baxter (see *ibid.,* IV, 262, and footnotes 1102 and 1307, above), and Franklin B. Sanborn — all from Boston — and T. W. H. Rolleston (see footnote 2662), finishing a translation of Whitman into German; and Charles Shepard would seem to be editor or on *The Long-Islander,* the weekly newspaper Whitman founded in 1838.
　　2673. There is much more on Whitman's health — such as "W. yesterday undoubtedly better than at any time in two weeks or perhaps a month" — in Horace Traubel's *With Walt Whitman in Camden,* III, 356–388 — on the period of 22–25 December 1888.
　　2674. Nathan Greeley of the *Kansas City Times*: letter from Whitman (if there was one) is missing, and Greeley is not otherwise identified.
　　2675. The eight-line poem, "Old Age's Ship & Crafty Death's," was published in *The Century,* XXXIX (February 1890), p. 553, in *Good-bye My Fancy* (1891), and *Leaves of Grass* (1891–92): see Comprehensive Reader's Edition, p. 543.
　　2676. Baxter's review in the Boston *Herald* pleased Whitman so much he wrote Baxter himself to thank him, wrote to Dr R. M. Bucke and to William Sloane Kennedy, using the word "splendid" several times — see *The Correspondence of Walt Whitman,* IV, 262–263 — and told Horace Traubel: "Baxter has been doing us up in fine style . . . so good, so sound, it might be us speaking instead of him! . . . it is certainly the best thing he has ever written: shows a firm hand: quotes liberally, finely. Evidently Sylvester recognizes the true function of a reviewer — to state what the writer purports to say — as far as possible to let him state it for himself . . . [The *Herald* review] is the best of all the reviews so far undoubtedly" (*With Walt Whitman in Camden,* III, 463).

Boughs
~~Copies~~ ($313:50 – deducting 5:59) – pays
me $307:91 – [2677]

12 Deposited 186:37 in Bank[2678]
Dr McAlister here (Dr Walsh sick)

duplicate – no value
10th from Edw'd Carpenter 174:37 originally
2d draft – destroy'd – no value   sent May 19
                                     (not lost[2679]

[364]

[Blank]

[365]

1889 – January   Camden
[Entry for 16 January written in pencil on larger sheet and pasted in the book:]

Jan: 16 '89
[Four words ink:] never so bad before   my own
A very bad of ∧ lapse   of ∧ memory.
Edw'd Carpenter sent me a bank draft
                    by Lou or Mrs: D   [in ink]
$174:37, last part of May, '88, wh' ∧ I de-
(I was very ill at the time bed fast)   [last two words in ink]
posited ∧ in Bank July 2.   Then in Jan:
 not hearing of the first draft & fearing it lost E C   [line in ink]
'89, ∧ sent me the same draft   in   duplicate,
                    I had not rec'd it
& I forgetting all ab't the first (& supposing ∧
&   & was credited
it lost) deposited it in Bank.   Of course
                    ∧
on presenting it for payment (to J M Shoe-

    2677. This money was for 950 copies of *November Boughs*: see Whitman's letter to Dr R. M. Bucke in *The Correspondence of Walt Whitman,* IV, 266.
    2678. This sum may be from David McKay's payment of 8 January 1889, or less likely from Edward Carpenter's $174.37 received two days later (see below).
    2679. See Whitman's thank-you letter, *The Correspondence of Walt Whitman,* IV, 266–267; and then Whitman telling Carpenter that this draft was a duplicate, which he was destroying, on 16 January 1889 (*ibid.,* IV, 269–270).

maker & Co. bankers) they spoke of the paid
Camden
original draft, & I gave the ∧ bank my cheque $174:37.[2680]

[Rest of page, nine lines, in ink:]
22 sent big book, letter &c to T W Rolleston
 Fairview, Delgany, Co: Wicklow rec'd [pencil] Ireland [2681]

22 the Gabriel ~~Sazzarin~~ Sarrazin article
 in Novelle Revue, May '88 Paris[2682]

23, '4, '5. the big book in half-calf, dark
 green binding ($1.24, binder's price) pleases
 me pretty well considering – (50 order'd)[2683]

Harper's Monthly Feb: has a friendlyish
 notice of Nov: Boughs & me by W D Howells[2684]

[366]

Wᵐ and Margaretta L Avery[2685]
Feb:'89   185 Sterling Place   Brooklyn
N Y

[367]

1889 Jan: & Feb:

2680. See previous footnote and letter to Carpenter, 16 January 1889.
2681. Letter to T. W. H. Rolleston is now lost; the big book Whitman sent him was his *Complete Poems & Prose* (see footnotes 2653, 2666, and 2672).
2682. For Sarrazin and the article, see footnote 2661.
2683. This binding was on one of the copies of *Complete Poems & Prose* that Whitman gave to Thomas B. Harned (see list over in *Daybook*); for more on the calf binding, see Whitman's letter to Dr R. M. Bucke ("not that I am overwhelmed or even entirely satisfied by it") in *The Correspondence of Walt Whitman,* IV, 274–275; and *With Walt Whitman in Camden,* IV, 11–12, 19–20, and 49–50.
2684. This same word, "friendlyish," Whitman used about William Dean Howells's review of *November Boughs* in the Editor's Study of *Harper's Monthly,* February 1889; Horace Traubel reported that Whitman "called it 'so-so' and 'friendly' but didn't in the least warm up over it" — *With Walt Whitman in Camden,* IV, 17. Howells, incidentally, first met Whitman at Pfaff's in 1860: see his "First Impressions of Literary New York," *Harper's Monthly,* XCI (June 1895), 65–70; *Literary Friends and Acquaintance* (New York, 1900), pp. 74–84; "Walt Whitman at Pfaff's," *The Conservator,* June 1895. Earlier, Howells had reviewed "Drum-Taps" in the *Round Table,* 11 November 1865, and had written on Whitman, Emerson, and Tolstoy in "Editor's Table," *Harper's Monthly,* LXXVI (February 1888), 478–479. See also William Sloane Kennedy, *The Fight of a Book for the World* (West Yarmouth, Mass., 1926), pp. 101–102, 275.
2685. William and Margaretta Avery (see footnote 115), cousins of Walt Whitman's mother, first visited him on 19 October 1876 (see entry of that date, above): a letter from Margaretta Avery to Whitman, 25 February 1889, is in the Library of Congress.

Jan:

25   sent portrait prints & photo's to Gabriel
                    all rec'd [in blue pencil]
        Sarrazin, Paris – had sent him a packet
        of printed personal & L of G. notice slips before

---

                                    rec'd [in blue pencil]
28 – sent Sarrazin the big book_∧ plain bd'g[2686]

---

        law
Feb: 1 – ∧ suit (over in Phila:) of Mary
        Davis for am't of W^m H Duckett's
        board bill: verdict for Mrs: D, $190:
        —— (Waln, att'y for Mrs: D) —
        the verdict was for her
        Waln p'd her $100 – then $40 more[2687]   [last three words in pencil]

---

    or 1
2 ∧   sent $45:50 to Mrs: M E Nichols
                    Blackwood, New Jersey
        Insane Asylum,_∧for Ed's board for
        three coming months.[2688]

---

4   rec'd "Magazine of Poetry" for Jan:
                    quarterly Buffalo N Y [2689]

---

14 sent big book to Dr Knortz rec'd [2690]   [last word in blue pencil]

2686. Letters accompanying this material, if there were any, to Gabriel Sarrazin (see footnote 2661) are missing; Whitman mentions, in a letter to William Sloane Kennedy (*The Correspondence of Walt Whitman*, IV, 276), sending this material. The "big book" is, of course, *Complete Poems & Prose* (1888). See also *With Walt Whitman in Camden*, IV, 2–3, with a facsimile of the first page of Sarrazin's article on Whitman, inscribed to the poet, dated 6 janvier 1889.

2687. This suit by Whitman's housekeeper against William H. (Billy) Duckett, is told, in part, in *With Walt Whitman in Camden*, IV, 64–66; and in Gay Wilson Allen, *The Solitary Singer*, p. 533. See also *The Correspondence of Walt Whitman*, IV, 278. Whitman felt betrayed by the boy, whom he had liked and who is mentioned several times in the *Daybook* (see footnote 2007) but who lied on the witness stand; Whitman's sympathies were with the charitable Mrs Mary Davis, who finally did collect, as seen here, $140 through her Philadelphia lawyer S. Morris Waln, whose name and address are above (see footnote 2645).

2688. This money was for Whitman's feeble-minded brother (see footnote 2602).

2689. This first issue of *The Magazine of Poetry*, I (January 1889), 14–23, contained a biographical sketch by Dr R. M. Bucke, and etching by Frank Fowler, and a photograph (from *November Boughs*). Whitman said to Dr Bucke: "all looks better than I w'd have anticipated — pictures, print, paper very fair — I see I appear quite largely — good biographic sketch f'm y'r pen I accept & like well" (*The Correspondence of Walt Whitman*, IV, 280); see also *With Walt Whitman in Camden*, IV, 85–86.

2690. See entry just below; for some reason, Dr Karl Knortz's name does not appear above in the list of those to whom Whitman sent his *Complete Poems & Prose*.

gave him copy big book
20 Jeff here – ∧ went home to St L to-night[2691]

      25 or 30
25 rec'd ∧ copies of "Grashalme"
          ab't 200 pages
    the little translation ∧ into German
    of some of L of G. by T W Rolleston
    & Karl Knortz pub: by Schabelitz,
    Zurich, Switzerland, 1889 (180 & 12 pp)[2692]

                                              [368]
                                               45
                                                4
                                              ────
                                              180

                                              [369]

Feb: 1889   March
25 Still sick – Kept in room – now 9ᵗʰ mo:

26 sent L of G and S D two vols. to Miss Langley
        37 London st.   Reading, Eng: paid[2693]

"   Dr Bucke here (the trouble, pain, &c. of left
        side is from diseased spleen.)[2694]

March
                            rec'd
8   sent $14 to J H Johnston for the ∧ watch[2695]

2691. Thomas Jefferson (Jeff) Whitman (see footnote 2665) had his name added to
the list of those receiving Walt Whitman's *Complete Poems & Prose*: the big book was given
to him, not sent to St. Louis.
2692. See footnotes 2662 and 2690.
2693. In January 1889 Horace C. Simmons wrote to Whitman (letter in the Feinberg
Collection), asking for a list of the poet's publications for a bookseller in Reading, England,
Miss Langley; Whitman must have replied, though the letter is now lost, for on 9 March
1889 (letter in the Feinberg Collection), she ordered copies of Dr R. M. Bucke's biography of
the poet and *November Boughs,* in addition to the *Leaves of Grass* and *Specimen Days,* which
he is sending her here; they were for "Mrs: General Faber" (see entry for 19 March 1889,
below).
2694. For a detailed account of Dr R. M. Bucke's visit to Camden, see Horace Traubel's
With Walt Whitman in Camden, IV, 224–370, with the visit to William Douglas O'Connor in
Washington occupying pp. 252–263. In addition to seeing the poet, Dr Bucke was concerned
with "the meter company & capital & manufacturing matter . . . the water-meter enterprise"
(mentioned in numerous letters during this period in *The Correspondence of Walt Whitman,*
IV, 294–304); he left for London, Ontario on 18 March 1889.
2695. On 19 March 1889, Whitman said to Traubel about John H. Johnston, the New

"   sun sets just at 6 [2696]

still ill– bladder – spleen – cold in the head –
– obstinate constipation – (no doctors here
for a month)[2697]
curiously mild winter so far —
    – the <u>meter</u> enterprise[2698]

---

11   sent big book to Stedman N Y by express[2699]

David McKay owes ⎫   25   March 22
      me for Big Books ⎬   12   3 copies
⎛ owes me $180 ⎞copies ⎧ paid
⎜ for 45 copies ⎟$4 each ⎨ $100   5   3 cop's Ap: 1
⎝ March 20 '89 [2700]⎠   ⎩

---

17 Sunday – Mrs: A H Spalding, Boston, call'd
      gave her the big book[2701]

York jeweler: "He was here about three weeks ago — came of a Sunday: I think only stopped off long enough to see me, then went back" (*With Walt Whitman in Camden*, IV, 378); but nothing is said anywhere about a watch, though this visit mentioned in the *Correspondence* (IV, 263) and in Traubel (III, 481) as of 20 minutes on Sunday, 6 January 1889.

2696.   There is no reason why anyone, especially a poet, shouldn't refer to the setting sun; however, Whitman doesn't very often, and when he does, as here, it's rather a dull, flat statement. He's more concerned with his health — see the next lines.

2697.   In saying "no doctors here for a month," Whitman of course excludes Dr R. M. Bucke; and Whitman's statement, which is accurate, is at variance with such of those as Gay Wilson Allen's in *The Solitary Singer* (p. 533): "The pattern of Whitman's life established in 1888 held for the remainder of his life . . . . a male nurse was on duty nearly all the time, a physician called almost daily."

2698.   This had to do with an invention, by William Gurd and Dr R. M. Bucke, which often was mentioned in letters during this period (see footnote 2694) — for example to William Douglas O'Connor on 27 February 1889, "Dr B[ucke] is full of *the meter* business (the invention patented & company forming)," and the next day, "Dr B[ucke] is here full of the water-meter enterprise — Keeps him busy enough (that's what he came for)" — *The Correspondence of Walt Whitman*, IV, 296, ff. Experts in Philadelphia tested the meter, and on 17 March Whitman wrote: "I rather think Dr [Bucke]'s meter business will be practically started, & will be a success — Horace Traubel will be Secretary" (*ibid.*, IV, 303). Finally, however, the next day: "The practical outset of the meter enterprise collapsed at the last moment for the want of capital investors (*ibid.*, IV, 304; see also *With Walt Whitman in Camden*, IV, 370–371, 402–403, 481–482, especially for Thomas B. Harned's connection with the enterprise).

2699.   Edmund Clarence Stedman wrote a praising letter about Whitman's *Complete Poems & Prose* on 27–28 March 1889 (Feinberg Collection, and published in *The Life and Letters of Edmund Clarence Stedman* [New York, 1910], II, 120–122); he also sent Whitman seven volumes of his *Library of American Literature* (New York, 1887–1889), in which Whitman was given more space than any other poet. See Whitman's letter to Stedman, 31 March 1889, in *The Correspondence of Walt Whitman*, IV, 315; and Horace Traubel's *With Walt Whitman in Camden*, IV, 446, 453, 454, 461, 471, 479, 486.

2700.   Dealings between the publisher David McKay and Whitman over the *Complete Poems & Prose* are mentioned numerous times in *With Walt Whitman in Camden*, IV, *passim*; in *The Correspondence of Walt Whitman*, IV, 309, *et passim*; and in the *Daybook*, see immediately below. Whitman's phrases "the big book" and *"Complete works"* refer to this volume, regarded as the eighth edition of *Leaves of Grass* (see footnote 2653).

2701.   Mrs A. H. Spaulding is mentioned in an account of Ernest Rhys's lecture on "The New Poetry" before the New England Woman's Club in the Boston *Transcript* of 6

Dr Bucke went back to Canada

---

19 sent Miss Langley Reading, Eng:
     for Mrs: General Faber 2 books
          paid [2702]

[370]

Complete works   big book
               furnished to Dave McKay
25 copies   March 22
12   "   all at $4 a copy
 5   "
 3   "
 3   "   April 1, the common binding
               $100 paid me on these
                    March 28 '89
               [Rest of page, six lines, in pencil:]
               ($92   due me Ap. 3)
                 \   paid   big books
                              all paid ∧ up
                         to date July 20
                              '89 [2703]

[371]

March   1889
20th   Still laid up in the 2d story room 328
          Mickle st: Camden (the 10th month)
          – Dr B. gone back to Canada[2704] – O'C pretty
          badly ill – room-fast & paralyzed in lower
               vomiting a good deal
          legs – ∧ has had some bad epileptic fits, but

March 1889 as having spoken in "eloquent praise of Whitman": see *The Correspondence of Walt Whitman*, IV, 155. Following the visit to Whitman recorded here in the *Daybook*, she wrote to the poet (letter in the Feinberg Collection, see *ibid.*, IV, 303), and Whitman noted on her calling card, "dear friend of L of G & me — a middle-aged lady — I sh'd say — *one of the real circle*" (also in the Feinberg Collection); and he told William Sloane Kennedy that she had called on him (*ibid.*, IV, 303); then on 28 March 1889 she sent Whitman "a beautiful bunch of flowers . . . they are scenting the room as I write" (*ibid.*, IV, 312). On 3 April 1889 Hamlin Garland wrote Whitman that "Mrs. Dr. Spaulding . . . is doing all she can for the acceptance of L. of G." (*With Walt Whitman in Camden*, IV, 491).

     2702.   See footnote 2693.
     2703.   See footnotes 2653 and 2700.
     2704.   For Dr R. M. Bucke's visit, see footnotes 2694 and 2698.

now over them[2705] — Horace T comes in faith –
fully – Ed Wilkins here – I sit here whiling
my time & imprisonment as well as I can –
– a terrible chronic constipation & palling
inertia – listlessness all the time fallen
upon me (like a great falling clinging net)
— My head heavy, bad, congested, to-day —
– a dark wet rawish day — it is ab't 11 a m
as I write – have had my mutton-broth
breakfast (late) – Ed is making up the
bed – H T has been in – otherwise I am
alone — I keep up, but these are dull
even miserable days[2706]

----

rec'd
23ᵈ sent big book to A N Brown, ∧ U. S. Naval
     Academy Library Annapolis Md by Express[2707]
                    paid

----

rec'd
sent also T B Aldrich, Boston, big book
             paid $25 [2708]

----

25 Dave McKay here — I adhere to my
    $333 proposition for the sheets – he declines
    then I shall fall back on supplying
    the first (boards) binding only[2709]

2705. Dr R. M. Bucke and Horace Traubel had been in Washington to see William Douglas O'Connor: see *With Walt Whitman in Camden*, IV, 252–263, and the numerous letters from Whitman to O'Connor in *The Correspondence of Walt Whitman*, IV, 284, 285, 286–287, 290–333. The final letter was written on 6 May 1889. Ellen M. O'Connor wrote on 9 May (letter in the Feinberg Collection): "The sad end is come. William passed peacefully to rest at 2 A. M. this day" (see *ibid.*, IV, 334n).

2706. This passage on Whitman's poor health and the assistance his nurse Edward Wilkins and Horace Traubel is giving him is one of the longest in the *Daybook*. In Traubel's account of these days, 20–22 March 1889, Whitman does not seem to be nearly so miserable as he described himself — *With Walt Whitman in Camden*, IV, 386–406. His letters in *The Correspondence of Walt Whitman*, IV, 305–308, to Dr R. M. Bucke, William Douglas O'Connor, and to William Sloane Kennedy, are also more cheerful.

2707. See Whitman's letters to Arthur Newton Brown in *The Correspondence of Walt Whitman*, IV, 305 and 310.

2708. In *With Walt Whitman in Camden*, both Arthur Newton Brown and Thomas Bailey Aldrich are mentioned by Whitman and Traubel. See also footnote 2650 for a brief note on Aldrich.

2709. See entries above for 11 March 1889, the following page of the *Daybook*, and footnote 2700.

26   bad news (thro' Dr B & Dr Hood's letter   ) for O'C [2710]
     two copies big book to Horace[2711]

[372]

[Clipping from a newspaper:]

. . . . Pickups in Fairmount Park: The willows
are getting perceptibly green; the red maple branches
are tipped with red; the spicewood bushes are blossoming. Catkins are common enough. Of the
birds, field larks, robins, flickers and song sparrows
have arrived. Of the wild flowers liverwort and
bloodroot are in bloom.

[In WW's hand:]   Phil Rec. April 6 '89 [2712]

[373]

March   1889   and April
26 – Am preparing for a special small ed'n (300)
     of L of G.   Annex & Backward Glance to commemorate
     my finishing the age of 70 – May 31 '89 [2713]

2710. Dr R. M. Bucke wrote Whitman on 23 March 1889, "We must make up our minds
to his [William Douglas O'Connor's] death" (*The Correspondence of Walt Whitman*, IV,
311n), and he enclosed a letter from T. B. Hood, O'Connor's physician, of 19 March, on the
lack of bed-sores but "within a few weeks the action of the heart is hurried" (*With Walt
Whitman in Camden*, IV, 425–426).
     2711. These copies of Whitman's *Complete Poems & Prose* were for Mrs Nora Baldwin
and John Herbert Clifford, a preacher of Germantown, Philadelphia, who visited Whitman in
Camden. See *With Walt Whitman in Camden*, IV, 427; also IV, 280–281, 452–453, 492–494.
     2712. Horace Traubel merely records that at 10:30 a. m. on 6 April 1889, "W[hitman]
reading Record," and there is no comment, either Whitman's or his young friend's (*With
Walt Whitman in Camden*, IV, 500).
     2713. Whitman spoke to Traubel on 22 March 1889 about a pocket edition: "I shall
supply it copiously with portraits. It has occurred to me that after all the best scheme would
be [to] make a special effort with this edition. It will be in a sense, or wholly, personal, in-
cidental to the moment, a commemoration of my birthday — the entrance upon my seventieth
year: therefore, it should be something peculiar, with an identity: perhaps after all a five-
dollar book if we get it richly bound: the purpose being to make it in all respects worth
while — undoubtedly consistent with the occasion" (*With Walt Whitman in Camden*, IV, 403).
Whitman also wrote to Dr R. M. Bucke about it: "L of G. with Annex & Backward Glance
(ab't 420 pp) . . . bound (probably) in handsome morocco, pocket-book style, six or eight
portraits, & autograph — $5 — (shall probably bring it out to commemorate my finishing my
70th year) — a little inscription on title — " (*The Correspondence of Walt Whitman*, IV, 309).
Numerous references to this long-cherished ambition of a handy pocket-size *Leaves* — a prefatory
note on the title page — bound in leather and printed on thin paper occur in *With Walt
Whitman in Camden*, IV, *passim*, and the *Correspondence*, IV, 311, 313, 317, 318, 320, 325,
327, 328, 330, 331, 333, 336, 338 (to Frederick Oldach on the binding), 339 (Whitman: "*press
work* . . . dont suit me"), and 343, most of this in letters to Dr R. M. Bucke. Coming between
the 1889 *Complete Poems & Prose* (eighth edition of *Leaves*) and the 1892 "Deathbed Edition"
of *Leaves of Grass,* this one has not come to be regarded as a new or separate edition. See William White, "Whitman's *Leaves of Grass*: Notes on the Pocketbook (1889) Edition," *Studies in
Bibliography*, XVIII (1965), 280–281.

paid the bill $65.28 of Oldach & Co: binding
  51 copies big book calf
also the bill $10.50 Photo Eng: Co. ("process")
  for making the ¾ portrait W W. f'm
    McKay's Photo[2714]

---

28 Dave McKay here pays me $100 on acc't
  of the copies (45) of the big books
               [In pencil:]
  (owes me $80)   (owes me $92   April 3)
  pays me   [in pencil]

∧ also $55. $\frac{64}{100}$ for royalty on my books

  L of G. and S D up to (or ab't to) date[2715]

April 1   three (3) more copies big book
    deliver'd to order David McKay[2716]

[Two lines in pencil:]
  3   paid gas bill $10.49 (bill 11.04)
    rec'd from p. o money orders 9 65

---

4   deposited $196.64 in bank by Ed:[2717]

17   send Dr B's WW and Nov: B (2 Vols:) to Miss Langley
    Reading, Eng: paid [2718]
  Nov: B to Albert E Johnston, N Y [2719]
  Nov: B to Mrs: Wᵐ Van Tassel [2720]
    Brooklyn   E D"

2714. See *The Correspondence of Walt Whitman,* IV, 311.

2715. See *The Correspondence of Walt Whitman,* IV, 312, and Whitman's comments and receipt and David McKay's account book entry in facsimile in *With Walt Whitman in Camden,* IV, 440–441.

2716. The young Philadelphia publisher was selling, for Whitman, *Leaves of Grass* (1881), *Specimen Days & Collect* (1882), *November Boughs* (1888), as well as the "big book," *Complete Poems & Prose* (1888).

2717. The fact that the *Daybook* is something of an account book makes it reasonable that Whitman should record such trivial as gas bills, money orders, and bank deposits made for him by Edward Wilkins, though the latter was mentioned in a letter of this date to Dr R. M. Bucke (why should he be interested in that?) — *The Correspondence of Walt Whitman,* IV, 316.

2718. For these purchases of Dr R. M. Bucke's *Walt Whitman* and *November Boughs,* see footnote 2693.

2719. Albert E. Johnston was the son of the New York jeweler John H. Johnston.

2720. Mrs William (Alice Hicks) Van Tassel was the great niece of Elias Hicks; her

[374]

[Clipped from larger sheet of lined paper, three lines in purple ink, not in WW's hand:]

Mrs Wm Van Tassel.

91 Furman Ave

Brooklyn, E. D.

[375]

April   1889   April and May

21 (Sunday) – Mont Stafford here[2721]
   Baby Harned " [2722]

 warm day

---

22 the 750 wreck'd Danmark crew <u>saved</u> [2723]

---

29 sent "Complete Works" by express, prepaid,
  to Will Carleton 420 Greene Av:
  Brooklyn (paid $10) rec'd [2724]

May 3 – Ed Stafford here[2725]

---

4 rec'd Sarrazin's handsome little book
  from Paris, 279 pp:[2726]

---

letter of acknowledgment of *November Boughs*, 28 April 1889, is in the Feinberg Collection. (See her address just below.)

 2721. There were two Montgomery Staffords: one was the brother (1820–1907) of the elder George Stafford, and the other, Harry Stafford's brother (1862–1926?). Because Whitman mentions Mont's visit in a letter to Mrs Susan Stafford, 25 April 1889, I assume this is the younger Mont, her son.

 2722. This visitor pleased Whitman very much: "I have had a call today from Tom and Mrs. Harned . . . And the baby at last! Herbert at last! Oh! and what a remarkable boy it is, too! — that big, clear, beautiful blue eye — a whole world of him, at least . . . And he is a specimen, too — nobly one; I was much taken, engaged, with him; it seemed to me I found in him the eligibility of any future in the calendar — highest, best — a bright, broad vista!" (*With Walt Whitman in Camden*, V, 62–63).

 2723. In a letter to Dr R. M. Bucke and another to William D. O'Connor he spoke of this: "Decidedly the best news of to-day is the saving of the wreck'd Danmark's 750 passengers & crew — out of the very jaws of death" (*The Correspondence of Walt Whitman*, IV, 324). And he added to Horace Traubel: "So after all they are safe — not a person drowned. Oh! what a relief that is to know!" (*With Walt Whitman in Camden*, V, 66).

 2724. Will Carleton, who read in one of the Camden churches on 22 April 1889, visited Whitman on 23 April with George William Curtis of the *Ladies Home Journal*; he mentioned having been forced to miss the 1887 reception for Whitman in New York (he also wrote Whitman about this, but the letter is now lost). Traubel described Carleton as "rather a handsome fellow — a good body and a splendid complexion — sunniness put into flesh" (*With Walt Whitman in Camden*, V, 72). The only other references to Carleton have to do with ordering or acknowledging Whitman books.

 2725. Edwin Stafford is Harry Stafford's brother.

wrote to Knortz, Dr B & card to Sar:[2727]

the pocket-book ed'n L of G. preparing[2728]

9 paid $12.30 to McCollin, Phila:
   for 307 photo-mounting for L of G [2729]

W^m O'C very ill – very – DIED 9th 2
a m[2730]
warm spell – 7th 8th, 9th

                    wrong
15 the wheel – chair. (a present from
   H L Bonsall and G Buckwalter)[2731]

17 – I get out every day – Ed pushes
   me in it – go down to foot of Cooper
   st to the river – sometimes up to the
   front of Hospital 6th St[2732]

2726. This book, *La Renaissance de la Poésie Anglaise 1798–1889*, with chapters on Wordsworth, Coleridge, Tennyson, Robert Browning, and Whitman, is described by Whitman as a "handsome 279 pp. book in the beautiful easy handy French style" (*The Correspondence of Walt Whitman*, IV, 330).

2727. These letters to Dr Karl Knortz, Dr R. M. Bucke, and Gabriel Sarrazin are in *The Correspondence of Walt Whitman*, IV, 330–332.

2728. See footnote 2713.

2729. McCollin had mounted several copies of the butterfly picture, which Horace Traubel had brought in on 6 May 1889, and Whitman liked them: "Are they all like this? . . . If they are, I shall be thoroughly satisfied . . ." (*With Walt Whitman in Camden*, V, 141).

2730. Thus ended one of Whitman's longest and closest friendships (see footnotes 2705 and 2710). The next day, 10 May 1889, Whitman wrote four short letters about William D. O'Connor's death to Dr R. M. Bucke, John Burroughs, Thomas B. Harned, and William Sloane Kennedy (see *The Correspondence of Walt Whitman*, IV, 335; see also IV, 336–340). See *With Walt Whitman in Camden*, V, 161–167, for Horace Traubel's account of this day with Whitman: " 'William is dead,' he [Whitman] remarked, 'you saw?' And then: 'It was in the papers. But I had two letters here about it — one from Nellie, one from James L. Sill.' He handed them to me, and took up the thread of his work again as I read. We said little after I finished, but W.'s whole look and tone were pathetic. 'Poor Nellie! Poor Nellie!' " (*ibid.*, V, 161).

2731. This wheelchair was one aspect of the citizens of Camden's testimonial to Whitman, with Geoffrey Buckwalter, Harry Bonsall, and Thomas B. Harned as heads of the committee; though the main event was to take place on the poet's 70th birthday, 31 May 1889, talk of the wheelchair began on 7 May (see *With Walt Whitman in Camden*, V, 145–146); Horace Traubel and Edward Wilkins found the chair they wanted at Wanamaker's on the next day (*ibid.*, V, 152, 154); and Whitman first tried it in his room on 10 May (*ibid.*, V, 167). On the 12th he wrote Dr R. M. Bucke: "Well I went out in the wheel chair yesterday afternoon & was probably out an hour & a half — every thing work'd well — the chair is a success & sits & goes easy — Ed [Wilkins] of course propell'd me — Shall go out again to-day — " (*The Correspondence of Walt Whitman*, IV, 336).

2732. There are many more details in *With Walt Whitman in Camden*, V, 168 *et passim*, about Whitman and his use of the wheelchair.

[376]

[Clipping from classified section of a newspaper:]

P HOTOGRAPHS PRINTED IN THE BEST MANNER. Photographs mounted, negatives developed. Sword Bros., 1520 Chestnut and 1412 Bouvier.

[In WW's hand:]   Phil: Press
                  May 25 '89 [2733]

[377]

May   1889   May   ~~and June~~
               L of G
18 – the pocket-book ed'n ∧ nearly done – all the
     work good with the exception of the <u>press-work</u>[2734]
     ————————   in the
     troubled all these days with the "cold ∧ head"
     feeling (?catarrh? a sort of gathering ∧ in the
     head) — half-buzzing – deafness, &c – constipation
     ————————————————————————∧rather bad [2735]
24   We all drank respects & health to Queen
     Victorio – (her birth day) [2736]

2733. Whitman may have clipped this advertisement out of the Philadelphia *Press* in connection with having his photograph mounted in an edition he was preparing, but he had just paid McCollin for mounting some pictures in the pocket-book (1889) *Leaves* (*With Walt Whitman in Camden*, V, 141, 155), which satisfied him. Sword Brothers: not mentioned in the *Daybook*, Traubel, or *The Correspondence*.

2734. Of the printing of the 1889 *Leaves* (see footnote 2713, above), Whitman said to Horace Traubel, "that vexes me — that is by no means up to the mark — neither registered well nor inked well. I should say, the ink not only very bad, but very sparingly used too. . . . Oh no! Ferguson has not done us up well this time" (*With Walt Whitman in Camden*, V, 189; see also V, 221).

2735. Twice during the day Whitman mentioned that something was the matter with his head: "It is my head — I have not been at all well today, though not giving up entirely . . . ," and later, "It keeps up an awful buzzing, sawing — keeps me deaf full half the time — oppresses, threatens, discomposes . . ." (*With Walt Whitman in Camden*, V, 195).

2736. Although Horace Traubel did not take part in the toast (as he was not there), Whitman wrote to Dr R. M. Bucke: "We broke a big bottle of good wine yesterday [24 May 1889] & all of us (seven — me at the head) drank health & respects to Queen Victoria — (it was her birthday you know —)" (*The Correspondence of Walt Whitman*, IV, 340–341). Whitman, Mrs Mary Davis, Edward Wilkins were three of the "seven"; among the others were Warren Fritzinger and an English sailor from a ship in the river. The next day, when Traubel asked the poet about the toast to the Queen, Whitman said, "Yes, we drank it — and heartily, too. Why not?" He said his friends were furious about his defending the monarchy, even William D. O'Connor. "A great many years ago, at Pfaff's," Whitman continued, "I got into a regular row by defending the Queen — and there were Englishmen present, too. But in my philosophy — in the bottom-meanings of Leaves of Grass — there is plenty of room for all. And I, for my part, not only include anarchists, socialists, whatnot, but Queens, aristocrats." (See *With Walt Whitman in Camden*, V, 227; see also V, 222, 223.)

25 Martin's Ship St Fillan f'm Bombay
East Indies. – bro't over copper ore f'm
Rangoon[2737]

---

paid $36.10 to Ferguson Bro's
"   7.65 to Billstein & Son[2738]

Sunday Evn'g: May 26 '89
the visit, nearly an hour, of the three
Hindus, in their native costumes – &
the gifts, (a large India silk handkerchief
&ᵃ cocoa-nut cane) – from the ship-crew
of the Saint Fillans, that bro't a
cargo of copper ore to Phila: f'm
Rangoon – I c'd talk a little with
them, & enjoy'd it all – [2739]

[378]

[Blank]

[379]

May   May 1889 / I begin on the
                         / other book from this

28 – Am sitting here alone in my room 328
Mickle st: Camden, bet: 8 and 9 a m.
– fair spirits but almost completely bodily
disabled – (Not so bad as that, either, for I

2737. Mrs Mary Davis and Edward Wilkins went down to the Delaware River to see some of the sailors, and an English ship with a crew of Hindus. One of the English seamen was a friend with whose family Warren Fritzinger had stopped in Liverpool, and they drank to the Queen (see footnote above) when they came to 328 Mickle Street. Whitman had wanted to see one of the Hindus, but "his father would not let him come for fear he would be spirited away for a museum!" (*With Walt Whitman in Camden*, V, 223). See also *The Correspondence of Walt Whitman*, IV, 340.

2738. These were bills for the printer (Ferguson Brothers, whose work Whitman did not like) and the plate printer (Henry Billstein, whose plates of a three-quarter Whitman the poet did like) of the special pocket-book (1889) edition of *Leaves of Grass* for the 70th birthday celebration (see footnotes 2713 and 2734).

2739. These three Hindus came to Mickle Street after Horace Traubel had, and Whitman told him about the peculiar visit (see also footnote 2737): "Three Hindu fellows came in — the fellows I spoke to you about: they could scarcely speak a word of English. They brought me this bamboo cane . . . And I have used it a good deal today — it is very nice — strong; Warren [Fritzinger] is going to have a ferrule put on it for me. They brought me also that gay handkerchief you see there on the chair," a gay dotted red and blue silk affair, over which Whitman laughed goodhumoredly: *With Walt Whitman in Camden*, V, 230–231.

have good use & volition of my right arm,
as shown by this writing) – bad eye-sight –
– brain very tender & easily wearied out
– my finish of 70th year of life (May 31)
is close at hand – There is to be (somewhat against my wish & advice) a 'public'
                    probably 200 people plus:
dinner, & speeches & company, ∧ to commemo-
rate it, to be held at 5 p m at Morgan's
hall here.
    Had a dish of big strawberries for breakfast[2740]

28th – a letter from Edw'd Carpenter[2741]
194:95 from E C., Bessie and Isabella
    Ford, & William, Ethel & Arthur Thompson
Good loving letter from J G Whittier
    to Horace Traubel – takes two tickets
        & encloses pay.[2742]
letter from "Mark Twain" [2743]

2740. Not since 20 March 1889 had Whitman written such a long entry in his *Daybook*, and there are not many of them; from notes here and in Horace Traubel's reports in *With Walt Whitman in Camden*, V, 234ff., one wonders if the birthday celebration were really against Whitman's wishes. Whitman's notes about the affair appear in the second volume that the poet kept as his *Daybook*; Traubel's account is in *With Walt Whitman in Camden*, V, 246–251; Gay Wilson Allen retells it briefly in *The Solitary Singer*, pp. 533–534; Whitman told about the dinner, the speeches, and his feelings in letters to Dr R. M. Bucke, William Sloane Kennedy, and J. W. Wallace — *The Correspondence of Walt Whitman*, IV, 342–345; and a fairly full report is in *Camden's Compliment to Walt Whitman, 31 May 1889: Notes, Addresses, Letters, Telegrams* (Philadelphia, 1889, 74 pp.), Traubel's first editing chore under his name.
    2741. This letter (now in the Feinberg Collection) is printed in *With Walt Whitman in Camden*, V, 256, mentioning the £40 he, the Fords and the Thompsons sent; Whitman wrote on it, "Seems to me one of the leading best missives I ever had — goes to my heart," and the letter also appeared in *Camden's Compliment to Walt Whitman*, p. 54. Whitman's reply to Edward Carpenter is in *The Correspondence of Walt Whitman*, IV, 341–342.
    2742. John Greenleaf Whittier (1807–1892), who wrote to Thomas Donaldson as late as 1885 that "I have been pained by some portions of W. W.'s writings, which for his own sake, and that of his readers, I wish could be omitted" (Thomas Donaldson, *Walt Whitman the Man* [New York, 1896], p. 175), told Traubel that he was too old and too ill to attend Whitman's birthday celebration but wished him "renewed health and many more birthdays, and [to thank God] for the consolation which must come from the recollection of generous services rendered to the sick and suffering Union soldiers in the hospitals of Washington during the Civil War" (*With Walt Whitman in Camden*, V, 231). It was Whitman's work in the hospitals that Whittier praised, also in the 1885 letter, not *Leaves of Grass*, though he did like the dirge to Lincoln — "O Captain! My Captain!" rather than "Lilacs." Whittier also liked "There Was a Child Went Forth" "better than anything else I wrote those days," Whitman said to Traubel, "in fact, I don't know but it's the only thing he likes it all" (*With Walt Whitman in Camden*, V, 311). Whitman, for his part, wrote William Sloane Kennedy, who was writing a book on Whittier, that the Quaker's verse "stands for *morality* (not its *ensemble* or in any true philosophic or Hegelian sense but) — as filter'd through the positive Puritanical & Quaker filters — is very valuable as a genuine utterance & a very fine one . . ." (*The Correspondence of Walt Whitman*, IV, 381).
    2743. Mark Twain had heard Whitman's Lincoln lecture in New York in April 1887 (see

29 – I am sitting 4.40 p m. in the 2ᵈ story
   room in Mickle Street.   Feeling so-so.
   – This book (memoranda, &c:) has ab't
                70ᵗʰ
come to an end, & my 69ᵗʰ y'r ditto
[In pencil:]
"   the pocket book ed'n 100 copies rec'd ²⁷⁴⁴

[380]

[Blank]

[381]

[In pencil:]
30ᵗʰ   sent pocket-book ed'n to Dr Bucke²⁷⁴⁵

[382]

[Blank]

[383]

1888   Bills, Moneys, &c: &c: paid out
W. W. Bennett (horse) April 7 '88 – $18.²⁷⁴⁶

April   '88 – lent to E E Harned   15 ²⁷⁴⁷

Whitman's brief letter to him, 14 June 1887, *The Correspondence of Walt Whitman*, IV, 101),
contributed to the horse-and-buggy fund in 1885, and cottage fund in 1888; but Traubel reported on 26 May 1889: "I received a four-page note from Mark Twain, full of generalities,
with practically no word about W. W. Have not yet referred to it in W.'s presence" (*With
Walt Whitman in Camden*, V, 229). This letter, to Traubel and not Whitman, must have been
seen by the poet, as it is mentioned here; yet this line in the *Daybook* and Traubel's short
comment are all we know of the reaction at 328 Mickle Street.
    2744.   This was the 1889 edition of *Leaves of Grass* made for Whitman's birthday affair
(see footnote 2713). Whitman was pleased with the book: "Everything seems just as it should
be — and there is the pocket, too, just as I wished it! I like the 'lay' of the book much!" And
he told Horace Traubel about distributing them on 31 May and mailing them to those not at
the celebration (*With Walt.in Camden*, V, 237).
    2745.   Whitman apparently sent no letter along with *Leaves of Grass*, but mentioned it
in letters to Bucke, 1, 2 and 4–5 June 1889 (see *The Correspondence of Walt Whitman*, IV,
343, 344, 345).
    Although the *Daybook* as a daily journal or diary — if that is what it ever was — ends
here, and Whitman began putting entries into the second volume of his *Daybook*, for the next
twenty pages in this first volume are to be found notations about money, bills, and financial
matters much the same as those Whitman made when he originally started the *Daybook* about
March 1876.
    2746.   This is also recorded for this date, above, but Whitman is not consistent about
this: sometimes he records in one place in the *Daybook*, sometime the other, and also sometimes (as here) in both the "front" and the "back" of the book.
    2747.   Could this be in error for Ezra H. Heywood, to whom Whitman did lend $15 on
23 March 1888 (see entry above, that date, and footnote 2558), which was repaid?

Ap. 28 – Mrs. M. Goodenough for Ed's b'd –   16

May   Bennet (horse)   18

June 6   "   "   18 [2748]

July 3 to Ferguson printer   50 [2749]

" 20 to Mrs. Stafford   25 [2750]

                    3 mo's
" 31 for Ed's board Blackwood∧ advance   45 [2751]

" 31 to Bennett (for horse)   36 [2752]

            f'm bank
Sept 5 drew out   for myself to pay   50
            bills &c &c

"   4 paid bill of Alexander Balfour
            Phila: for paper   240.10[2753]

" 12 Ferguson's printer's bill   246.98 [2754]

" 13 Bennett (horse)   22.29 [2755]

Dec. 20 – drew.cash to pay bills, Christ-
            mas presents, &c &c –   100.[2756]

    27 to Ferguson printer   84.75 [2757]

    31 to Oldach bookbinder   34.86 [2758]

    2748. The payments to Mrs Goodenough and the Bennett in May are mentioned above, but not the June payment for the keep of Whitman's horse Nettie.
    2749. This was for printing *November Boughs* (see entry for this date, above, and footnotes 2589 and 2597).
    2750. Susan Stafford visited Whitman in Camden on 20 July 1889 (see *The Correspondence of Walt Whitman,* IV, 189), but this $25 is not referred to in the *Daybook* (except here); in a letter to her on 21 July, he asked "did you get the money all right at the bank?" (*ibid.,* IV, 190). A loan, gift, or payment for something?
    2751. See entry for 1 August 1888 for more of this, and footnote 2602.
    2752. For keeping Nettie for two months — not listed elsewhere.
    2753. The paper was used for printing *November Boughs* (see entry of 5 September 1888), on which date he also recorded the $50 which Mary Davis, Whitman's housekeeper, drew from the bank to pay taxes and other bills.
    2754. More money for *November Boughs* — paid by check (see entry that date).
    2755. This was the final payment for the boarding of Nettie, for Whitman had just sold his horse (see footnote 2629).
    2756. Except for $10 each to Whitman's sisters (see entries above, for 20 December 1888), this $100 is accounted for in the bills below.

"   to W H Adams, steel plate printer   6.32

[384]

[Blank]

[385]

       Bills, Moneys, &c: &c: paid out

ø

Oct. 24 '88 – Medallion plate, (frontispiece Complete Works, Vol)
                           Phila
   Photo-Eng. Co: 728 Chestnut st: 11.50 [2759]

'89
March 27, '89 – Photo-Eng: Co. for the
    ¾ length figure "process"   10.50 [2760]

April 6 – extra money for eng: 3.

'89
May 25, '89 to Ferguson Bro's: for
   printing &c: pocket b'k ed'n L of G.   36.10

May 25, '89 to Billstein & Son, 925
   Filbert st: Phila: for plate printing
   for pocket-b'k ed'n L of G   7.65 [2761]

[386]

[Blank]

[387]

      Bills, Moneys &c: &c: Paid

Bill W C Hamilton & Sons, paper dealers
  Phila: for paper for the 70th year
                 April 6 '89
  Ed'n L of G – (cheque to Horace) $49.[2762]

2757. So far Whitman had paid Ferguson Brothers and Company in 1888 $381.73 for printing *November Boughs* and *Complete Poems & Prose.*
  2758. See *The Correspondence of Walt Whitman,* IV, 242 for Whitman's binding order to Frederick Oldach.
  2759. This and the previous bill above for plates are not mentioned elsewhere.
  2760. See entry above for 26 March 1889 and *The Correspondence of Walt Whitman,* IV, 311.
  2761. See entry above for this date and footnote 2738.
  2762. See *With Walt Whitman in Camden,* IV, 503.

April 3   Gas bill for Jan. Feb. &
    89   March, '89   10.49 [2763]
                to   bill.
                    for ¾ figure "process"   10.50 [2764]

[388]

[Written in WW's hand on an envelope of Ferguson Bros. & Co.:]

Ferguson's foremen
Myrick
            in composition room[2765]
Brown in press room[2766]
James Electrotype room

[Other material pinned to page]

[Five lines in pencil:]   [389]
    May 29 '88 – have sent copy "A
Backward Glance o'er Travel'd Roads,"
for "Nov: Boughs" by Horace T
to Ferguson, printer – Evn'g (x)[2767]

─────────────

30 – Note to Ferguson[2768]

Expenses on the two Books

1888   "November Boughs" & the big Book[2769]

2763. See entry above for this date.
2764. This is repeated, perhaps by mistake, from a few lines above.
2765. Myrick, the foreman in Ferguson Brothers printing plant, was the man Horace Traubel dealt with in printing the 1889 *Leaves of Grass* and other books: see *With Walt Whitman in Camden,* V, 2, 5 ("I am surprised, knowing Myrick's good taste as I do, that he ever consented to pass such a page as that other"), 6, 8, 24, 48, 349, 350 (Myrick's good qualities), 396.
2766. Brown, whose first name is never given (nor was Myrick's), was also at Ferguson's, and Traubel was with him often: see *With Walt Whitman in Camden,* V, 78, 81, 92, 102, 113, 144, 153, 158, 221, 268, 369, 377, 383, 401, 403, 407; and sometimes there were difficulties between him and Traubel and Whitman. Another man at Ferguson's printing establishment, simply called James here, is not named in Traubel's volume, and one cannot know if James is his first or last name.
2767. As early as 18 March 1886 Whitman wrote to John Burroughs, "Want to scoop up what I have (poems and prose) of the last MSS since 1881 and '2, & put in probably 200 page book (or somewhat less) to be called perhaps *November Boughs* —" (*The Correspondence of Walt Whitman,* IV, 22); but it was not published until October 1888 (see footnote 2589, above), and included of course "A Backward Glance O'er Travel'd Roads" on pp. 5–18 (see *ibid.,* IV, 36n).
2768. This note to George Ferguson, also mentioned under 30 May 1888 in the *Daybook,* is missing.

Money paid July 3 to Ferguson	$50:
engraving Elias Hicks	4:50
frontispiece	11:
copies	
printing the frontispiece 1775	11:75
White paper 1100 copies"Nov- ember Boughs" & 600 big Book }	240:10
Sept: 12 paid Ferguson's bills	246.98
money to Horace to pay	
bills	15:
to Ferguson	
paid ∧ Dec: 27 '88 ——in full	84:75
Dec	
" to Oldach & Co binders 31	34.86
Adams plate printer – Dec 31	6.32 [2770]

                                                      [390]

[Blank]

                                                      [391]

by letter from Edw'd Dowden,		[In red pencil,
Winsted, Temple Road,		sideways:]
Rathmines, Dublin	$69:25	all rec'd
Feb. 16		
sent the books – 6 sets – by express		
March 2ᵈ [2771] [In red pencil:] — all rec'd —		

March 5
by letter ∧ from W M Rossetti,
£5, each
∧ for himself & Mrs. Gilchrist   £10.

    2769. In addition to *November Boughs,* Whitman was bringing out his *Complete Poems & Prose,* which he always calls "the big book" (see footnote 2653, above). Some of the expenses listed here on the several lines below are also under their "regular" dates in the *Daybook,* 3 July 1888, 5 and 12 September 1888.

    2770. Whitman's bookkeeping is odd, to say the least: these three December bills are not recorded under their dates, above in the *Daybook,* but they appear twice — see a few lines just above here — in the back of this book.

    2771. This shipment of six sets of *Leaves of Grass* and *Two Rivulets* is recorded under 2 March 1876, near the beginning of the *Daybook* (see footnote 9).

_____ 5 Vols   [In red pencil,
sent <u>him</u> L of G. & 2 <u>T. R.</u> _{altogether}   sideways:]
rec'd

– Mrs G.   L. of G & T. R.[2772]

April 13 from E. C. Stedman   [In red pencil,
80 Broadway N Y. $30   sideways:]
sent books, slips photo   rec'd
&c[2773]

April
21 / Edwd Carpenter (see back 1st page) }
sent 1 set books (rec'd)[2774]   } $21.97

books furnished   [vertically written]
from Joaquin Miller for a set, Two Vols. $10:

(sent through Mr. Johnston, 150 Bowery
N Y [2775]

[392]

[Clipping of an 1880 advertisement of Spring Lawn, Glen Mills, Delaware
Co., Pa., for country boarding, Wm. V. Montgomery.]

[In WW's hand, down the side and in bottom half:]

March 23'– 1881 – Ed went
to board – $16 a month

April, May, June paid –
N [?]   [?]   [erased]

Sept '81 paid $16 [2776]   [in blue pencil]

2772. These letters and shipments of *Leaves of Grass* and *Two Rivulets* for William
Michael Rossetti and Mrs Anne Gilchrist go back to 15 March 1876 (see early pages of the
Daybook and footnotes 14 and 15), the first mention of these two important people in Whitman's later years.
2773. See 13 April 1876, above, the first mention of Edmund Clarence Stedman. See
footnote
2774. See 21 April 1876, above, and footnote 20.
2775. See 19 April 1876, above, and footnote 24. (One wonders why these five entries for
Dowden, Rossetti, Mrs Gilchrist, Stedman, Carpenter, and Miller were recorded twice — at the
beginning of the *Daybook* and at the end.)
2776. These are only a few of the monthly payments Whitman made and recorded
throughout the *Daybook* — see first one this date, above, to William V. Montgomery, Glen
Mills, Pennsylvania — for the upkeep of Edward Whitman, the poet's helpless brother.

~~first~~ first visit to Kirkwood

     April 1, '76 [2777]

    ☞   [In pencil, figures:]

'80	'81
32	23
10	30
20	30
20	10
25	30
107	123 [2778]

    June & July 1873 – Commenced living in Camden. June, July, Aug. Sept. Oct. Nov. & Dec. '73 — the first four months paid $30 monthly – the rest $15 monthly

1874 – paid 15 or $16 monthly cash

1875   "   "   "   "   [In pencil:]

[four lines in pencil:]   See back

1876–'7–'8 "   "   "   "   in this book

                                        1881

    June, 1883 – For Ed (from March 23, ~~up~~ up to date June 1883 – my share nine months) have paid ab't $140 –

June 1 1887 — for the last 6 or 7 years I have paid nearly $400 for Ed's board [2779]

                                                         [393]

Board Acc't[2780]   July 12 '78 – $12

    2777. Although the *Daybook* was being kept by Whitman at this date, he was not recording such items at that time as his visits to the Stafford farm at White Horse, near Timber Creek, Kirkwood, Glendale, New Jersey. (See Gay Wilson Allen, *The Solitary Singer*, pp. 474ff., who says Whitman's first stay was "some time in late April or early May of 1876," but the *Daybook* here says 1 April 1876.)

    2778. The pointed finger (toward Kirkwood) seems to indicate that these figures for 1880 and 1881 are sums which Whitman may have paid Susan Stafford for his stays at their farm; it is more likely that the Staffords did not take money from him for the 44 days in 1880 and 26 days in 1881 (according to the *Daybook*) he was at White Horse, and thus this $107 and $123 Whitman paid to Louisa Whitman for boarding with her and George in Camden — which is what occupies the next few lines here. This is confirmed by entries on the next pages, plus some for his brother Edward's board.

    2779. In Whitman's "scattered" bookkeeping system, we have now shifted to his payments for his brother Edward's board.

    2780. *"Board Acc't"* refers mainly to money Whitman paid his sister-in-law Louisa Whit-

[Six lines in pencil:]   Aug 10 '78 – $7 [in pencil]
1879   Nov. 13 '78 –   20 [in pencil]
Jan 13 – paid Lou $10   March 30 – '78 – Paid L $50 [in pencil]
Feb 28 "   " $10   July   2 – '78 – $20   [in pencil]
March 24 "   " $20   April 2 '78 – $20 [in pencil]
                                    ⎰ absent in N Y
                                    ⎱ from April 9 to June 14 ⎱
                                        – ten weeks   ⎰

last of April (or in May) $10 (from N Y for Ed)

July 2 – paid Lou $10

                                    2ᵈ to 9ᵗʰ
Aug 1.   "   " $10. (was down at Glendale a week
                    & alone a week) two weeks ∧

[Rest of page, 15 lines, in blue pencil:]
   Sept 3 $20
          Colorado & Missouri trip   [in ink]
       (absent ∧ from Sept 10 to Jan 5)

1880 – Feb 27, $32 (March 6 to 12 down Glendale)

   "   March $10 (for Ed)

   May 6 – $20 (pays up to April 30)

         Summer in Canada   [in ink]

   Aug 25 $20   for Ed (from Canada)
         (in Canada 1880 from June 3ᵈ to Sept 31)   [last two words in ink]

Nov 19 – $25 – pays up to date
  ─────────
Jan 6 '81 – $20   pays up to date

Feb 28 '81 $30 – 5 for Ed pays up to date

man, a few sums for his brother Edward's room and board, and the days when Whitman was
away from Camden (in New York or out West) and did not have to pay Louisa for his meals.
For more on his visits to New York, Glendale, Colorado, Missouri, and Canada, see the *Daybook*
entries above for the relevant dates.

March 23 '81 – Ed went to board at   Glen
Mills[2781]

May 28 '81 – $30   pays up to date
                    [three lines in ink:]
July 2 '81 – $10 to Lou   ) left Canada July 23
                            / returned Nov 3
July 3 a visit at Glendale (gone about 15 weeks

[394]

[Year in red:]

on
1884   – paid Mr & Mrs: Lay – cash — board acc't[2782]

March _____ $4 –

April $2   – $2 — $2 ———   6

_____   see $\frac{last}{page}$ [in pencil]

    paid 2 every week (occasionally, (rarely) 1.50)
    every week for nearly a year

[395]

[Written in red ink vertically (two lines) in   In Boston printing 7th Ed'n
left margin:]   L of G. Sept. & Oct. 1881 [2783]

[Line in blue pencil:]
1881 – Left Camden July 23 '81 – on to N Y.

— at Woodside, (Queens Co: L I) 23 to 29th July

– at West Hills, 29th July to Aug. 1 –

– in N. Y.   some days at Edgar Smith's 5 E 65th st[2784]

2781. This was the place in Pennsylvania where Edward Whitman was cared for by William V. Montgomery, Spring Lawn.

2782. Mr and Mrs Lay lived in Whitman's house at 328 Mickle Street, Camden — the poet paid them for his meals — but the arrangement worked only for about a year (see footnotes 1792 and 1796).

2783. These dates and other details are written here by Whitman mainly to help him figure out how many days he was away from Louisa Whitman's house, and did not have to pay for his board: he was meticulous about payments to his sister-in-law. Payment for his brother Edward's keep also crept in here once. More information about these visits to New York City, Long Island, and Boston are given in the *Daybook* for 1881, above.

2784. For Edgar M. Smith, briefly, see *The Correspondence of Walt Whitman*, III, 234n, 236n, and *Daybook*, 1 August 1881.

– N Y   Mott av. & 149th st. 6ᵗʰ Aug. to 19ᵗʰ ²⁷⁸⁵

Sept '81 paid $16 to Montgomery for Ed – [line in blue pencil]

– in Boston 19ᵗʰAug. to Oct. 22

                         nearly
– in N Y Oct. 22 to Nov. 3 – gone ∧ 15 weeks altogether
    absent nearly 15 weeks

[Three lines in pencil:]
Dec 9   I must pay Lou at least $30 – which will pay
          up to Dec. 10 \

Dec 10 '81 – paid Lou $30 – (pays up to date)
    Dec 29 – to Jan 9 – at Glendale – 11 days²⁷⁸⁶

Jan 25 '82 – paid Wᵐ V Montgomery $16 for Ed

[Four lines in pencil:]
'82 Feb 16 – paid Lou $25 (pays up to Feb 18)
       3½ weeks at Glendale – one week, from 24ᵗʰ to
                                 31st March
☞   5 days at Glendale (22ᵈ to 27ᵗʰ April)
(☞ calculate from 6ᵗʰ March, with 2 weeks out)

                       [Five words in pencil:]
May p 8 – paid Lou $25   pays up to May 10

July 15   paid Lou $30 (pays up to date)

[one line in pencil:]
Aug 29 – paid Lou $10 – ~~pay 18 more Sept 29~~

    2785. Mott Avenue and 149th Street was the summer address of the John H. Johnstons, Mott Haven: see the *Daybook,* 7 August 1881; *The Correspondence of Walt Whitman,* III, 236n; and Whitman's article, "City Notes in August," New York *Tribune,* 15 August 1881.
    2786. This line is repeated here — it is also in its appropriate date above — so that Whitman would know how much to deduct from his board payments to Louisa Whitman. Three other lines about Glendale (the Stafford farm, where Whitman often visited) are cited below for the same reason.

Sept 9 '82 – paid Lou $15 pays up to date

Nov: 11 – paid L $30 – pays up to date

Jan 4 '83 – paid " $25 – pays up to date

March 6 '83 "   30 "   "   "   "

May 5, 83   "   30 "   "   "   "

July 3 '83   "   25 "   "   "   "

3ᵈ to 17ᵗʰ (two weeks) down at Glendale

[Two lines in red ink:]
Aug 4 to 28 (24 days) at R P Smith's[2787]

Sept 1 " 3 (12 ") "   "

[396]

[In purple pencil:]   10 weeks to Feb 16 [2788]

[397]

1883
Sept 22 '83 – paid Lou $22 – pays up to date

Sept 26 to Oct 10 – (two weeks) down at
    Ocean Grove, N J.[2789]

[Three words in red ink:]
Dec 8   paid Lou 30   pays up to date ab't
                                      8½ weeks

    [One line in red ink:]
    15, 16, 17, at R P Smith's[2790]

2787. For these two visits to Robert Pearsall Smith's in Germantown, Philadelphia, see footnote 1697 — the lines here are repeated from above (4 to 28 August 1883) to keep his financial transactions straight with Louisa Whitman. (This was not his first stay at the Smith house: that was on 23–25 December 1882 — see footnotes 1622 and 1638.)
    2788. This is the only line on this page, and as no money is indicated the date may have been entered earlier as one on which Whitman planned a payment.
    2789. Recorded here for days not requiring board payments to Louisa Whitman, this trip to Ocean Grove — Sheldon House on the seaside, with John Burroughs — is mentioned above and far more fully in footnote 1714.
    2790. See footnote 2787.

five days at Mr & Mrs Williams Germantown[2791]

1884 – Jan 5, 6, 7, & 8 at R P Smith's – Germantown

Feb   Feb 19

     paid $30 ∧ pays up to date   8 weeks 2d   [line in purple pencil]

–   " $14 to Lou [in pencil]   (12 days out [in purple pencil]

[398]

premises 328 Mickle street Camden N. J.
    bought of Rebecca Jane Hare, April 3, 1884 [2792]

purchase money – cash –	1750.00
Lougheed's bill, plumbing – gas & water	134.
Schellinger's bill carpentering	27.50
Gas Co. connecting street main (paid July 9 '84)	14.75
Ivins – carting &c.	3.25
Recording Deed – – – – – – – –	1.50
Carpentering Schellinger and others [in pencil]	35.
Paper hanging back room 2ᵈ story	3.50
Water permit	3.33
Searches, County offices, Taxes &c	9.
Johnson	
June 7 paid Chas J̶o̶h̶n̶s̶o̶n̶, carpentering	10.
Joshua Killingbeck mason, (bricklaying)	10.90
Chas Johnson	10.50
Schellinger March '85	3.50 [line in pencil]
Plumbing – "	18.50 [line in pencil]
Water Bill (March 26 1885)	5.
Gas up	
Sewer Culvert	
(paid June 30	
back taxes (1884) left unpaid '86)	23.40
water tax '86	8. [?]
Gas up to July 1, '86	3.00

2791. For the Francis Howard Williamses, see footnote 1765.
2792. Other data about the purchase of this house are given in the *Daybook* proper for this date, above, and in footnote 1799; but recorded below are many of the specifically financial transactions, permits, repairing, and taxes.

[399]

\Copy of schedule handed Lou March 23, '84   /
    \rough statement[2793]

Came to Camden June 1873

from that time till end of March 1884 is 560 weeks
during that time absent & away, (Kirkwood,
    New York, Mrs. Gilchrist's, Western trip, Canada,
    Boston, Germantown) 143 weeks —

Leaves 417 weeks I have boarded

[Rest of page, 19 lines, in purple pencil:]

	Paid – 1873 –	$135	
	'74 –	175	
	'75 –	170	Absences
	'76 –	150	absent 9 weeks
	'77 –	90 – 26 weeks, N. Y.	
		Mrs. G's &c[2794]	
	'78 –	120	19 weeks
	'79 —	90	28 weeks altogether[2795]
	'80 –	107	2X weeks
see items	'81 –	123	24 " Boston &
			N Y
on other	'82 –	135	9 weeks
sheet	'83 –	162	9 weeks
	'84 –	44	
		1501	

ab't $3.60 a week for the time boarded

——————

            $208 up to March '84   [line in pencil]
(of course my payments∧ for Ed's board
    \ are _not_ included above
        ∕ not copied here
    ∕ on a second sheet with above were
        the items for 1880, '81, '82, '83 & '84

—————————————

2793. In this "rough statement" for eleven years, one can certainly trace Whitman's movements, with some additional details for the last nine years in another part of the *Daybook*. Then, along with Horace Traubel's *With Walt Whitman in Camden* and *The Correspondence of Walt Whitman*, we have as full a record of Whitman's activities as anyone could possibly need or want.

2794. There were many long visits — a month or so — to the Staffords in Glendale,

[400]

[Blank]

[401]

[Newspaper clipping:] Mr. Benjamin Whitman, of Erie county, de-
clines to be considered a candidate for any elec-
tive office this year; but if the Democrats of Erie
county should nolens volens send him to the
Legislature they would do themselves a credit
and the State at large a favor. Men of his experience and ability are sadly needed at Harrisburg.[2796]

[Sideways in red ink, in margin in WW's hand:]   Phil:
Record
Aug 16 '86

[402]

[Long clipping, pinned to the page, headed: A Story of Whitman. / How the
Good Gray Poet Was Vindicated by / a Stubborn Jury. /. With a notation
in WW's hand: July 2 –/87 –.]

A STORY OF WHITMAN.

**How the Good Gray Poet Was Vindicated by
a Stubborn Jury.**

From the New York World.

The story that Walt Whitman is infirm and poor calls to mind a story of
the early days, when the author of "Blades of Grass" lived with his father in
Babylon. The old gentleman occupied the Minturn Place, West of the village
about a mile and a half. It was in 1840. The budding poet, then about 18
years of age, had just returned home after his venture in journalism in Huntington. His success had not been marked; in fact, it is questioned whether it
should not be put down as a miserable failure.

Walt Whitman, as described by the old ladies of the village, was a handsome youth, full of life, pert in his manner and brisk in his walk. He was
broad-shouldered and muscular, always walking erect, with a sailor swing

and numerous evenings when Whitman had dinner with Mrs Gilchrist at her place in
Philadelphia.
    2795. Whitman was in New York from 9 April to 14 June 1879, and from 10 Septem-
ber until the end of the year on his trip to St. Louis and Colorado.
    2796. Relationship to Walt Whitman doubtful.

of easy independence. His dress suggested a "water dog." His collar was cut low and his shirt front was usually rolled back, exposing his robust breast. A short sailor jacket and wide trousers contributed an air of salt water, and suggested a jolly marine out for an airing. Captain Simon Cooper is reported as saying: "I can smell salt water ten miles away just on seeing Whitman."

He was a popular favorite among both sexes in the village, and many jolly yarns are told of those days which, no doubt, the now aged and suffering poet can recall with pleasure.

One of the stories called to mind is the arrest of the poet for an assault upon a young man named Benjamin Carman. The Carman farm joined the farm occupied by the Whitmans. A trout pond formed the boundary. In this pond Walt delighted to fish. On a certain day while Whitman was sitting in his boat angling, young Carman conceived the idea of annoying him. He first threw stones so as to disturb the water near the fisherman. Seeing no effect on the stolid fisherman, he got in his own boat and commenced leisurely rowing around in the vicinity of the poet, to the total destruction of fishing. Even this annoyance failed to call forth any reproof or remonstrance, and Whitman fished on as though nothing was annoying him. At first the lad was careful to keep beyond the reach of the fishing-pole, but finally, his suspicions being quieted by the manner of the fisherman, who in a casual sort of way plied him with various questions, asking if he were not a namesake of Benjamin Frank-

lin, and engaging him in cheerful conversation, the boy edged nearer and nearer, until, coming within the swing of Whitman's fishpole, the poet caught him unawares and thrashed him unmercifully, breaking his pole and inflicting quite severe injuries upon the boy, dismissing him with the admonition that the next time to refrain from interfering with his fishing.

But this was not destined to be the last of the matter. The elder Carman, in rage at the castigation of his son, swore out a warrant for Whitman's arrest before Justice Joel Jarvis, of Huntington. In those days Babylon was a land of "rum and romance," and many quaint characters clustered about the village. The news of the important arrest traveled like wildfire, and when the constable produced the prisoner before the magistrate the little seven-by-nine courtroom was crowded. General Richard Udall, afterwards member of assembly from Suffolk, appeared as attorney for Carman, while Whitman pleaded his own case. The jury was made up of men who thought more of common sense than of law. The foreman was John Edwards, an Englishman, full of stubborn persistence, prepared to insist upon having his own way. The progress of the trial was not devoid of interest; in fact, for years the case of "The People against Walt. Whitman" was one of the most celebrated on the "merry old South side." General Udall made a clear case. The evidence was not disputed. Whitman, when he summed up his defense, told the jury the facts in the case. He admitted he had trounced the boy, but plead in justification that Carman had interfered with his vested rights and had made himself a nuisance, and the nuisance had simply been abated. The jury filed out. They were out but a few moments and returned into court.

The Justice resettled his steel-bowed spectacles so that he could more readily look over them and asked: "Gentlemen of the jury, have you agreed upon your verdict?"

"We 'ave," said Edwards.

"What is it?" asked His Honor.

"We find 'e did not 'it him 'ard enough," said the foreman.

The uproarious laughter which greeted this verdict the Justice was unable to quell, and in his righteous indignation broke his spectacles in his endeavor to sufficiently express his disapproval. When quiet was restored he explained to the jury that they must find a verdict of "guilty" or "not guilty," when the spectators were again convulsed by the answer of the sturdy Yorkshire gentleman, who stubbornly insisted that the only verdict of the jury was that "Whitman 'ad not 'it 'im 'ard enough," and after repeated attempts to get the matters right, the prisoner was discharged and the verdict stands to-day that "the plaintiff was not hit hard enough."

Whitman's father was a coarse, large-boned, very tall and powerful man. His mother is recalled as a slight, refined, lady-like woman of most prepossessing manners.

[Line in red ink:]
1884   (Ed commenced boarding away March 23, 1881 [2797]
[Rest of page, 12 lines, in purple pencil:]
My payment for Ed's board
        Maggie B Goodenough   [in ink]
    at Mrs: Margaret Goodenoughs

(Mt Laurel N J)   Moorestown N J.
        p. o.
April 1st 1884 – Up to this date I
    have paid thirteen months at $16
                a month $208

2797. At this time Edward Whitman was being cared for by William V. Montgomery, Glen Mills, Pennsylvania; then he went to Mrs Margaret Goodenough's, Moorestown, New Jersey; and on 1 August 1888 to the Insane Asylum, Blackwoodtown, New Jersey (see footnote 2602).

May is my turn but it is already paid   10

 [pointing finger in pencil]

August is my next turn   paid July 30   16 [last four words in ink]

Mrs Goodenough   Mt Laurel road
                        Moorestown – her p.o. is
                                    Mt Laurel

[Upside-down, written by turning book over:]
May 4 rec'd $10 by check from Laura Curtis
        Bullard, 35 east 39th st. N Y for 1 set books[2798]
                [In pencil:] books sent & recd

                                                [403]

[Blank]

                                                [404]

[On a large sheet, pinned to the page, written in WW's hand:]

        Moneys &c paid   Mr. and Mrs. Lay[2799]

March 8 '84 – to Mr. L — $5
    " 13 "   "   "   10
    " 21 "   to Mrs. L   4
April 5,12,19,26 $2 each —   8
May 3,10,17,24,& 31. – $2 each –   10
June 7,14,21,& 28. $2 each —   8
July 5,12,19,26   2 each —   8
Aug. 2,9,16,23,& 30. $2 each   10
Sept. 6,13,20,27 $2 each   8
Oct 4,11,18,25, $2 each   8
Nov. 1,8,15,22,29, $1 each   5
Dec. 6,13, $1 each   2
                                   ____
                                   $84:
Rent 10 months @ $10 —   100
Gas — 9 months @ 2 —   18
                                   ____
Paid Tasker $20 [in pencil, erased] 202
    Cash, $1 $5 Jan 23—   6
                                   ____
                                   $208

    Paid Tasker $20
to Mrs L – $2 – 2 – 2 – 2 —
41 weeks from March 29 '84 to Jan 4 '85

[405]

[Back cover Daybook One: blank]

[Daybook Two: inside front cover: blank]   [2:0]

                                                                      [2:1]

for Johnstown goods to be mark'd
  Care J V Patton, Sup't B & O
    Johnstown Penn:
    send to Pier 12 north wharves, Phila:[2800]

                                                                      [2:2]

[Blank]

                                                                      [2:3]

    C W P is located (July 24 '90) at 3819 Lancaster av: Phila
                  real estate office[2801]

This Memorandum Book was a present
  from my dear young friend,   what has become [two lines in pencil]
  Clayton Wesley Peirson   of him?
bro't to me by him Evn'g of March 22, 1887 –

May 31   Write this ab't 11 a m in my big ratan chair
1889   in Mickle street Camden.   Have just had a
                              Camden
    wash & bath – a newspaper reporter, (News, ~~Phila:~~)
    has call'd, but I am tired & head-sore & thick
    & I cut the interview short.   It is cloudy & looks
    like rain. The "public dinner" is to come off

2798. Laura Curtis Bullard wrote Whitman on 3 May 1876 (letter in *With Walt Whitman in Camden*, III, 555-556; his reply is now lost); this sale is recorded on the early pages of the *Daybook* — why repeat it here?

2799. This final entry in the *Daybook's* first volume, actually pinned in, records the $2 a week from March through September 1884 that Whitman paid Mr and Mrs Lay for boarding him in his own house, 328 Mickle Street, Camden (see footnotes 1792, 1796, and 2782).

2800. This has to do with goods to be sent to victims of the Johnstown flood, about which Whitman was asked to write a poem, which became "A Voice from Death," New York *World*, 7 June 1889 (see *Daybook* entry below for 1 June 1889; also for 7 June).

2801. This line was written some years after the line just below here about Clayton Wesley Peirson, who gave Whitman this new *Daybook* on 22 March 1887, and Whitman later asked, "what has become of him?" On 25 February 1887 Peirson took the original *Daybook* to be rebound; and in a letter to Thomas Donaldson, 14 January 1889, Whitman asked about the boy (see *The Correspondence of Walt Whitman*, IV, 269).

at & after 5 p m.[2802] To-day finishes the 70th year
of my life.   Have had a bad year past, nearly
all the time imprison'd in this room.   But
here I am yet, with my head above water.
       (and some gloomy enough,)
Big time-marks, ∧ the late ones. My dear friend
William O'Connor is dead & buried.[2803] My big
book, "complete works" is printed: the best
ed'n "Leaves of Grass" (pocket book binding)
                                 422 pages
with "Sands" and "Backward Glance" included, ∧ is out.[2804]
I shall try to get around & show myself &
speak a short word, to my dear friends at the
       to-night.[2805]
dinner ∧   The event itself, & what is done &
said, will show what ɪt all amounts to.
— The old memorandum book being now
fill'd, I henceforth write in this.

sent pocket-b'k edn's L of G to

Sarrazin, France	Frank Williams rec'd
Dowden, Ireland, 2 copies	Herbert Gilchrist rec'd
rec'd	
Lou rec'd	Sylvester Baxter rec'd
Armstrong	
Judge Garrison rec'd (bo't)	Mrs. Stafford (Glendale)
Clifford rec'd	Dr Bucke (three)
Horace 2 copies	W S Kennedy [in pencil]
R W Gilder rec'd	Phillips Stewart
John Burroughs rec'd	Mr Bancroft (Wash'n)[2806]
T B Harned rec'd	

2802. For the birthday celebration, see, among other items, footnote 2740.
2803. See footnote 2730.
2804. For Whitman's *Complete Poems & Prose* — as the title reads on the title-page —
see footnote 2713. Although he here called the *Leaves* with the "pocket book binding" the
"best ed'n," it is not now even considered a separate edition of the *Leaves,* merely one that
was printed between the *Complete Poems & Prose* (1888) and the "Deathbed" printing of 1892.
2805. Whitman's remarks were printed in a full report of the testimonial dinner in the
Philadelphia *Press,* 1 June 1889.
2806. Most of those on this list were not at Whitman's birthday celebration and he
wanted them to have copies of the pocket-book (1889) printing of *Leaves:* Gabriel Sarrazin,
the French critic whom the poet had lately praised; Edward Dowden, the Irish scholar and
long-time admirer; the poet's sister-in-law Louisa Whitman; John Burroughs the great
naturalist; Sylvester Baxter the Boston journalist; Mrs Susan Stafford, at whose Glendale,

[2:4]

[Printed card: Edward W. Searing, Counsellor at Law, 25 Chambers Street, New York. Notary.] 2807

[2:5]

    Camden Mickle street   June   1889

June 1 The most pervading & dreadful news this
    m'ng is of the strange cataclysm at Johns-
    town & adjoining, Cambria County, Penn: by wh-
        of people   [in pencil]
    many thousands ʌ are overwhelm'd, kill'd by drowning
    in water, burnt by fire, &c: &c: x all our hearts, the
    papers & the public interest, are fill'd with it —
    – the most signal & wide-spread horror of the
    kind ever known in this country – curious that
    at this very hour, we were having the dinner festivities &c
    – unaware2808

2 – the dinner, speeches, &c: all get good praise –
    – certainly, for a Quaker racket (as some one
    has call'd it) – and for Camden, and for a gen-

New Jersey farmhouse Whitman spent so many days and weeks; Dr Richard Maurice Bucke, who remained in London, Ontario; William Sloane Kennedy, who also was out of town at his home in Belmont, Massachusetts; Phillips Stewart, who was from Toronto, visited Whitman on 1 July 1889 (see entry that date, below); and George Bancroft the historian, whom Whitman had never met (see *With Walt Whitman in Camden*, II, 16). Six others whose names are here were at the 31 May 1889 affair in Camden: Judge Ambler Armstrong, who bought a copy of the book and who was a substitute on the program for Lyman Abbott, the rationalist preacher; John Herbert Clifford, the Unitarian minister from Germantown, Philadelphia, who also spoke at the dinner; Richard Watson Gilder of *The Critic*, and now *The Century*; Thomas B. Harned, one of Whitman's closest associates and Camden's leading lawyer; Francis Howard Williams, the Quaker poet and dramatist with whom Whitman stayed in Germantown; Herbert Gilchrist, the artist now painting on Long Island.
    2807. Edward W. Searing's card is here because he apparently ordered a copy of *November Boughs,* which Whitman sent him on 7 June 1889 (his letter now lost, as is Whitman's if there was one): see entry below.
    2808. Whitman wrote Dr R. M. Bucke on 4–5 June 1889 how "gloomy" they all were about the Johnstown flood, "the more we hear, the worse & more destructive & deadly it proves" (*The Correspondence of Walt Whitman,* IV, 345); and he spoke of it to Horace Traubel, "It is beyond all precedent — almost incredible" (*With Walt Whitman in Camden,* V, 257; see also V, 261). Then on 5 June C. H. Browning of the New York *World* was asked by Julius Chambers to go to Whitman in Camden and get "a threnody on the Johnstown flood" for publication in the *World* (see *With Walt Whitman in Camden,* V, 265–267; and *The Correspondence of Walt Whitman,* IV, 346). Whitman wrote the poem, "A Voice from Death," which appeared in the New York *World,* 7 June 1889, p. 1. See *Leaves of Grass,* Comprehensive Reader's Edition, pp. 551–553; the poem appeared in *Good-bye My Fancy* before its inclusion in the 1891-92 *Leaves.* A full account of the Johnstown flood and "A Voice from Death" is told in William White, "Whitman's Poem on the Johnstown Flood," *Emerson Society Quarterly,* No. 33 (IV Quarter 1963), 79–84.

unine & quiet affair, the most successful of the

now

kind ever known. — the project∧ is to make a
little 72 page book, pub'd by Dave McKay, Phila:
(50cts) printing nicely the whole affair, speeches, &c:
<u>edited by</u> <u>Horace Traubel</u> – (I <u>endorse</u> the <u>proj</u>ect) – [2809]

4   Tuesday-just p m – Nothing special – I write
with no special purpose – a cloudy, warmish,
still day – half-ill (even for these times) to-day.
– O this dreadful horror around Johnstown! [2810]

£

5   recd from the p o the   10 and $4.99 . . . Lou here last
evening[2811]

7   "A Voice from Death" my poem on the Conemaugh
        1/3^d of a column $25
Cataclysm   printed in N. Y World, this mn'g (pay rec'd [2812]
sent Nov: B to E W Searing   Paid $2 [2813]
paid
sent 6 L of G – & 6 Nov: B. to Judge Garrison $19.50 [2814]
Am sitting in the old 2^d story room in Mickle st.
– Every thing smooth & prosperous enough – Have just

2809. For Whitman's letter to Horace Traubel on *Camden's Compliment to Walt Whitman*, see *The Correspondence of Walt Whitman*, IV, 343–344; see also *With Walt Whitman in Camden*, V, 259–260, 262, 274, 278, 283, 284, 303, 313, 408, 440–441, 454, all of them brief comments on the title or the contents; further comments, about 25 or 30 of them between June and 29 October 1889 (when the book came out, though Whitman wanted it in a few days after the testimonial dinner), are scattered through *The Correspondence*. See also footnote 2740, above. "Traubel's dinner book," Whitman called it: *The Corerspondence*, IV, 372.

2810. The Johnstown flood: see footnote 2808.

2811. The £10 came from J. W. Wallace of Bolton, England, as a gift (letter in the Feinberg Collection); Whitman's letter of thanks is in *The Correspondence of Walt Whitman*, IV, 345; the $4.99 was from William Sloane Kennedy (see *ibid.*, IV, 344), a facetious way of ordering the pocket-book *Leaves of Grass*; Traubel mentions that Mrs. George (Louisa) Whitman and the poet were talking when he (Traubel) approached about 8 p. m. — he was advising her about some sewing (*With Walt Whitman in Camden*, V, 262).

2812. See footnote 2808.

2813. Searing was a New York City attorney, whose calling card Whitman pasted in the *Daybook* (see a few entries above, and footnote 2807).

2814. Judge Charles G. Garrison, who had been one of the several speakers at the birthday celebration in Morgan's Hall, Camden, had written to Thomas B. Harned on 3 June 1889 for these half-a-dozen copies of *Leaves of Grass* and *November Boughs*; his talk is in *Camden's Compliment to Walt Whitman*, pp. 34–36. (See *The Correspondence of Walt Whitman*, IV, 348.) Whitman spoke to Horace Traubel of the "extreme kindliness of the Garrison family — women and men" (*With Walt Whitman in Camden*, V, 261).

envelop'd for mailing to Europe and to Dr B the "Voice"
(correctly printed in today's N Y World)²⁸¹⁵ – At present
my physical botherations are this catarrhal, and
trouble
(to some extent) the bladder — weather sunny, coolish,
pleasant – (W'd this heavy disagreeable feeling, head,
be remedied any by more abstinence & care in eating?)²⁸¹⁶

[2:6]

[Written in WW's hand on part of an envelope from Hannah & Hogg, Wholesale Liquors, 220 S. Clark Street, Chicago, Illinois:]

[On the page in pencil, in WW's hand:]

(Cavalry soldier in War
5ᵗʰ reg't – I call'd him
"Cody"
I sent the letter to Dr B)²⁸¹⁷

Mirrors
615 north 2ᵈ st Phil

[On clipped corner of a letterhead of R. S. Nickerson:]

M C Reed
222 So: Clark st
    wrote him a card June
                    9
Chicago Ill:

419 Cooper st
June 25 '89

[On the page in WW's hand:]

[Clipping, with WW's notation:]

Ledger   June 12 '89

ORIGIN OF THE "ARABIAN NIGHTS."
— The origin of "The Ten Thousand
and One Nights" is almost as difficult
to trace as that of the "Iliad" or the
"Pentateuch." These are all not
products of single minds, but masses
of literature, shaped anew from generation to generation; the beginning
of them wrapped in obscurity because there was no one to chronicle
the first silent growths. — *The Atlantic.*

Phillips Stewart
112 College street
    Toronto
        Canada²⁸¹⁸

[Clipping, with WW's notation:]

Phil
Ledger
Aug 3
'89

Clayton W. Peirson and Howard
P. Gore, trading as the West Philadelphia Real Estate Agency, have
dissolved partnership. Mr. Peirson,
having purchased the interest of Mr.
Gore, continues the business under
the old firm name at 3819 Lancaster
avenue.²⁸¹⁹

2815. This refers to "A Voice from Death," Whitman's threnody of the Johnstown
flood disaster, the New York *World*, 7 June 1889 (see footnote 2808); Whitman bought

[Clipping of an advertisement of
Putnam & Co., 8 & 10 Beach St., Boston, Brass Bedsteads and Fine Bed-
ding, with WW's notation:]

Boston Christian Register
Aug: 22 '89

[2:7]

Camden   June   1889

9th– Sunday – warm, quiet – sit here in my 2d story
room in Mickle st: wrote poemet "My 71st year"
yesterday – (Ed, Harry, Warren, & Martin)

accepted [2820]

sent "My 71st year" to Gilder (Century N Y) $12 paid
– the champagne & ice (from Tom Harned's) [2821]
— am sweating freely — warm temperature

have written to Donaldson for Irving's cheque [2822]
"   "   "   Dr B & to TBH. for the wine [2823]

eleven copies of the paper and found only two commas out of place (*With Walt Whitman in Camden*, V, 270).

2816. Whitman said nothing whatever to Traubel on this day of his "physical botherations" — so how serious were they? (*With Walt Whitman in Camden*, V, 270–274).

2817. This letter (now in the Feinberg Collection) was from Milford C. Reed, 1 June 1889 — his name is given here on the next line — and Whitman's reply of 9 June is missing. Reed, who served in the 5th U. S. Cavalry, was befriended by Whitman in the Armory Square Hospital in Washington: "you used to take me into a Restaurant and give me a good square meal," he wrote Whitman; "I have often passed through Camden, and had I have known it was your home I should surely have stopped to see you, that I might once more have grasped you by the hand and looked into that kindly face . . ." And Whitman wrote to Dr Bucke about this letter "from a western soldier boy of twenty-four years ago, was with me a good deal, bringing back hospital & war scenes of long ago" (*The Correspondence of Walt Whitman*, IV, 346). Although he lived in Chicago, this is not likely the one of whom Whitman said to Dr Bucke on 9 June 1889: "A good Illinoisian & wife came to see me last evening — bo't a big book — (enthusiastic ab't L of G.)" (*ibid.*, IV, 347).

2818. Phillips Stewart is one of the 16 people to whom Whitman sent the pocket-book (1889) edition of *Leaves of Grass* (see entry, giving the list, and footnote 2806).

2819. Clayton Wesley Peirson was the one who gave Whitman this *Daybook* (see footnote 2801).

2820. "My 71st Year," *The Century Magazine*, XXXIX (November 1889), 31, a 6-line "poemet" published in *Good-bye My Fancy*, then in the 1891–92 "Deathbed" *Leaves of Grass*: see Comprehensive Reader's Edition, p. 541. The four men listed here are Edward Wilkins, Harry and Warren Fritzinger, but Martin ? (first or last name?).

2821. Whitman said to Horace Traubel: "Tom [Harned] was in today for a short visit — very short; and he brought along a bottle of champagne, which set me up wonderfully. I think this brand Tom has is the best that ever was known — I know no other like it. What . . . do you know of the history of champagne? Who invented it? When? Is it a modern drink? Sitting here today, I have wondered. Then I have been asking, what of the California Champagne?" (*With Walt Whitman in Camden*, V, 277).

2822. This letter to Thomas Donaldson (*The Correspondence of Walt Whitman*, IV, 348) has to do with a gift of $50 and $25 from Henry Irving and Bram Stoker, which Whit-

10 hot spell, day & night

---

                                                            return'd
                                                                    $10
11 sent "Bravo, Paris Exhibition!" to Herald

            sent to World, June 13, $6 [2824]

        – Lou here – bro't my new blue gown[2825]

        – hot, still, cloudy day — John Burroughs new book[2826]

                                                rec'd
                                                        rec'd

    sent pocket-b'k edn: to John Burroughs & R W Gilder
            both with the Sarrazin slips[2827]

12ᵗʰ & 13ᵗʰ – pleasanter cooler half- rainy

[Three lines in purple pencil:]
18 sent L of G to Th D 3444 3ᵈ Av.   N Y p'd $1.50 [2828]

    the 72 pp: pamphlet ab't dinner, speeches, &c is being
    prepared by Horace Traubel – to be pub'd by McKay[2829]

---

man expected (see *With Walt Whitman in Camden*, V, 271). Donaldson wrote on 16 September 1889 he would bring the check to Camden (letter in the Feinberg Collection), and on 1 October (see *Daybook* that date, below) Whitman received the $75. (See also Thomas Donaldson, *Walt Whitman the Man*, p. 98.)

2823. For the letter to Dr R. M. Bucke, see *The Correspondence of Walt Whitman*, IV, 347–348; for the letter to Thomas B. Harned, see *ibid.*, IV, 349. About the wine, Whitman wrote: "I drank the whole bottle (except for a little swig I insisted on Ed [Wilkins] taking for going for it) . . . , it has done me good already (for I was sort of 'under the weather' the last 30 hours.)."

2824. "Bravo, Paris Exposition!" *Harper's Weekly,* 28 September 1889, was in *Good-bye My Fancy* and the "Deathbed" (1891–92) *Leaves of Grass*; see Comprehensive Reader's Edition, pp. 544–545. The Paris Exposition, including the Eiffel Tower, ran 6 May–6 November 1889. Both the New York *Herald* and New York *World* apparently rejected the poem; Whitman sent it to *Harper's Weekly* on 18 September 1889 (see *Daybook* that date, below); it was accepted by John Foord the next day — his letter is in the Feinberg Collection (Whitman's letters to these magazines are all lost). "Bravo, Paris Exposition!" was reprinted in *Le Temps* (Paris), a copy of which Whitman sent to Dr R. M. Bucke on 6 November (see *The Correspondence of Walt Whitman,* IV, 394); see *Daybook* for 18 September 1889.

2825. He had written Louisa Whitman on 9 June 1889 (see *The Correspondence of Walt Whitman*, IV, 348) and mentioned the gown.

2826. This was *Indoor Studies*: all that Whitman said about it was that Horace Traubel should take it and read it — "of course you'll want to!" Which he repeated three days later (see *With Walt Whitman in Camden*, V, 282, 291).

2827. No letters are extant which accompanied these copies of the 1889 *Leaves of Grass*, with offprints of Gabriel Sarrazin's article on Whitman from *La Nouvelle Revue*, LII (1 May 1888), 164–184.

2828. "Th D" is not Thomas Donaldson, who lived in Philadelphia; it could be Thomas Davidson, mentioned several times in *With Walt Whitman in Camden* for his lectures in Philadelphia; he also reviewed Ignatius Donnelly's *The Great Cryptogram* in the New York *World,* 28 August 1887.

2829. This is *Camden's Compliment to Walt Whitman*: see footnotes 2740 and 2809, above.

[Line in blue pencil:]
20 sent the big book (complete W) to Rudolf Schmidt[2830]
                                        rec'd [in ink]

---

26 Buckwalter, E A Armstrong, Mr Derosse call'd paid me
     ab't $125 (in gold) the surplus of the dinner
                 the wheel-chair ($30) paid for by "dinner money"[2831]
    N Y World paid me $25 for the poemet[2832]
                                        Asbury
    Mrs: Davis goes on a three days' visit to ~~Doylesburg Pa:~~
                Mrs: Mapes here[2833]

                                        Sylvester
27 deposited 261.45   10 to W H D[2834]   Baxter
                                        here[2835]

2830. Rudolf Schmidt (see footnote 81), to whom Whitman sent his *Complete Poems &
Prose* (1888), and whose address is in the *Daybook*, below, introduced Whitman to Scandinavian readers; he is quoted in *Camden's Compliment to Walt Whitman*, pp. 53–54; his
letter to Whitman, 8 July 1889, is in the Feinberg Collection, and Whitman's letter to
Schmidt, 24 December 1889, is in *The Correspondence of Walt Whitman*, IV, 408.
2831. Geoffrey Buckwalter was one of Whitman's Camden friends and an organizer
of the birthday celebration in Morgan's Hall, and also spoke at the affair; so did E. Ambler
Armstrong (Traubel said he was "simply clap-trappy, telling in a style laboring to be
pathetic and personal, things of W[hitman] of a very dubious authenticity" — *With Walt
Whitman in Camden*, V, 249); Derosse (Traubel spells his name Derousse — *ibid.*, V, 327)
cannot be otherwise indentified; for the wheelchair, see footnote 2731, above; and of course
by "dinner money" is meant the money left over, after expenses, from the 31 May 1889 event
— see *ibid.*, V, 327.
2832. By "poemet" is meant Whitman's "A Voice from Death" in the *World* on 7
June 1889 (see footnotes 2808 and 2815).
2833. Mrs Mary Davis, Whitman's full-time, live-in housekeeper, was often assisted by
Mrs Mapes, who is mentioned in only a few places in either Traubel's five volumes or the
Correspondence (she was left $20 in the poet's will).
2834. Despite Mrs Mary Davis having had to sue William H. (Billy) Duckett and
Duckett's lying about Whitman in Mrs Davis's suit for the unpaid board bill, Whitman
still let the young man have $10. Traubel reports the occasion: "Bill Duckett came up
as I sat there. Had had a sister die. W[hitman] gave him 10 dollars. 'I am more interested
than you know, Bill,' he said, 'when you get settled in the city, write me how you like it,
or come see me.' After Bill had gone, W. spoke feelingly of the sudden death of the sister
and explained the condition of things" (*With Walt Whitman in Camden*, V, 329–330). The
last known letter from Duckett to Whitman is dated 20 December 1889 (Feinberg Collection), in which he asked for a loan.
2835. For Sylvester Baxter, Boston journalist, see footnotes 1102 and 1307; of this
particular visit, Whitman was full of enthusiasm, telling Horace Traubel, he is "a splendid
fellow — handsome, a typical American. He is a Boston man now — connected with the
Herald there — is now on the way South. A young man — or not very young, either, probably thirty-one or along there — but young in spirit; and he is all ardor — has it in his
bonnet that the world needs reforming — is a theosophist, Socialist, Anarchist, — yes, even Anarchist . . . ardent enough to touch even me, I do believe! He has been a good deal about
in the world — has been for some years located with the Boston Herald: the paper now
sends him down there." Whitman also said he advised Baxter, "hold your horses — hold
your horses!" He added that Baxter is very enthusiastic about the South, "goes to Kentucky

28 bad depress'd physical condition these times – 2 or 3 days
    weather xx warm, oppressive, bad upon me 2 days

---

sent Sarrazin's book "Poesie Anglaise" by Horace
  to Morris, Phila: to have the article ab't me
      [six words in pencil:]
  English'd first part trans: (2^d part also: book return'd [2836]
             & furnish'd me) [in pencil]

---

29 bad spell continued – hot oppressive weather
                                           continued

July 1 hot weather – bad spell yet – Phillips Stewart
    f'm Toronto Canada here [2837] – $7 in purse to Mrs. M.
    – 5 to Mrs. D for Mrs. M's mother's dress &c. 4. for gas[2838]
    Horace's piece ab't O'Connor in "Unity" [2839]

and Tennessee — seems embued with a faith that the South is the greater America . . . And certainly, Horace, Sylvester is our man — I am sure of it — ain't you? — he belongs to us, we to him" (*With Walt Whitman in Camden*, V, 326–327). More briefly, Whitman wrote Dr R. M. Bucke the same thing: see *The Correspondence of Walt Whitman*, IV, 352.

2836. Harrison Smith Morris (1856–1948), author of *Walt Whitman: A Brief Biography, with Reminiscences* (Cambridge: Harvard University Press, 1929), first published as *Walt Whitman the Poet of Democracy* in Italian (Florence: Bemporad, 1920), also wrote several articles on Whitman, beginning with "The Poetry of Whitman," *The American*, XVI (7 July 1888), 183–184, and then a review of Gabriel Sarrazin, "A French Critic on Walt Whitman," *The American*, XIX (16 November 1889), 89–90, of which an excerpt was in *The Critic* of 21 December 1889; see "Walt Whitman's Method of Composition," *Harper's Weekly*, XXXVI, (2 April 1892), 318; a letter on Whitman's funeral, *Mercure de France*, 1 February 1914; and "Reminiscences of Whitman in Mickle Street," *Camden Post-Telegram*, 17 November 1923; and his address at the unveiling of Whitman's bust at the Hall of Fame 14 May 1931 (New York University Press, 1931). In his book he writes of his first meeting Whitman on 8 June 1887, though Whitman does not mention the visit in his *Daybook* under that date. Dr John Johnston and J. W. Wallace, *Visits to Walt Whitman in 1890–1891 by Two Lancashire Friends* (London, 1918), p. 171, report Whitman describing Morris as "A nice fellow — nervous, literary — snatched from the ranks of the enemy through Horace." Morris's several visits to Whitman in the last two or three years of the poet's life are referred to in letters — see *The Correspondence of Walt Whitman*, V, 106, 109, 178, 207, 254 (a brief letter from Whitman to Morris), 259 — and Horace Traubel's five volumes have more than fifty references to Morris, whose relationship with Whitman became close enough for him to be one of the 26 pallbearers to Whitman's funeral. After Morris had translated Sarrazin's letter for *Camden's Compliment*, Traubel suggested, on 25 June 1889, that Morris also translate Sarrazin's essay on Whitman in *Poesie Anglaise* (*With Walt Whitman in Camden*, V, 319–320), which Morris agreed to do (*ibid.*, V, 324). The first parts were sent to Whitman on 1 August 1889 (*ibid.*, V, 403, 408), then the second and final parts (*ibid.*, V, 422, 444, 475, 492), which Whitman read and commented, "it impresses me more than ever."

2837. Phillips Stewart was one of the few people to whom Whitman sent copies of the 1889 pocket-book *Leaves of Grass* on 31 May (see footnote 2806).

2838. The money here refers to household matters at 328 Mickle Street, the $7 for Mrs Mapes, who had taken care of the house while Mrs Mary Davis went to Asbury for three days, 26–29 June 1889; the $5 to Mrs Davis was for Mrs Mapes's mother's dress — a trivial matter, but Whitman recorded it anyway.

2839. Horace Traubel's obituary of William Douglas O'Connor appeared in *Unity*, XXIII (29 June 1889), 138, a dozen copies of which he brought to Whitman (*With Walt

[2:8]

[In WW's hand on a scrap of paper:]
Edward Bertz
litterateur
~~of "Deutsche Presse"~~
Holzmarkt Str 18
    Potsdam
      Prussia[2840]

[On the page itself:]

Ruth Goldy   Guthrie
          Ind. Terr:
p o box ~~91~~ 466
    Topeka   Kansas[2841]
Sidney Morse
  374 E Division st
    Chicago Ill:[2842]

July '90
[In pencil, on a slip of paper:]

    Rudolf Schmidt
      Blaagaardsgade 16 B
        Copenhagen N[2843]

[In WW's hand:]
  Prof: Dowden
Winstead Temple Road
    Rathmines
Dublin   Ireland[2844]

Thos: Donaldson
      39th
326 north xxth St
    Phila:[2845]
[Four lines in pencil:]
Charles W. Eldridge
  Internal Revenue agent
    room 11 Appraiser's Building
  San Francisco Cal[2846]

[Clipping of an ad: William Wiler, Brass Bedsteads and Cribs, Philadelphia. And another ad: Salter's Handsome Mirrors, 911 Market Street.][2847]

Whitman in Camden, V, 333), one of them going to Ellen M. O'Connor (*The Correspondence of Walt Whitman,* IV, 353).

2840. Eduard Bertz (1853–1931), a German scholar, first wrote "Walt Whitman zu seinem siebzigsten Geburtstag," *Deutsche Presse,* II (2 June 1888), 177–179, which he sent to Whitman — see Bertz's letter in *With Walt Whitman in Camden,* V, 330–331 (see also V, 415–416); on 2 July 1889, Whitman sent him his *Complete Poems & Prose* (1888) — see entry below — and five days later Dr R. M. Bucke's *Walt Whitman* (Philadelphia, 1883), also recorded in the *Daybook.* For Bertz's thank-you letter, see *The Correspondence of Walt Whitman,* IV, 352n, and the Feinberg Collection. His later writings on Whitman include: an account of Whitman's life and work in Spemann's *Goldenes Buch der Weltliteratur* (1900); "Walt Whitman: Ein Charakterbild," *Jahrbuch für sexuelle Zurschenstufen,* VI (1905), 155–287; *Der Yankee-Heiland* (Dresden, 1906); *Whitman-Mysterien* (Berlin, 1907); and "A propos de Walt Whitman," *Mercure de France,* CIV (1 July 1913), 204–210; CV (1 October 1913), 654–655; CVI (1 November 1913), 219; and CVII (1 January 1914), 222–223. Whitman said of Bertz: "He bids fair to be, or rather is, one of the first class friends of L of G" (*The Correspondence of Walt Whitman,* IV, 362).

2841. Ruth Goldy was Mrs Susan Stafford's daughter and Harry's sister, who married William C. Goldy on 19 August 1884 (see footnote 1857); her Kansas address is given here because Whitman had just received a letter from her (now lost), which he sent to her mother on 30 July 1889 — see *The Correspondence of Walt Whitman,* IV, 361.

2842. Sidney Morse (see footnote 2336) was the sculptor whose bust of Whitman was used as a frontispiece for *Camden's Compliment to Walt Whitman.*

2843. For Rudolf Schmidt, see footnote 2830.

2844. Whitman received a letter from Edward Dowden, his Irish friend, on 17 June 1889 ("quite full of meat"), and another on 7 July 1889 ("his letter is very warm — very

[2:9]

Camden   July   1889

[One line in pencil:]

July 2   Sent Edw'd Bertz, Germany, the big book – rec'd [2848]

$12. (7 in purse, & 5 for her mother's dress &c) to Mrs M [2849]

3   paid $4.56 for gas bill [2850] – still cloudy, half rainy 4ᵗʰ day
                                                    rec'd
slightly easier of the bad spill – sent miscel: to E Bertz[2851]

5   McKay pays $75 – (the bill was 92, balance due
on big books Mc had – but the deduction was made
for bills against me, right –)[2852]

7   sent Edw'd Bertz, Potsdam, Dr Bucke's book
                                    rec'd [2853]

[Rest of page, 22 lines, in pencil:]

8   Monday – hot weather spell – a week now –
– ill feelings – head and abdominal – sit here
in Mickle street – hot, uncomfortable, ill –
– breath short – Harry F   poorly in health – [2854]
– July at present quiet – I write this at noon

enthusiastic") — see *With Walt Whitman in Camden,* V, 301, 303, 352 (the letter of 26 June is in the Feinberg Collection).

2845. For Thomas Donaldson, see footnote 2822; see also *With Walt Whitman in Camden,* V, 376.

2846. Charles W. Eldridge is an old Washington friend; on 27 August 1889 Whitman wrote Ellen M. O'Connor that Eldridge "is in San Francisco, no d[oubt] as U S Revenue Ag't," and again on 19 September that he was sending him a copy of Horace Traubel's obituary in *Liberty* of 7 September 1889 (which is in *Walt Whitman in Camden,* V, 333–334): see *The Correspondence of Walt Whitman,* IV, 367, 375.

2847. The fact that there are clippings here and on the previous right-hand page of the *Daybook* for bedsteads and mirrors suggests that Whitman was looking for these items for his house.

2848. See footnote 2840.

2849. This line is almost exactly the same as that of 1 July 1889, above (see footnote 2838).

2850. Hardly worth mentioning once, but Whitman records this twice (see above for 1 July 1889).

2851. See footnote 2840; Whitman's letter to Eduard Bertz is missing, but see his letter to Whitman, 20–22 July 1889, in the Feinberg Collection.

2852. It's hard to tell just which Whitman book that David McKay is paying royalties for: the 1888 *Leaves of Grass, November Boughs* (1888), or the 1889 pocket-book *Leaves.*

2853. See footnote 2840.

2854. Harry F is the elder of the Fritzinger brothers (Warren, Whitman's nurse, is the other), who were the sons of the sea captain that Mrs Mary Davis nursed in Camden before she became Whitman's housekeeper. As for the poet's health it had been fairly good, for he

19 cloudy – a shade better this forenoon – stopt taking
the "tonic" yesterday – Chas Eldridge at San
Francisco Internal Agent again (his old place).[2855]
— John Burroughs temporarily at Hobart N. Y.[2856]
— no sale worth mentioning of my books by myself
McKay off west drumming[2857] — I go down to foot
of Cooper st. to river side in the wheel chair
at sunset, (propell'd by Ed) – enjoy it quietly
– Horace T. comes regularly[2858]

20th Big book ("complete works") safely rec'd by Rudolf Schmidt[2859]

23d sent big book to J W Wassall 208
    Dearborn ave: Chicago, by Express
                                    paid $6 [2860]

30th still warm – plenty of rain – death of Pardee[2861]
10 days ago – I stick it out here in Mickle

wrote Dr R. M. Bucke on 3 July 1889 that he hadn't taken medicine for a long time and no doctors had come to 328 Mickle Street for three or four months (*The Correspondence of Walt Whitman*, IV, 353); probably the heat made him feel bad.

2855. Eldridge was mentioned on the previous page of the *Daybook* (see footnote 2846), Whitman having received a letter, dated 13 July 1889, from him (now in the Feinberg Collection), Whitman's letter: *The Correspondence of Walt Whitman*, IV, 358.

2856. Whitman's letter, of this date, to John Burroughs is in *The Correspondence of Walt Whitman*, IV, 357; he was to send it to Dr R. M. Bucke, with Charles Eldridge's letter, just received.

2857. David McKay had left on 8 July 1889 for a trip as far west as Denver for about six weeks (see *With Walt Whitman in Camden*, V, 348); McKay had left all details to *Camden's Compliment to Walt Whitman* in Horace Traubel's hands. On 10 July, when someone suggested that McKay was publishing Whitman's books just as a business act, Whitman said, "Dave at that time rescued us, whatever else is to be said — he appeared just in the nick of our trouble. That is not to be forgotten — we must not forget it!" (*ibid.*, V, 359). By 18 August, McKay was back in Philadelphia from his "business & drumming tour west": see *The Correspondence of Walt Whitman*, IV, 354, 365.

2858. Whitman many times had words of praise for Horace Traubel, who — after his working hours in the Farmer 7 Mechanics Bank, 427 Chestnut Street — invariably came by to see Whitman and do all sorts of errands; his five volumes (all so far published) on Whitman run from 28 March 1888 to 14 September 1889.

2859. See footnote 2830.

2860. In his letter to Dr R. M. Bucke of 24 July 1889, Whitman said: "Have just sold to Chicago purchaser one of the big book (three the last week, but that is exceptional) —" (*The Correspondence of Walt Whitman*, IV, 359). The "big book" is of course Whitman's *Complete Poems & Prose* (1888). Nothing else is known of Wassall.

2861. Timothy Blair Pardee, one of Dr R. M. Bucke's good Canadian friends, was in Camden on the way to Florida on 31 January 1888 (see entry that date); he was the Commissioner of Crown Lands, and Whitman had stayed at his home in Sarnia, Ontario, 19–24 June 1880, when he made his trip to Canada to visit Dr Bucke (see *Daybook* of that date). More recently, on 7 May 1889, Whitman told Thomas B. Harned he had a letter from Dr Bucke, who said that Pardee "is very sick — almost dead — dying. This dying is a long process, often — but dying he is" (*With Walt Whitman in Camden*, V, 147). Dr Bucke wrote Horace Traubel about Pardee's death, saying he had gone to the funeral in Sarnia on

street so far – (p c to Blackwood to know
who to send the cheque for Ed's board)[2862]

[2:10]

for Ed's board /

C F Currie, Sup't Asylum, Blackwood New Jersey
paid $45.50 Aug. 1 '90   paid $45:50 Aug: 2 '89   for Ed's board
Aug. Sept. & Oct. '89 – p'd $45.50 for Feb.M.& A.'90[2863]

Billstein
Billstein & Son: plate printers 925 Filbert St Phila:[2864]

L W Ingram Molalla Corners, Clackamas Co: [in pencil]
Oregon[2865]   [in pencil]

[Name and address on a small scrap:]

Wm Melligan
  Asbury Station
    Hunterdon Co:
      New Jersey[2866]

Walt Whitman Reynolds
  Jones & Co's Mills
    45 Broome St.
      New York City[2867]

25 July 1889: "It is well — his mind had been completely gone for weeks — did not know a single soul — could not speak a word — absolute eclipse." When Traubel told Whitman, the poet exclaimed, "Oh! I had heard nothing of that. Poor Pardee! Gone at last!" Then he reminisced about Bucke's friend — "a brainy man — a man of parts, intellectuality . . . Nor was he old, either — probably 60 . . . Poor Pardee! It is the end of the drama, for him!" (*ibid.*, V, 389–390). Whitman's full comment to Dr Bucke in his letter of 26 July: "A word first for Pardee — gone over then to the majority, where we are all steadily tending 'for reasons' — blessed be his memory!" (*The Correspondence of Walt Whitman*, IV, 360).

2862. This letter, to C. F. Currie (?), is lost
2863. These sums are, of course, Whitman's usual payments for the room, board, and care of Whitman's helpless brother Edward. For some reason Ed is not even mentioned in Vols. IV and ·V of *With Walt Whitman in Camden*, only once in Vol. III, and three times each of Vols. II and I; apparently he did not talk to Horace Traubel about his brother in the asylum.
2864. Henry Billstein, whom Whitman met on 3 February 1889 (Traubel spelled his name then as "Bilstein" — *With Walt Whitman in Camden*, IV, 78 — and here in the *Daybook* it is spelled two ways), and who made the plates for the pocket-book (1889) *Leaves of Grass* (see *Daybook* entry for 25 May 1889 and footnotes 2738 and 2761), has his name here because Whitman now wanted him to make plates for a collection of *pictures from life of W W*: see *With Walt Whitman in Camden*, V, 406–407, 412, 416, 421, 428, 439.
2865. L. W. Ingram may be a relative of William Ingram; he is listed above, in the *Daybook* for September 1888, with his full name, Louis William Ingram (see footnote 2644).
2866. William Melligan may have been someone Mrs Mary Davis met or knew in Asbury, where she had been 26–29 June 1889.
2867. Walt Whitman Reynolds: undoubtedly the son of an admirer of the poet or of a Civil War veteran whom Whitman cared for in Washington. He visited Whitman on 1 September 1889 — see *Daybook* entry, below.

[Printed calling card of
Charles W. Eldridge, Internal
Revenue Agent, Appraiser's Building,
San Francisco.] [2868]

[Letterhead of Charles J. Cohen,
envelope manufacturer, wholesale
stationer, 617 Market Street.]

This '89–'90 Congress is the 51st –
 – when the new four western
states come in the Union
there will be 42 states
Forty Two States

[Not in WW's hand, written on a scrap:]

My address will be
Care Charles E. Legg,
146 Devonshire St.
    Boston, Mass.

coffee
one third Mocha – two thirds
                    Java
——————————(Sept. '89

H M Alden
p o box 959
New York city [2869]

John Foord   same [2870]

[Clipping: ads for King's Book Exchange,
Great Chair Depot, I. H. Wisler & Sons,
and Clement H. Moore, 835 Market Street,
Manufacturer of Blank Books.]

[2:11]

    Camden   August   1889

July 31 – Wednesday – early p m — rainy, rainy, these
            days – hard pours last night & this forenoon
            – (marked perturbations in the weather for a year
            I believe both here & the old continent) –
            – Am feeling fairly well to-day – continue to eat
            & sleep middling fairly (not markedly ill) wh- is
            a great blessing – fair bowel action this forenoon –
            – very quiet as I sit here alone in my room

    2868. Charles W. Eldridge had just written to Whitman (see footnotes 2846 and 2855,
above).
    2869. Henry M. Alden, editor of *Harper's New Monthly Magazine,* wrote Whitman
on 25 August 1889, asking for a poem, which the poet sent on 30 August: "Death's Valley."
Harper's paid him $25 on 1 September (see *Daybook* entries below for those two dates and
19 September and 9 December). The poem, however, was not publishd until after Whitman
had died: see "Death's Valley," *Harper's Monthly,* LXXXIV (April 1892), 707–709, *Leaves
of Grass,* Comprehensive Reader's Edition, pp. 580–581; and *The Correspondence of Walt
Whitman,* IV, 368. Whitman's poem was to accompany a picture of a painting by George
Inness, "The Valley of the Shadow of Death" (see LeRoy Ireland, *The Works of George
Inness* [1965], pp. 98–99), which it did. See also Horace Traubel, *With Walt Whitman in
Camden,* V, 471, and following 242, for a facsimile of part of the MS of the poem.
    2870. John Foord was editor of *Harper's Weekly,* to whom Whitman sent "Bravo,
Paris Exposition!" on 18 September 1889 (see entry below, that date, and footnote 2824).

Mickle street – the "forecast" gives us clear
skies &c: this evening – so to morrow begins
the last hot summer month – have stood it
all pretty well here in my den so far –
wonder if I am going to pull thro' it all?
– I could migrate to some mountain or sea-
coast quarters of course (I have money enough)
– but I am used to my den, locale, a hundred
little personal adjustments, & am doubtless best
without change & here as things are, (the heat
& stale air worst) considering all.[2871]

(rec'd)

Aug. 2   sent Dr Bucke two copies ∧ little morocco b'd L of G [2872]

(rec'd)

paid C F Currie, Sup't, Blackwood, $45:50
for Ed's board for ensuing Aug:, Sept:, & Oct.[2873]

(rec'd)

paid $13 ⟨q⟩ for "process" pict: "laughing philosopher" [2874]

4   pleasant, quiet Sunday – good long letter
from Edward Bertz, Potsdam, Germany[2875]

6   went over in a carriage to Gutekunst's,
Philadelphia & had photo: sittings

2871. A remarkably long entry for the *Daybook* — on the weather and the general state of Whitman's health and his attitude — different from Horace Traubel's report on that day in *With Walt Whitman in Camden*, V, 400-401; but see Whitman's letter to George and Susan Stafford in *The Correspondence of Walt Whitman*, IV, 360-361.

2872. These were two of 20 copies of the 1889 pocket-book *Leaves of Grass* without the flap, which Horace Traubel brought to Whitman on 1 August 1889: see *With Walt Whitman in Camden*, V, 403; Whitman noted that Oldach, the binder, did not follow his directions about margins on the picture-page, but the next day (he had given Traubel an inscribed copy, too), Whitman said of the books, "they pleased me very well — very well indeed" (*ibid.*, V, 406). See *The Correspondence of Walt Whitman*, IV, 361.

2873. See footnote 2863.

2874. The "laughing philosopher" is a photograph of Whitman taken in 1887 by George C. Cox in New York; it had been used in *The Century*, and Whitman told Traubel that "it seems to me so excellent — so to stand out from the others — that something ought really be done with it — something more than has been done" (*With Walt Whitman in Camden*, V, 261); so Traubel wanted it for *Camden's Compliment to Walt Whitman*, or the poet thought it might be reduced in size and used in *Leaves of Grass*. For comments and discussion, and two letters about the picture, see *With Walt Whitman in Camden*, V, 268, 301, 305, 312, 314, 377, 387, 400; and *The Correspondence of Walt Whitman*, IV, 351; the photograph is reproduced in *ibid., IV,* following 278; and in *With Walt Whitman in Camden*, V, foll. 242.

2875. This letter, dated 20–22 July 1889 is in the Feinberg Collection; Whitman wrote Dr R. M. Bucke on 3-4 August about Bertz, who had been in America and wrote good English: see footnote 2840, above.

(Mr Buckwalter and Ed: Wilkins with me
– got along very well)[2876]

[Four lines in pencil:]
13th   Mr G. sent specimens – big heads ("panel"
size) – a big half-length, sitting, no hat, (big pict.
but less than "panel") – this 2[d] one I like – & a number
of others – [2877]

[2:12]

J E Kingsley, Continental Hotel, Phila:[2878]

Charles L Webster & Co: 3 East 14th St: New York[2879]

[Five lines in pencil:]
Adrian M Jones, News newspaper office
    Tex Galveston   Texas

Mrs Mary E Mapes,
    care Frank J Ingram
    Downs   Osborne   Co: Kansas[2880]

[In pencil, on card:]   [Clipping of an ad: F. Dodd & Co.,
                                   Fashionable Hatters, 126 N. Ninth St.,
Horace L. Traubel   Philadelphia]
Farmer & Mechanics
    Bank
427 Chestnut[2881]

2876. Photographs of Edward Wilkins, Whitman's nurse from Canada, and Geoffrey Buckwalter, who had arranged the 1889 birthday celebration (with others), are in *With Walt Whitman in Camden,* V, opp. 243; and F. Gutekunst was regarded by Whitman as "on top of the heap" (*ibid.,* V, 338). The account of this trip to Philadelphia is in Traubel (*ibid.,* V, 416–418; see also 394, 420, 421); the picture was reproduced in *The New England Magazine,* IV (May 1891), 290; *The Correspondence of Walt Whitman,* IV, following 278 (see also IV, 364); and in the *Walt Whitman Review,* XV (March 1969), 64, from the original in the Feinberg Collection, under which Whitman wrote: "My 71st year arrives: the fifteen past months nearly all illness or half illness — until a tolerable day (Aug: 6 1889) & convoy'd by Mr. B[uckwalter] and Ed: W[ilkins] I have been carriaged across to Philadelphia (how sunny & fresh & good look'd the river, the people, the vehicles, & Market & Arch streets!) & have sat for this photo: wh- satisfies me. Walt Whitman."
2877. As Traubel wrote in *The New England Magazine* (see footnote above): "Whitman has been photographed as often perhaps as any public man who ever lived, and the photographs are in the main better than any oil or crayon portrait. The Gutekunst picture reproduced with this paper is the very latest (taken within a year) and satisfies Whitman as fully, perhaps, as any."
2878. J. E. Kingsley: unidentified.
2879. Charles E. Webster and Company was the publishing house which issued, of course among other books, Edmund Clarence Stedman's *The Library of American Literature,* in which Whitman received more space than any other poet.
2880. Mrs Mary E. Mapes was a friend of Mary Davis, Whitman's housekeeper, and she either helped Mrs Davis or took her place at 328 Mickle Street when Mrs Davis was away (see footnotes 2833 and 2838).
2881. This was the Camden bank where Traubel was employed.

Tom Harned can telephone

[Clipped from a card: "The Nineteenth
Century," 1 Paternoster Square, London,
E. C.[2882] Written upwards, not in
WW's hand: Whitm.]

[Receipt for payment of $3.15 by Walt Whitman to Sun Fire Office of Lon-
don, United States Branch, Philadelphia, 10 August 1889, for premium on
$300 insurance on Stock, 8 August 1889 to 8 February 1890, 1213/1215 Filbert
Street, on which Whitman has written:]

<u>Expires Feb 8 '90</u> [2883]

[2:13]

Aug: Camden   August   1889
   8   superb weather now 3 days & nights

[Six lines in pencil:]
   11   Sunday – a delightful quiet sunny soothing day
                   wrote to H and sent a little money

   14   sent over photo: to Gutekunst – ask'd 12 [2884]

   16   paid $3.15 for insurance for $300 on stock at 1213
          Filbert st. wh- is continued on to Feb: 8 '90 [2885]

          sent one copy big book to McKay[2886]

   17   sent big book by Express to Sara McGee
                   Adams Hotel, Washington st. Boston – paid $5
          (also address 112 College Av: Toronto Canada
          — Phillips Stewart also there)[2887]

2882. On 3 November 1889 (see entry, that date, below) Whitman sent to *The Nineteenth Century,* edited by James Knowles (letter now lost), a group of poems called "Old
Age Echoes," which were rejected. See *The Correspondence of Walt Whitman,* IV, 385n.
2883. Whitman also recorded this insurance payment of $3.15 just below, under the
date of 16 August 1889.
2884. This photograph was the one F. Gutekunst took in Philadelphia on 6 August
1889 (see entry, that date, and 23 August, below, and footnotes 2876 and 2877).
2885. See receipts just above.
2886. David McKay had not yet returned from his western trip (see footnote 2857),
but someone in his office "who writes much like him" (*With Walt Whitman in Camden,* V,
439) had ordered a copy of Whitman's *Complete Poems & Prose* (1889).
2887. Phillips Stewart, who is listed among those to whom Whitman sent copies of
the 1889 pocket-book *Leaves of Grass* (see footnote 2806), visited the poet on 1 July 1889,
recorded in the *Daybook.*

sent big book to J H Clifford, Farmington, Maine

paid

4

by Express, (for Dr O W True) JHC is to bring me $4 [2888]
fine weather, 16th, 17th, 18th

[Nine lines in pencil:]

23   sent over to Gutekunsts for 6 more picts
      sent over the 6 to be "copyrighted," (get the pattern
      —————————————————————— again) [2889]

      have had a bad week – one of the worst, (tho't
      sometimes it might be the <u>close</u>) – but am
      a little easier to-day – 21st & 22^d hot[2890]

24   the <u>princip</u>al tax on my shanty – $25.28!
                        & Greece
      (then there are 7 or 8 others) – in Italy∧ they
      have a dis-illegal banditti – <u>here</u> we have
      a regular legal one, & numerous & remorseless[2891]

27   easier & better (a little, but perceptible) after 8 or 9
                                      days quite ill [2892]

28   very perceptibly cooler
      paid the water tax bill $8.40 (Ed p'd it – City Hall) [2893]
      Dick Flynn here[2894]

2888. John Herbert Clifford, the Unitarian minister whose name is mentioned about fifty times in *With Walt Whitman in Camden,* V, wrote to Whitman late in July (see *ibid.,* V, 394) about a friend in Farmington, Maine, who wanted *Leaves of Grass* but "seemed staggered at its price," so Whitman let Clifford have the book, *Complete Poems & Prose* for $4 (*ibid.,* V, 409, and also V, 459 for Clifford's letter); the friend was a minister, Dr O. W. True, who had written Whitman on 9 January and 1 September 1889, somewhat incoherently (both letters in the Feinberg Collection).

2889. For an account of these pictures, see footnotes 2876 and 2877.

2890. In his conversation with Traubel, Whitman merely said he was "poorly" (*With Walt Whitman in Camden,* V, 447); but he did write Mrs Susan Stafford on 22 August 1889 that he had "one of my worst spells" (*The Correspondence of Walt Whitman,* IV, 366).

2891. If Whitman had had more outbursts like this one about taxes, this *Daybook* would be much more interesting reading. He complained to Dr Bucke also about paying $40 to the "banditti who *govern* our city" (*The Correspondence of Walt Whitman,* IV, 369).

2892. If one compares this statement, "8 or 9 days quite ill," with Whitman's letters during these days, and his conversation with Traubel, it does appear to be at least a slight overstatement.

2893. Edward Wilkins, among other things, went to the City Hall to pay Whitman's water tax and other bills.

2894. Richard Flynn, who was 24 years old when Whitman met him in 1880 in London, Ontario, was employed by Dr R. M. Bucke at his asylum from 1875 to 1885 as a messenger, gardener, watchman, and stoker. Whitman described him as "a modest, reticent sort of

30   rec'd the photo's – twelve – big, seated, ¾ length
          no hat – head of cane in right hand – good pict's[2895]
          – one sent to Dr Bucke by Dick Flynn (rec'd)[2896]
       feel pretty easy comparatively – superb weather
       sent "Death's Valley" to Alden, Harper's Monthly[2897]

Sept: 1   "Death's Valley" accepted & paid for ($25)[2898] also
          rec'd the proof — & have rec'd proof "My 71st year" &
          sent back to "Century"[2899]
       went to Mr & Mrs: Harned's – drank a bottle of
          champagne[2900]
       young Walt Whitman Reynolds here f'm N Y to see me[2901]

[Across this page and previous one is a tax bill, The City of Camden, 1889, for 328 Mickle, 20 x 100, valued at $800, $20.83 tax, personal property valued at $100, $4.45 tax, total $25.28 ($1.26 deduction), making $24.02 which Whitman paid. His notations in upper corners read:]

Paid)   paid   paid (by Ed)
             Sept 17 '89   Sept: 17, 1889 [2902]

[2:14]

[Tax bill of Department for Supplying the City with Water, City Hall, The City of Camden, March 1, 1889, water rent for year 1889, 328 Mickle St., $8.40, with WW's notation in upper corner:]

       paid

fellow, disinclined to self. I remember I praised him once or twice up there, and he resented it — did not like it at all — sort of drew himself up — so I did not venture often on that line. He would say, when I spoke of something he had wisely done — planting, digging, whatnot — that it was no credit to him — that he was only working, only making a living: though it was true he liked, loved, his work! We got along very well . . ." (*With Walt Whitman in Camden*, V, 461). Flynn visited Whitman for a few days, went to Philadelphia with Edward Wilkins (who was also from London, Ontario), and returned to Canada, bringing Dr Bucke one of the Gutekunst pictures — the one that is now in the Feinberg Collection and its autograph is described in footnote 2876. Whitman wrote Dr Bucke, 30–31 August 1889: "Dick [Flynn] is very quiet — we all like him here — he has left & will get there before this [letter]" — *The Correspondence of Walt Whitman*, IV, 369; see also III, 190n.

2895. See footnote 2876.
2896. See footnote 2894.
2897. See footnote 2869.
2898. But it took 2½ years before it was published in April 1892 (see footnote 2869).
2899. See footnote 2820.
2900. There's no question about how Whitman felt about champagne: on 9 June 1889 (see entry of that date, above) Thomas B. Harned sent the poet a bottle and ice, and Whitman drank it all, "which set me up wonderfully" (see footnote 2821).
2901. For a conjecture on Walt Whitman Reynolds, see footnote 2867.
2902. How Whitman felt about this tax, and the banditti who collected it, see *Daybook* entry for 24 August 1889.

[2:15]

Camden   September   1889

2^d Monday – middling fair – good weather enough
       – Rush call'd – look'd well – was very thankful
       eulogistic, full-hearted – is just out of prison,
       is just off to his parents in the country[2903]

       _____

                    Harned
3^d T B and Frank ∧ and Horace Traubel & Herbert Gil here
       _____ evening[2904]

[Four lines in pencil:]
5,6,7   Depress'd – ill – Ev'ng's easier

       _____

8   – Sunday – a shade better – T B H and Mr Green
       a young English Unitarian Minister here
       big photo to T B H – I sit all day in 2^d story room[2905]

9   furnish'd McKay with one big book (he now owes me
       big photo: to T B H.[2906]   for two copies[2907]

       _____

10   Tuesday – cloudy, rainy, cooler – sitting here stupidly
       in 2^d story room   Mickle st – noon

       _____

11 12 bad storm – New Jersey coast devastated
       _____ Atlantic City specially[2908]

2903. This story of George Rush, Jr, of Concordville, Pennsylvania, seems to have had a happy ending, beginning with William Ingram's visit to Whitman on 3 August 1888 (see entry of that date, above, and footnote 2587). See Whitman's letter to Ingram, 2 September 1889, in *The Correspondence of Walt Whitman*, IV, 370–371, which repeats what is, in the *Daybook*; but a footnote quotes from Rush's letter of 13 February 1890 from Missouri, where he was an entertainer and called his prison term "a gross injustice" (letter in the Feinberg Collection).
     2904. This visit with Thomas B. Harned, his borther Frank, Herbert Gilchrist and Horace Traubel is fully told in *With Walt Whitman in Camden*, V, 477–480.
     2905. Horace Traubel was out of town on this day, so we know no more about this visit by Thomas B. Harned and Mr Green, who is not further identified in Whitman's letter to Dr R. M. Bucke in *The Correspondence of Walt Whitman*, IV, 372.
     2906. Why mention giving the Gutekunst portrait to Thomas B. Harned twice?
     2907. Because this copy of *Complete Poems & Prose*, which Whitman let David McKay, his publisher, have, is a matter of business, the poet recorded it here; but more interesting on this date is Traubel's brief account of McKay sending over to Whitman a copy of the first (1855) edition which McKay had got from W. C. Angus in Scotland, and which he wished Whitman to sign. See *With Walt Whitman in Camden*, V, 493–494; and also IV, 198–199, for Angus's letter to Whitman, 26 October 1888, asking Whitman to sign the book, which he intended to give to a public library.
     2908. Storms, floods, shipwrecks, and other disasters all had a strong effect on Whitman; "There is still no word from the shore. Oh! it is to be hoped that there will be no

13 Sir Edwin Arnold here[2909]

17 paid Tax Bill (by Ed) $24.02 ($25:28, 5 per cent deducted)

rec'd note from T Donaldson – Irving sent ʌme 50 &
Bram Stoker 25 wh- T D (who has been badly
hurt & laid up) will soon bring over to me[2910]

cloudy & moist continued – hard rain last night

18 sent "Bravo! Paris Exposition!" to Harper's Weekly $10 & 10 papers

accepted
19 sent proof (revise) "Death's Valley" to H M Alden   paid [2911]
markedly cooler   p o box 959 New York City[2912]

broken uneasy nights

21 sent the big book to Addington Symonds
Davos Switzerland [2913]

me
23 two young women visited   – bo't 3 Nov. Boughs[2914]

more Johnstown disasters — one is enough for a century!" he told Traubel — *With Walt Whitman in Camden,* V, 503.

2909. Sir Edwin Arnold (1832–1904), whose best known work is *The Light of Asia* (1879) on Buddha, wrote Whitman on 12 September 1889, asking to visit him (Feinberg Collection; see also The Boston *Traveller,* 5 October 1889, a different letter from New York than the one from Washington): see *The Correspondence of Walt Whitman,* IV, 372n, 373, 373n, 374; Horace Traubel's *With Walt Whitman in Camden,* V, 506, 509–510; and Sir Edwin Arnold, *Sea and Lands* (New York, 1891), pp. 75–79. Whitman told Dr R. M. Bucke that Arnold was "a tann'd English traveler — I liked him," and said to Traubel, "He was a hearty, jovial, fine sample of a middle-aged man. He stayed with me from three quarters of an hour to an hour. We talked quite a good deal. Oh yes! he was very flattering — said a great many eulogistic things — like most all of 'em nowadays. I liked the style of the man very much," and the next day Whitman added to this, that Arnold may have been "too eulogistic — too flattering. He was very frank in his expression of his own views with respect to Leaves of Grass — of his decided friendliness — of his particular friends' friendliness over there . . ."

Horace Traubel, *With Walt Whitman in Camden,* ends Vol. V with this date; there is enough MS material for three more volumes, but publication has not yet (1976) been ascertained.

2910. See footnote 2822 and entry, below, for 1 October 1889, when Thomas Donaldson brought over the $75 from Henry Irving and Bram Stoker. Donaldson's letter of 16 September 1889 is in the Feinberg Collection.

2911. See footnote 2824. The letter to *Harper's Weekly* is missing.

2912. For notes on this poem and Henry M. Alden, editor of *Harper's Monthly,* see footnote 2869. Whitman's letter with the proof, if there was a letter, is now lost.

2913. Whitman told Dr R. M. Bucke, "Quite a strong 'last word' from J A Symonds f'm Switzerland — you will see it in Horace's book" (*The Correspondence of Walt Whitman,* IV, 375). Traubel's book is *Camden's Compliment to Walt Whitman:* see p. 73. The book Whitman sent Symonds is *Complete Poems & Prose* (1889).

2914. On the basis of information now available, the two women who bought *November Boughs* are not known.

[Four lines in purple pencil:]
28   John Burroughs here[2915]

29   <u>Sunday</u> – Sitting here in my "den" in Mickle
    Street – main physical botherations – head
    (catarrhal) – & the bladder – dull enough –

[Three lines in pencil:]
Oct 1 sent photo to Lounger   Critic[2916]

    rec'd   75 f'm Thos: Donaldson: viz:
        (50 f'm Irving   25 f'm Bram Stoker)[2917]

                                      [2:16]

             Moneys
               paid to

         Subsequent to
           Oct. '89   [in purple pencil]
           $2.20   [in purple pencil]
           50.
           12
            6
           13
            5
           13   86   [in purple pencil]
           20   [in purple pencil]
           13.40
           10   E.M O'C [2918]
            2
            5
            2
           2.50
           28
           15.25
           7.14
            2

2915. In his letter to Dr R. M. Bucke, Whitman added a little to this: that Burroughs had been to Asbury Park, New Jersey with his wife Ursula and son Julian, who had gone back to Poughkeepsie, New York, "& John jaunts on here, & to New York to-night, & back to West Park [New York]. J is well, & looks well, works in his vineyard & farm, & feels well" — *The Correspondence of Walt Whitman,* IV, 377.
2916. This letter to *The Critic* is now lost.
2917. For more on Thomas Donaldson and this money, see footnotes 2822 and 2910.
2918. The initials of Ellen M. O'Connor (William Douglas O'Connor's widow) are

Camden   October   '89

3 sent pictures to Johnny Wroth Jesus Maria
                    Chihuahua   Mexico   reached him
_____   safely[2919]
   Mrs. Mapes and Glenny gone to Kansas   arrived
_____   safe
   [Four lines in purple pencil:]   Sat. night[2920]
   got in a cord of oak wood – $8 paid
       have a fire
   _____

   principal physical troubles head (catarrhal   I
     suppose) and bladder – health 2/3ds   off – [2921]
   _____

[Two lines in blue pencil:]
   paid   Oldach, binder $50 [2922]

               photo-mounter $12 [2923]

7   sent pocket-b'k edn. L of G to W H Bustin Jr (pd)
       p o box 3096 Boston, Mass: & Charles Louis Palms (pd)
       713 Cambridge st.   Cambridge Mass:[2924]
   _____

[Three lines in pencil:]
8   paid $13 for stuff for house repairs and work[2925]

here, opposite an entry for $10, because Whitman gave her this money on 13 November 1889 (see entry, that date). What are all these other small sums of money?

2919. John W. Wroth was the grandson of Mrs Caroline Wroth, wife of a Philadelphia importer, at whose home, 319 Steven Street, Camden, Whitman took his meals in July 1881 (see *The Correspondence of Walt Whitman*, III, 232n). Wroth wrote Whitman on 2 June 1887 about his western trip (letter in the Feinberg Collection); three other Wroth letters (Feinberg Collection), 27 October 1889, 18 December 1889, and 1 January 1891, acknowledge receipt of the photo, send Christmas greetings, and New Year's wishes.

2920. Mrs Mapes (see footnotes 2833, 2838, and 2880) was a friend of Whitman's house-keeper.

2921. In his letters of this date and 29 September 1889 (see entry just above) Whitman does not seem to complain quite so much — "Matters ab't as usual with me"; "Nothing very new in my condition" — but he did tell William Sloane Kennedy that he was "altogether disabled" (*The Correspondence of Walt Whitman*, IV, 377, 378).

2922. This payment to Frederick Oldach is most likely for binding morocco *Leaves of Grass* pocket-book editions, though it could be for *Camden's Compliment to Walt Whitman*, being printed at the time (not yet bound).

2923. For the Gutekunst photo of Whitman.

2924. No letters either to or from Whitman are extant in connection with the sales of these 1889 pocket-book editions of *Leaves*; also, purchasers unidentified.

2925. This was paid to William H. Johnson, plus $20 on 12 October and more on 19 October 1889 (see entries for these dates below); Whitman wrote Dr R. M. Bucke that "the old shanty [was in] some danger of sagging, tumbling &c." (*The Correspondence of Walt Whitman*, IV, 381).

letter f'm C L H. Hannah very ill jaundice
— next day letter, "much better" – sent $6 [2926]

---

9   David McKay paid me $88:56 for royalty &c[2927]
      [One line in blue pencil:]
          Harry Stafford here[2928]

---

11   deposited $282.71 (seven cheques) in bank[2929]

---

12   paid $20 to W™ H Johnson the carpenter[2930]
          ~~paid back~~
          ~~don't forget to return the 20 to Mary D~~ [2931]   [in purple pencil]
17   drew $80 for self f'm bank

---

18   sent <u>Old age's voices</u> to H M Alden, 100 (sent back to
                    rejected   me[2932]

2926. Charles L. Heyde, Whitman's brother-in-law and wife of Hannah, wrote the poet from Burlington, Vermont in October? (letter in the Trent Collection); see *Daybook* entries below for 31 October 1889 and 8 and 18 November about "the miserable whelp" — Whitman's attitude toward Heyde is quite clear, and his begging for money hardly helped. Here Whitman sends him $6.00. A good summary of Whitman's attitude toward Heyde is in *The Correspondence of Walt Whitman*, IV, 390n–391n.

2927. This does not represent much of a royalty payment for six months.

2928. Harry Stafford, Susan's son who had been very close to the poet from 1876 to about 1885 (Harry was married in 1884), had not seen Whitman for some while — in his letter to the young man's parents on 30 July 1889, Whitman wrote, "I have not heard from or seen [Harry] in a long time" (*The Correspondence of Walt Whitman*, IV, 361); and in the five volumes of Traubel's *With Walt Whitman in Camden*, which runs from 28 March 1888 to 14 September 1889, Harry Stafford is hardly mentioned. On 22 August 1889, Whitman did tell Susan Stafford he was "glad to hear f'm Harry" (*The Correspondence of Walt Whitman*, IV, 366). Though the relationship obviously waned, Harry did visit the poet to the very end, Whitman writing Dr R. M. Bucke on 5 December 1891, "H Staff[ord]'s wife & children (fine ones) call this mn'g" (*ibid.*, V, 269); Harry himself had seen Whitman on 18 November 1891. He was of course living in New Jersey near Camden.

2929. If Whitman's royalty payments were low, he was at least getting some money from other sources: from the birthday testimonial, from newspapers and magazines, from more affluent friends.

2930. See footnote 2925 and entry below for 19 October 1889.

2931. This entry, apparently regarding a $20 loan(?) from Mrs Mary Davis, Whitman's housekeeper, was merely a reminder to himself; when he paid Mrs Davis he crossed out the entry.

2932. Henry M. Alden, editor of *Harper's New Monthly Magazine,* rejected this cluster of poems because the "thought is worthy of a more careful texture in its parts & a more shapely embodiment as a whole" (letter, dated 24 October 1889, in the Lion Collection — see *The Correspondence of Walt Whitman,* IV, 385n). After *Nineteenth Century* also turned the verses down (see entry below for 3 November 1889, where the title is given as "Old Age Echoes"; and 9 December 1889 entry), Whitman broke up the cluster. "To the Sun-Set Breeze," one of them, was published in *Lippincott's Monthly Magazine,* XLVI (December 1890), 861. See *Leaves of Grass,* Comprehensive Reader's Edition, p. 546. Others of the "3 or 4 sonato poemets," which he mentions in the 9 December *Daybook* entry, were eventually published elsewhere.

19   sent pk't-b'd L of G. ($5) by Express c o d to W H
         Front St
     Raymeaton 38 ∧ Worcester, Mass: <u>paid</u> ²⁹³³

---

     paid W H Johnson $13.40 – $33.40   altogether
        scamp & fraud   15   for lumber²⁹³⁴

---

21   Monday – Ed has left me – gone back to Canada²⁹³⁵
        I sent Dr B a big parcel of portraits

     [One line in pencil:]
     big book supplied to McKay   he now owes me for
     _____   3 paid
                                              all ²⁹³⁶

22   Warren F   now my nurse & helper
                 (good massages)²⁹³⁷

---

23   sent p'k:b'k L of G.   to Edmund B Delabarre
        14 Trowbridge Place   Cambridge   Mass:²⁹³⁸
                      paid

                                              [2:18]

[Two lines in pencil:]
– Office Physicians Cor: 13ᵗʰ & Locust

2933. Apart from what David McKay was doing, Whitman continued to sell the various editions of *Leaves of Grass* himself: here the pocket-book edition of 1889 to W. H. Raymenton of Worcester, Mass., President of the Natural History Park, who wrote Whitman, "For years you have been to me a Living Presence." This letter, 18 October 1889, is in the Princeton University Library and is reproduced, with Whitman's marginal comment, in the *Walt Whitman Review*, XIX (December 1973), 172.
2934. See footnote 2925.
2935. For Edward Wilkins, who was now going back to Veterinary School in Toronto, see footnote 2657; Whitman was sorry to see him go, he wrote Dr R. M. Bucke — "the nurse-dislocation bothers us (but all goes into a life time) —" (see *The Correspondence of Walt Whitman*, IV, 385–386). The "big parcel of portraits" mentioned here on the next line were taken by Wilkins to Dr Bucke in London, Ontario.
2936. The big book is the *Complete Poems & Prose*, the eighth edition of *Leaves of Grass* (1888).
2937. As Whitman wrote to, as usual, Dr R. M. Bucke this same day, "Warren Fritzinger, one of Mrs D[avis]'s sailor boys, is acting as my nurse & helper — I have just had a good massage — get along fairly —" (*The Correspondence of Walt Whitman*, IV, 386).
2938. Once again, Whitman writes to his London, Ontario friend: "One of the Cambridge, Mass: College fellows has just sent to get L[eaves] of G[rass], the pk't b'k ed'n — sent the money — several have been b't there before —" (*The Correspondence of Walt Whitman*, IV, 387).

headquarters   Male nurses
137 King Street
Ed: Wilkins 556 Hamilton Road London Ont:[2939]

C

Col: John A Cockerell [2940]

H Buxton Forman, 46 Marlborough Hill, St John's Wood
London N W [2941]

[Clipping:]   The grand jury has handed in indictments against Joseph Pulitzer, John H. Cockerell, Julius Chambers and James F. Graham, of the New York *World,* for criminal libel, on complaint of ex-Judge Hilton.

[On slip on paper, not in WW's hand:]

Frank R. Stockton[2942]
Convent Station
New Jersey.

_____

Send a 2^{oc} Copy L.

of G. – Autographed.

[Notation in blue pencil in WW's hand, written upwards:]

book
sent
Nov: 8

2939. This address was either written before Edward Wilkins left Camden, or the change was possibly made after Warren Fritzinger heard from Wilkins on 31 October 1889 from London.

2940. Col. John A. Cockerill was an important New York newspaperman, and I doubt that Whitman ever met him; his name may be here because of the clipping just below about his being indicted with Pulitzer, Chambers (whom Whitman did know) and Graham of the New York *World.* Both Whitman and the newspaper (below) misspell his name.

2941. For H. Buxton Forman, see footnote 248; he wrote Whitman on 26 September 1888 about George Eliot and *Leaves of Grass* — see Horace Traubel, *With Walt Whitman in Camden,* II, 433–434, and *The Correspondence of Walt Whitman,* IV, 218n — and later on 4 and 16 June 1890 (see footnote 3060, below). Why is his address here now?

2942. Frank R. Stockton (1834–1902), Philadelphia novelist, short story writer, and editor of *St. Nicholas* (1873–1881), is perhaps best known for his "The Lady or the Tiger?" in *The Century* in 1882, and his fantastic novel *Rudder Grange* (1879). This slip here in the *Daybook* is his order for *Leaves of Grass,* which Whitman sent him on 8 November 1889 (see entry below, that date). Stockton did not seem important enough for Whitman to tell Dr R. M. Bucke that the novelist had bought a copy of *Leaves.*

[Calling card, printed:]

Sidney H. Morse, Sculptor,
374 E. Division Street,
Chicago.[2943]

[Long clipping: Peculiar Colors and Cutting. / How the Lapidary Shapes and Pol-/ishes the Diamond — Rubies, Sap-/phires and Spinels — The / Story of the Pearl. /. A leaf from a book: A Gem for every Month.]

[2:19]

Camden   Oct: and November   '89

26 had the old tree cut down – it was dead & no
        sap, no leaves – "why cumbereth it the ground?"
        (how long before I go too?) – it stood in the front
        of my old ranch in Mickle st: must have been
        40 or 50 yr's old – Jo Jackson (color'd man, Centre-
        ville) cut it down this forenoon smooth'd the ground
        & paved the walk over with bricks & placed the
        white stone carriage step (with W W on, a present f'm
        R Pearsall Smith) in better middle position – $2:50 – gave
        Jo a good glass of Sherry wine – [2944] (rather moderate temper-
        ature – cloudy – looks like rain) – am feeling so-so – might
        be worse – & probably shall be – head & bladder trouble –
        . . . W F nursing & helping me now – Ed in Canada[2945]
    sent p'k-b'k L of G. to Walter Delaplaine Scull, 2 Langland
        Gardens, Frognal, Finchley Road, London, N w. England
        Alys Smith here – good sunshiny visit[2947]   paid
                                                                          $6 [2946]

2943. For Sidney Morse, see footnote 2336; he spent considerable time in the summer of 1887 sculpting Whitman, and a print of his bust was used as a frontispiece in *Camden's Compliment to Walt Whitman,* which Horace Traubel was now seeing through the press (a reproduction of this bust is in *The Correspondence of Walt Whitman,* IV, foll. 278).

2944. A somewhat similar account of cutting this tree down — "was afraid it w'd fall & perhaps hurt some one" — is in Whitman's letter to Dr R. M. Bucke, *The Correspondence of Walt Whitman,* IV, 388.

2945. For Warren Fritzinger taking Edward Wilkin's place, see footnotes 2935 and 2937.

2946. Walter Delaplaine Scull was a young English artist who ordered a copy of the pocket-book (1889) edition of *Leaves of Grass*: his letter of 14 October 1889, doing so, is in the Feinberg Collection.

2947. Alys Smith, daughter of Robert Pearsall Smith, and sister of Logan and Mary (Whitman's "bright particular star"), was over from England, where the family had moved from Germantown, Philadelphia (see footnote 1622). Whitman wrote to Bucke, misspelling her name, "Alice Smith, the dear delicate cheery girl, is over this afternoon & pays me a good long sunshiny visit — " (*The Correspondence of Walt Whitman,* IV, 388); he also wrote her sister, Mary Smith Costelloe (*ibid.,* IV, 389) about Alys.

28   paid $2.50 for cutting &c: the old tree in front[2948]
        cloudy, dark, damp, rainy, three days

31   Recd: $25 f'm R Pearsall Smith f'm England [2949]
        Sister Han has had a bad spell illness – jaundice
                is now easier[2950]
        Dr Hawley here – bo't two big books[2951]
        extra bad feeling in head (catarrhal?)

[Three lines in pencil:]
Nov:
    1   Friday evn'g – "My 71st Year" in Century – slips sent[2952]
        – pictures & note sent to R P Smith, London[2953]
        – rec'd letter f'm Dr B – Ed arrived in London, Canada[2954]

                                                £
    3   sent "Old age Echoes" to 19th Century –   20 & 20 slips
                                                        sent back
        four pieces – intended to make a page (rejected)   to me[2955]

    8   sent L of G. (author's ed'n – green bdg) to F R Stockton
            Convent Station N J.   paid $2 [2956]
        cloudy – half rainy – feeling fairly – snivelling letters
        continued (apparently endlessly) f'm the miserable
        whelp C L H (he knows I can't help myself – I never
        answer them   I feel as if I could crush him out
        like an offensive bed-bug wh' he is) – [2957]

2948. Why mention the $2.50 price twice (just above, too): is it that important?
2949. This letter, dated 13 October 1889 (Feinberg Collection) also said that Mary Smith Costelloe, whom Whitman had just written on 27 October (see footnote 2947), "is under a nervous break-down — not suffering much but compelled to great quiet." She herself wrote again on 26 October (Feinberg Collection) of her plan to visit Spain for her health.
2950. See footnote 2926.
2951. Dr W. A. Hawley (of Syracuse, New York) had ordered a copy of *Leaves of Grass* to be sent to A. A. J. Züllig about 24 October 1888 — the letter of Whitman's about the book is now lost, but see entry for that date and footnote 2654. The two big books he now buys are copies of *Complete Poems & Prose* (1888).
2952. For "My 71st Year," see footnote 2820.
2953. This letter to Robert Pearsall Smith is now lost, but see footnotes 2947 and 2949.
2954. Letters of 29 and 30 October 1889 from Dr R. M. Bucke are in the Feinberg Collection; for Edward Wilkins, see footnote 2935; Whitman worried about Wilkins and kept asking Dr Bucke if he had arrived back in London.
2955. For "Old Age Echoes," originally called "Old Age's Voices" in the *Daybook*, see footnote 2932.
2956. For Frank R. Stockton, see footnote 2942.
2957. These comments, not typical certainly for the *Daybook*, are typical of Whitman's attitude toward his brother-in-law Charles L. Heyde: see footnote 2926, above.

[Six lines in pencil:]
Horace T. here   this   evn'g – Read a letter f'm
    F B Sanborn ab't the scurrilous Note in Edw'd
    Emerson's book "R W E was habitually looking
    at a matter f'm many sides or points of view
    – & this might have been one – but it was not
    the one" – &c &c[2958]

---

                                              her
13   visit f'm Mrs: E M O'Connor   gave $10 [2959]

[2:20]

Dec. 9 – London Eng: <u>Nineteenth</u> <u>Century</u> has (I sent to 'em)
    "Old Age Echoes" (?Voices)   3 or 4 sonato poemets
    [First word in pencil:]   rejected – sold to Lippincott
"To the Sunset Breeze" to be pub'd Nov: '90   paid $60 [2960]
          my MS
<u>Harpers' Monthly</u> has a poemet illustrating "the Valley
    of the Shadow of Death" picture by Innes – paid $25 [2961]
    pub'd [in blue pencil]

pub'd { <u>Century</u> has "Old Age's Ship & Crafty Death's" 8-line poemet
                                   paid $10 – pubd Feb
           pub'd   [in blue pencil]   '90 [2962]
       S S McClure has "A Christmas Greeting f'm a Northern
                       pub'd & copied largely in Europe
           Star: group to a Southern"   – paid $11 [2963]

[Clipping of label: "From / Billstein & Son, / Printers, / Nos. 925 and 927
Filbert Street, / Philadelphia. /." WW's notation:] [2964]

          plate   (good
       & other

2958. Horace Traubel read Franklin B. Sanborn's letter to Whitman about Edward
Emerson's reference to Whitman in *Emerson in Concord: A Memoir* (Boston, 1889), p. 228n:
"When Leaves of Grass appeared at a later period than that of which I speak, the healthy vigor
and freedom of this work of a young mechanic seemed to promise so much that Mr. Emerson
overlooked the occasional coarseness which offended him, and wrote a letter of commendation
to the author, a sentence of which was, to his annoyance, printed in gold letters on the covers
of the next edition. But the first work led him to expect better in future, and in this he was
disappointed. He used to say, this 'Catalogue-style of poetry is easy and leads nowhere,' or
words to that effect." This footnote is reprinted in Horace Traubel, *With Walt Whitman in
Camden*, V, 172. Whitman first said, when Traubel showed him the passage on 11 May 1889,
"Well it makes no difference" (*ibid.*, V, 172); the next day, Whitman was vehement, "It is a
lie!" and 'it is the concoction — I know unconscious of Edward, of Ellen. The two put their
heads together — produced it. Ellen [Edward's sister] hates me like the devil — always did. This

[2:21]

Camden   Nov: &   Dec: 1889

18 Monday – Warren F. my friend & nurse, (the massages)[2965]
– Mrs: O'C   she probably returns to Wash'n (f'm quite a long
visit in New Eng: & three days here) to day —[2966]
– rainy & dark to-day — am sitting here penn'd up, as
        eigh
now for ~~nine~~teen months (since 1st of June 88)
– do I not feel a shade better, stronger lately?
– letters continued from that miserable whelp C L H – he
is the worst nuisance & worriment of my illness – keeps me
back (his damnable letters) ab't the worst factor of all –
                him
– always whining & squeezing me for more money – damn
                him
– he ought to be crush'd out as you w'd a bed-bug[2967]
– sent morocco L of G. to Harrison S Morris[2968]

---

note — this was never Emerson!" Whitman was also contemptuous of "or words to that effect" and felt the book had no value as biography (*ibid.,* V, 176). Again on 13 May 1889, Whitman told Traubel, "The note was undoubtedly lugged in — inexcusably lugged in — an attempt to force an utterance of disdain from me"; and he further called R. W. Emerson's second wife "a hideous unlikely woman," and Ellen "a hag! She is a hag! . . . She is repulsive to me beyond utterance . . ." (*ibid.,* V, 178–179). Whitman said of Sanborn's letter that Traubel "will some-day tell you [Dr Bucke] more fully ab't it, but S[anborn] don't want it published (? at present) — is ab't Edw'd Emersons sneaking lying *note* anent of me in his late b'k ab't R W E — B [Sanborn] is cool & collected & conservative but I consider him a real honest permanent friend of self & L of G —" (*The Correspondence of Walt Whitman,* IV, 396).

2959. See footnote 2918, and *The Correspondence of Walt Whitman,* IV, 397.
2960. For "Old Age Echoes" and "To a Sun-Set Breeze," see footnote 2932.
2961. For "Death's Valley," which Whitman wrote for the picture, see footnote 2869.
2962. For "Old Age's Ship and Crafty Death," which Whitman sent to the magazine on 4 January 1889, see footnote 2675.
2963. "A Christmas Greeting," subheaded "From a Northern Star-Group to a Southern, 1889–'90," was sent to John Foord, *Harper's Weekly,* on 19 December 1889, rejected, then sent to S. S. McClure but publication details are not known. See *Leaves of Grass,* Comprehensive Reader's Edition, p. 548.
2964. Henry Billstein was the plate printer of the 1889 pocket-book *Leaves of Grass* (see footnote 2738); he called on Whitman on 3 February 1889 and the poet liked him — see *With Walt Whitman in Camden,* IV, 78.
2965. For Warren Fritzinger, see footnotes 2935 and 2937.
2966. Whitman wrote Dr R. M. Bucke on 16 November 1889 that Mrs Ellen M. O'Connor, William Douglas O'Connor's widow, was to leave Philadelphia on 18 November for Washington; she wrote Whitman from there on 20 November — see *The Correspondence of Walt Whitman,* IV, 399 and 401. (Her letter is in the Feinberg Collection, and his reply, published in *The Correspondence,* is in the Berg Collection.)
2967. How Whitman did stew about Charles L. Heyde, his sister Hannah's artist husband; just a few lines above, on 8 November 1889, Whitman lashed out in the *Daybook*; see also footnote 2926.
2968. For Harrison Smith Morris, to whom Whitman has just sent one of the newly bound 1889 printings of *Leaves of Grass,* see footnote 2836.

19   sent big book by Express to R F Wormwood
        Fryeburg, Maine – paid $5 – rec'd   (& the $1 p'd)[2969]
     dark rainy day – feeling tolerable – good massages
              welcoming the Brazil republic
     sent the little poemet ∧ "A north star to a south"
                                          return'd
        to John Foord, "Harper's Weekly" – $10 & ten papers
                                    rejected [2970]

25   Monday – dark, rainy – feeling so-so – word rec'd
     f'm Ellen O'C, Ed W. & Mrs: Mapes[2971] – poor day –

Dec: 4 sent "A Christmas Greeting f'm a Northern Star:
                            accepted
        Group to a Southern" to S S McClure N Y. $11 – paid – [2972]
        Death of poor old Mrs: Curtz $5 [2973]   (Cold and sunny
                                          weather   )

 9   am sending out a few adv: circulars of the 3 issues[2974]
     sent pocket b'd L of G to Grace Johnston N Y.[2975]

11   D McKay sends $12 for the three copies "Complete Works"
        pays for all them had by him up to date.[2976]
     Jefferson Davis buried at New Orleans[2977]

2969. See Whitman's letter to Wormwood about the *Complete Poems & Prose* in *The Correspondence of Walt Whitman,* IV, 400.

2970. See footnote 2963.

2971. For Ellen M. O'Connor, see footnote 2966; for Edward Wilkins, whose letter to Whitman is now lost, see footnotes 2657, 2935, and 2939; for Mrs Mapes, whose letter is also missing, see footnotes 2833, 2838, and 2880.

2972. For this poem, also mentioned just above on 19 November 1889, see footnote 2963. Whitman's letter: *The Correspondence of Walt Whitman,* IV, 402.

2973. Mrs Henry Curtz was the wife of the eccentric printer — "an effete person — seems as if left over from a very remote past" who had a "queer little office, the Washington press, the old faced letters, the wood type . . . he's the last of his race" (*With Walt Whitman in Camden,* I, 180; mentioned several times in Horace Traubel's five volumes). Whitman apparently sent $5 to her husband?

2974. This was a circular to advertise *Complete Poems & Prose* for $6, the small 1889 *Leaves of Grass* for $5, and the autographed *Portraits from Life* for $3; a copy of the circular is in *Camden's Compliment to Walt Whitman,* and a facsimile of Whitman's MS for the printer is in *With Walt Whitman in Camden,* V, following 242. The very last entry in the *Daybook,* which must have been written about this time, contains a list of 13 people to whom Whitman sent the circular.

2975. Grace Johnston, who brought Whitman some roses on 19 May 1889 (see *With Walt Whitman in Camden,* V, 201), was, as far as I can discover, the stepdaughter of Mrs Alma Johnston (J. H. Johnston's wife) of New York City.

2976. See the transcript of Whitman's letter in *The Correspondence of Walt Whitman,* IV, 405.

2977. Whitman had strong feelings about the Confederate president in a letter of 7

13   Robert Browning died [2978]

---

14   laid in a fresh cord of cut wood

---

16   composing "Old Poets – (and other things)" [2979]

---

19   sent big book (complete works) to Mrs: E C Waters
                paid – 6:40 by p o order   rec'd[2980]
      Sag Harbor by p o. (stamp'd 40^cts) – Sunny day
      sent H L H   Burlington Vt. 10 (5 for C)   all rec'd [2981]
      also to Mary,   Greenport   10   rec'd [2982]

[2:22]

Mrs: William Patterson
   167 N Mercer street
      New Castle Pa:[2983]

[On a scrap of paper, first two
lines in pencil:]

Thos: Donaldson
   326 n 39
      cor: Baring[2984]

[Printed on a scrap from an
envelope:]

   Rudolf Schmidt,
   Blaagaardsgade 16. B.
      Kjebenhavn, N.[2985]

Bernard O'Dowd

      Supreme Court Library
         Melbourne   Victoria
            via San Francisco[2986]

[Clipping:]

   Walt Whitman was out in the sun
shine riding yesterday. He went to
Harleigh Cemetery to see the lay of the
ground and to pick out a burial lot. He
resolutely passed by all the show parts
and lawns, and chose a place back on a
woody side hill, where he is to have a
plot 20x30 feet, and where a solid gray
stone monumental vault will be con-
structed.[2987]

[WW's notation:]

   Camden Post, Dec 26 '89
rec'd the deed April 29 '90

December 1889: "So Jefferson Davis is dead — the papers to day are full — he stands, will remain, as representative for a bad *even foul* move — & himself a bad & foul move — that's the
deep final verdict of America's soul" (*The Correspondence of Walt Whitman*, IV, 403).
   2978. Whitman, who said very little of Browning in *Prose Works 1892*, wrote to Dr
R. M. Bucke: "So Browning is dead — as it has happen'd I never read him much — (Does he not
exercise & rather worry the intellect — something like a sum in arithmetic?)" (*The Correspondence of Walt Whitman*, IV, 405). He told William Sloane Kennedy he had no "inherent opinion" of Browning (*ibid.*, IV, 406).
   2979. "Old Poets" was a prose essay, which Whitman was still "pottering over" on 5
January 1890 (*The Correspondence of Walt Whitman*, V, 18); in October 1890 he sent it to the

[2:23]

Camden N Y   328 Mickle st: Dec: '89 and Jan: '90

Dec:

24   3 p m – Have been out in a cab & open wagon to
Harleigh Cemetery – all around & back through
roads &c: and to the Cooper's creek north bound
– have selected & designated my cemetery

North American Review (*ibid.,* V, 101), where it was published, CLI (November 1890), 610–614, and reprinted in *Good-bye My Fancy* (1891). See *Prose Works 1892,* II, 658–662.

2980.   Mrs E. C. Waters not identified.

2981.   This $10 was the usual Christmas present Whitman sent to his sister, Mrs Hannah L. Heyde; but could "5 for C" mean that he also sent $5 to her husband Charles after the strong words he had to say of him above, "miserable whelp" and "offensive bed-bug"?

2982.   A Christmas gift, the usual one, of $10 to Whitman's sister Mary Van Nostrand. The letters to Whitman's sisters are both missing.

2983.   Mrs William Patterson not identified.

2984.   For recent Donaldson-Whitman activities see footnotes 2822 and 2910, and the *Daybook* entry for 1 October 1889.

2985.   For Rudolf Schmidt, Whitman's Scandinavian friend, to whom he wrote on 24 December 1889, see footnotes 81 and 2830.

2986.   Bernard O'Dowd (1866–1953), Australian poet, is here first mentioned by Whitman, although the earliest known letter from O'Dowd is dated 12 March 1890 (see entry below for 16 April 1890). Whitman's first known letter, [12] July 1890, is in *The Correspondence of Walt Whitman,* V, 62. O'Dowd's correspondence with Whitman and their relationship through letters is told in A. L. McLeod's "Walt Whitman in Australia," *Walt Whitman Review,* VII (June 1961), 23–35, and his *Walt Whitman in Australia and New Zealand: A Record of His Reception* (Sydney: Wentworth Press, 1964). Son of an Irish policeman and brought up as a Roman Catholic, O'Dowd was a lonely and loveless child who became a free-thinker, a teacher (for a time), and a poet who also drifted from job to job and considered himself a failure; for him Whitman became a father-figure. As quoted in Mr McLeod's book above (p. 23): "Had Carlyle added another chapter to his 'Hero Worship' the 'Hero as Nurse' with Walt Whitman as subject would have worthily capped his dome." O'Dowd's fervor is shown in this comment quoted by Edwin Haviland Miller in *The Correspondence of Walt Whitman,* V, 3: "I can hardly think it is not a dream that I am writing to Walt Whitman. Take our love, we have little more to give you, we can only try to spread to others the same great boon you have given to us." Between April 1890 and November 1891 he wrote 11 letters to O'Dowd — all published from originals in the Feinberg Collection in *The Correspondence,* V, 62, 98–99, 112–113, 138–139, 142–143, 150–151, 167–168, 176, 201, 260 — and seven of the Australian's extant letters to Whitman (also in the Feinberg) are in *Overland,* No. 23 (April 1962), 9–18; or in McLeod's book, pp. 19–33, 38–39. As Whitman told his young far-away correspondent, "you please me more than you know."

2987.   This paragraph from the Camden *Post* reads as if Whitman himself wrote it, for the same information is in his letter to Dr R. M. Bucke of 25 December 1889: "Yesterday went out (two hours drive) to Harleigh Cemetery & selected my burial lot — a little way back, wooded, on a side hill — lot 20 x 30 feet — think of a vault & capping all a plain massive stone temple, (for want of a better descriptive word) — Harleigh Cemetery is a new burial ground & they desire to give me a lot — " (*The Correspondence of Walt Whitman,* IV, 408). "Give" may apply to the lot, but not to the tomb, for Whitman signed a contract for construction of the tomb without agreeing on the cost; when Thomas B. Harned learned that the contractor was going to charge several thousand dollars, he settled for $1500, which, says Gay Wilson Allen, Harned probably paid himself. (See *The Solitary Singer,* p. 540. Professor Allen also says that Whitman wanted a mausoleum so that the remains of his father and mother could be removed there; as well as Hannah, George, Louisa, and Edward.) Although it is not mentioned in the *Daybook,* as there is no entry for that date, Whitman first went to Harleigh Cemetery on 7 December 1889 (letter to Dr Bucke, *The Correspondence of Walt Whitman,* IV, 403). J. B. Wood, Harleigh Cemetery, wrote to Whitman on 24 December 1889 (letter in the Feinberg Collection).

lot 20 x 30 feet in area, on a wooded knoll
in[2988]

25   sent a big envelope with the 6 or 8 portraits
       to J A Symonds Davos Platz Switzerland [2989]

26   sent morocco b'd L of G to Alma Johnston N Y.   paid
                                              5 [2990]

27   a little cold – four days now of fine sunshine
       – out in the wheel-chair every afternoon
       – call'd at Mr Traubel's & saw the pictures[2991]

31   sent to C L H $2 [2992] – letter to Ed Wilkins[2993]

1890   1890

Jan: 1   Am writing this – 9 p m in my room Mickle
street – pretty feeble, & gradually failing to
all appearance (& f'm inherent feeling) —
– grow weaker in my legs – dull and weighty
in head – eyes dimmer – almost deaf at times[2994]

2   paid $15.25 Billstein & Co: Plate Printers   925
                                                Filbert St[2995]

"   7.14 to Camden Gas Office

"   2   to C L H [2996]

2988.   See previous footnote.

2989.   No letter to John Addington Symonds extant for this date; the portraits were undoubtedly those Whitman planned for *Portraits from Life,* which he was to sell for $3. Symonds's letter of 9 December is in the Feinberg Collection; it is No. 1761 in *The Letters of John Addington Symonds,* edited by Herbert M. Schueller and Robert L. Peters (Detroit: Wayne State University Press, 1969), III, 424–426.

2990.   There do not seem to be any extant letters to or from Whitman and Mr or Mrs John H. Johnston, his well-to-do New York friends, for this period.

2991.   Whitman referred to Horace's father, Maurice Traubel as "Mr Traubel."

2992.   This sum of $2 was sent to Charles L. Heyde in Burlington, Vermont, though he was no great favorite of Whitman's; letters from Heyde to Whitman of 27 December and December ? are in the Trent Collection; Whitman's to him of 31 December 1889 is lost.

2993.   Whitman's long and pleasant letter is in *The Correspondence of Walt Whitman,* IV, 409–410.

2994.   Though anything but a well man, Whitman managed to struggle on for more than two years, continued to write more than 500 letters, some material for publication, and even made his Lincoln address on 15 April 1890 in Philadelphia.

2995.   This was for *Portraits from Life,* the autographed collection of the poet's picture which he was selling for $3. (See footnote 2864.)

2996.   All three of these bills, for the plates, for the gas in Whitman's house, and the $2 for Charles L. Heyde (whom he had just sent $2 on 31 December 1889), are recorded again at

                            u
8   sent "A Death-Boquet" to Franklin File[2997]
        Sun office N Y.   (1205 Broadway too)
            paid $10   publish'd [2998]

26   sent "Osceola" to Melville Phillips, "Press"   paid $10
                                                        off:
            [Line in pencil:]   pub'd "Munyon's Ill: World" April [2999]

27   sent big book (mail) to J V Blake 21 Laflin
        st Chicago   paid $6.40 [3000]

29   visit f'm Mr Munyon, Melville Phillips & the two
        photographers – the latter "took me" in my room
        – (bo't two big books)[3001]

                                                    [2:24]

[Clipping: "The Three Americas", a 66-line newspaper article on Central
and South America.]

                                                    [2:25]

            Camden Jan:& February   1890
Feb: 3   sent "the Commonplace" poemet, and "the Voice" prose
            & ¶(ab't common school teachers) $20 due me[3002]

the very end of the *Daybook*. Letters from Heyde for 1, 2 and 6 January 1890 are in the Trent
Collection; Whitman's to him is missing.
    2997. Franklin File, whose real name was Franklin Fyles, was the drama critic of the
New York *Sun* and the author of several plays; Whitman's letter to him, sending this article,
is missing.
    2998. "A Death-Bouquet," a prose piece, was published in the New York *Sun* and Whitman
was paid $10 for it, according to the *Daybook,* but it has not been found in the *Sun,* nor in
the Philadelphia *Press* for 2 February 1890, where Whitman told Dr R. M. Bucke it was
printed (*The Correspondence of Walt Whitman,* V, 24 and 25); William Sloane Kennedy, *The
Fight of a Book for the World,* p. 271, also says it was in the *Press.* It was reprinted in *Good-Bye
My Fancy* (1891) and is in *Prose Works 1892,* II, 671–673.
    2999. This 10-line poem, "Osceola," on the death of a Seminole Indian, was sent to Mel-
ville Philips at the Philadelphia *Press,* although it was for publication in *Munyon's Illustrated
World* (Philadelphia), where it appeared in April 1890, Vol. VI, p. 7; the same issue con-
tained "Walt Whitman's Life." See *The Correspondence of Walt Whitman,* V, 24n and 27–28;
see also V, 201, for another letter to Philips about further contributions by Whitman. For
"Osceola," which was reprinted in *Good-bye My Fancy* (1891), see *Leaves of Grass,* Comprehensive Reader's Edition, pp. 550–551. (A file of *Munyon's* has not been found.)
    3000. The Rev. James Vila Blake was a Unitarian minister who visited Whitman in
March 1889 (see footnote 2650).
    3001. This visit has to do with the publication of "Osceola" and "Walt Whitman's Life"
in *Munyon's Illustrated World* (see footnote 2999). Whitman misspelled Philips's name here
and above. The books they bought were Whitman's *Complete Poems & Prose* (1889).
    3002. "The Commonplace," an 8-line poem, appeared in *Munyon's Illustrated World,* in
MS facsimile in March 1891 (see text, *Leaves of Grass,* Comprehensive Reader's Edition, pp.

sent "Compliment" book to Ed: Wilkins   rec'd [3003]

---

sent pk't-b'd L of G. to Bancroft Wash'n   (rec'd)[3004]

---

6   sent big book to Prof: John W Cook Normal, Ill:
        paid
        bill ∧ (6.40) to Wm Hawley Smith, Peoria, Ill
                                [In pencil:]   pay – rec'd [3005]
        postal to Dr Hawley 308 Warren St   Syracuse N Y [3006]

---

sent request to James Knowles, Nineteenth Century MS. return'd [3007]

[Line in pencil:]   £
10   Rec'd letter f'm Leonard Morgan Brown, Eng: 5   note enc: [3008]

553–554); "the Voice" refers to a prose piece, "The Human Voice," also published in *Munyon's*, VI (October 1890), 2, reprinted with the title "The Perfect Human Voice" in *Good-Bye My Fancy* (1891) — see *Prose Works 1892*, II, 673-674. Whitman mentioned these in a letter to Dr R. M. Bucke this same date, 3 February 1890: *The Correspondence of Walt Whitman*, V, 24. The paragraph "ab't common school teachers" cannot be identified. The letter to *Munyon's* is missing.

3003.   Edward Wilkins, Whitman's former male nurse who had returned to Canada, wrote to Whitman about this date (the letter is now lost); the book which Whitman sent is *Camden's Compliment to Walt Whitman* (see footnote 2809), edited by Horace Traubel in 1889. See the poet's letter to Wilkins: *The Correspondence of Walt Whitman*, V, 30-31.

3004.   George Bancroft (1800–1891), to whom Whitman sent the pocket-book (1889) edition of *Leaves of Grass* (see footnote 2806) and of whom he told Traubel: "No — we never met — though I have seen him [in Washington] many times. If the way had been open I would have introduced myself. Even as it is, today, were I eligible, I would take the trouble to write, if do no more by him. Bancroft is a man of sagacity — honest — rather prosy and slow: a plodding hewer of wood and drawer of water — yet an indispensable collector — a man going before to gather materials for philosophy." As far as Whitman knew, Bancroft had no opinion of *Leaves of Grass*. (Horace Traubel, *With Walt Whitman in Camden*, II, 16.)

3005.   Other than what we know here, Professor John W. Cook is unidentified; but Whitman wrote to William Hawley Smith on 23 December 1890 about another copy of *Complete Poems & Prose*, which Smith sent to S. R. Henderson in Los Angeles; Whitman's letters to him on 27 January and 2 March 1891 are missing; a letter from Mrs Smith to the poet, 11 March 1887, is in the Feinberg Collection.

3006.   Dr William A. Hawley of Syracuse's letter from Whitman is missing, as is one of 24 October 1888, when Whitman sent him one of his books. (See footnote 2951.) Dr Hawley had written Whitman at the Attorney General's office as early as 10 August 1869 that he (Hawley) was *"entombed* in the church and never had a breath of the pure, free air of heaven till I was thirty-five years old. Swedenborg first opened the sepulchre . . . but it remained for you to breathe upon the *dry bones* and make *them* live. To you alone I owe the discovery that 'Divine am I inside and out' — that the 'body is not less sacred than the soul.' . . . [Y]ou have lifted up and made happy a brother . . . I would I could grasp your hand, look in your eyes and have you look in mine. Then you should see how much you have done for me." (Horace Traubel, *With Walt Whitman in Camden*, IV, 365.)

3007.   Whitman's letter to the editor of *Nineteenth Century* is in *The Correspondence of Walt Whitman*, V, 25-26; he had sent "Old Age's Echoes," a cluster of short poems, in November, and Knowles returned them on 21 February 1890 (letter in the Feinberg Collection). They were published in *Lippincott's Magazine*, XLVII (March 1891), 376 and after Whitman's death, with some composed later, as "Old Age Echoes," in the 1897 *Leaves of Grass* — see Comprehensive Reader's Edition, pp. 575-582.

3008.   Whitman to Leonard Morgan Brown, 7 February 1890, thanking him for $25: *The Correspondence of Walt Whitman*, V, 25; see also *ibid.*, IV, 132-133, for Whitman's letter

sent $45.50 to Mr Currie, Blackwood, for Ed's board[3009]
2 to Han – 2 to Mrs. Mapes[3010]

---

26   poemet "A Twilight Song" accepted by <u>Century</u>[3011]
paid $25

---

bo't new cord oak wood

March 11   – sent answers to "Illustrated American" N Y [3012]

---

20   the piece by young Mr Cate in "Morning News" [3013]
I sent copies to many friends

April 3 paid the gas bill $7 (7.36, 36 off)

---

presented Dr Brinton with big book[3014]

---

of 19 November 1887, thanking him for a previous $25; but on 9 May 1891 Brown wrote Whitman (letter in the Feinberg Collection), regretting that he could not send his annual gift. For more on Brown, see footnote 2403, above.

3009. This was for Edward Whitman's expenses at the asylum for three months. These are accounted for at the end of the *Daybook* again.

3010. Whitman's gifts to his sister Hannah Heyde were small but fairly regular; Mrs Mary E. Mapes, whom Whitman also helped, had been a housekeeper for him on Mickle Street when Mrs Davis was away.

3011. First called "Unknown Names," for "the masses of common slain soldiers buried after the Secession battles" — as Whitman described the poem in *The Correspondence of Walt Whitman*, V, 24 — it became "A Twilight Song" in *The Century Magazine*, XL (May 1890), 27. See *Leaves of Grass*, Comprehensive Reader's Edition, p. 549.

3012. Maurice M. Minton, of *The Illustrated American*, had written Whitman on 9 March 1890 (letter in the Feinberg Collection), for some verse to accompany a photograph; he sent three lines from "Song of Myself," Section 16, published in facsimile on 19 April 1890; Whitman was called "The greatest figure — almost without question — in contemporary American literature." (See *The Correspondence of Walt Whitman*, V, 39n.) On 2 April — not recorded below — Minton asked Whitman to answer, "Why am I a bachelor?" (see letter, Feinberg Collection). No reply is known. In its issue of 30 August 1890 *The Illustrated American*, in a Ruskin article, reprinted Whitman's letter to William Harrison Riley, of 18 March 1879 (*The Correspondence of Walt Whitman*, III, 148–149).

3013. Whitman mentioned the piece about him in the Camden *Morning News* in his letter to Edward Wilkins (*The Correspondence of Walt Whitman*, V, 30); but instead of naming those to whom he sent copies, this time he merely wrote in the *Daybook*, "many friends."

3014. Dr Daniel Garrison Brinton (1837–1899), who was the author of *Giordano Bruno: Philosopher and Martyr* (Philadelphia, 1890), with Thomas Davidson, which is mentioned here on the next line; the book contains a brief one-paragraph preface by Whitman, "Inscription for a Little Book on Giordano Bruno," reprinted in *Good-bye My Fancy* (1891) and *Prose Works 1892*, II, 676–677. Dr Brinton taught American linguistics (Indian languages) and archeology at the University of Pennsylvania, visited Whitman often in Camden, and was called by the poet "a master-man — stern, resolute, loyal — yes, what I like (in the best sense) to call adhesive: a good comrade, a ripe intellect" (Horace Traubel, *With Walt Whitman in Camden*, I, 128, with Brinton's picture opposite). He was one of the five speakers at Whitman's funeral. His letter of 12 April 1890, thanking Whitman for this *Complete Poems & Prose*, is in the Feinberg Collection.

4   ab't 3 p m have sent copies of Dr Brinton's <u>Bruno</u>
  to Symonds, Tenyson, Sarrazin, Rolleston,
  Dr Bucke, Wm M Rossetti[3015]
  – Have had a very bad week, night & day,
  probably the grip – two or three days ab't as sick
  & dismal as I have ever been — this afternoon
      fair
  better, even pretty – sweated freely the last 30 hours[3016]
    [In pencil:]   Canada gray cloth sent me by Dr B
  new togs (coat, vest, trousers) of the ∧ grey cloth
  ——————————————⌐ tailor'd by   [in pencil]
         ⌐ f'm ∧ young Harry Twoes[3017]

    till May 1
8,9,10,11,12 – grip continued ∧ – bad nightmare fit night 11th
  Tom Donaldson here evn'g 11th (Warry was over there
  to his house, cor: 39th and Baring – 13th) s. w. cor:[3018]

14. 13 easier but bad enough yet – told H T[raubel] I sh'd
  try to deliver the <u>Lincoln Death Piece</u> in Phila:[3019]

  Tuesday night (may break down tho')   was out in
               wheel chair
               40 minutes

14   continue better – ate 4 raw oysters for breakfast
  Melville Phillips and Mr Munyon here – took the
  two big books – paid $10[3020]

3015. See footnote 3014 about the *Bruno* book; the recipients are too well known for comment: John Addington Symonds, Alfred Lord Tennyson, Gabriel Sarrazin, T. W. H. Rolleston, Dr R. M. Bucke, and William Michael Rossetti — no Americans.

3016. However, Whitman wrote Dr R. M. Bucke, "I am quite sure nothing serious or at all alarming — will probably blow over this coming week," and though the grip continued, he was able to make his Lincoln talk in Philadelphia on 15 April (see *The Correspondence of Walt Whitman*, V, 33).

3017. The Twoes had been making clothes for Whitman for years.

3018. For Thomas Donaldson and his previous and latest Whitman relationship, see footnotes 2822 and 2910, and the *Daybook* for 1 October 1889; "Warry" refers to Warren Fritzinger, who had been helping care of Whitman on Mickle Street — he told Dr R. M. Bucke, "Warren is very good & kind" (*The Correspondence of Walt Whitman*, V, 33–34).

3019. Despite his having a bad time at the moment and his doubts about giving his Lincoln lecture, Whitman wrote William Sloane Kennedy "Astonishing [what] one can stand when put to your trumps" (*The Correspondence of Walt Whitman*, V, 37), and Dr R. M. Bucke, "Horace [Traubel] came & I told him I w'd try to go thro' the Lincoln Death Piece Tuesday night (I can't bear to be *bluff'd off* & toward the last, even in minor ways) — But I by no means know how it will go off — or but I sh'l break down — no strength no energy — " (*ibid.*, V 37). As it turned out, Whitman did deliver his lecture in Philadelphia (see entry on 15 April 1890 below) and all went well — it was the 13th and last time.

3020. Melville Philips was apparently connected with *Munyon's Illustrated World*, which

David McKay here pays me $58:15 Royalty
(See Statement this date)[3021]

---

15   Eveng went over in carriage (Mrs. D and Warren with
me) to Phila. to Art Gallery, Broad St.
& deliver'd the "Death of Lincoln" piece – all
went well – this must be the 13th time & is probably the last[3022]

[2:26]

J M Stoddart   Lippincotts 715 Market
Phila:[3023]

Critic   52 Lafayette Place   New York[3024]
Amid my many buffets[3025]

[2:27]

Camden   1890   April

16 April   Letter & proposition (offer, request) from
Dodd, Mead & Co. 753 Broadway, New York, to
write book (60,000 words) ab't Ab'm Lincoln

Munyon obviously published, and to which Whitman recently contributed (see footnote 3002). Whitman's *Complete Poems & Prose* was the big book they purchased. For more on Philips, see Whitman's letters to him, *The Correspondence of Walt Whitman*, V, 27–28, 201.

3021.   David McKay's royalty statement is not now in the *Daybook*.

3022.   A clipping from the Philadelphia *Record* reads: "The aged poet sat during his address and his readings from his poems. His voice was so distinct and steady that all of the audience, which filled the room to overflowing, could hear every word. His well-known venerable appearance was heightened by a shaded lamp placed beside him to light his manuscript." And he wrote to Dr R. M. Bucke: "The piece [Lincoln lecture] went off all right — got thro' all without dishonor — feel my sight & voice not what they were — presence (self-possession &c) perfect — audience large & very cordial — It is probably my 'last public appearance' — " (*The Correspondence of Walt Whitman*, V, 38–39; see also footnote 3018, above and 3030, below)..

3023.   Joseph M. Stoddart (1845–1921) visited Whitman on 21 April 1890 (see entry that date, below); and as will be seen in the entry for 24 April, Whitman sent four poems to *Lippincott's Magazine* (they were "Old Age Achoes," which had been rejected by *Nineteenth Century* — see footnote 3007, above), to be published separately (see entry for 28 April), for which he was paid $60. "To the Sunset Breeze," was published in *Lippincott's*, XLVI (December 1890), 861; "Sounds of the Winter," "The Unexpress'd," and "After the Argument," *Lippincott's*, XLVII (March 1891), 504 — the last three, with "Sail Out for Good, Eidólon Yacht!" under the general title of "Old-Age Echoes." See *Leaves of Grass*, Comprehensive Reader's Edition, pp. 546, 548, 556, 621, and 539. Whitman's letter to Stoddart: *The Correspondence of Walt Whitman*, V, 41.

3024.   *The Critic*, XVI (24 May 1890), 262, was soon to print "For Queen Victoria's Birthday," a poem which appeared two days earlier in the Philadelphia *Public Ledger*, and also in the *Pall Mall Gazette*, 24 May 1890: see *Leaves of Grass*, Comprehensive Reader's Edition, pp. 620–621. *The Critic* was also to print this year, two prose pieces, "An Old Man's Rejoinder," XVII (16 August 1890), 85–86, and "Shakspere for America," XVII (27 September 1890), 160, from *Poet-Lore*, II (September 1890), 492–493; now in *Prose Works 1892*, II, 655–658, and 674–675. See also *The Correspondence of Walt Whitman*, V, 46, 67, 68, 70.

3025.   Source of these four words?

– pay to be to me 10^{cts} – 10 per cent – on the
books sold – or $500 in lump[3026]
rec'd letter f'm (& answer'd ~~sent pictures in big envelope~~)
Bernard O'Dowd, Supreme Court Library
Melbourne, Victoria[3027]
sent paper with picts in

18   three bad deadly – feeling days — 19, 20, 21
same 22-to 27

21   Stoddart comes, inviting me to write
for Lippincott's magazine[3028]
Horace T. comes with the item (f'm a
letter seen by Frank Williams, Phila.
of Tennyson's criticism on L of G.)[3029]

22   the piece "W W's last public" in <u>Post</u> f'm the
Boston <u>Transcript</u> — (I sent off copies)
Same piece printed in London Eng: Pall Mall Gaz: May 24 [3030]
quite a number of   [in pencil]
~~Many~~ ᴧoffers   f'm publishers, magazine editors,
& heads of newspaper syndicates these times[3031]

3026. This letter from Dodd, Mead, 15 April 1890, is in the Feinberg Collection. He wrote almost exactly the same *Daybook* words to Dr R. M. Bucke, 17 April: "Publishers Dodd, Mead, & Co: N Y have written for me to furnish them in MSS a new book (60,000 words) on Abm Lincoln, for a series *Makers of America* — my pay to be 10 per cent on sales, or $500 in lump — I think favorably — " (*The Correspondence of Walt Whitman*, V, 39). But of course Whitman was unable to do the book.

3027. For Bernard O'Dowd, see footnote 2986. This letter of 16 April 1890 to O'Dowd is missing; O'Dowd's, 12 March 1890, is in the Feinberg Collection.

3028. For Stoddart and Lippincott's, see footnote 3023.

3029. In connection with this piece that Horace Traubel brought from Francis H. Williams, the minor poet and dramatist — see *Walt Whitman Review*, XIV (March 1968), 31 — Whitman wrote Bucke, "Did you know Tennyson has been talking *very strongly* in favor of L of G?" (*The Correspondence of Walt Whitman*, V, 42). The English poet's remarks appeared in the Philadelphia *American* on 26 April 1890.

3030. This piece, "Walt Whitman's Last' Public,'" was first published as "Walt Whitman Tuesday Night" in the Boston *Transcript* of 19 April 1890; and William Sloane Kennedy (*The Fight of a Book for the World*, p. 270) writes: "Sent to us at *Transcript* office by W. W. in his own MS., with request to me to return the MS., which I did. It is an account of his Lincoln lecture in Philadelphia, and is now included in his complete prose works." After its *Pall-Mall Gazette* printing Whitman included it in *Good-Bye My Fancy* (1891): see *Prose Works 1892*, II, 684–685. For the lecture, see footnotes 3019 and 3022.

3031. Aged, ill, and in his last two years of life, Whitman was able to publish prose pieces in the Camden *Daily Post*, *The Critic*, *North American Review*, *Lippincott's Magazine*, *Pall-Mall Gazette*, Boston *Transcript*, New York *Morning Journal*, *Munyon's Illustrated World*, *Poet-Lore*, *Engineering Review*; and poems in *The Century Magazine*, *Munyon's Illustrated World*, *Lippincott's*, *The Critic*, *Youth's Companion*, *Truth*, and *Home Journal* (New York).

sounds of

24   sent "Old Age Echoes" (4 pieces, "Signs f'm winter"
         "the unexpress'd," "to the sunset-breeze" and
         "after the argument") – to Stoddart, Lippincott's

paid

         to make a full page – $60 & 12 copies –   rec'd [3032]
         the third warm day

27   sent MS "O Captain! My Captain!" to Horace Furness[3033]

28   rec'd Deed for Cemetery Lot – (Harleigh C)[3034]
leave
         note f'm J M Stoddart, asking to print the
paid $60 [3035]
         four poemets separate — ans'd yes
         the American (Phil. April 26) with Tennyson's criticism[3036]

[Last three words in pencil:]
29   100 from Dr S Weir Mitchell & Horace Furness[3037]

May 1   sent Complete works (big book) – the MS of
            "O Captain" – & an envelope with portraits to
            Dr Mitchell 1524 Walnut st: Phila[3038]
            the May Century publishes "A Twilight Song" [3039]

[2:28]

Herbert calls May 10 / 1890 [3040]

3032. For these four poems, see footnote 3023. For letter to Stoddart: *The Correspondence of Walt Whitman*, V, 41.
3033. For Horace Howard Furness, see footnote 369; Furness and his father, then 88, visited Whitman on 10 April 1890: "Horace very deaf, gets along sort o' with ear trumpet — both real friends of mine & L of G" — *The Correspondence of Walt Whitman*, V, 35. If a letter accompanied this MS., it is now lost.
3034. For the Harleigh Cemetery and Whitman's lot, see footnote 2987; Whitman wrote to Dr R. M. Bucke, "— they have sent me *the deed* for the cemetery lot (so that is settled for) — I rather think I shall have a plain strong stone vault merely made for the present —" (*The Correspondence of Walt Whitman*, V, 43).
3035. See entry above for 24 April 1890 and footnotes 3023, 3032.
3036. See footnote 3029.
3037. For Furness, see footnote 3033; for Dr Mitchell, see footnote 76. See Whitman's thank-you letter to him, 30 April 1890: *The Correspondence of Walt Whitman*, V, 44 ("Your splendid contribution to me has been rec'd by the hands of Horace Furness & is hereby deeply thank'd for [$100] & is opportune & will do me much good.").
3038. Whitman's *Complete Poems & Prose* and some pictures, as well as a reprint of his "A Twilight Song" in *The Century Magazine*, XL (May 1890), 27, he mentions in his letter to Dr Mitchell (see previous footnote); but not the "O Captain" MS — he sent Horace Furness a MS of this poem on 27 April 1890 (is this another MS?).
3039. For "A Twilight Song," see footnote 3011.
3040. This entry and next few lines refer to Mrs Anne Gilchrist's son Herbert Gilchrist,

[Next lines not in WW's hand (on a slip pasted to page):]

This address ⎞ Herbert H. Gilchrist,
will find me ⎪   The Moses Jarvis Farm,
for year & a ⎬ (Centre Port Cove)
half from   ⎠   Centre Port Suffolk County,
the 10ᵗʰ of May Long Island   New York
  1890.

[In WW's hand:]

  H. calls it "paradise"   it is a stone throw f'm L I Sound

[On another slip of paper:]

        David L. Lezinsky   [not WW's hand] ³⁰⁴¹
              box 211 Berkeley   left
[not WW:]   Cal: May 18
16Q7 Post   May 13 1890
      in R
    Edward Stead   [Printed matter:
  2226 Jefferson st Phila:³⁰⁴² Illustration of hotel,
  ──────────────────────   Aldine, Decatur Street, First House from Beach,
  C H Luttgens³⁰⁴³   Cape May City, N. J.] ³⁰⁴⁴
      Hammonton New Jersey

---

who was attempting to make his living as an artist. Whitman told Dr Bucke, "Herbert Gilchrist has gone to Centreport (L I near Huntington) for a long stay" (*The Correspondence of Walt Whitman,* V, 47). From time to time he came to Camden to visit Whitman.

3041. David L. Lezinsky visited Whitman on 17 May 1890 and was on his way to California by way of Chicago; the poet wrote to Dr R. M. Bucke: "I could not make any thing very definite or satisfactory from his talk (wh' was very profuse) & I told him finally & summarily I guess I was exhausted, & to *write* plainly what he proposed & send me, when I w'd give him categorical reply — (If he writes, proposing any thing I will first show it you, & probably to Horace too) — " (*The Correspondence of Walt Whitman,* V, 49). On 4 June 1890 (see *Daybook* entry below) Whitman sent Lezinsky a copy of his *Complete Poems & Prose* at Butte City, Montana, and also wrote him, but the letter is missing now, as are other letters, except for two of 28 October and 30 November (see *The Correspondence of Walt Whitman,* V, 106–107, 125), in which he tells young man, an 1884 University of California graduate and poet, about his health, what he had sent him, his housekeeper, Dr Bucke, Traubel, and Jeff Whitman, and what he was writing and eating — nothing about Lezinsky's "proposition." In January 1891 he writes Dr Bucke that he had heard from Lezinsky, "my California (?Jewish) friend" (*ibid.,* V, 158): see *American Literature,* VIII (1937), 437n.

3042. Edwin R. Stead, whose address is given here, was the driver on a long three-mile outing on 14 May 1890 (see entry below) in a comfortable hansom, sent by a friend (Stead was a coppersmith): see *The Correspondence of Walt Whitman,* V, 47. Stead also took him for a drive to Gloucester on 19 May, again recorded in the *Daybook,* and the poet last saw him on 20 August 1890, as he told David Lezinsky (*The Correspondence of Walt Whitman,* V, 125); see also *Daybook* entry below for that date. Stead did write Whitman on 10 December 1890 (letter in the Feinberg Collection), and Whitman replied on 6 January 1891: see *The Correspondence of Walt Whitman,* V, 146, 395.

3043. C. H. Lüttgens is mentioned below in the *Daybook* on 8 July 1890 as sending Whitman some honey, though on 5 July he tells Dr R. M. Bucke that he "bo't some *real honey*

[Calling card: J.H. Johnston & Co., Diamonds, Watches, Jewelry and Silver Ware, 17 Union Square Cor. Broadway & 15th St., New York. Fine Printings, Bronzes and Porcelains.] [3045]

[2:29]

Camden   1890   May

May 1 fine sunny day – good temperature – a sort of let-up to-day – but my head (physical brain no doubt) a little sore and achy.

---

10 proofs of "Queen Victoria's Birthday" &
                                    rec'd
      "On, on the same, ye jocund twain!" f'm Curtz[3046]
      Fred: Vaughan here[3047]

---

12 sent "On, on the same, ye jocund twain" to Gilder
            rejected   out in
      Century – 20 [3048]   sent $2 to H [3049]   – wheel chair[3050]

---

13 David L Lezinsky — (a short drive in the hansom)[3051]

(wish I c'd send you some)" — presumably the same honey (*The Correspondence of Walt Whitman*, V, 59).

3044. This is the hotel where Dr R. M. Bucke was staying when he was in Cape May, New Jersey in May: see the *Daybook* entry for 13 May 1890. Thomas B. Harned and his family were also in Cape May in July.

3045. Bertha Johnston, the daughter of J. H. Johnston, always one of Whitman's staunchest friends, visited Whitman in Camden on 4 June 1890.

3046. Curtz, according to Edwin Haviland Miller (*The Correspondence of Walt Whitman*, V, 46–47n), was a compositor at 104 South Second Street, Philadelphia: Whitman's note to him (in *ibid.*, V, 46) is written on the verso of a heavily corrected proof of "For Queen Victoria's Birthday" (see footnote 3024). "On, on the same, ye jocund twain!" was rejected by *The Century Magazine* (see entry below for 12 May 1890), and on 22 November 1890 by *The Arena* (see entry below for that date; on 21 May 1891 Whitman received $10 for this poem and another from *Once a Week* (see *Daybook* that date). The poem may have appeared in *Once a Week*, but Sculley Bradley and Harold W. Blodgett say in *Leaves of Grass*, Comprehensive Reader's Edition, pp. 540–541, that it was first published in *Good-bye My Fancy* (1891).

3047. Fred Vaughan (see footnote 66) was an old friend of Whitman, whom he first knew as a New York driver at least as early as 19 and 21 March 1860 — letters from Vaughan in the Feinberg Collection, and others of 9 and 30 April and 21 May 1860, 2 May 1862 and 11 August 1874.

3048. See footnote 3046.

3049. This letter to Whitman's sister Hannah Heyde is missing; he does not record this $2 that he sent her at the back of the *Daybook*, but he does record $5 he sent on 8 July and 20 August 1890.

3050. Whitman mentioned this — Warren Fritzinger took him in the wheel chair — in a letter to Dr R. M. Bucke, whom he was writing almost every other day (*The Correspondence of Walt Whitman*, V, 46).

3051. David L. Lezinsky: see footnote 3041.

3052. Mary Davis, Whitman's housekeeper, on a short holiday.

Mary D gone to Doylestown[3052]
at   [in pencil]
Dr Bucke here ("Aldine"   Cape May)[3053]

driving[3054]   [in pencil]
14 went out in the hansom (Ed: Stead) to Westmont – to the toll gate (Cline's) — call'd at the
Cemetery – how beautiful it all looks! [3055]
a long drive on the Haddon road – I enjoy'd it –
the longest "outing" for two years, nearly —
– warm day – slight west breeze – feeling pretty well

17 a good long drive in hansom to Pea Ridge Shore
the imminent accident (dangerous) at Market St: wharf.[3056]
deposited $160 in bank

18 paid Oldach & Co $44.41 in full to date[3057]
Sunday – bright, sunny
Dr B's piece "L of G. & Modern Science" in "Conservator" [3058]

19 Monday – drive to Gloucester   [On slip of paper:]
— warm – gave Two Riv: Stead
S   Edwin R Pease
to Ed – the fourth day   – 2226 Jefferson
of feeling fairly[3059]   st
                                         Phila:

3053. Dr R. M. Bucke's address for 12, 14, 15 and 18 May 1890 was the Aldine Hotel,
Cape May, New Jersey.
3054. For Edwin R. Stead, see footnote 3042.
3055. For the Harleigh Cemetery, where Whitman had a lot and was to be buried on
30 March 1892, see footnotes 2987 and 3034. Whitman expressed these same feelings in this
entry in the *Daybook* in his letter to Dr R. M. Bucke: *The Correspondence of Walt Whitman*,
V, 47.
3056. This imminent (dangerous) accident was the reason, Edwin Haviland Miller
thinks, for Whitman to tell Dr R. M. Bucke on 18 May 1890: "It is probable I shall not see
the hansom any more" (*The Correspondence of Walt Whitman*, V, 49).
3057. This sum, also recorded at the back of the *Daybook*, was for binding Whitman's
most recent editions of *Leaves of Grass* and (probably) *Camden's Compliment to Walt
Whitman*.
3058. This same article in this newly started periodical, "*Leaves of Grass* and Modern
Science," *The Conservator*, I (May 1890), 19, was reprinted in *In Re Walt Whitman* (Philadelphia, 1893), edited by Dr R. M. Bucke, Horace L. Traubel, and Thomas B. Harned. Whitman
read proof: see his letter of 28 April 1890 in *The Correspondence of Walt Whitman*, V, 43.
3059. *Two Rivulets*, which Whitman gave to Edwin R. Stead (see footnote 3042), was
published by Whitman in Camden in 1876; it is surprising that he still had any copies left.

22   sent H. Buxton Forman, London, a package by

rec'd   for

express – books & pictures — paid ∧ by him[3060]

---

26   recd letter f'm Edw'd Carpenter $203 $\frac{65}{100}$ f'm

him, Misses Ford, Wm Thompson & Mr & Mrs: Roberts[3061]

letter f'm J Johnston & J W Wallace, Anderton, near

£

Chorley, Lancashire, Eng: 12 [3062]

---

31   Saturday Evn'g – Complimentary Birthday Supper

in Phila: 5thSt: Reisser's resterant – 7 to 10

p m – 30 to 35 at table – Ingersoll's grand

speech, never to be forgotten by me – [3063]   [last two words in pencil]

[2:30]

[City of Camden, Water Rent for the year 1890, 328 Mickle St., $8.00: paid 18
June 1890; Camden Gas Light Company, 1 April to 1 July 1890, $4.10: paid;

3060. H. Buxton Forman's letters to Whitman of 4 and 16 June 1890 are in the Feinberg
Collection; see also footnote 248. Whitman's letter to him is missing.

3061. For Whitman's reply to this letter, see *The Correspondence of Walt Whitman*, V,
50.

3062. Dr John Johnston and J. W. Wallace formed "Bolton College" in Bolton, England,
of Whitman admirers; Wallace wrote Whitman on 27 June 1890 that Johnston was coming to
Camden and to Long Island to see places mentioned in *Specimen Days* (letter in the Feinberg
Collection) and to bring back a report to England. On 15 July 1890 Whitman wrote Wallace
briefly about Dr Johnston's visit — see *The Correspondence of Walt Whitman*, V, 62–63 —
to which Wallace replied on 1 August that "the main privilege" of his life was to be able to
communicate with the poet and "to personally tender you my deep reverence and love." Dr
Johnston also went to Brooklyn, where he talked to a ferry pilot who knew Whitman, visited
the poet's birthplace and saw older residents in West Hills and Huntington, Long Island, wind-
ing up his tour by seeing John Burroughs. Then Wallace came over to America in 1891, talked
with the poet, collected more information, and reported as Dr Johnston had done to "Bolton
College" members. What the men learned and said of Whitman was published as *Visits to
Walt Whitman in 1890–1891* (London, 1917), which Gay Wilson Allen, in *The Solitary Singer*
(p. 537), calls "one of the most interesting of the early books on Whitman's life." The correspondence actually began in May 1887 (see *The Correspondence of Walt Whitman*, IV, 95,
96, 345; and in 1890–1892 Whitman wrote 72 letters to Dr Johnston and 28 to Wallace. See
footnote 2344, above.

3063. Whitman's health seems to have improved enough for him to go to Philadelphia.
After Robert Ingersoll's speech, which lasted 45 minutes, Whitman — who admired Ingersoll's
eloquence but not his agnostic views of immortality — asked him: "Unless there is as definite
object for it all, what in God's name is it all for?" (Henry Bryan Binns, *Walt Whitman*, London, 1905, p. 332). "Ingersoll's Speech," from the *Camden Post*, 2 June 1890, was included in
Good-bye My Fancy (1891) and in *Prose Works 1892*, II, 686–687, which quotes Whitman,
"What is this world without a further Divine purpose in it all?" The Philadelphia *Inquirer*
of 1 June 1890 had a piece about the birthday party on p. 1, and Traubel wrote "Walt Whitman's Birthday," *Unity*, XXV (28 August 1890), 215. Whitman's clippings from the *Camden
Post* and other papers were attached to the next page of the *Daybook*.

Statement of the Amount, Valuation and Description of Property at 328 Mickle, 1 H. 20 x 100, value of real estate 850, tax for 1890; various clippings (one with WW's notation, "Camden Post / June 2 1890"), "Ingersoll's Speech. / He Attends the Celebration of Walt / Whitman's Seventy-second Birthday."; another from The Philadelphia Inquirer, 1 June 1890, headed "Honors to the Poet / Walt Whitman's Friends Help/Him Celebrate His Birthday. / Colonel Robert G. Ingersoll / Makes an Eloquent Address. / A Pleasant Discussion of the Peculiar / Religious Tenets Held by the / Great Orator — The Author of / 'Leaves of Grass' States His / Views on Immortality."][3064]

3064. The full texts of the clippings follow.

HONORS TO THE POET

**Walt Whitman's Friends Help
Him Celebrate His Birthday.**

**COLONEL ROBERT G. INGERSOLL
MAKES AN ELOQUENT ADDRESS.**

**A Pleasant Discussion of the Peculiar
Religious Tenets Held by the
Great Orator — The Author of
"Leaves of Grass" States His
Views on Immortality.**

Walt Whitman, the author of "Leaves of Grass," "Drum Taps" and other volumes of poems, entered yesterday upon his 72d year. His Philadelphia admirers thought the occasion a most favorable one to testify their respect for the venerable poet, and followed up the recent demonstration in his honor in the city of his residence with a birthday banquet, to grace which they secured the presence of Colonel Robert G. Ingersoll, who divided with the band the honors of the evening.

The entertainment took place at Reisser's Restaurant, Fifth street, above Chestnut. Dr. Daniel G. Brinton presided, and the company congratulated themselves on having with them, as some of them said, the "greatest poet and the greatest orator in America."

Colonel Ingersoll made the first speech, congratulating Walt Whitman — nobody called the poet by any other name — on being the first true poet of democracy and showing to the American people the poetry that is in common things, in every-day employments, in the common people. He was the modern American Homer, inasmuch as his poems were a perfect mirror of the times in which he lived. "If," said the colonel, "an antiquarian a thousand years hence should desire to know what America was between 1860 and the centennial days, and should by chance come upon 'Leaves of Grass,' he would find there every interest and every occupation of the period fully depicted, from the forests of Maine to the turpentine woods of North Carolina.

THE ORATOR'S WORD PICTURES.

"Whitman had taught the American people the dignity of manhood and womanhood. He had written years beyond his time. We wanted somebody to talk about the things of every day and to make them poetic. There is not a man in the world who ever painted a beautiful picture of a palace. It can't be done; there are too many straight lines. When we want the picturesque we paint a cottage, and as you look at that cottage you don't think there's a mortgage on it, but you admire its vine-clad beauty and think of the happy fireside within. No man ever painted a beautiful picture of a queen in her robes; the woman is lost in drapery. Let me give you a picture: An old blacksmith and his wife have gone to see their white-robed, flower-crowned daughter made Queen of May, and as they look at her with wonder in her fresh young loveliness, they ask themselves how ever did it come to pass that we are the parents of such a beautiful child? And so may you take the children of the average man's brain and dress them in words — not beyond recognition, but so that what you write will look beautiful to him. That is what the great poet does, that is what the great orator does. Nothing more, nothing less.

"In every country somebody, from the earliest times to these, has been cringing before somebody else. Even here in America there is a tendency to bow down before the President, the servant of the people; hired at so much a day — and the people, by the way, are usually very glad to pay him off and discharge him when his time is out. But there is that tendency to cringe, and it needed somebody to teach the nation that man and woman are the highest titles — plain man and plain woman, and that you, Walt Whitman, have done and I thank you for it."

He congratulated the poet on having outlived detraction, and on having lived long enough to prove the intellectual inferiority of his detractors, and to find himself cordially appreciated.

THE COLONEL'S RELIGION.

Colonel Ingersoll took occasion to ventilate his peculiar theological views, but with gentleness and courtesy, avoiding any offensive slurs upon that faith in immortality which Whitman is known to cherish. He hoped, he said, that everybody would find his wishes realized, provided those wishes were good; and those who hoped for immortality might attain it. He did not deny the possibility of a future life; indeed, for aught he knew, there might be one.

"I believe," said he, "as firmly as I believe that I am, that all men do as they must, and that that is the only possible justification for the human race. There may come a time — there may be another world, when we shall be great enough to look back upon this and see why all things, vices and virtues, could not have been otherwise than as they were."

These remarks were chiefly interesting because after the other speeches they led to a discussion, Walt Whitman having evidently been turning the subject over in his mind.

Colonel Ingersoll was followed by Dr. Buck[e], of Canada, and he by Dr. S. Weir Mitchell, who said that the first he knew of "Leaves of Grass" was receiving the book as a present from a friend. While he was looking over it his little son, then aged 6, sat on his knee, and he read to the child the poem, describing the battle between the Serapis and the Bonhomme Richard, upon which the little fellow delivered this criticism:

"Papa, the man who wrote that must be a buster."

Speeches were also made by Frank Williams, Hon. H. C. Harned, Harrison Morris, Horace Traubel and Dr. Brinton.

THE POET'S FEELING WORDS.

After the speaking Mr. Whitman reverted to Colonel Ingersoll's tribute to his poems, pronouncing it the culmination of all commendation that he had ever received. Then, his mind still dwelling upon the colonel's doubts, he went on to say that what he had in his mind when he wrote "Leaves of Grass" was not only to depict American life, as it existed, and to show the triumphs of science and the poetry in common things, but also to show that there was behind it all something which rounded and completed it. "For "what," he asked, "would this life be without immortality and the infinite? It would be but as a locomotive, the greatest triumph of modern science, with no train to draw. If the spiritual is not behind the material, to what purpose is the material? What is this world without a Divine purpose in it all?"

Colonel Ingersoll repeated his former argument in reply, taking the opportunity to pitch into orthodoxy.

Among those present were: Cornelius Stevenson, Mrs. Baldwin, Professor Felix E. Shelling, Mr. and Mrs. Talcott Williams, John J. Boyle, the sculptor; Wm. Henry Walsh, Carl Edelheim, Wilson Eyre, Lewis C. Smith, Mrs. Balch, Judge Boyle and others.

— *Philadelphia Inquirer,* 1 June 1890, p. 1

INGERSOLL'S SPEECH.
He Attends the Celebration of Walt
Whitman's Seventy-second Birthday.

Walt Whitman is now in his seventy-second year. His younger friends, literary and personal, men and women, gave him a complimentary supper last Saturday night, to note the close of his seventy-first year, and the late curious and unquestionable "boom" of the old man's

[2:31]

June   Camden   June   1890   &   July
1   Sunday – To-day I commence my 72^d year.
      Dr Bucke left here for Danbury Conn: He is due
      in home London on Wednesday next June 3^d
      I am feeling stupid and very sluggish, but no particu-
      lar pain or physical bother – eat my meals heartily

---

3   sent books by Express to Mrs: J M Sears, Southborough
              paid rec'd   paid   [last word in pencil]   Mass:[3065]

---

      by Express   also letter
4   sent $\wedge$ books to David L Lezinsky $\wedge$ care O K
                                              rec'd
      Lerris Hotel, Butte City Montana – paid [3066]

wide-spreading popularity and that of his "Leaves of Grass." There were fifty or sixty in the room, mostly young, but some old or beginning to be. The great feature was Ingersoll's utterance. It was probably, in its way, the most admirable specimen of modern oratory hitherto delivered in the English language, immense as such praise may sound. It was 40 minutes long, in a good voice, low enough and not too low, style easy, altogether without mannerism, rather colloquial (over and over again saying "you" to Whitman who sat opposite,) sometimes impassioned, once or twice humerous, amid his whole speech, from interior fires and volition, pulsating and swaying like a first-class Andalusian dancer.

And such a critical dissection, and flattering summary! The Whitmanites for the first time in their lives were fully satisfied; and that is saying a good deal, for they have not put their claims low, by a long shot. Indeed it was a tremendous talk. Physically and mentally Ingersoll (he had been working all day in New York, talking in court and in his office,) is now at his best like mellowed wine or a just ripe apple; to the artist-sense, too looks at his best, not merely like a bequeathed Roman bust or fine smooth marble Cicero-head, or even Greek Plato; for he is modern and vital and veined and American, and (for more than the age knows,) justifies us all.

We cannot give a full report of this most remarkable supper (which was curiously conversational and Greek-like) but must add the following significant bit of it.

After the speaking and just before the close, Mr. Whitman reverted to Colonel Ingersoll's tribute to his poems, pronouncing it the culmination of all commendation that he had ever received. Then, his mind still dwelling upon the colonel's religious doubts, he went on to say that what he himself had in his mind when he wrote "Leaves of Grass" was not only to depict American life, as it existed, and to show the triumphs of science and the poetry in common things, and the full of an individual humanity, for the aggregate, but also to show that there was behind all something which rounded and completed it. "For "what" he asked, "would this life be without immortality? It would be as a locomotive the greatest triumph of modern science, with no train to draw. If the spiritual is not behind the material, to what purpose is the material? What is this world without a further Divine purpose in it all?"

Colonel Ingersoll repeated his former argument in reply.

— *Camden Post,* 2 June 1890, p. 1

At the top of the clipping, Whitman has written: "Camden Post / June 2 1890." This news account has, in part — certainly the next-to-last paragraph — been taken from the *Philadelphia Inquirer,* even the typographical error of an extra quotation mark in "what" being repeated. The author of this was actually Whitman himself, for it is reprinted in *Prose Works 1892,* II, 686–689.

3065. Mrs Sears's acknowledgment is in the Feinberg Collection.

3066. For David L. Lezinsky, see footnote 3041; Whitman's letter to him is missing.

great heat to-day –   three hot days 4th 5th & 6th & 7th
Dr B arrived safe home in Canada[3067]

8th Sunday – pleasantly cool – out in wheel chair two hours

11 sent letter to "City Surveyor" ab't wrong number next door[3068]
hot day – thunder shower at night

12 sent MS "O Captain" and portraits to Chs Aldrich
[One word in purple pencil:]
Des Moines Iowa   rec'd   paid me $5 [3069]

13 sent pocket book ed'n to Col: Ingersoll N Y.
R G I sent me the beautiful "prose poems" book[3070]

18 paid water bill for 1890 – $8 [3071]
18, 19, & 20th fine days, sunny, cool enough

21 sent morocco L of G. to E S Marsh, Brandon Vt.   paid [3072]
Some hot weather – go out at sunset in
wheel chair

30 sent pocket b'k ed'n L of G to Peter Eckler 35 Fulton
st
N Y City[3073]

July 1 sent the big book & morocco b'd pocket bk form
L of G. to Miss Drewry 143 King Henry's Road
rec'd
South Hampstead, London, Eng.   paid – £ 2–8[s] [3074]

3067. Dr R. M. Bucke's letter of 5 June 1890 is in the Feinberg Collection; Whitman wrote to him on the same day, a rather long letter: *The Correspondence of Walt Whitman,* V, 52.
3068. This letter is now missing.
3069. Whitman's acknowledgment of $5 from L. A. McMurray for Charles Aldrich is in *The Correspondence of Walt Whitman,* V, 57.
3070. Colonel Robert G. Ingersoll had spoken at Whitman's birthday celebration, 31 May 1890 (see footnote 3063). Ingersoll's letters of 5 and 16 June 1890 are in the Feinberg Collection. The book Ingersoll sent was *Prose-Poems and Selections from the Writings and Sayings of Robert G. Ingersoll,* either the edition published by C. P. Farrell in Washington in 1884 or in New York in 1888.
3071. This bill is attached to the previous page of the *Daybook* and its payment is also noted at the end of the *Daybook.*
3072. Edward Sprague Marsh's letter, 14 June 1890, ordering the book, is in the Feinberg Collection.

3   paid gas bill $4.10 for April, May & June 1890 [3075]
        hot hot weather (good rain yesterday & last night)
        – lots of blackberries

---

                                                     rec'd [3076]
8   hot – hot – hot, – send 5 to H and 5 to Mrs: M
        rec'd honey f'm Lüttgens, Hammonton [3077]
        go out sunset time wheel chair

---

10   Wyoming admitted to-day – with Idaho now
        there are 44 States in the U S [3078]

---

                                                       rec'd
11   sent Dr Bucke's W W to O'Dowd, Melbourne ⋀ Vict: [3079]
     Visit f'm J E Reinhalter & Ralph Moore ab't
        vault for cemetery — design of J E R [3080]
        — sent letter to B O'D July 12 [3081]
     "W W's Quaker traits" by K in "Conservator" [3082]

                                                    [2:32]

[On a calling card of P. Reinhalter & Co., Monumental Manufacturers, Philadelphia:]

call'd early in July '90 & left the plan
            of vault

3073. Peter Eckler: unidentified, no known letters to or from Whitman.
3074. Louisa Drewry's letter, 20 June 1890, ordering *Complete Poems & Prose* and the pocket-book *Leaves,* is in the Feinberg Collection; a transcript of Whitman's letter to her, 1 July, is in *The Correspondence of Walt Whitman,* V, 58. She is mentioned in H. Buxton Forman's letters (see footnote 3060).
3075. These are attached to the previous pages of the *Daybook* and payment is also noted at the end of the *Daybook.*
3076. These payments went to Whitman's sister Hannah Heyde and Mrs Mary E. Mapes, both also recorded in the back of the *Daybook.*
3077. For C. H. Lüttgens, see footnote 3043.
3078. This is one of the very few historical notes in the *Daybook*; no comment on the two new states here, in *The Correspondence,* or elsewhere.
3079. For Bernard O'Dowd, see footnote 2986; for a transcript of Whitman's letter to O'Dowd, [12] July 1890, see *The Correspondence of Walt Whitman,* V, 62.
3080. For Harleigh Cemetery, see footnotes 2987 and 3034; for J. E. Reinhalter & Co., see *The Correspondence of Walt Whitman,* V, 95, 105, 203n, 225, 264n. Mr Reinhalter was the cemetery superintendent, and Moore was the monument architect who (Whitman told Dr R. M. Bucke) was "to have control & charge under my name & be my representative." See entry below for 11 July 1890.
3081. See footnote 3079.
3082. This was William Sloane Kennedy, "Quaker Traits of Walt Whitman," *The Conservator,* I (July 1890), 36, reprinted in *In Re Walt Whitman* (Philadelphia, 1893), pp. 213–214.

[Also in WW's hand, not on the card:]

$$\left(\begin{array}{c} \text{Immanuel} \\ \text{God – with – us} \end{array} \right)^{3083}$$

[On a slip, not in WW's hand: J. Johnston and J. W. Wallace, with addresses; printed on a small piece of paper: Rome Brothers, Printers, 76 Myrtle Avenue, Brooklyn, N. Y. Between them, in WW's hand:]

Dr J here July 15 '90

return'd

safely to Eng: [3084]

[Printed on a small slip: David McKay, Publisher and Bookseller, No. 23 S. Ninth St., Philadelphia. – Old Books Bought and Sold. Clipping from a news-paper:]

— It may be just as well to mention that Uncle Sam's dominion extends a little more than half way around the globe. Therefore, when any of Her Majesty's subjects get off that chestnut about the sun never setting on the British dominions, we can brag of the same thing too. The distance from the easternmost point in Maine to the westernmost island in Behring Sea, is a little more than 196 degrees of longitude, so that it is full sun up in Maine before it is sundown in Behring Sea. [Spring-field Republican.

[In WW's hand:]

Mrs: Margaretta L Avery[3085]

185 Sterling Place Brooklyn New York

[Long clipping on Julius Chambers, editor of the Sunday edition of the New York *World,* and other newspaper people.[3086] Clipped from the envelope of

3083. See footnotes 2987, 3034, and 3080; also entry below for 11 July 1890.

3084. For Dr John Johnston and J. W. Wallace, see footnotes 2344 and 3062, and entries below for 15 and 17 July 1890. The Rome Brothers were the printers of the first (1855) *Leaves of Grass.* Andrew Rome's wife was the cousin of Dr Johnston's wife. Rome wrote Whitman 12 July 1890 (letter in the Feinberg Collection).

3085. For Margaretta L. Avery (see footnote 115); she was a distant cousin of Whit-man's. She visited Whitman on 13 October 1890; letters from her and William A. Avery, 16 September 1891, and 1 March 1892, are in the Library of Congress and the Feinberg Col-lection.

3086. Julius Chambers (see footnote 2808) was the representative of the New York *World* who sent C. H. Browning to Camden to ask Whitman for the poem on the Johnstown

J. H. Johnston & Co., Diamond Merchant and Jewelers, 17 Union Square, New York[3087]; Charles L. Webster & Co., Publishers, 3 East 14th Street, New York.]

[In WW's hand in blue pencil:]	[Address not in WW's hand:]
Harrison	227 So. 4" Street
S Morris[3088]	Philada. Aug. 11/90.
Erastus Brainerd [3089]	
Press newspaper. Seattle Wash'n	

[2:33]

Camden   July & August   1890

July 11 pleasant – not hot – J E Reinhalter & Ralph
            Moore call – the cemetery mauseloum design[3090]
        feeling pretty well these days

_____

15   Dr Johnston here – hot, hot day

_____

17   still hot – Dr Johnston left this afternoon[3091]
            return'd to Eng: safely
        for Brooklyn (Andrew   Rome's) not at Dr B's[3092]

_____

                                    rec'd [3093]   fine
20 sent $5 to H Burlington   Vt   19th, 20th two cool days
        20th, 1st, 2d, 3d 4th   very pleasant, cool enough

_____

flood on 5 June 1889.

3087.   There are four letters from J. H. Johnston in September 1890 in the Feinberg Collection; Bertha Johnston, his daughter, saw Whitman on 4 June 1890; and on 17 September 1890 Bucke wrote to Whitman about Johnston's getting up a benefit lecture for the poet — see *The Correspondence of Walt Whitman*, V, 86n.

3088.   For Harrison S. Morris, see footnote 2836.

3089.   Erastus Brainerd was on the staff of the Philadelphia *Daily News* in August 1887 when Whitman wrote two brief letters to him: see *The Correspondence of Walt Whitman*, IV, 113, 115. There is evidence (see *ibid.*, III, 170n) that he was on the Philadelphia *Press* in December 1879; and here — from the address below his name — he may have gone to the Seattle *Press*.

3090.   See footnote 3080.

3091.   For Dr John Johnston, see footnote 3084.

3092.   Dr John Johnston did visit Andrew Rome, one of the Brooklyn printers of the 1855 *Leaves of Grass*, but did not go to London, Ontario, to see Dr R. M. Bucke, as he had intended (see *The Correspondence of Walt Whitman*, V, 63, 71); he was back in Bolton, Lancashire, England by 19 August 1890.

3093.   Another $5 for Whitman's sister Hannah Heyde, 20 Pearl Street, Burlington, Vermont, also recorded in the back of this *Daybook*. He sent $2 on 30 July 1890, not recorded but mentioned in his letter — *The Correspondence of Walt Whitman*, V, 67.

25   the Dr Bucke W W book came back f'm P O & I
     put 9^{ct} more postage (21 ^{cts} altogether) – to go to
          Bernard O'Dowd, Melbourne – (went thro' safe rec'd at last)[3094]

---

28   sent big book to Wm Payne Woodleigh, the Thicket,

$\pounds$ s

     Southsea, Portsmouth, Eng: Paid   1 •11 [3095]
     Diet – bread & honey, (good); potatoes, onions & green beans,
          stew'd mutton & rice, moderate supply of meat, pie, &c.

Aug: 1   Paid Ed's board at Blackwood $45.50 to Mr Currie[3096]
          two fearfully hot days

---

4   sent "an old man's rejoinder" to Critic ($10 & 20 slips)[3097]
                                            ($10 rec'd)
          letter to W S K   proof rec'd Aug.12   all paid [3098]

     due me $20 f'm Munyon's Weekly   Phil
     for "the unexpress'd" & "the voice" [3099]
                     paid
     & $6 for Morning Journal   N Y., 162 Nassau St N Y [3100]

---

5   the baby   Ethel   Col kitt call'd

---

8   drew p o money orders $24.24

---

12   rec'd $58.80 f'm R Pearsall Smith (thro A L

3094. For Bernard O'Dowd, see footnote 2986.
3095. William Payne's letter of 16 July 1890 is in the Feinberg Collection.
3096. This payment for Edward Whitman's keep for August, September and October 1890 is recorded in the back of the *Daybook*, and Whitman's letter to C. F. Currie is in *The Correspondence of Walt Whitman*, V, 67.
3097. For "An Old Man's Rejoinder," see footnote 3024; the letter to *The Critic* is in *The Correspondence of Walt Whitman*, V, 67 (see also V, 63–64). This essay had to do with John Addington Symonds's "Democratic Art, With Special Reference to Walt Whitman," in his *Essays Speculative & Suggestive* (London, 1890), II, 30–77.
3098. Letter to William Sloane Kennedy: *The Correspondence of Walt Whitman*, V, 68. The "proof" must refer to the piece in *The Critic* (see footnote 3097).
3099. For "The Human Voice," see footnote 3002; it is a prose piece in *Munyon's Illustrated World*, VI (October 1890), 2. For "The Unexpress'd," see footnote 3023; it is a poem published, with others, under "Old-Age Echoes," in *Lippincott's Magazine*, XLVII (March 1891), 504, although, as indicated here, it may have first appeared by itself in *Munyon's*, a file of which has not been located.
3100. The New York *Morning Herald* published Whitman's "Old Brooklyn Days," a short essay, on 3 August 1890; reprinted in *Good-bye My Fancy* (1891) and *Prose Works 1892*, II, 687–688, 773–774.

Smith 3045 Chestnut st. 1305   Arch st
Phila) for twelve copies pocket b'k   bd
                              13th 14th   delightful
L of G.[3101]   11th, 12th   pleasantly cool   change   [in pencil]

---

13   sent big book to D McKay, (he has now – two)[3102]

---

17   (Sunday) – "An Old Man's Rejoinder" in yesterday's
     Critic – instigated by the essay "Democratic Art"
     in J A Symonds's new vol – nothing very new –
     my old points reiterated[3103]   (hot day)

[2:34]

James   J. M. K.   Cattell   [2 lines not in WW's hand,
          Morton, Del Co. Pa.[3104]   on a small slip]

[Printed address, clipped, of David McKay, Publisher and Bookseller, No. 23
S. Ninth St., Philadelphia.][3105]

[In WW's hand:]   David L Lezinsky   box 62 211
                        Berkeley, Cal.[3106]

[Receipt from Adams Express Company, Camden, N. J., for one bdl from
W Whitman to R P Smith, London, Eng, 19 August 1890.][3107]

[2:35]

     Camden   August   Sept: 1890
Aug 19 McKay sends over to know the price of fifty
     copies in sheets complete Works, plates, &c
     I send word $3 each ($150 the lot 50)   27th order[3108]
                              paid   the 50

3101. For Whitman's letter about these books, see *The Correspondence of Walt Whitman*, V, 69–70; it was Logan Pearsall Smith who bought the copies of *Leaves of Grass*.
3102. Whitman told Dr R. M. Bucke that he occasionally sells copies of the *Complete Poems & Prose* — "likely they have nearly repaid the expense of their printing & binding, & I have ⅜ths left" (*The Correspondence of Walt Whitman*, V, 70).
3103. For "An Old man's Rejoinder," see footnotes 3024 and 3097.
3104. Professor (of psychology) James McKeen Cattell, University of Pennsylvania, 1888–1891, sent Whitman a basket of seckel pears about 19 September 1890, some of which the poet sent to old and sick neighbors ("best tasting pears ever was" — *The Correspondence of Walt Whitman*, V, 87–88). Cattell later became editor of *The Psychological Review*, *Scientific Monthly*, and *School and Science*.
3105. Whitman's publisher had recently bought copies of *Complete Poems & Prose* (the "big book").
3106. For David L. Lezinsky, see footnote 3041.
3107. This is for the 12 copies of *Leaves of Grass* mentioned above in the entry for 12 August 1890 (see footnote 3101).
3108. This exchange of information must have been through Horace Traubel or

sent off by Express the parcel directed to
    R P Smith, 44 Grosvenor Road, the Embankment
    London Eng – 14 pkt bk bd L of G   (all rec'd
[In purple pencil:]
(books paid)   2 complete wks for Edw'd Carpenter
         1   "   "   "   R P S 2^{d} one for
                                    Symonds[3109]
[Two lines in blue pencil:]   recd
sent letter (answer) to Symonds (see envelope)[3110]
busy at 2^{d} annex[3111]

20   sent $5 to H[3112]   (rainy yesterday last night & to-day)
[Line in pencil:]
    Ed Stead here – young lady – good impression – widow[3113]

27   rec'd order f'm D McKay for 50 copies in sheets
    Complete Works ($150) – wh' I sent to Oldach
                                          packages
    binder 1215 Filbert st: to make up   mad up &
                                          sent away[3114]

                                      paid[3115]
28   sent pocket-b'k L of G. to J W Wallace Eng:

someone else, as no letters — if there were any — are known. See entry below for 27 October 1890.
    3109. This shipment is referred to twice above, in the entry for 12 August 1890, and in the receipt for 19 August (see also footnotes 3101 and 3107). The exact number of books sent is not clear; in the former entry 12 is the figure given, here 14 copies of the pocket-book (1889) *Leaves of Grass,* plus two *Complete Poems & Prose* for Edward Carpenter, one more for Robert Pearsall Smith, and another for John Addington Symonds — 18 in all.
    3110. This letter to John Addington Symonds — with R. W. Emerson's 1855 letter the most famous one to or from Whitman — is (in draft form) in *The Correspondence of Walt Whitman,* V, 72–73, with a fairly full discussion by Edwin Haviland Miller. It deals with Whitman's attitude toward Symonds's interpretation of the "Calamus" poems and homosexuality; and it has the often-quoted comment by the poet, "Tho' always unmarried I have had six children . . ." For more information, largely bibliographical, and a facsimile, see "My 'Six Children': Whitman to Symonds," *Walt Whitman Review,* XVI (March 1970), 31, and *ibid.,* XV (June 1969), 125–126.
    3111. By "2^{d} annex," Whitman meant *Good-bye My Fancy,* first published separately in 1891, and then published from the plates as a Second Annex to the 1891–1892 *Leaves of Grass*; it contained a "Preface Note to 2d Annex: Concluding L. of G. — 1891," and 31 poems, most of them first published in periodicals.
    3112. This money for Hannah Heyde, Whitman's sister, is also recorded at the end of the *Daybook.*
    3113. For Edwin R. Stead, see footnote 3042; the young widow, obviously a friend of Stead's, is not otherwise identified.
    3114. This matter was previously discussed on 19 August (see entry above).
    3115. For J. W. Wallace, see footnotes 2344 and 3062; Whitman's letter to Wallace, 30 August 1890, is in *The Correspondence of Walt Whitman,* V, 79.

29   sent the Hollandisk mems to W S K [3116]

Sept: 1 – paid the City Taxes, $24.92 [3117] ("labor day"
                                                 fine day – sunny
                                                          cool

---

8   sent pk't-b'k L of G. to Geo: Horton, Chicago   rec'd
     care Herald newspaper[3118]

---

9   sent Horton's little poem in Press to various addresses[3119]

---

11   sent p't-b'k ed'n L of G. to J W Wallace   paid
            also p c[3120]   cooler – wet & cloudy
     Mrs: D started for Downs, Kansas[3121]

---

13   wrote to Dr Bucke, Dr Johnston & J A Symonds[3122]
      14th (Sunday) champagne & oyster dinner at Harned's[3123]

            Sent $5 [3124] 16th
14   – Mary in Kansas – Harry and Becky married (15th   [3124a]

3116. By "Hollandisk mems," Whitman means William Sloane Kennedy's piece, "Dutch Traits of Walt Whitman," which appeared in *The Conservator*, I (February 1891), 90–91, and was reprinted in *In Re Walt Whitman* (Philadelphia, 1893), pp. 195–199. See Whitman's letter to Kennedy about the article, *The Correspondence of Walt Whitman*, V, 78.

3117. This city tax bill is also recorded at the end of the *Daybook*.

3118. George Horton's poem, "An Old Man Once I Saw," Chicago *Herald*, 18 September 1890, was reprinted in *In Re Walt Whitman* (Philadelphia, 1893). See *Daybook* entries below for 9 and 16 September 1890. On 5 August 1891, Horton asked Whitman for a poem about the forthcoming world's fair in Chicago (letter in the Feinberg Collection), which I doubt was ever written.

3119. This poem must have been reprinted from the Chicago *Herald* (see footnote 3118); it is not known just whom Whitman sent copies to, for there are no letters extant for this date, and Whitman does not comment of the poem in later letters.

3120. This is a second copy of the pocket-book (1889) edition of *Leaves of Grass* he sent to J. W. Wallace, who telegraphed Whitman for it, as it was to be a birthday present for a member of the Bolton College (see the letter of this date in *The Correspondence of Walt Whitman*, V, 83).

3121. Mrs Mary O. Davis, Whitman's housekeeper, who planned to be gone for two weeks — see *The Correspondence of Walt Whitman*, V, 85–86, for his long letter to her, dated 15 September 1890.

3122. Letters to Dr R. M. Bucke and Dr John Johnston are in *The Correspondence of Walt Whitman*, V, 84–85; the letter to John Addington Symonds is missing.

3123. Whitman had not been to Thomas B. Harned's in Camden for some time; he mentioned the dinner in his letter to Mrs Davis (footnote 3121).

3124. This $5 was for Mrs Mary O. Davis (see footnote 3121), who left Camden on 11 September (see entry above).

3124a. Harry Fritzinger, who was getting married, was Mrs Mary Davis's adopted son, and one wonders why she was in Kansas at the time; Whitman wrote her about it: "Harry was up with me yesterday noon to talk ab't it — I felt quite solemn ab't it (I think more of the boy, & I believe he does of me, than you knew) — He kissed me & hung on to my

15   – 16th I sent "Poet-Lore" with the Shakspere bit to
                                                several
16   – Mrs: Doughty and Maggy here[3126] Symonds, Kennedy
         rainy spell – 4 days   & Bucke[3125]
                                                        Chicago
     little poemet "to Walt Whitman" Geo: Horton –
                                                        Herald [3127]

19   Lou & Jessie here   talk ab't Burlington visit[3128]
         letter f'm Mary Davis Kansas[3129]
     sent pk't-b'k L of G. to Dr Johnston Bolton   paid [3130]

21   composing (finishing) Preface to O'Connor's posthumous
                              book[3131]
         cool day   my letter with $5 to Kansas rec'd safely[3132]

                       in bank   it
23   deposited 63.80 ∧ (sent by Warry)[3133]   fine sunny day cool enough

[Inserted between this page and the previous one is a large bill, Office of the
Receiver of Taxes — City Hall, The City of Camden, Dr. 1890, to Walt Whitman for 328 Mickle, 26   20x100, $850 (Value of Real Estate), $100 (Value
of Personal Property), taxes $20.83 and $4.45 – $25.28 (minus 1.26), $24.02,
which Whitman paid and wrote on the sheet:]

                       Paid Sept 1 '90 [3134]

neck — O if he only gets a good wife & it all turns out lasting & good (Mary, I think more
of Harry than you suppose) — at any rate one first-rate point, it may anchor him in a way
that nothing else might, & give him a definite object & aim to work up to — (& perhaps
he needs that) — " (*The Correspondence of Walt Whitman,* V, 86).

3125. This was "Shakspere for America," *Poet-Lore,* II (September 1890), 492–493. (See
footnote 3024, above.) Kennedy's letter from Whitman is in *The Correspondence of Walt
Whitman,* V, 86–87.

3126. Mrs Doughty and Maggy (her daughter?) took Mrs Mary O. Davis's place in
fixing Whitman's meals and taking care of him while the latter was in Kansas.

3127. For George Horton and his poem to Whitman, see footnote 3118.

3128. Louisa Orr Whitman, the poet's sister-in-law, and their niece from St Louis,
Jessie Louisa Whitman, told Whitman about seeing Hananh Heyde, who was ill in Vermont.

3129. This letter from Whitman's housekeeper, away for two weeks, is missing.

3130. Dr John Johnston's report of his visit to Whitman had apparently stirred up
some sales in Bolton — this is the third copy of the pocket-book (1889) *Leaves of Grass*
Whitman had sent in the last few weeks.

3131. William Douglas O'Connor's book was *Three Tales,* and Whitman's piece,
"Preface to a Volume of Essays and Tales by Wm. D. O'Connor, Pub'd Posthumously in
1891," appeared also in *Good-bye My Fancy* (1891): see *Prose Works 1892,* II, 689–691.

3132. This went to Mrs Mary E. Mapes ($2) and Mrs Mary O. Davis, Whitman's house-
keeper: see his letter to her, *The Correspondence of Walt Whitman,* V, 85–86.

3133. Warren Fritzinger, who had become very helpful to Whitman at this time.

3134. This tax is also recorded as paid at the back of the *Daybook.*

[2:36]

10 Rue Troyon Paris France
M. Gabriel Sarrazin, magistrat.
[Two lines in red ink:]
Hotel Caramie
Noumea
153 Boulevard St Germain
Nouvelle   Caledonie
(Colonies Françaises)

letter f'm G S f'm Noumea
[Three lines in red ink:]
dated July 3 1890   M. Gabriel Sarrazin
care M Leon Sarrazin a Saint – Front – la – riviere
par Saint   Pardoux   (Dordogne)[3135]

[On a calling card of John Harrison, Manager, Wyckoff, Seamans & Benedict, 834 Chestnut Street, Philadelphia:]

call'd on me Sept: 9

[Address from envelope, printed: Oldach & Co., Bookbinders, 1215 Filbert Street, Philadelphia.]

[Written by WW on half a discarded postcard:]

L M
Dr ∧ Bingham
110 College street
Burlington
Vermont[3136]

Mrs: Church

[In WW's hand:]
visited Camden Sept: '91 – goes to
Providence R I[3137]

3135. This letter from Gabriel Sarrazin, 3 July 1890, is in the Feinberg Collection; for Sarrazin, see footnote 2661, above. Whitman sent Sarrazin's New Caledonia letter to Dr R. M. Bucke on 11 September 1890, as he had replied to Sarrazin on 5 September: see *The Correspondence of Walt Whitman*, V, 80.

3136. Dr L. M. Bingham, whose letters to Whitman of July, 6 August, and 16 November 1890 are in the Feinberg Collection, was Hannah Heyde's physician, and he is mentioned in several letters Whitman wrote to his sister.

3137. Mrs Church is unidentified: a Camden neighbor? She is not mentioned elsewhere in the *Daybook* or in Whitman's letters.

Mrs: E M O'Connor
112 M st N W
    Washington D C [3138]

Sept: '90   ———————

          Curtz 104 South 2ᵈ cor Bridge av
—————————————

      Poet-Lore 1602 Chestnut Phil:[3139]
          Charlotte Porter[3140]
          Helen A Clarke[3141]

[Printed slip: Catalogue of Mineral Curiosities . . . , J. G. Hiestand, Manitou, Colo.]

                                  [2:37]

    Camden   Sept: & Oct: 1890
Sept: 28 Supper at T B Harned's – John Burroughs[3142]
—————————————

  29 letter f'm Mrs: O Connor[3143]   cold spell
—————————————

  30 sent the p'k't – b'k of L of G. to Wallace, Eng: for the friend [3144]
                                    paid
        the talk of Ingersoll's address   Phila.[3145]
—————————————

3138. Whitman's letter to Ellen M. O'Connor, of 21 and 25 September 1890, are addressed to 1015 O Street N W, Washington; but on 29 September he told Dr R. M. Bucke that she had moved to 112 M Street N W, and had a two months' appointment in the Census Bureau.

3139. Curtz was a compositor at 104 South Second Street, Philadelphia, and apparently set type for the magazine *Poet-Lore,* which published Whitman's essay "Shakspere for America" in September 1890 (see footnote 3024).

3140. Charlotte Porter was to write, with Helen A. Clarke, "A Short Reading Course in Whitman," *Fellowship Paper,* No. 13 (1895); and "The American Idea in Whitman," *The Conservator,* VII (July 1896), 73–75.

3141. Helen A. Clarke, in addition to the piece with Charlotte Porter, wrote "Walt Whitman and Music," *The Conservator,* V (December 1894), 153–154; "Passage to India," *The Conservator,* VI (March 1895), 7–10; "Does Whitman Harmonize His Doctrine of Evil with the Pursuit of Ideals?" *The Conservator,* VI (May 1895), 39–43; "An Ideal of Character Drawn from Whitman's Poetry," *The Conservator,* X (June 1899), 56–58; and "The Awakening of the Soul: Whitman and Maeterlinck," *The Conservator,* XI (June 1900), 58–60.

3412. Whitman added a few details in a letter to Dr R. M. Bucke: "I was out to Harned's to supper ½ past 5 yesterday — John Burroughs is here to see me — was at the Supper — is well & in good spirits — has grown quite gray — left here to-day — was down some days at R U Johnsons at Babylon L I, & thinks of going on to see Herbert Gilchrist at Centreport — " (*The Correspondence of Walt Whitman,* V, 95).

3143. Mrs Ellen M. O'Connor actually wrote two letters, both now missing; but Whitman's reply is in *The Correspondence of Walt Whitman,* V, 96, dealing in part with his preface to W. D. O'Connor's *Three Tales* (see footnote 3131).

3144. This is the fourth copy this month to be sent to J. W. Wallace in Bolton (see entries in *Daybook,* above, and footnotes 3120 and 3130).

3145. Robert Ingersoll's address, which his bibliographer — Gordon Stein, *Robert G. Ingersoll: A Checklist* (Kent, Ohio, 1969), pp. 18, 53, 54 — says was first called "Testimonial

Oct: 1   rode   out to Harleigh Cemetery (Ralph Moore's rig)
           to see the beginning of the burial tomb building
           – two men were at it digging – it is to be set back
           15 or 20 feet from the lane – saw the architects there –
           – told them to have nothing artificial or ornamental
      must be
           ʌ consistent with the plain natural place, the turf
           the simple trees & rock, fallen leaves, (death & burial) &c:
           – perfect sunny day – rode on some two miles –
           – enjoy'd all – R M very kind – good company –³¹⁴⁶

3   Sent copies of the big book, Dr B's W W. & J B's Notes
           (with portraits W W in envelope] to Col: Ingersoll N Y.³¹⁴⁷
           rec'd good letter f'm B O'D   Melbourne (sent letter to him)³¹⁴⁸

6   sent the big book to Edw'd Browne, 7 Norland Place
           Holland Park   London, W. Eng – paid³¹⁴⁹
           p'k't – b'k L of G. to R K Greenhalgh, Bank of Bolton,
           Bolton, Lancashire, Eng: paid³¹⁵⁰

9   rec'd $44.80 for royalty, f'm D McKay³¹⁵¹
           cooler   sunny
                          "Liberty in
           the Ingersoll lecture, ~~Literature and~~ Literature"
           preparing to be given Evn'g Oct: 21, Horticultural
           Hall, Phila: (R G I & all behave splendidly)
                          I send I: letter & suggestion³¹⁵²

to Walt Whitman," and given to Camden on 31 May 1890, was expanded and published in *Truth Seeker*, XVII (1 November 1890), 690–693, 700; Whitman, here in the *Daybook*, only gives its later title, "Liberty in Literature" (for "Liberty and Literature") — see entries below for 9 September, 22 and 28 October 1890, where Whitman gives, for him, considerable detail and opinion.

3146. Whitman on his own burial vault and the cemetery — see also footnotes 2987, 3034, 3055, and 3080 — is unexpectedly candid; "R M" refers to Ralph Moore, the monument architect at the cemetery. See also *The Correspondence of Walt Whitman*, V, 98.

3147. Whitman sent to Robert G. Ingersoll his *Complete Poems & Prose* (1888), Dr R. M. Bucke's *Walt Whitman* (Philadelphia, 1883), and John Burroughs's *Notes on Walt Whitman as Poet and Person* (New York, 1867, more likely the second edition, 1871).

3148. This letter from Bernard O'Dowd (see footnote 2986), dated 1 September 1890, is in the Feinberg Collection and published in *Overland*, No. 23 (April 1962), 12, and A. L. McLeod, *Walt Whitman in Australia and New Zealand* (Sydney, 1964), pp. 24–26; Whitman's reply is in *The Correspondence of Walt Whitman*, V, 98–99.

3149. Edward Browne: unidentified.

3150. R. K. Greenhalgh, another member of Dr John Johnston and J. W. Wallace's "Bolton College": see footnotes 3120, 3130, and 3144.

3151. The last royalty payment David McKay made was on 14 April 1890 for $58.15.

3152. For more on Robert G. Ingersoll's earlier lecture on Whitman, see footnote 3145;

sent off "Old Poets" to N A Review – N Y.   W H Rideing
paid $75 & 25
slips[3153]

13   sent pk't – b'k L of G to J. W. Smith care W H
Crossman 77 Broad st N Y. $5 due paid   rec'd [3154]
visit f'm Margaretta Avery[3155] – also Capt: Nowell [3156]

17   bo't & got in a cord of saw'd wood $8
fine sunny day   cool enough

18   rec'd, read, & sent back proof of "Old Poets" to N A
Rev:[3157]

20   last night somehow a very bad night with
me – no sleep – dull & poorly to-day —
– the prospect, for the Ingersoll meeting
to-morrow night looks well – Horace has
work'd like a beaver – Dr B is here – I feel
in the midst of my best staunchest friends[3158]

[2:38]

[Blank]

[2:39]

Camden   October   1890
Oct: 20 sent pk't-b'k L of G. to Edward J Baillie, Woodbine,
Upton Park, Chester, Eng: paid [3159]

Whitman's letter to Ingersoll is missing.
3153. A transcript of this letter to the Editor, *The North American Review,* is in *The Correspondence of Walt Whitman,* V, 100; William H. Rideing, who was the assistant editor, had asked for a 4000-word article on American literature (letter in the Feinberg Collection) — see *ibid.,* V, 99. Whitman received proofs of the article "Old Poets" on 18 October (see *Daybook* of that date, below), and it was published in *The North American Review,* CLI (November 1890), 610–614; in *Good-bye My Fancy* (1891), and *Prose Works 1892,* II, 658–662.
3154. Neither J. W. Smith nor W. H. Crossman identifiable.
3155. For Margaretta Avery, a cousin, see footnotes 115 and 3085.
3156. If and when later volumes of Horace Traubel's *With Walt Whitman in Camden* are published, we may learn more about Capt. Nowell and others mentioned in the *Daybook.*
3157. See footnote 3153, above.
3158. Colonel Robert G. Ingersoll's lecture, "Liberty and Literature," given in the Horticulture Hall, Philadelphia, was mentioned in several letters to Dr R. M. Bucke — see *The Correspondence of Walt Whitman,* V, 97–98, 100, 101, 102, 103 — and Whitman wrote Ingersoll twice before the lecture, letters now lost (see *ibid.,* V, 100n; see also *Daybook,* footnote 3145, above). Ingersoll's letters to Whitman, 12 and 20 October 1890 are in the Feinberg. The lecture was published at least nine times, in periodicals and as a short book, *Liberty in Literature* (New York: Truth Seeker Co., 1890, 77 pp.; London: Gay & Bird, 1891). See Whitman's letter to him, *The Correspondence of Walt Whitman,* V, 104.
3159. Three letters from Baillie, a disciple of the poet, to Whitman, 17 September 1890, 10 October 1890, and 19 January 1891, are in the Feinberg Collection.

21   furnish'd D McKays (order) 50 (fifty) full sets
          in sheets of <u>complete</u> <u>book</u> ($3 a copy)
          – in addition to the 50 furn'd Aug: 27:

          — sent McKay also a copy big book   he now owes me
                                              for 3 ($12)[3160]

22   Well the Ingersoll lecture came off last
          evn'g in Horticultural Hall, Broad st: Phila:
          – a noble, (very eulogistic to W W & L of G)
          eloquent speech, well responded to by the audience
          There were 1600 to 2000 people, (choice persons,)
          one third women (Proceeds to me $869.45)
          I went over, was wheeled on the stage in my
                              at the last
          ratan chair, and ∧ spoke a very few words —
          – A splendid success for Ingersoll, (& me too.)
          Ing: had it written, & read with considerable fire,
          but perfect ease.   Warren & Mrs. D with me.
          Fine weather.[3161]

23   Dr B and Horace leave Phila: by RR for Canada[3162]
          Deposited $930.65 in Nat: St: Bank   Camden[3163]
                    cloudy rainy day
          have rec'd (& been reading all through) the well
          printed complete essay of R G Ingersoll "Liberty
          and Literature" – & it permeates & satisfies &
          explains itself splendidly to me, brain & heart –
          – (after all, I want to leisurely read & dwell
          on any profound or first-rate piece – one
          thing is, my hearing is not to-day real good,
          & another thing probably is I am rather slow
          any how)[3164]

    3160. The book which Whitman "furnish'd" to his publisher, David McKay, was *Complete Poems & Prose* (1888); Whitman also referred to this edition as the "big book."
    3161. For more on the Ingersoll lecture, which followed the birthday dinner, see footnotes 3145 and 3158. According to the *Camden Post,* 50 or 60 people attended the dinner; the 1600 or 2000 heard the lecture.
    3162. Whitman wrote to his two great friends, Dr R. M. Bucke and Horace Traubel, this same day in London, Ontario: see *The Correspondence of Walt Whitman,* V, 103–104.
    3163. Most of this money, which Whitman told Dr R. M. Bucke and Horace Traubel, "Ain't that enough to take y'r breaths away, both of you," came from the proceeds of the Ingersoll lecture (see footnotes 3145, 3158, and 3161).
    3164. This long comment and the one just above, certainly not usual for the entries

25   signed & gave the contract for <u>the burial</u>
     <u>house</u> in Harleigh Cemetery with Reinhalter
     Bros: 18 South Broad st: Phila.   Ralph Moore
     to be my representative & have charge &
     control   Ralph Moore here[3165]
          Fine sunny forenoon – Horace in Canada[3166]

[2:40]

E C Stedman 137   west 78th st New York[3167]
               Nov, 1890
Logan Pearsall Smith, 13 Museum Terrace Oxford
                    Eng:[3168]

[Two clippings:]
44   "W. S." — The new States are North
states   and South Dakota, Washington, Montana,
now   Idaho and Wyoming. Their capitals are,
         respectively, Bismarck, Pierre, Olympia,
         Helena. As the State Governments of
         Wyoming and Idaho have not yet been
         formed, their capitals have not been
         chosen.

         Mme. Alboni celebrated the completion of her
         seventy-fourth year last week at her house in the
         Cours la Reine, Paris. Notwithstanding her years,
         Mme. Alboni, it is said, sang the air from "The
         Prophet" with a powerful dramatic sentiment and a

in the *Daybook,* are fuller than almost anything else in these pages; it is, perhaps, largely a tribute to Robert G. Ingersoll's oratory and his great reputation at this time. Ingersoll actually gave two lectures on Whitman — one on the poet's birthday, the other on 21 October 1890.

3165. Whitman was greatly concerned with "the burial house," as seen in the *Daybook* entries: see footnotes 2987, 3034, 3055, 3080, 3146.

3166. See Whitman's letter to Dr R. M. Bucke and Horace Traubel in London, Ontario, 24 October 1890: *The Correspondence of Walt Whitman,* V, 104–105; to Dr Bucke, the next day, Whitman virtually repeated word by word, what he wrote above, in the *Daybook,* about the burial vault.

3167. Whitman had not corresponded with Edmund Clarence Stedman since May; but Stedman's son Arthur — whose address (the same as his father's) is also written on this same page below — may have now begun his own Whitman "activities." Arthur Stedman was to edit *Autobiographia: Selected from Whitman's Prose Writings* (New York: Charles L. Webster & Co., 1892, 205 pp.) and Whitman's *Selected Poems* (New York: Charles L. Webster & Co., 1892, 179 pp.).

3168. Logan Pearsall Smith, Robert's son and sister to Mary and Alys, had written Whitman from Oxford on 27 October 1890 (letter in the Feinberg Collection), which the poet sent to Dr R. M. Bucke on 8 November: see *The Correspondence of Walt Whitman,* V, 115.

superb voice that recalled the brilliant triumphs of
this incomparable Fidès.[3169]

Mrs: Mapes now Mrs: M E Stanley 717 M street Atchison
Kansas[3170]

Jessie   2437   2ᵈ Carondelet Av: St Louis[3171]

[Small clipping:]
    — The new States are North
and South Dakota, Montana, Washington, Idaho and Wyoming.

Arthur Stedman
137 west 78ᵗʰ st
New York City[3172]

Moncure D Conway, 230 west 59ᵗʰ st: N Y City[3173]

[2:41]

Camden   Oct: and   November   1890
Oct: 28 sent 4 big book by Express (with letter by mail)
  directed Mr Adams   bookseller Fall River Mass[3174]
  cloudy & cool $16 due   paid
  heavy, congested, stupid & dull to-day
sent letter to David L De Lezinsky, p o box 63, Berkeley, Cal:
  with paper[3175]
R G Ingersoll's address "Liberty and Literature" is pub'd
  entire in "Truth-Seeker" weekly paper 28 Lafayette
  Place, New York City, Nov: 1, 1890 – got 30 of them[3176]
letter f'm Bernard O'Dowd – letter to him f'm me[3177]

Nov. 4 Gleeson White f'm London, Eng: here[3178]

3169. These two clippings are of course concerned with two areas of great interest to Whitman: "these states," with which was carrying on a lifelong love affair, and the opera, the poet's favorite cultural activity.
3170. Mrs Mary E. Mapes (now Mrs Stanley) had worked for Whitman briefly as his housekeeper and he often sent her money, such as $5 on 8 July 1890 (see entry in the *Daybook* for that date).
3171. Jessie was the daughter of Whitman's brother Thomas Jefferson Whitman; he died on 25 November 1890 while she was in New Jersey (see entry that date below).
3172. See footnote 3167.
3173. Moncure D. Conway (see footnote 36), an American who lived in England, visited Whitman on 12 September 1891; at the time of this entry he obviously was in New York City, however, and may have written Whitman (letter now lost, if there was one).
3174. See Whitman letter and bill to Robert Adams, *The Correspondence of Walt Whitman*, V, 106.
3175. For David Lezinsky, see footnote 3041; Whitman's letter to him, 28 October 1890, is in *The Correspondence of Walt Whitman*, V, 106–107.
3176. On Robert G. Ingersoll's lecture, see footnotes 3145 and 3158.
3177. For the Australian, Bernard O'Dowd, see footnote 2986; O'Dowd's letter of 29 September 1890 is in the Feinberg Collection and A. L. McLeod's *Walt Whitman in Australia and New Zealand* (1964), pp. 27–30, and Whitman's, 3 November 1890, in *The Correspondence of Walt Whitman*, V, 112–113.
3178. Gleeson White had written Whitman on 2 November 1890 for permission to

big

5   rec'd $16 f'm Rob't Adams, Fall River, Mass. for 4 books [3179]
        sent rec't & letter & note to Miss Fenner[3180]
    big book sent to F Townsend Southwick 31 w 55th St
        N Y City – by express – b'k paid for – I p'd expressage[3181]
    sunny, cool weather – a persistent belly-ache
                                        night & day

6   deposited $97.40

7   sent off "National Literature" to W H R North American
        Review, $75 & 30 slips[3182]
    a long fine wheel-chair jaunt to-day to Cooper's Point
    Warry down to Blackwood to see Ed yesterday[3183]

8   sent over by express 300 first sheets (autographs)
        to Oldach, bookbinder 1215 Filbert st. with
        order to bind up 100, & fold & tie up the rest
        (194 I believe) in sets, folded complete[3184]
    rec'd 30 Truth Seekers with Ingersoll's lect: complete[3185]
        another fine day – Indian Summerlike – bad grip &
                                                 bladder trouble

visit him (letter in the Feinberg Collection); the poet obviously gave him permission, but no letter is extant. In his letter of 8 November to Dr R. M. Bucke, Whitman referred to "a lively gent visitor day before yeterday f'm Eng. — gives strong acc't of L of G receptivity & popularity am'g choice circles, students, (the big colleges) & younger folk there — middle aged man very gentlemanly & pleasant — " (*The Correspondence of Walt Whitman,* V, 115). White had written Whitman on 4 March 1889 (Feinberg Collection) for information about the poet for a piece in an English magazine for girls, an article, if published, I have not located.

3179. See footnote 3174, and letter to Robert Adams, *The Correspondence of Walt Whitman,* V, 113.

3180. All of these are now lost.

3181. F. Townsend Southwick, to whom Whitman sent his *Complete Poems & Prose* (1888), was the director of a school of oratory; he had written Whitman *circa* 1890 for permission "to select & edit a number of your poems for class use & recitation" (letter in the Library of Congress: see also *The Correspondence of Walt Whitman,* V, 117n). On 2 June 1891 he asked for leave to visit Whitman (letter in the Feinberg Collection); no reply is extant.

3182. Whitman wrote the editor of *The North American Review* — which had recently published his "Old Poets" — on 4 November 1890 about this article, "Have We a National Literature?" which was published in the *NAR,* CLII (March 1891), 332–338. It was used in *Good-bye My Fancy* (1891) and *Prose Works 1892,* II, 663–668, with the title "American National Literature," and sub-title, "Is there any such thing — or can there ever be?"

3183. This refers to a visit by Warren Fritzinger, acting as a male nurse to Whitman, who visited the poet's feeble-minded brother Edward.

3184. See Whitman's letter to Frederick Oldach & Company, 5 November 1890, in *The Correspondence of Walt Whitman,* V, 113–114.

3185. "Testimonial to Walt Whitman," *Truth Seeker,* XVII (1 November 1890), 690–693, 700; see footnotes 3145, 3158, 3164.

9   continued belly-ache

18   sent "W W's Thanksgiving" to J C "World" N Y. paid $10 [3186]

22   sent off (for two pp: <u>Arena</u>) Old Chants – ~~Sail~~ On on
     the Same Ye Jocund Twain, – Sail out for good, Eidolon
     Yacht – L of G.'s purport – my task – & For us two, reader dear
     (six poemets) – $100 – 25 slips – I reserve future printing
     to I N Baker 45 Wall st: N Y – rejected
                                     sent back to me [3187]

23   D McKay sent two copies Nov: Boughs to
     Library Congress, Washington D C to
     secure the Copyright [3188]

     the N Y World, (Julius Chambers) sends
                                     pays $10
     for the Thanksgiving poemet [3189]

                                                              [2:42]

R Pearsall Smith   44 Grosvenor Road
     Westminster embankment   London   S W [3190]
                              Horace Tarr
                              86 Liberty st
                         New York   city [3191]

3186. "Walt Whitman's Thanksgiving," New York *World* (Julius Chambers), 23
November 1890, included a preface, not reprinted (except in part in *The Correspondence of
Walt Whitman,* V, 118n), and "Thanks in Old Age" (see *Leaves of Grass,* Comprehensive
Reader's Edition, p. 527).
     3187. These six poemets, sent to Isaac N. Baker of *The Arena* and rejected by B. C.
Flower, the editor, 2 December 1890 (see his letter in the Feinberg Collection, in which he
says he would prefer an essay, though this was never sent by Whitman), were all published
in *Good-bye My Fancy* (1891). Earlier publication of "Old Chants" was in New York *Truth,*
X (19 March 1891), 11; and "Sail Out for Good, Eidólon Yacht!" *Lippincott's Magazine,*
XLVII (March 1891), 376, with other poems as "Old Age Echoes." Whitman's listing here of
"L. of G.'s Purport," "My Task," and "For Us Two, Reader Dear" confirms Sculley Bradley's
and Harold W. Blodgett's guess (*Leaves of Grass,* Comprehensive Reader's Edition, p. 555n)
that "L. of G.'s Purport" in *Good-bye My Fancy* (1891), p. 44, was first projected as three
separate short poems. For texts of these six poems see *Leaves of Grass,* Comprehensive Reader's Edition, pp. 547, 540–541, 539, and (the last three as one) 555-556.
     3188. This is not wholly clear: Whitman had printed, at his own expense, *November
Boughs* in September 1888; in October McKay purchased 950 copies for $313.50, with the
privilege of printing further issues until the end of 1890. Why is McKay now, in November
1890, sending two copies to the Library of Congress to secure copyright when Whitman had
copyrighted *November Boughs* in 1888?
     3189. See entry for 18 November 1890 and footnote 3186.
     3190. Whitman had sent Robert Pearsall Smith, of the Transatlantic and Germantown
Smiths, staunch friends of Whitman's, a bundle of books about 2 November 1890; Smith was
also among the 14 people to whom Dr John Johnston was asked, on 2 December 1890, to
send copies of his *Notes of a Visit to Walt Whitman* (Bolton, England, 1890).
     3191. Horace Tarr, on *The Engineering News,* had written Whitman on 1 and 13

[Corner of the envelope, printed: The Engineering & Building Record, P.O. Box 3037, No. 277 Pearl Street, New York. Receipt, dated 15 December 1890, to WW from Oldach & Co., for $22. Another, dated 19 May 1890, for $64.41 from Oldach.] [3192]

[2:43]

Nov: Camden   Nov: and December 1890
24   Sunny, dry, cold – belly ache – bad head – bad di-
                                                gestion

---

25   My brother Jeff died at St Louis, Mo:
                                        heart attack
            typhoid pneumonia   at last[3193]
in his 58ᵗʰ year – born July 18 1833
Geo: went on to St: L – Jessie who was in N J:
            got there the 2ᵈ day after the death

26, 27, 28, 29, 30   cold, cold

---

29   sent p'kt:b'd L of G. to Rev'd T B Johnstone 116
            Chorley, New Road, Bolton, Lanc, Eng.   paid rec'd [3194]

L
30   Long letter f'm David Lezinsky, Berkeley, Cal: ans'd [3195]
            Sunday – noon – Sun out – cool – Warry[3196] gone to Doylestown
            – am feeling poorly enough – bladder trouble, grip,

December 1890 (letters in the Feinberg Collection) about writing an obituary of Whitman's brother Jeff, who died on 25 November (see *Daybook* entry) and sending a picture of Jeff. Whitman's letter to Tarr, 13 December 1890, is in *The Correspondence of Walt Whitman,* V, 131. (This name and address were obviously written after Jeff's death, recorded on the next page of the *Daybook*.)

3192. These dates and sums differ from those to Oldach the binder listed by Whitman at the end of the *Daybook*.

3193. Whitman, who was 16 when Jeff was born, was greatly attached to Jeff until the younger brother's marriage, as he says in his letter to Dr R. M. Bucke, 28 November 1890 (see *The Correspondence of Walt Whitman,* V, 123), and his letters to his sister Mary, his brother Edward, and his niece Jessie Louisa (*ibid.,* V, 122, 123, 124). Whitman's obituary of Jeff, "An Engineer's Obituary," *Engineering Record* (New York), 13 December 1890, was reprinted in *Good-bye My Fancy* (1891) and *Prose Works 1892,* II, 692–693.

3194. Whitman refers to the Rev. Mr Johnstone, one of the "Bolton College" group in his letters to Dr John Johnston, 29 November 1890 and 5 January 1891 — *The Correspondence of Walt Whitman,* V, 124 and 145. Johnstone himself wrote to Whitman, but the letter is not extant.

3195. The long letter is in *The Correspondence of Walt Whitman,* V, 125; for more on David Lezinsky, see footnote 3041.

3196. Warren Fritzinger, now Whitman's male nurse.

& (probably) catarrh of bowels – (out in chair
                                    Harry F [3197]
George here – just ret'd f'm St Louis[3198]
wrote to Jessie St L.[3199]   (capsules f'm Dr. Mitchell f'r bladder
                                               trouble)[3200]

sunset feeling easier

Dec: 1 letter to H. ($2)[3201] – sent big book to D McKay
    – this makes the 4th one unacc'ted (unpaid) for
    but one of the four may have been for the sheets
    sent to Eng:[3202]   (gastric uneasyness)

---

4   sent portraits (three big) in large envelope
       to Mrs: R G Ingersoll   New York – rec'd [3203]

---

gloomy days – death of Jeff — [3204]

---

5   – proof type writing "Off-hand talk between
       W W & R W Ingersoll" Talcott Williams[3205]

"grip" – bladder-trouble – catarrh of bowels – h'd ache

3197. Harry Fritzinger, who was Mary Davis's adopted son, as was Warren; Harry took care of Whitman when Warren was out of town.
3198. George Whitman, Walt's brother who lived in Burlington, New Jersey, had gone to St Louis, Missouri, for the funeral of their younger brother Thomas Jefferson, who died 25 November 1890 (see entries above).
3199. Whitman's letter to his niece is in *The Correspondence of Walt Whitman,* V, 124.
3200. This was Dr J. K. Mitchell, the son of Dr S. Weir Mitchell, of whom Whitman wrote to Dr R. M. Bucke on 25 November 1890: "Young Dr Mitchell (he said his father sent him) was here f'm Phila. yesterday — fine y'ng fellow — no medicine (at least yet) — " (*The Correspondence of Walt Whitman,* V, 121–122).
3201. This letter to Whitman's sister Hannah Heyde is missing.
3202. As seen here, the *Daybook* continued to be Whitman's account book too; this time for copies of *Complete Poems & Prose* (1888) to his publisher.
3203. Though the letter to Mrs Robert G. Ingersoll, wife of the orator, if Whitman wrote a letter, is missing, the portraits were gifts, as he wrote Dr R. M. Bucke, "Am to send Mrs: Ingersoll 400 5th av: N Y. some good photos of self in big handsome envelope for Christmas present" (*The Correspondence of Walt Whitman,* V, 121.).
3204. That Whitman should mention Jeff's death twice in the *Daybook,* a rare occurence, is evidence of how deeply Walt felt his loss. Gay Wilson Allen, *The Solitary Singer* (New York, 1955, 1967), pp. 537–538, agrees that Jeff's death was Walt's saddest event of 1890 and a very severe shock.
3205. Whitman wrote to Dr R. M. Bucke, 8–9 December 1890: "Talcott Williams (Phil: Press) had a stenographer there at Reisser's evn'g May 31 '89, & took down the conversation bet'n Ingersoll and self (ab't immortality &c) after supper it seems — & is now typewriting it out & to send me copies, one of wh' I will surely forward to you soon as he does — " (*The Correspondence of Walt Whitman,* V, 130); and on 16 December Whitman wrote William that "the type-written report of the Ing[ersoll] conversation has not reached me — " (*ibid.,* V, 133). Whether this conversation was published in the Philadelphia *Press* or distributed in some form I do not know.

8   Horace T. back f'm N Y – f'm seeing Ingersoll and J H Johnston[3206]

9   sent big book (paid $6) to J H Johnston N Y. f'r Agnes Schilling[3207]
     snow on ground – have not been out for four days – sunny to-day

11   sent Phil: Press, of Dec. 8 with item ab't "Good-Bye My Fancy" to
     various foreign (& home) names[3208]

12   paid Oldach bookbinder $22 in full by Horace[3209]

13   sent photo of Jeff: to Horace Tarr N Y for print[3210]

17   sent 4 poemets (Old Chants, Great is the Seen, Death dogs

     my steps & two lines) to Scribner's N Y
                                              [Three words and date in red ink:]
                price $100 and 20 copies   rejected
                                              sent back
     wind gales   Jan: 23 '91 [3211]
     dark ∧ raining, cold (but hardly freezing)
     Mr Sheppard (friend of Frank Harned) call'd – bot 2 books[3212]

     the snivelling, sickening, letters of the meanest cuss

3206. There is more on this in Whitman's letter of Dr R. M. Bucke on this same date:
"Horace [Traubel] has been here back from his brief N Y trip — he saw Ingersoll at I's
splendid Wall st offices, surrounded with his clerks & Mr Baker, & had a long talk, varied &
animated & interesting — was at (Jeweler) Johnston's — staid there — had good confabs &
good meals there — went to the Ethical Convention &c &c &c —" (*The Correspondence of
Walt Whitman*, V, 129).
3207. This sale of *Complete Poems & Prose* (1888) is mentioned both here and in a
letter to Dr R. M. Bucke (*The Correspondence of Walt Whitman*, V, 130).
3208. *The Critic* for 29 November 1890 had announced the forthcoming *Good-bye My
Fancy,* with an appendix containing essays by Sarrazin, Rolleston, and Ingersoll (an idea
later abandoned); and the Philadelphia *Press* likely picked this up in its issue of 8 December.
It is not known to whom Whitman sent copies of the *Press,* for they are not named
here; no letters mention the *Press,* and no letters from Whitman dated 11 December 1890
are extant.
3209. This receipt is attached to the *Daybook* on the previous page.
3210. For Tarr, see footnote 3191; he wanted the picture of Thomas Jefferson Whitman,
who died on 25 November 1890, for publication in *The Engineering News.*
3211. "Old Chants" had been rejected by *The Arena* (see footnote 3187) but was published in *Truth,* X (19 March 1891); "Grand Is the Scene" was first published in *Good-bye
My Fancy* (1891; see *Leaves of Grass,* Comprehensive Reader's Edition, p. 556); "Death Dogs
My Steps" became lines 10, 11, and 12 of "L. of G.'s Purport" in *Good-bye My Fancy* (1891:
see *Leaves of Grass,* Comprehensive Reader's Edition, p. 555n); the "two lines" cannot be
identified, but may be "After the Argument" (see footnote 3215, below).
3212. Frank Harned was the brother of Camden lawyer Thomas B. Harned, who became one of Whitman's literary executors; Frank was a photographer; for more of his friend
Sheppard, we must await later volumes of Horace Traubel's *With Walt Whitman in Camden.*

Nature ever spawn'd – C L H, Burlington Vermont[3213]

– still continued – now over a year –

[2:44]

[Bill to Whitman from Ferguson Bros. & Co., 15 North Seventh Street, Philadelphia, May 1891, for *Good-bye My Fancy,* typesetting, $106.39, printing 1000 copies, $43.40; *November Boughs,* 400 copies, $43.00 (total bill $192.79).]

[Calling card from S. Elmer Wright, with E. H. Parry, Hatter, S.E. Cor. Tenth & Market Sts., Philadelphia.]

[Bill from Adams Express Company, Camden, N. J., 27 December 1890, for shipment to B. O'Dowd, Melbourne, Victoria, Value $25.00, freight paid $7.50.]

[Bill to Whitman from the Camden Gas Light Company, for gas from 1 October to 1 January 1891: $8.96 less .45 (5% for prompt payment), $8.51.]

[2:45]

Camden   December '90   and   Jan: '91

18   rec'd word f'm W H R, N. A Rev: that Nat. Lit. will not be in
                                                    Jan: number[3214]

---

20   got in cord of split oak wood

---

21   finishing "Some Personal Memoranda" for Stoddart
                                                    Lippincott's[3215]

3213. No letter from Charles L. Heyde, Whitman's detested brother-in-law, of 15 or 16 December 1890, is extant; but his letter to Whitman, 24 December, is in the Feinberg Collection. Despite Whitman's feelings about Heyde, when he (Whitman) wrote his sister Hannah on 22 December (see *The Correspondence of Walt Whitman,* V, 134–135, and entry in *Daybook*) he sent her $10 and said, "you might give one of the 5s to C[harles]."

3214. William H. Rideing, assistant editor of *The North American Review,* wrote Whitman on 16 December 1890 (letter in the Feinberg Collection) that "Have We a National Literature" would not appear as announced in the January 1891 issue but "probably" in the February; it actually was printed in March 1891 (see footnote 3182).

3215. Whitman wrote Dr R. M. Bucke, 19 December 1890 that Joseph M. Stoddart "wants (proposes) to make his March number [*Lippincott's Magazine*] what he calls *a Whitman number* with articles (some of mine, with name) & picture — " (*The Correspondence of Walt Whitman,* V, 134). "Some Personal and Old Age Memoranda," *Lippincott's Magazine,* XLVII (March 1891), 377–381, was reprinted in *The Critic,* 28 February 1891, and in *Good-bye My Fancy* (1891) as "Some Personal and Old Age Jottings"; the magazine also printed, p. 376, under "Old Age Echoes," four poems, "Sounds of Winter," "The Unexpress'd," "Sail Out for Good, Eidólon Yacht," and "After the Argument." For the prose piece, see *Prose Works 1892,* II, 699–706, 774–776; for the poetry, also printed in *Good-bye My Fancy* (1891), see *Leaves of Grass,* Comprehensive Reader's Edition, pp. 548, 556, 539, and 621. Horace Traubel's "Walt Whitman: Poet, Philosopher and Man" was in *Lippincott's,* XLVII (March 1891), 382–389.

22   resolutions & memorial speech in honor of Jeff
            f'm St Louis Engineers' Club Dec: 17 1890 [3216]
                    rec'd   recd
            sent $10 to Han — $10 to Mary[3217]

---

box 838

23   sent big book p o to S R Henderson,   Los Angeles, Cal ^paid [3218]
            wrote to J N Johnson, Ala:[3219]

---

24   recd $300 fm David McKay for the 100 sets of books
            sheets – sent to England [3220]
        a big book sent to McKay   now 5th copy (but
            one of them may have gone in the sheets)
        sent pkt-b'k L of G. to Fred Wild   Bolton Eng: paid [3221]

                                                        *

25   sent <u>sixth</u> big book to David McKay[3222]

---

27   sent four big books & some pictures to
            Bernard O'Dowd, Sup. Ct. Lib: Melbourne Victoria
            by Express, paid $7.50   rec'd [3223]

---

30   sent MS of "Some Personal Memoranda" and poemet "Sail
            out for good Eidólon Yacht" (to fill out page) to Stoddart

3216. E. D. Meier wrote Whitman on 19 December 1890, thanking him for material about Jeff. These resolutions and the memorial speech were published?
3217. Whitman's letter to his sister Hannah Heyde is in *The Correspondence of Walt Whitman,* V, 134–135 (see footnote 3213, above); his letter to his other sister Mary Van Nostrand, 22 December 1890, is missing. Both $10 listed in the back of the *Daybook.*
3218. The $6.40 for *Complete Poems & Prose* (1888) was sent by William Hawley Smith: see *The Correspondence of Walt Whitman,* V, 136.
3219. Letter missing; for John Newton Johnson, of Mid, Alabama, a colorful eccentric who often wrote to Whitman, see footnote 9a.
3220. These 100 copies, undoubtedly of the 1888 edition of *Leaves of Grass,* appeared in England with a different binding from the American edition; but bibliographical details have not been recorded yet.
3221. Wild was one of Dr John Johnston and J. W. Wallace's "Bolton College" group — Whitman mentioned sending the book in his letter to Dr Johnston: see *The Correspondence of Walt Whitman,* V, 135; Wallace described Wild as "not literary" but "not without appreciation of the *best* literature. He has an artist's eye for the beauties of Nature . . . but prefers Nature at first hand . . . He has a wild native wit of his own, and is frank, outspoken, and free" (*The Correspondence of Walt Whitman,* V, 156n); his letter to Whitman, 5 March 1892, is in the Feinberg Collection.
3222. Whitman, here and two lines above, kept careful account of every copy of *Complete Poems & Prose* (1888) his publisher received.
3223. For Bernard O'Dowd, see footnote 2986; Whitman's letters to O'Dowd, 26 and 27 December 1890, are in *The Correspondence of Walt Whitman,* V, 138–139.

Lippincotts – $50 and 30 numbers mag: ($50 paid me)[3224]

Elmer Wright, f'm Parry's hat store, cor. 10th & Market   [three words

Phil. came to see ab't the hat, gave him the order,   in red ink:]

dimensions, &c: to be done in ab't a week – price ab't $5[3225]   hat

_____   rec'd

31   deposited $321[3226]   good

Jan 1 '91 glum and dark & wet & foggy   *middling cold

the grip (cold & stopt in head) – bladder trouble

¼ after 4 – have eaten a hearty good meal, turkey &c: half light

_____ evn'g[3227]

3   sent little morocco L of G to Gen. Cassius M Clay Whitehall

rec'd ackn'gd   Ky[3228]

glum physique & spirits

_____   accepted – paid

4   sent "the Pallid   wreath" to Critic – $5 & 10 slips   & printed[3229]

_____

5   paid the gas bill $8.52 (for Oct. Nov & Dec. '90)[3230]

Lou here   Harry Stafford here[3231]   Mont at Elwood

on Atl RR line[3232]

_____

3224. See footnote 3215.

3225. Rather a mundane matter to write about, so minor he did not mention it to Dr R. M. Bucke, to whom he seems to have written about everything.

3226. Most of this was from the $300 which David McKay paid him on 24 December 1890 for 100 sets of sheets (see *Daybook*, above).

3227. Whitman writes about all these things — weather, bladder trouble, and what he ate — to Bernard O'Dowd, 1 January 1891: *The Correspondence of Walt Whitman*, V, 142–143.

3228. Depuis Macellus Clay acknowledged receipt of the book on 6 January 1891 (letter in the Feinberg Collection). Cassius M. Clay had written Whitman on 9 July 1887, noting receipt of a book and sending an address he made at Yale (also in the Feinberg Collection); of Clay, Horace Traubel reported on 12 July 1889: "W[hitman] sitting at parlor window reading life of Cassius Clay. Asked me, 'Did you ever know anything of Cas Clay? — ever see him, meet him?' Adding, 'He was a great man in his day — must be a very old man now!'" (*With Walt Whitman in Camden*, V, 361).

3229. See Whitman's letter to Joseph B. and Jeannette L. Gilder, *The Critic*, in *The Correspondence of Walt Whitman*, V, 145. The poem, "The Pallid Wreath," *The Critic*, XV (10 January 1891), 18, was reprinted in *Good-bye My Fancy* (1891): see *Leaves of Grass*, Comprehensive Reader's Edition, p. 542.

3230. This is also listed in the back of the *Daybook*.

3231. Whitman wrote to Dr John Johnston, Bolton, England, 5 January 1891, about "a rush of visitors to-day & last evn'g" (*The Correspondence of Walt Whitman*, V, 145–146), by which he meant his sister-in-law Louisa (George's wife) and Harry Stafford (see footnote 2928, above), who had been Whitman's great young friend from 1876 to 1885 but visited the poet far less frequently now. See *The Correspondence of Walt Whitman*, V, 155n about his current (January 1891) activities; he visited the poet again on 3 February.

3232. Mont is Montgomery Stafford, Harry's brother, who last visited Whitman 21 April 1889.

6   proofs sent the page of poemets to Stoddart Lippincotts[3233]
      & "pallid wreath" to Critic[3234]
      $50 rec'd from Lippincotts – [3235]   cold, sunny day

---

7   cold, sunny * 1½ p m – seems to me as I come f'm the
      wash-room I am perceptibly stronger more than
      for two years (may be but an accidental evanescent
      whiff, or imaginary) but it comes to me

[2:46]

[Clipping of an ad for window awnings. Bill to Whitman from Thos. H.
McCollin & Co., Photographic Supplies, 635 Arch Street, Philadelphia, 21
January 1891, paid 1/27/91, 50 prints, 50 prints, 118 unmounted, and 1 nega-
tive, $18.41.] [3236]

[2:47]

      Camden   January   1891
8   sent "quaker traits" "science & L of G" and personal
      letter to Stoddart (Lippincott)   all rejected [3237]

---

10   letter to H $2 [3238] — pieces to Stoddart (Lippincott) we will
      see what comes of them all [3239] – sent pict to Stead, London[3240]

3233. These were "Sounds of Winter," "The Unexpress'd," "Sail Out for Good, Eidólon
Yacht," and "After the Argument" — see footnote 3215.
3234. See footnote 3229.
3235. This was for the four short poems, mentioned above and published as "Old Age
Echoes."
3236. Not that Whitman needed an excuse, but one wonders why Whitman needed
this many pictures, though on 28 January 1891 he sent four to Dr R. M. Bucke (see *Daybook* entry, below).
3237. See Whitman's letter to Joseph M. Stoddart in *The Correspondence of Walt
Whitman*, V, 147-148. "Quaker Traits of Walt Whitman," by William Sloane Kennedy, was
in *The Conservator*, I (July 1890), 36; so Whitman could have meant Kennedy's "Dutch
Traits of Walt Whitman," then unpublished but later in *The Conservator*, I (February 1891),
90–91 — both reprinted in *In Re Walt Whitman* (1893), pp. 213–214, 195–199. "*Leaves of
Grass* and Modern Science," by Richard Maurice Bucke, had also appeared earlier: in *The
Conservator*, I (May 1890), 19, and reprinted in *In Re Walt Whitman* (1893), Whitman
here have been attempting to give the two articles wider distribution than afforded by *The
Conservator*.
3238. See Whitman's letter, sending the $2, to his sister Hannah Heyde in *The Corre-
spondence of Walt Whitman*, V, 148.
3239. On 8 January 1891 Whitman seems merely to have written Joseph M. Stoddart
that he intended sending the pieces by W. S. Kennedy and Dr R. M. Bucke (and also one
by Horace Traubel), and here on 10 January he sends the three pieces — see footnote 3237.
Traubel's piece — also reprinted in *In Re Walt Whitman*, pp. 202–211 — was actually published in *Lippincott's Magazine* (see footnote 3215 in the *Daybook*, above).
3240. See Whitman's letter to William T. Stead, 6 January 1891, in *The Correspondence of Walt Whitman*, V, 146. Stead's periodical, *The Review of Reviews*, reproduced this

11   Sunday – dark, rainy, glum, not very cold – sent $2 to Mrs: D
                                              and picture to Mrs. B [3241]

---

                              paid $75
12   sent off proof "American National Literature" to N A Review[3242]

                                                              Aunt
      a very depress'd bad week days & nights – $10 to Mrs: S – $2 to Hannah[3243]

---

18   sent $5 to Mr Lay (Mrs: Lay's burial, Phila:)[3244]

---

19   recd $15 f'm <u>Youth's</u> <u>Companion</u> for "Ship Ahoy!" [3245]

---

24   poemet-page rejected "Old Chants" &c: by <u>Scribners</u>
          and sent back to me.[3246]
      the little Ingersol – lecture-pamphlet, pub'd by
          N Y T<u>ruth</u>-S<u>eeke</u>r, rec'd – well-done, printing &c:[3247]
      Horace T going to N Y this afternoon   fine sunny
      Mrs: D [3248] gone to Doylestown for the day   day
          H T. ret'd evn'g[3249]

---

post card in facsimile, III (February 1891), 163, and published the picture which Whitman
sent, IV (August 1891), 197, with a review of *Good-bye My Fancy;* excerpts from published
Whitman pieces were in the Christmas 1890 issue, in III (March 1891), 249, and III (June
1891), 570–571.

3241.   Neither the letter with $2 for Mrs Mary Davis (?) nor the one with the picture for Mrs R. M. Bucke are extant.

3242.   For "Have We a National Literature?" see footnotes 3182 and 3214.

3243.   Though this entry is undated, it most likely is 16 January 1891, when he wrote to Mrs Susan Stafford — see *The Correspondence of Walt Whitman,* V, 152 — and sent her the money. By "Aunt Hannah," Whitman may be being playful about his sister Hannah Heyde, to whom he often sent money; he had a grandmother, Hannah Brush Whitman, who died in 1834, but no Aunt Hannah — there is no letter of this date (16 January 1891) to help identification.

3244.   Mr and Mrs Alfred Lay lived in Whitman's house on Mickle Street when he bought it in March 1884 (see footnotes 1792 and 1796); the letter here to Alfred Lay is now missing.

3245.   Whitman's poem, "Ship Ahoy!" *The Youth's Companion,* LXIV (12 March 1891), 152, was reprinted in *Good-bye My Fancy* (1891), p. 28; see *Leaves of Grass,* Comprehensive Reader's Edition, p. 620. See Whitman's brief letter to the editor of the magazine, *The Correspondence of Walt Whitman,* V, 153.

3246.   "Old Chants" had previously been rejected by *The Arena* (see entries for 22 November and 17 December 1890, and footnotes 3187 and 3211, above).

3247.   For Robert G. Ingersoll's lecture, see footnotes 3145 and 3158. *Liberty in Literature* (New York: Truth Seeker Co., 1890, 77 pp.) was reprinted six times; when Truth Seeker Co. reprinted it in 1892, the book also contained Ingersoll's address at Whitman's funeral. See Gordon Stein, *Robert G. Ingersoll: A Checklist,* p. 18.

3248.   Mrs Mary O. Davis, Whitman's housekeeper.

3249.   While Horace Traubel was away Whitman wrote him a note on the final page of the galleys of Traubel's "Walt Whitman: Poet and Philosopher and Man" (to be in the March 1891 *Lippincott's*): see *The Correspondence of Walt Whitman,* V, 156.

27   sent off the little Ingersoll "Liberty in Literature"
       book to various persons by mail [3250]
      sent big book by mail to Charles E Barrett Atchison,
       Kansas, (paid) - p c to W H Smith, Peoria, Ill:[3251]

28   bad physical cond'n - bad constipation long -
       - catarrh in head - gastric & bladder cond'n bad
             rec'd
      sent 4 pictures to Dr B - $2 to H - paper to Jessie[3252]

29   sent proof Dutch piece to Kennedy – ret'd [3253]
                   rec'd
Feb: 2 paid C F Currie, Supt: $45.50 ∧ for Ed's board [3254]

 3   sent big book by mail to W^m J Nicolay, Minier,
               paid
      Ill: 4.40 due ∧ f'm Truth Seeker 28 Lafayette place
                                              N Y.[3255]

10   got in cord of oak wood $8 paid
      "Dutch Traits of W W" by Sloane Kennedy[3256]

16   bad continued constipated spell the worst yet
       heavy dizzy dull headache - dark rainy to-day
                        not cold
      "The New Spirit" book rec'd f'm Havelock Ellis[3257]

3250. See footnotes 3145, 3158, and 3247.
3251. This post card to William Hawley Smith is missing; earlier, on 23 December
1890, Smith paid for another copy of Whitman's *Complete Poems & Prose* (1888) — see
footnote 3218, above.
3252. The four pictures to Dr R. M. Bucke most likely were from those Whitman
bought on 27 January 1891 (see receipt above); the $2 for the poet's sister Mrs Hannah
Heyde (see his letter to her, *The Correspondence of Walt Whitman*, V, 157–158); and Jessie
was·his niece in St Louis, Missouri, whose father Jeff Whitman had died on 25 November
1890, and whom he had written on 1 and 2 January 1890 (see *ibid.,* V, 142, 143–144). Whitman told Hannah, "Just sent papers &c: to Jessie, St Louis — dont hear much, but suppose
she is there & [takes?] up affairs &c: & is well —" (*ibid.,* V, 157).
3253. *"Dutch piece"* refers to William Sloane Kennedy's "Dutch Traits of Walt Whitman" (see footnote 3237).
3254. This money for the keep of Whitman's feeble-minded brother Edward at the
asylum in Blackwoodtown, New Jersey is also recorded at the end of the *Daybook.*
3255. A confusing entry: did the *Truth Seeker* (New York) owe Whitman $4.40
(which was paid: for what?), or did William J. Nicolay pay this money? *Truth Seeker* was
both a magazine which printed Robert G. Ingersoll's pieces and a publishing house which
issued his books.
3256. Of William Sloane Kennedy's piece, "Dutch Traits of Walt Whitman" (see
footnote 3237), Whitman wrote Kennedy: "it is the best thing of its kind yet" (*The Correspondence of Walt Whitman*, V, 164).
3257. Havelock Ellis (1859–1939), renowned English psychologist, published his essay,

                                    another one the 8th
19   sent big book to D McKay, the 7th copy ∧ he has
          now to acc't to me for
      getting "Good – Bye my Fancy" copy ready for printer[3258]
      – easier last evn'g & to-day – (or fancy I am)

_____

20   sent letter to Bernard O'Dowd [3259]

                                                        [2:48]

            Co:
Geo: Ferguson ∧ ~~Bros.~~Printers 15 north 7th st
                            Phila:[3260]

                                                        [2:49]

      Camden   February   &   March   1891
Feb: 21   bad way continued – four weeks – gastric & bladder
      – dark wet glum weather — finishing touches copy
      "Good-bye my Fancy" – (goes to printers in two days)[3261]
      send off Ing:'s little book to Sarrazin[3262]
      – looking yet for March Lippincott[3263] — ~~sent~~[?] the good
      little "Dutch Traits" by Kennedy, out & sent to many[3264]

_____

23   sent copy "Good:Bye my Fancy" pp: 3 to 42 inclusive

"Walt Whitman," in *The New Spirit* (London: George Bell & Sons, 1890); but Whitman here received the revised edition (London: Walter Scott, 1891), pp. 89–132; since reprinted (New York: Boni and Liveright, 1921; Boston: Houghton Mifflin, 1926). Ellis wrote Whitman, 3 February 1891 (letter in the Feinberg Collection): "It is a feeble attempt to express the help & delight that your work has given me." Dr R. M. Bucke, 22 February (Feinberg Collection) said he had seen the book a year ago and found the essay "mostly good — had some bad shots in it"; and William Sloane Kennedy, in *The Fight of a Book for the World* (West Yarmouth, 1926), p. 39, felt that Ellis was friendly, "but the chapter contains a wofully mistaken and beastly idea of the Calamus poems. One understands from such utterances as this why Symonds in his book found it necessary to defend Whitman's Calamus doctrine." Whitman's copy of *The New Spirit* is now in the Feinberg Collection. See *The Correspondence of Walt Whitman*, V, 166n, 167n.
    3258. As will be seen below in entries for 21 and 23 February, 15 March, and 6, 17, and 24 April, 6 and 17 May, and in numerous letters, Whitman was busy with the publication of *Good-bye My Fancy,* which contained both poetry and prose, some printed in periodicals, some published for the first time. Application for copyright was made on 18 May 1891, and the 66-page book printed and presswork all done by that date. George Ferguson Company, Philadelphia, was the printer.
    3259. Letter: *The Correspondence of Walt Whitman*, V, 167–168.
    3260. The firm was now printing *Good-bye My Fancy* (see footnote 3258).
    3261. See footnote 3258.
    3262. The little book which Whitman sent to his French enthusiast and critic Gabriel Sarrazin was Robert G. Ingersoll's *Liberty in Literature* (see footnote 3247).
    3263. This issue of *Lippincott's* was virtually a Whitman number (see footnote 3215, above).
    3264. "Dutch Traits of Walt Whitman," *The Conservator*, February 1891 (see footnotes 3237 and 3256).

to Ferguson, printer, (by Horace)[3265]
fine sunny day – bo't injection (enema) pipe – fair success
– badly constipated nearly four weeks – head glum[3266]

27   the March Lippincott & the "Dutch Traits" piece
        sent out liberally by mail [3267]
    get & take the prescription of Dr B. f'm Druggist Brown[3268]

March 2 – sent big books to O J Bailey, Peoria
        Illinois &
    Alfred P Burbank care Lotos Club,
        New York City   both paid (12.80) by W^m
        Hawley Smith,   Peoria, Ill. (letter sent to him)[3269]
    extra bad condition day & night — sharp cold weather

4   N A Rev. paid $75 for "National Literature" [3270]

5   sent Two Riv. to John F Burke, law office, Milwaukee
        Wis. $2.50 due   paid [3271]   fine sunny day   cold
    sent Nat. Lit. to several [3272]
        Copyright bill pass'd [3273]

                                    rec'd safely
7   sent the three big books to Jessie   St Louis ∧ by express[3274]

3265. See footnote 3258.
3266. See Whitman's letter to Dr R. M. Bucke in *The Correspondence of Walt Whitman*, V, 169; and Dr Bucke's reply, *ibid.*, V, 168n–169n.
3267. See footnotes 3263 and 3264.
3268. See Whitman's letter to Dr R. M. Bucke, 28 February 1891, in *The Correspondence of Walt Whitman*, V, 170–171.
3269. William Hawley Smith, who had had Whitman send copies of his *Complete Poems & Prose* (1888) to Prof. John W. Cook (6 February 1890), S. R. Henderson (see *Daybook* entry for 23 December 1890 and Whitman's letter to Smith, *The Correspondence of Walt Whitman*, V, 136) and Charles E. Barrett (see *Daybook* entry for 27 January 1891), seems to be "promoting" Whitman. His letter to Smith, 2 March 1891, is missing.
3270. For "Have We a National Literature?" see footnotes 3182 and 3214.
3271. Whitman published *Two Rivulets* himself in 1876 and apparently as late as 1891 still had copies to sell; his letter to John F. Burke, 5 March 1891, is missing (Feinberg Collection has only the envelope).
3272. Whitman's essay in *The North American Review*: see footnotes 3182 and 3214.
3273. In his letter to Dr R. M. Bucke, 5 March 1891, Whitman wrote, "— we have got the international copyright law pass'd here—" (*The Correspondence of Walt Whitman*, V, 173); that Whitman mentioned the bill is an indication that he thought it important, but one regrets the lack of a comment (he commented so little on anything in the *Daybook*).
3274. Jessie was Whitman's niece (see footnote 3252); but what are the three big books (one was undoubtedly *Complete Poems & Prose*, 1888)?

sent big book to Signor Enrico Nencione

3 portraits

viate Galileo 9 Firenze Italy[3275]

---

finished   sent

15   finishing (sending off) the poetic, (20 pp:) proofs of
"Good-Bye my Fancy" & to-day 12 or 14 pp: of
copy for prose part of G-B   F.[3276]   (the fearful
constipation continued essentially unbroken)
fine sunny day   cool
sent "Old Chants" to <u>Truth</u> by yn'g Mr Stoddart $12 [3277]

---

17   deposited 168.60 [3278] – cold, sunny
sent $2 L of G. to Chs F Carter, Waterbury Conn.   pd

[2:50]

[Bill to Whitman from Department for Supplying the City of Camden
with Water, 1 March 1891, 328 Mickle Street, for the year 1891, $8.00, with
WW's notation:]

Water Rent
for 1891
<u>Paid</u>

[2:51]

Camden   March   April   1891

March 19 Dr Longaker 652 N Eighth st: Phila
– had a long talk – used the catheter first time

3275. Enrico Nencione (or Nencioni) wrote of Whitman in *Nuovi Orizzonti Poetica*
(Fanfulla), 1881; "Walt Whitman," *Fanfulla della Domenica,* 7 December 1879; "Walt
Whitman, il poeta della democrazia," *ibid.,* 18 November 1883; "Mazzini e Whitman," *ibid.,*
20 April 1884; "Walt Whitman," *Nuova Antologia,* August 1885 (reprinted *in Saggi Critici
de Letterature Inglese,* Florence, 1897, pp. 110–123; see also pp. 204–230, which reprints "Il
Poeta della Guerra Americana," *Nuova Antologia,* 1 December 1891). Whitman wrote Dr
R. M. Bucke, 10 July 1890, "There is a book ab't American Poets (I don't know the name)
by (Prof. I believe) Enrico Nencione, Florence, Italy, in wh' is a chapter devoted to L of G
& me quite appreciative & favorable — must have been pub'd (say) two y'rs ago — you might
have in mind, & be on the look out for — Prof. E N is (I believe) in the University at
Florence" (*The Correspondence of Walt Whitman,* V, 61). See also Gay Wilson Allen, *Walt
Whitman Abroad* (Syracuse, New York, 1955), pp. 187, 278.
3276. See footnote 3258.
3277. "Old Chants," *Truth,* X (19 March 1891), 11 (see footnotes 3187 and 3211).
3278. Since his last deposit on 31 December 1890, Whitman had received $5 from
The Critic, $50 from *Lippincott's Magazine,* $75 from *The North American Review,* $15
from *The Youth's Companion,* and $12 from *Truth* (a total of $157 for his writing); so the
rest of the money must have come from book sales.

my general first impression of Dr L & the affair, good – [3279]
sent pictures &c in big evelop to Dr Thos C Whitman
    Brooksville Fla:[3280]

22   sent "Old actors" to "Truth" 140 Fifth av:
                        proof rec'd
    N Y. $16 (intended for April 2ᵈ) April 10
                         return'd [3281]

24   sent big book to Henry S Tuke, Swanpool,
        Falmouth, Cornwall, Eng: paid [3282]
sort of edging toward bowel action after
    nine or ten weeks essential inaction
    – take Dr L's pills – have taken 14 or 15 – [3283]
good & frequent letters f'm Dr J & J W W. Eng:[3284]
– am reading the prose proofs "Good-Bye" [3285]

              see below – same
25   gave D McKay order ʌ for six (6) sets
    sheets big book complete works a$3.20 [3286]

3279. Dr Daniel Longaker, here first mentioned, became Whitman's physician for the rest of the poet's life; he is referred to numerous times, especially in letters to Dr R. M. Bucke, and Whitman seemed to like him. We have three letters from Whitman to Dr Longaker, 15 April, 10 May, and 7 June 1891 (*The Correspondence of Walt Whitman*, V, 191–192, 199, and 209). The physician was paid from a fund for Whitman's nursing care, as Dr Bucke wrote to Horace Traubel on 1 April 1891: "My idea is that the 'Fund' should pay Dr Longaker and I increase my subscription to meet this [by $5], I calculate that Dr L. should have $30.00 or $40.00 a mth. *f'm now on (?)*" (*ibid.*, V, 177n; letter in the Feinberg Collection).

3280. No relative, but not identified.

3281. "Old Actors and Singers [Shows, &c., in New York]" was scheduled to be published in *Truth* (New York) 2 April 1891 (though Whitman says here he returned the proofs on 10 April); no file of the magazine has been found. The essay was included in *Good-bye My Fancy* (1891): see *Prose Works 1892*, II, 693–699, for text from the book.

3282. Henry S. Tuke's letter, 9 March 1891, ordering *Leaves of Grass, Complete Poems & Prose* (1888) is in the Feinberg Collection; a transcript of Whitman's letter of 24 March is in *The Correspondence of Walt Whitman*, V, 180–181. Tuke wrote Whitman: "I cannot tell you what a blessed thing it was to me when I found your poems, & I could say the same of several other young Englishmen I know."

3283. Misspelling his doctor's name, Whitman wrote Dr R. M. Bucke, 23 March 1891, "Dr Forkaner came yesterday — I like him"; and again on 27 March, "Getting along still — Dr Foraker here yesterday (comes ab't every 2d day) — am taking medicine pills (I suppose to placate the digestive parts & produce evacuation) — " (*The Correspondence of Walt Whitman*, V, 180, 181).

3284. Most of these letters from Dr John Johnston and J. W. Wallace, of Bolton, England, are in the Feinberg Collection, and Whitman's frequent replies are in *The Correspondence of Walt Whitman*, Vol. V.

3285. For *Good-bye My Fancy, 2d Annex to Leaves of Grass* (Philadelphia: David McKay, 1891) see footnote 3258, above.

3286. There is no letter extant for this date to David McKay, but there is a note in

27   sent $2 edn L of G. to Joseph M Pratt, Saybrook Conn:
                    paid

29   sent two big books to care of Miss C Reynolds,
            Newnham College Cambridge   12.80 due
                & letter to Miss C R – paid [3287]

31   Six copies big book complete in sheets to McKay
            a 3.20 – owes me $19.20 for them   (see below
        ab't 190 big books complete in sheets now at Oldach's
                            bindery[3288]

                    Apr. 9 2ᵈ copy pk't bk L of G – rec'd
Apr: 1 sent pk't-book ed'n L of G. to Cushing & Co: ∧ Booksellers
        34 W Baltimore st: Baltimore Md: paid – stolen en route[3289]

3   deposited $51 in bank
            calls f'm D McKay
        "   W R O'Donovan, N Y, sculptor
        "   "   Dr Longaker[3290]
    paid gas bill $8.51 the last 3 months[3291]

4   statement f'm D McKay   paid $127.87
            pays up (does it?) to date
                everything – (inc'ng the 6 sets above)[3292]

The Correspondence of Walt Whitman, V, 185, for Horace Traubel, 31 March 1891 (see entry in *Daybook,* below) about this matter. See Whitman-to-McKay letters, 3, 5, and 6 April, *ibid.,* V, 186, 187.

3287. Whitman's letter to Miss Clare Reynolds is now lost; her letter to him, 13 April 1891, enclosing payment, is in the Feinberg Collection.

3288. See entry above, 25 March 1891, and footnote 3286.

3289. None of this correspondence about the pocket-book edition of *Leaves of Grass* (1889) is now extant.

3290. The calls by David McKay, Whitman's publisher, and Dr Daniel Longaker, his physician, might be called routine; but of William R. O'Donovan, the poet wrote to Dr R. M. Bucke: "Mr O'Donovan, N Y, sculptor of repute, has been here to arrange f'r sculpting me — I told him I w'd submit — we'll see what comes of it — " (*The Corresponence of Walt Whitman,* V, 186). O'Donovan started working on the sculpture on 17 April 1891, was in Camden off and on until 29 July, when Whitman told Dr Bucke, "O'Donovan, the sculptor, continuing — he is to bronze it (*nous verrons*) — " (*ibid.,* V, 231; see also pp. 190, 192, 193, 200, 207, 209, 222, 225, and 226 — Whitman described O'Donovan as "a fine fellow, splendid magnetic fellow," but continued to say what he first said, "we will see what it all comes to"). His name does not come up in Whitman's letters after 29 July 1891 or in the *Daybook.*

3291. This is repeated, with other gas bills, at the end of the *Daybook.*

3292. On this matter, see *The Correspondence of Walt Whitman,* V, 185–187, and Edwin Haviland Miller's accompanying footnotes.

6   reading proof "Good-Bye" pass'd the 51st page[3293]
         Herbert Gilchrist here[3294]
            Dr L here[3295]

[2:52]

Eakins' studio
            1330 Chestnut st[3296]
O Donovan
         M H Spielmann[3297]

[On clipped letterhead of Samuel B. Foster, Local Attorney, Chamber of Commerce Bldg., Chicago:]
            sent Circ
         books sent
                    paid
      May 2
               by express[3298]

[Bill to Whitman, 328 Mickle, from Camden Gas Light Company, for gas from 1 April to 1 July 1891, $4.80, minus .24 (5% for prompt payment) — $4.56.]

[2:53]

         Camden   April   May   1891
7   bright sunny day out – spring like – fluctuating
         grip – gastric – head &c: troubles continued bad
            now, five or six months – nearly all that
               time cribb'd in this room & chair – [3299]

3293. See footnotes 3258.
3294. Herbert Gilchrist, the artist son of Anne Gilchrist, who herself was one of the most interesting of Whitman's women friends, came often from his Centreport, Long Island, studio to visit the aging poet; he was both unhappy and unsuccessful (see the comment in *The Correspondence of Walt Whitman,* V, 174n, and numerous references by Whitman to him in letters).
3295. For Dr Daniel Longaker, see footnote 3279.
3296. Thomas Eakins's portrait of Whitman, the poet wrote to Dr R. M. Bucke, on 24 January 1891, "is among the great show Penn: Art Exhition Phila —" (*The Correspondence of Walt Whitman,* V, 155); and wrote him on 14 May that William R. O'Donovan (see footnote 3290, above), the sculptor, "is in Eakins's studio, 1330 Chestnut st: Phil: —" (*ibid.,* V, 200). Eakins visited Whitman on 6 June 1891, and on 7 June Whitman wrote Horace Traubel, then in Lonon, Ontario, that "Eakins says O'D[onovan] wants the presence of that oil portrait while sculpting" (*ibid.,* V, 209).
3297. H. M. Spielmann (see footnote 2502), editor of the *Magazine of Art* (London), wrote Whitman on 16 March 1891 (letter in the Feinberg Collection) to thank him for sending a copy of Horace Traubel's periodical *The Conservator.*
3298. See fuller entry in the *Daybook,* 2 May 1891, below.
3299. Two slightly variant accounts of his health are seen in Whitman's letters on this date to Dr R. M. Bucke ("Keeping on fairly I guess . . . — take medicine every day — bowels moderately loose — inertia & headache quite heavy — appetite so-so [no nausea] —

14   sent p'k't b'k ed'n L of G. to Mary R Cabot
            Brattleboro Vermont   paid
        $2 to H L H [3300]   * – sweating – warm

15   got out a short jaunt out door in wheel chair – eyes blinded [3301]

16   weak as death – strange, depress'd day

17   warm the last three days & nights
        O Donovan, the sculptor, here, making preparations[3302]
        — finishing the proofs   Good-Bye   66 pp:[3303]

20   sent "Two Riv:" (gift) to W H Healy, 503 Avery
            av: Syracuse   N Y.   rec'd[3304]
        The big Presidential trip South & West
            in Galveston, Texas, yesterday[3305]

24   the hand sculping[3306]   Warren gone to Doylestown[3307]

27   sent mor –b'd L of G. to J W. Wallace, Anderton
                            paid
            near Chorley, Lanc. Eng. for Wentworth Dixon[3308]

sleep middling") and to J. W. Wallace ("keeping on much the same — no worse I guess . . .
Am sitting here [listless & stupid as a great log] in my den — take medicine every day") —
The Correspondence of Walt Whitman, V, 187–188. Whitman was an old and ill man, and
less than a year later he died.

3300. See Whitman's letter to his sister, Hannah L. Heyde, in *The Correspondence of
Walt Whitman*, V, 191.

3301. Whitman wrote Dr Daniel Longaker the same thing: "Went out in wheel chair
fifteen minutes; warm, bright sun, flustered, headache — eyes badly blurred — (first time out
in four months)" — *The Correspondence of Walt Whitman*, V, 191; see *ibid.*, V, 192, for a
similar letter to Dr R. M. Bucke.

3302. For William R. O'Donovan, see footnote 3290.

3303. See footnote 3258.

3304. Why Whitman is sending *Two Rivulets* (1876) as a gift to W. H. Healy is not
quite clear.

3305. Whitman asked Dr R. M. Bucke, "Do you follow President [Benjamin] Harrison's trip south &c? — it is quite curious — he is going 10,000 miles all in our own settled
demesne — " (*The Correspondence of Walt Whitman*, V, 193). The poet's earlier opinions of
Harrison: "we have an unprecedently humdrum President & big m'n" (22 January 1890,
ibid., V, 21); "the damnable diseased policy the Harrison gov't typif.es call'd protectionism —
thats the bottom of it, below every thing else — probably the world never saw such a mean
dog-in-the-manger principle so thoroughly attempted & made the base of a great party" (13
September 1890, *ibid.*, V, 84). But by 10 May 1891 Whitman was saying to J. W. Wallace:
"Do you keep at all the American presidential trip Pacific-ward & south west ward? with the
tip top off hand speeches of Prest: Harrison? All curious & significant & satisfactory to me —
a lunch-trip of 10,000 miles '& all on our own land' — " (*ibid.*, V, 199).

3306. This was being done by William R. O'Donovan (see footnote 3290).

3307. Warren Fritzinger, Whitman's male nurse, probably went to Doylestown, New
Jersey, to see his grandfather, who was "very low, may be dying" (*The Correspondence of
Walt Whitman*, V, 195).

3308. J. W. Wallace's letter, 13–14 April 1891, is in the Feinberg Collection; Bolton's

May 2 – sent a bundle, two big books, one '76 L of G.
and one Dr B's W W. & also photo W W 1890, 4 books
& photo, by express, to Saml B Foster, attorney,
Chamber of Commerce Bldng, Chicago.   paid [3309]
big book by mail to J G Dempsey M d   65
           u
Dalymont   Phibsboro, Dublin Ireland

6   big book to F H Herrick, Adelbert College
Cleveland, Ohio. $6.40 due.   paid

12   Paid Reinheilter $500 toward the tomb[3310]

16   send unb'd "Good-Bye" to Symonds, Dr Johnston
Kennedy, Melville Phillips[3311]
17   Tennyson, Sarrazin ∧
sent previously to Dr B – Dr L here yesterday[3312]

18   sent formal application for copyright for Good-Bye
to Librarian Congress ($1 enc'd) rec'd & copyright
Entered [3313]

"   big book to D McKay[3314]
Sheets Good-Bye (66 pp:) printed – presswork paper &c.
· good [3315]

Whitman admirers continued to buy copies of *Leaves of Grass,* the morocco bound edition (1889) and others.

3309. Without Samuel B. Foster's letter, missing, one cannot know the reasons he bought Dr R. M. Bucke's *Walt Whitman* (1883), *Leaves of Grass* (Centennial Edition, 1876), and two copies of *Complete Poems & Prose* (1888).

3310. For more on Whitman's tomb, see footnotes 2987, 3034, and 3080. See also his letter to William Sloane Kennedy in *The Correspondence of Walt Whitman,* V. 197.

3311. Of these seven people who were sent unbound copies of *Good-bye My Fancy,* four were in Europe—John Addington Symonds, Dr John Johnston, Alfred Lord Tennyson, and Gabriel Sarrazin—Dr R. M. Bucke of course in Canada, William Sloane Kennedy in Boston, and Melville Phillips (Philips) on the Philadelphia *Press* and with *Munyon's Illustrated World.* See Whitman's letter to Dr. Bucke, 14 May 1891, in *The Correspondence of Walt Whitman,* V, 200; see also, *ibid.,* V, 201, his letter to Bernard O'Dowd, in Australia, to whom he also sent an unbound copy.

3312. Dr Daniel Longaker was ill for ten days during the first of May but was now coming every few days.

3313. See footnote 3258.

3314. It would seem to be bothersome to send David McKay copies of Whitman's *Complete Poems & Prose* (1888) one at the time.

3315. Whitman was so pleased with printer George Ferguson's work that he wrote him, "The *press work* paper &c: of the little 'Good-bye my Fancy' make a first rate, good, satisfactory job—& the press work is capital. If worth while I sh'd like the pressmen, foreman &c: to see this" (*The Correspondence of Walt Whitman,* V, 202).

[2:54]

W^m H Taylor, 321 High st. Newark, N J [3316]
    Reeves & Turner publishers
     Fleet street London Eng:[3317]

[Clipping:]   "A.J.W." — (1) The United States flag
after July 4 of this year will have forty-
four stars. There will be four rows of
seven stars and two rows of eight stars
each, the latter in the upper and lower
rows. (2) There are now forty-four States
in the Union.

Miss Isabella O Ford
  Adel Grange, Leeds, Eng:[3318]

[2:55]

   Camden May June 1891
21 sent "On, on ye jocund twain" & "unseen buds" to Melville Phillips for Nugent Robinson "Once a Week"
        $10
   rec'd pay ($10) f'm Melville Philips [3319]

27 sent big book to G & C Merriam & Co: Springfield
              Mass: [3319a]

  masks to Spielmann[3320]

3316. William H. Taylor (see footnotes 374 and 388) was an old Brooklyn friend and Broadway omnibus driver and policeman who wrote Whitman on 15 June 1891 (letter: Feinberg Collection) to ask if he wanted Taylor "to see some of our old friends" in New York, such as George Storms, "as you used to ride more with him than any one else" (*The Correspondence of Walt Whitman*, V, 215n). Storms named a son after Whitman.

3317. Dr R. M. Bucke wrote to Horace Traubel in August 1891 from London, England about Reeves & Turner becoming Whitman's British publishers (see *The Correspondence of Walt Whitman*, V, 252n).

3318. Isabella Ford was an English friend of Edward Carpenter, who was among those giving birthday gifts to Whitman (see *The Correspondence of Walt Whitman*, V, 207); on 12 May 1891 she wrote Whitman (letter in the Feinberg Collection) about a book he had sent her.

3319. See Whitman's letter to Melville Philips in *The Correspondence of Walt Whitman*, V, 201. "On, on the Same, Ye Jocund Twain" and "Unseen Buds" may have appeared in *Once a Week* (Whitman was paid $10, but this money was for a poem in the Philadelphia *Press*, and not for *Once a Week*); William Sloane Kennedy and Emory Holloway do not list them in their bibliographies, and *Leaves of Grass*, Comprehensive Reader's Edition, pp. 540 and 556, where their texts are printed, says they were first published in *Good-bye My Fancy* (1891). In his letter to Philips, Whitman asked that Nugent Robinson *"publish them before"* they appear in *Good-bye My Fancy* early in June 1891; apparently they were not.

3319a. G. and C. Merriam & Co. is best known as publishers of *Webster's International Dictionary*; they seem to have exchanged a *Dictionary* for Whitman's *Complete Poems & Prose* (1888) — see entry below for 29 May 1891.

3320. For H. M. Spielmann, see footnotes 2502 and 3297; Whitman also sent a mask

28   Horace Traubel married [3324]

29   Dr Bucke here[3322]
      rec'd big International Dictionary (Merriam & Co:)[3323]

30   went out to Harleigh[3324]

31   evn'g birth day party good success[3325]

June 2 sent big book to Dr Fletcher Army Medical Museum
       Wash'n D C. by express   paid
       Dr B back to Canada – Horace & Annie
                        with him[3326]

            many
       sent ∧ papers   Post (birth-day spree acct)[3327]

to Dr John Johnston in Bolton on 1 June 1891 (see letter, *The Correspondence of Walt Whitman*, V, 206).
    3321. As so often in the *Daybook*, Whitman fails to comment on events; in his letter to Dr John Johnston, Bolton, the poet said simply, "Horace T is married" (*The Correspondence of Walt Whitman*, V, 206). Traubel and Anne Montgomerie were married in the poet's bedroom; it was she who suggested that Traubel keep records of his conversations with Whitman. Whitman himself devised the wedding ceremony; J. H. Clifford, of the Germantown Unitarian Church, Germantown officiated. After the ceremony, according to Gay Wilson Allen's account (*The Solitary Singer*, 1955, 1967, p. 538), "Walt kissed the bride (or she him) and gave the young husband and wife his blessing — a simple and unpremeditated gesture, but, like so many of his final acts, proper conduct for a venerable 'prophet.'" Dr R. M. Bucke, who came to Camden the next day and was at Whitman's small birthday party with the two young Traubels and about 40 others, went with Horace and Anne to Canada; they returned to Camden on 14 June 1891 from the short honeymoon.
    3322. Dr R. M. Bucke came from London, Ontario, in part for Whitman's 72nd birthday, 31 May 1891; he returned home to Canada with Horace Traubel and his bride Anne Montgomerie on their honeymoon by way of Niagara Falls.
    3323. See footnote 3319, above.
    3324. It was at Harleigh Cemetery that Whitman's tomb was being built: on 12 May 1891 he made a payment of $500 and on 10 July he paid $1000 (see entries in the *Daybook* for those dates, as well as footnotes 2987, 3034, 3080, 3310, and 3361).
    3325. In contrast to the parties on Whitman's 70th and 71st birthday, 1889 and 1890, this affair was a quiet one: "ab't 40 people [attended], choice friends mostly — 12 or so women — Tennyson sent a short and sweet letter over his own sign manual — y'r [Dr John Johnston, of Bolton, England] cable was rec'd & read, lots of bits of speeches, with gems in them — we had a capital good supper (or dinner) chicken soup, salmon, roast lamb &c: &c: &c: . . . a big goblet of first-rate iced champagne — I suppose I swigg'd it off at once — I certainly welcom'd them all forthwith . . . — so I added ('I felt to') a few words of honor & reverence for our Emerson, Bryant, Longfellow dead — and then for Whittier and Tennyson 'the boss of us all' living (specifying all) — not four minutes altogether — then held out with them *for three hours* — talking lots, lots impromptu — " (*The Correspondence of Walt Whitman*, V, 205–206).
    3326. See footnotes 3321 and 3322.
    3327. Whitman could well have written the piece in the Camden *Post* himself, just as he had sent the *Post* an account of Robert G. Ingersoll's speech for the 2 June 1890 *Post*; and it too might have appeared in *Good-bye My Fancy* if this book were not already printed, or at least in type.

7   sent "Good-Bye" to J W Wallace[3328]
      Horace T. in Canada[3329]
      easier (negative) to day
      poor Han sick at Burlington, Vermont (bad)[3330]
      Horace and Annie ret'd all safe[3331]

15   sent big book to J Francis Shephard,
            12 rue Pergolése Paris   France
      hot weather – cooler spell – then heat again

26   Dr Bucke starts for Eng: leaves N Y July 8
            in the Britannic[3332]
      rec'd
      the   fine facsimiles of my letter to Dr J
            of June 1 [3333] – hot dry weather
      ink & stands f'm Carter, Dinsmore & Co:
            438 Pearl st: N Y
      Ch's W Eldridge here[3334]

30   Paid Water Rent $8 City Hall [3335]
            bro: Geo: here – Hannah better[3336]
      I have head-ache all the time

                                              [2:56]

Aug 8.   181 copies big book   complete works
          175   "   pocket-b'k-edition[3337]

3328. Whitman had sent unbound copies of *Good-bye My Fancy,* just published, to Dr John Johnston, Wallace's Bolton, England, friend, on 17 May 1891.

3329. For Horace Traubel's marriage, see footnote 3321; Horace and Anne Montgomerie Traubel returned to Camden on 14 June 1891 (see entry below, though undated, must have been written on this date).

3330. See Whitman's letter to his sister Hannah L. Heyde, 8 June 1891, in *The Correspondence of Walt Whitman,* V, 210; and another of 16 June (*ibid.,* V, 214–215).

3331. See entries just above about the Traubel's; undated, this entry is for 14 June 1891.

3332. Dr R. M. Bucke was going abroad in the interest of his water meter, which he mentions over and over again but Whitman ignores — see *The Correspondence of Walt Whitman,* V, 216n, and 217–238, for letters to Bucke which the poet sent to England, and for material on Dr Bucke's visit to Bolton, to see Dr John Johnston and J. W. Wallace, and of his seeing Tennyson. Bucke returned to New York on 2 September 1891.

3333. See *The Correspondence of Walt Whitman,* V, 219.

3334. Charles W. Eldridge (see footnote 116), publisher of the 1860 *Leaves,* who helped Whitman get his Washington job and one of the poet's oldest friends.

3335. This sum is also entered at the end of the *Daybook.*

3336. Whitman refers to George's long visit in his letter to Dr R. M. Bucke in *The Correspondence of Walt Whitman,* V, 221; see the letter to Hannah L. Heyde, 7 July 1891, *ibid.,* V, 223.

3337. These figures on the left-hand page of the *Daybook* (where Whitman did

?10 copies since in sheets big book to D McK [3338]

[Calling card, printed: Dr. G. E. de Schweinitz, 1401 Locust Street.[3338a]]

[2:57]

Camden   July   &   Aug: 1891
July 9 sent morocco L of G. to Dr D J Doherty 143 North av:
Chicago Ill: by mail: $5 due.
sent $50 to Dr Bingham Burlington. 40 for Hannah[3339]

10   call f'm Reinhalter and Ralph Moore
altogether
paid Reinhalter $1000 – wh'makes ∧ $1500 paid cash[3340]
(500 May 12)

14   Deposited $219.43 in bank

15   hot wave – now 3ᵈ day – am beginning to feel
it badly – hot 16ᵗʰ,'17ᵗʰ, 18,19,20,21,'3,'4,'5

17   Dr B arrived in Eng: Cable this mn'g f'm Dr J.
f'm Bolton – (B there)[3341]
21   to McKay (to Oldach & Co:) six copies com-
[Five words in red ink:]
now owes
plete works (big book) in sheets   me for 7 [3342]

not make his day-to-day diary entries) seem to be an inventory of copies of *Complete Poems
& Prose* (1888), which he called "the big book," and the pocket-book edition of *Leaves of
Grass* (1889) Whitman had on hand as his own publisher — though David McKay's imprint
was on the title-page.

3338. See entries below for 21 July, 1 and 4 August 1891 on books that David McKay
got from Whitman, copies of *Complete Poems & Prose* (1888).

3338a. See footnote 3352.

3339. Dr L. M. Bingham, who had been physician to Whitman's sister Hannah Heyde
for years, acknowledged the $50 (letter in the Feinberg Collection) and asked the poet to
discount Charles Heyde's accounts of his wife's condition; on 6 August 1891 Dr Bingham
said Hannah's health was better: see *The Correspondence of Walt Whitman,* V, 232, 232n–
233n. Whitman's letter to Dr Bingham is missing. According to Whitman's note (see back
of the *Daybook*) $40 was for Hannah, and $10 for Dr Bingham.

3340. On the Whitman tomb: see footnotes 2987, 3034, and 3080; also *The Correspondence of Walt Whitman,* V, 225, where Whitman tells Dr R. M. Bucke that the bill for the
tomb was $4000, though the receipt from P. Reinhalter & Company was for only $1,500
(the figure given here, also) — see *An Exhibition of the Works of Walt Whitman* (Detroit,
1955), p. 41.

3341. See Whitman's letter to Dr John Johnston, *The Correspondence of Walt Whitman,* V, 227, on Dr R. M. Bucke's arrival.

3342. Whitman's letters to David McKay, his publisher, and/or to Oldach & Company,
book-binders, are missing. McKay wanted copies of Whitman's *Complete Poems & Prose*
(1888), the latest edition of *Leaves of Grass,* because he was making "a trade jaunt" out
west (*The Correspondence of Walt Whitman,* V, 230).

[Line in red ink:]

23   sent pict of tomb & others to Dr Johnston[3343]

28   Dr Bucke in England – letter f'm him at Bolton[3344]

Aug. 1 a big vol. to McKay – he now owes me for 2 b'd
          & 7 unbound copies, 8 altogether[3345]
       paid C F Currie $45.50 for Ed's board [3346]

   4   big book to D McK – now the 9th
          he owes me for 3 bound & 6 unb'd copies[3347]

  25   after 10 days & nights of depressing heat to-day
          is quite tolerable   even pleasant – my eyes
          growing dimmer[3348]

Aug 30 – Mrs: O'Connor here – Dr Bucke & J W W at
          sea, en route to America – cooler weather
          set in after a hot Aug: I am half blind
                                        & deaf [3349]
       Mrs. O'C goes back to Wash'n
       Dr B and (5 days afterward) J W W here[3350]

3343. See letter to Dr John Johnston of Bolton, England, in *The Correspondence of Walt Whitman,* V, 229–230.

3344. Letters from Dr R. M. Bucke in England, 18, 23, 26, and 31 July; 4, 10, and 16 August 1891 are all in the Feinberg Collection.

3345. See footnote 3342.

3346. This sum (also entered at the back of the *Daybook*) was for three months' board at the Blackwoodtown Asylum for Edward Whitman, the poet's feeble-minded brother.

3347. See footnote 3342.

3348. Although Whitman made no *Daybook* entries between 4 and 25 August 1891, he was well enough to write Dr R. M. Bucke, Dr John Johnston, Sylvester Baxter, and William Sloane Kennedy eight letters — see *The Correspondence of Walt Whitman,* V, 234–237.

3349. Mrs Ellen O'Connor, widow of William Douglas O'Connor, was in town to see a friend; she wrote Whitman of her visit on 26 August (letter in the Feinberg Collection); Whitman wrote Dr John Johnston that she was to be the guest of Horace and Anne Traubel to see Dr R. M. Bucke, expected back from England (*The Correspondence of Walt Whitman,* V, 238). Also coming from England was J. W. Wallace, Dr Johnston's close friend from Bolton, and the reports of the two Englishmen were to be published as *Visits to Walt Whitman in 1890–1891* (London, 1917). (See footnote 2344.) In his letter to his sister Hannah Heyde, 1 September 1891, Whitman repeated what he wrote here, "I am half blind and deaf" (*The Correspondence of Walt Whitman,* V, 238). Mrs O'Connor remained in Camden a week and returned home to Washington on 7 September.

3350. J. W. Wallace (see previous footnote) came later than Dr R. M. Bucke, arriving at Whitman's on the afternoon of 8 September 1891. After visiting Dr Bucke in Canada, Wallace saw Andrew Rome in Brooklyn, and was back in Camden on 15 October, spent two days with the Staffords at Timber Creek, and took the "City of Berlin" back to England on 3 November 1891.

Sept. 11 they are now in Canada – all well
    pleasantly cool weather – feel comfortable
    am getting the new printed pp: &c for the
    really <u>completed</u> L of G. (438 pp)[3351]

16   Talcott Williams & Dr Schweinitz oculist M D
    1401 Locust st: here – my eyes not seriously diseased
    not threaten'd with blindness (accd'g to Dr S)[3352]

[2:58]

Ernest Rhys   Sept. '91
   Geinen Hir   [Three lines in red ink:]
    Llangollen   Frank Williams
     N Wales[3353]   333 Drexel B'ld'g
                    Phila[3354]

English publishers } Mr Heinemann
                  Wolcott Balestier
                  John W. Lovell
                      nster
    2 Deans Yard, Westmin~~er~~   Abbey
        London England [3355]

3351. This was to be Whitman's final printing of *Leaves of Grass,* dated 1892 on the title-page but copyright 1891; it was a two-volume edition, with the two annexes and all the collected prose, including *November Boughs* and *Good-bye My Fancy,* plus "An Executor's Diary Note, 1891." This *Leaves of Grass* is generally known as Whitman's "Death-bed Edition," but his true deathbed edition was a limited and private one of about a hundred copies, prepared by Horace Traubel and others in the poet's closest circle because they did not think he would live to see bound copies of the 1892 printing. See Gay Wilson Allen, *A Reader's Guide to Walt Whitman* (New York: Farrar, Straus & Giroux, 1970), pp. 1110–12.

3352. Talcott Williams (see footnotes 277 and 799) was a Philadelphia *Press* staff member and another long-time Whitman friend who suggested on 14 September 1891 (letter in the Feinberg Collection) that Whitman have his eyes examined — note the poet's remark, "I am half blind and deaf." So he and Dr G. E. de Schweinitz of Philadelphia came over, and Whitman wrote to Dr R. M. Bucke that the physician "impress'd me favorably, made a quite varied examination, result much more comfortable than I anticipated (I have been dreading blindness or close on it) — T C [Williams?] will get more propitious glasses — (with these I have my sight blurs badly) —" (*The Correspondence of Walt Whitman,* V, 244).

3353. Ernest Rhys (see footnote 1978), an English friend from 1885, had recently written Whitman a letter from Wales (letter now lost), which he had sent to J. W. Wallace in London, Ontario, with the comment, "he must be having good times — (he is a hand-some smart *litterateur* worthy of a better fate) —" (*The Correspondence of Walt Whitman,* V, 242).

3354. Francis H. (Frank) Williams, another Philadelphia friend of the 1880s — see *Walt Whitman Review,* XIV (March 1968), 31, and footnotes 277 and 1765 in the *Daybook* — visited Whitman on 28 October 1891.

3355. See *Daybook* entry for 18 October 1891, below, and *The Correspondence of Walt Whitman,* V, 253 and 252n, and V, 267.

[Tiny Clipping:] JOHN W. LOVELL COMPANY, PUBLISHERS,
30 WORTH Street, New York.[3356]

---

new address   Oct: '91
Edw'd Carpenter, Millthorpe, Holmesfield,
near Sheffield, Eng:[3357]

[Clipping:]

Wolcott Balestier, who has collaborated with
Rudyard Kipling in the new novel which the *Cen-
tury* will begin publishing in November, is a young
American now living in London. He is a writer and
a business man as well, being a member of the re-
cently organized firm of Heinemann & Balestier, of
Leipsic, which is publishing a series of copyrighted
English and American novels on the continent of
Europe in the fashion of the Tauchnitz editions.
He was formerly the editor of the New York hu-
morous weekly, *Time*.[3358]

[2:59]

Sept: Camden   Sept: &   Oct: 1891
         D McKay   @
22   supplied ∧ ten (10) copies comp. works b'd 3.50 $35

26   rec'd $68 f'm D McKay for books (p'd up to date)[3359]

28   sent H. B Forman   complete works
         Burroughs' Notes   paper Dem Vistas
         As a Strong Bird   "   German Grashelme
      "Good Bye" sheets 2 [3360]
      paid City Tax Bill $24.47

3356. John W. Lovell has to do with the same matter discussed in the entries referred
to in footnote 3355.
    3357. Edward Carpenter (see footnote 20), who goes back in Whitman's life to 1874
and who visited Whitman in 1877 and 1884, saw Dr R. M. Bucke in England in August
1891; see Whitman's letter to Carpenter, 20 October 1891, in *The Correspondence of Walt
Whitman*, V, 255–256.
    3358. Balestier was being considered as a publisher of Whitman in England — see en-
tries discussed in footnotes 3355 and 3356.
    3359. These two entries have to do with David McKay's taking copies of Whitman's
Complete Poems & Prose (1888) on his trip to the west to sell books (see footnote 3342).
    3360. For H. Buxton Forman, see footnote 248; see also Whitman's letter to him, 27

Oct. 1   Reinhalter Bro's here [3361] – Cool change
          D McKay's big books &c: up to date paid
          supplied McKay with big book $4

     5   paid the gas bill $2.57 (discount 13^{cts})
          another big book to D McKay – the 2^d one[3362]

10 to   J W Wallace in Brooklyn & West Hills[3363]
    13   letters f'm him – Andrew & Tom Rome – the Jarvis
                  & Place people &c at W H — Charles Velsor – [3364]
                  – Herbert Gilchrist[3365]

    14   J W Wallace & Andrew Rome here – talk ab't
          Brooklyn, West Hills, folks, places, changes,
          fortunes &c – the good lunch of Chesapeake
          oysters and Rhine wine – & I and Warry – [3366]

    16   J W W here – [3367]

    17   sent the big book to Charles Velsor[3368]

September 1891, in *The Correspondence of Walt Whitman,* V, 247. (See *ibid.,* V, 253 and footnote there.) Forman wanted Whitman's *Complete Poems & Prose* for his son Maurice to take to Egypt.

3361. Reinhalter & Company were building Whitman's tomb (see footnote 3324), which was completed on 27 October 1891; there is one more entry in the *Daybook* — and that a very brief one of four words — on 30 October. For a fuller discussion, see Whitman's letter to Dr R. M. Bucke, 12–14 November 1891, *The Correspondence of Walt Whitman,* V, 265, and especially Edwin Haviland Miller's long footnote, *ibid.,* V, 264n–265n; and also *ibid.,* V, 267.

3362. Though very ill, and the entries in the *Daybook* soon to draw to a close, Whitman was still keeping track of single copies of his *Complete Poems & Prose* his publisher was picking up.

3363. J. W. Wallace, of Bolton, England, deals with his visits in his book, which he wrote with Dr John Johnston, *Visits to Walt Whitman in 1890–1891* (London, 1917); see Whitman's references to Wallace in *The Correspondence of Walt Whitman,* V, 250, 251, 252, 253.

3364. There are no less than 22 letters from J. W. Wallace to Whitman, between 11 September and 14 October 1891, in the Feinberg Collection; Whitman wrote four letters to Wallace — see especially the one of 9 October in *The Correspondence of Walt Whitman,* V, 251–252. W H, of course, refers to West Hills, Whitman's birthplace, and Charles Velsor was a relative on his mother's side of the family.

3365. For Herbert Gilchrist, see footnote 3294, above; he may have been among those J. W. Wallace saw on Long Island at this time.

3366. Whitman talks about this visit with Wallace and Andrew Rome, and Warren Fritzinger in his letters to Dr R. M. Bucke and Dr John Johnston, but says hardly anything significant or in any detail at all — *The Correspondence of Walt Whitman,* V, 253–254.

3367. We must wait for future volumes of Horace Traubel's *With Walt Whitman in Camden* to get any details on J. W. Wallace's day with Whitman on Mickle Street.

3368. See footnote 3364; Whitman refers to Charles Velsor in his "A Week at West

18   sent H B Forman, 46 Marlborough St.
     St John's Wood, London, Eng: letter empowering
     him to bargain with Heinemann ⎫
                      Wolcott Balestier ⎬ pubr's
                      J W Lovell ⎭
     2 Dean's Yard, Westminster Abbey
     to pub. my books – enc'd Gilder's letter[3369]

19   2ᵈ (supplementary) letter – <u>three</u> vols: suggested [3370]

20    $96.71   f'm D McKay for royalty

21   deposited $203.21 in bank (sunny day)[3371]

24   Jeannette L Gilder here[3372]
     J W W down at Glendale[3373]

     by express
27   sent ∧big book   to Arthur Joburus, Leisenring
     Fayette Co: Penn – order of Funk & Wagnalls
     18 Astor Place N Y. $4 due f'm them   4 paid

Hills," New York *Tribune,* 4 August 1881 (see *Prose Works 1892,* I, 353), among his friends and relatives.

3369. This letter to H. Buxton Forman is missing; for more on these matters, see footnotes 3355, 3356, 3358, 3360 and the entries to which they refer. Joseph B. Gilder's letter is also missing. On 24 October 1891, Whitman told Dr R. M. Bucke, "the English 'nibbling' pub'rs are Heinemann & Balestier (& it w'd seem J G Lovell N Y) & I have written to Forman, asking him to prospect & negotiate with them — have given him absolute power" (*The Correspondence of Walt Whitman,* V, 257; earlier reference, *ibid.,* V, 256; but see a more important later one, V, 267).

3370. This letter is also missing (see previous footnote).

3371. On 14 July 1891, Whitman deposited $219 in the bank (see that date, above); since then, according to *Daybook* entries, which obviously are not complete, Whitman received $68, $4, and $96.71 (a total of $168.71), and paid out $45.50, $24.47, and $2.57 (a total of $72.54), leaving a balance of $96.17. Where did the other $107.04 come from?

3372. Jeannette Gilder was editor of *The Critic,* which published at least 28 prose pieces by Whitman between January 1881 and 17 October 1891, and five poems; Whitman wrote to Dr R. M. Bucke on this date, "Jeannette Gilder N Y & three charming girls just here — I consider J G & Jo[seph B. Gilder] & the *Critic,* old & real & valuable friends — (have never halted or wavered) — " (*The Correspondence of Walt Whitman,* V, 257).

3373. J. W. Wallace wrote about this visit to the Staffords in *Visits to Walt Whitman in 1890 and 1891* (see footnotes 3349 and 3363), pp. 184–190; Whitman simply told Dr R. M. Bucke, "J W W has just ret'd f'm a good (two days) visit to the Staffords (& Timber Creek) — " and to Dr John Johnston, "J W W has ret'd f'm a pleasant visit to the Staffords (Glendale, Camden Co: N J) — is well, has just gone over to Philadelphia — " (*The Correspondence of Walt Whitman,* V, 258).

[2:60]

[Clipping of printed poem, title and author's name missing. Stanza five emendations (three words and a letter) by WW:]

"Whose steps are those? Who comes so late?"
  "Let me come in — the door unlock."
" 'Tis midnight now; my lonely gate
  I open to no stranger's knock.

"Who art thou? Speak!" "Men call me Fame.
  To immortality I lead."
"Pass, idle phantom of a name."
  "Listen again, and now take heed.

" 'Twas false. My names are Song, Love, Art.
  My poet, now unbar the door."
"Art's dead, Song cannot touch my heart,
  My one Love's name I chant no more."

"Open then, now — for see, I stand,
  Riches my name, with endless gold —
Gold and your wish in either hand."
  "Too late — my youth you still withhold."

"Then, if it must be, since the door
  In   Stands shut, my last true name do know.   t
  me   ~~Men call me~~ Death. Delay no more;
  find   I bring the cure of every woe."

The door flies wide. "Ah guest so wan,
  Forgive the poor place where I dwell —
An ice-cold hearth, a heart-sick man,
  Stand here to welcome thee full well."

67 big books
Warry's count Nov: 17 [3374]

Oldach has 81 copies
in sheets Nov. 19 '91 [3375]

3374. Since the last "inventory" in the *Daybook,* 8 August 1891, when Whitman reported 181 copies of his *Complete Poems & Prose* (1888), he must have sold or given away 114 copies, according to Warren Frizinger's count; this may account for the bank deposit on 21 October.

3375. On 31 March 1891 (see entry, above) Oldach had 190 copies in sheets — this means 109 *Complete Poems & Prose* (1888) were bound.

lo – cale (ló-kál)
mahab bār a ta[3376]

[Written in blue pencil by WW on a slip of paper:]

Mrs O'Connor
34 Benefit st
Providence
R I [3377]

[2:61]

Camden   Oct: &   Nov & Dec: 1891

Oct. 27   J W W ret'd f'm Glendale, (matters as usual there)[3378]

Nov. 2   Sir Edwin Arnold, John Russell Young & Major Pond here[3379]

recd [3380]

3   sent big books to Dr Bingham   & Prof. Hale
        care Hamlin Garland, Roxbury, Mass:[3381]

16   sold to D McKay 50 sets big book sheets
        a $3 – ($150)[3382]

29   depress'd condition   bad all thro Nov:

3376. Even in his last days Whitman was jotting down material for "studying" words and pronunciation.

3377. Mrs Ellen O'Connor, whose husband William Douglas O'Connor died on 9 May 1889, left Washington some time before 12 November 1891 to live in Providence, Rhode Island (Whitman's letter to her of that date is addressed to her there — see *The Correspondence of Walt Whitman,* V, 264); in March 1892 she married Albert L. Calder.

3378. For J. W. Wallace at the Stafford's, see footnote 3373.

3379. For Sir Edwin Arnold, see footnote 2909, above; for John Russell Young, see footnote 1528, above; for Major James B. Pond, who was associated with Whitman's 14 April 1887 lecture on Lincoln in New York, see *The Correspondence of Walt Whitman,* IV, 84, 86, 91. On this 1891 visit, Whitman merely wrote Dr R. M. Bucke, in his brief way at this time, that the three men "paid me a visit yesterday — all went right" (*The Correspondence of Walt Whitman,* V, 260 and also V, 262); but see Edwin Haviland Miller's comments (*ibid.,* V, 260n–261n) on the Philadelphia *Press,* 3 November 1891 article, "A Poet's Greeting to a Poet."

3380. Dr L. M. Bingham was Hannah L. Heyde's physician in Burlington, Vermont (see footnote 3339). Bingham acknowledged Whitman's *Complete Poems & Prose* (1888) on 16 November 1891 (letter in the Feinberg Collection).

3381. For Hamlin Garland, see footnote 2604, above; in a letter to Dr R. M. Bucke, 22 January 1890, is a clipping from the 18 January Boston *Evening Transcript* about a series of lectures to be given by Garland, "The Genre and Landscape Poetry by Whitman" (*The Correspondence of Walt Whitman,* V, 21n); in May 1891 Whitman sent Garland two copies of *Good-bye My Fancy* (1891), for which he had paid $5 (this letter is missing; though a letter dated 15 April 1890 is in the Feinberg Collection).

3382. These were to go to some English dealer, Whitman wrote Dr R. M. Bucke (*The Correspondence of Walt Whitman,* V, 266); this is the last mention of David McKay in the

30   the two Reinhalters here³³⁸³   cold spell
        letters f'm Dr J & J W W ³³⁸⁴

Dec 1   sent J Wᵐ Lloyd 563ᵈ East St: N Y. big book by mail ³³⁸⁵
        $3 paid   340 due   clear cool

2   * 4ᵗʰ *   2ᵈ, 3ᵈ day & night g't suffering³³⁸⁶

[2:62–264]

[Blank]

[2:265–268]

[Clipped out]

[2:269]

Aug: 28 '89 – paid Water Tax, $8.40 (by Ed: Wilkins)

Sept: 17 '89 – paid Tax Bill   24.02 (by Ed: W)

Oct: '89   paid W H Johnson carpenter ᵣₑₚₐᵢᵣₛ ₕₒᵤₛₑ $48.40

Jan 2 '90 – paid Billstein & Co: $15.25
        Camden Gas office –   714
        C L H   2

Daybook, although he is mentioned once more in a letter to Dr Bucke, 27 January 1892; "McK[ay] was here — paid me $283 — " (*ibid.,* V, 275).

3383. This visit was on the matter of Whitman's tomb: see footnote 3361 for other references.

3384. These letters from Dr John Johnston and J. W. Wallace, the Bolton pair, are in the Feinberg Collection; Whitman, who certainly does not list all of their letters in the *Daybook,* actually got, during October and November 1891, 10 letters from Wallace and 12 from Dr Johnson (all are now in the Feinberg Collection).

3385. J. William Lloyd's letters, 30 November 1891 and 1 December, ordering and acknowledging Whitman's *Complete Poems & Prose* (1888), are in the Feinberg Collection.

3386. There is no question that Whitman was very ill, and his remarks in letters to Dr R. M. Bucke — "Bad days & nights with me, no hour without its suffering" (*The Correspondence of Walt Whitman,* V, 270) — in almost every letter expand on this "g't suffering" entry; though Dr Daniel Longaker, who himself was too sick to see Whitman, was more cheerful: "I hope, before many days, to see you again and that, in the meantime, you will steer along cheerfully, hopefully, without my captaincy, if I for the moment may assume such role" (*ibid.,* V, 269n).

The diary, or *Daybook,* as Whitman called it, actually ends here for its day-to-day entries, though Whitman wrote 19 more letters between 2 December 1891 and 17 March 1892, the date of his last letter (to his sister, Hannah Heyde). He died on 26 March 1892 and was buried on 30 March in Harleigh Cemetery. The remaining entries in the *Daybook* had all been made earlier, between 28 August 1889 and 8 August 1891, and almost all of them deal

Feb 10 '90 paid $45.50 to Mr. Currie for Ed's board 3 mo's

April 3 '90 Gas Bill $7.36   paid

May 18 '90 paid Oldach binder $44.41

June 18 '90   paid Water Bill $8

      '91

July 24ʌ – paid (thro' Horace) Ferguson, printer⎫203.19
        Billstein & Co: 925 Filbert st: ⎬
      & McCollin & Co: 635 Arch   ⎭

July 3 '90 – paid gas bill $4.10

Aug 1 '90 – paid Ed's board $45.50 (3 mo's) to Mr Currie, Black
                                            wood

Aug 20 '90 sent $5 to H, Burlington Vt

Sept. 1 '90 paid the city tax bill $24.02

Dec. 12 '90   paid Oldach binder $22 (by Horace)

Dec 22 '90   sent $10 to H, Burl'n Vt
   " " "   " $10 to Mary

                                                 [2:270]

[Blank]

                                     [2:271–274]

[Clipped out]

                                             [2:275]

Jan 5 '91   paid the gas bill $8.52

Feb 2 '91   paid Currie $45.50 for Ed's board

with money he paid out: for taxes, house repairs, printing various books of his, gas bills, for Edward Whitman's board, his sister Hannah Heyde, the $1500 for his tomb, water, plumbing, gifts to Mrs Mapes and to Mrs Colkitt. Many of these items are also listed in their proper place, by date, in the *Daybook* earlier.

Apr: 3 '91 paid gas bill $8.51

ei
May 12 '91   paid Reinhalter $500: on the tomb

June 30 '91   paid water rent $8

July 9 '91   sent Dr Bingham, Burlin Vt 50 – (40 for H, 10 for himself)

July 10 '91   paid Reinhalter $1000 more on tomb
($1500 paid altogether)
paid Ed's board Blackwood $45.50 to C F Currie

Aug 8   paid $4 to Wm Longhead plumber

[2:276]

1890
July 8 – sent $5 to H, Bl'ton
"   "   "   5 to Mrs M
Kansas

"   18   " $5 to Mrs Colkitt

"   20   " $5 to Han B'l't'n

[2:277]

[Blank flyleaf]

[2:278]

[On flyleaf]
Sent the (three books) Circular printed Dec: '89 ³³⁸⁷
R P Smith, London
W M Rossetti
Josiah Child
Sloane Kennedy
Alys Smith

3387. The list of 13 people here, most of them mentioned in other places in the *Daybook*, many of them on numerous occasions, were sent a circular about *Complete Poems & Prose* (1888), *Leaves of Grass* (pocket-book edition, 1889), and *Portraits from Life*. See entry for 9 December 1889, above, and footnote 2974.

one to Maurice Stoddart
       Sag Harbor L I
4 to Dr Bucke
3 to Edw'd Carpenter
H Buxton Forman
C W Eldridge
Robt Adams
    bookseller Fall River
Mrs: O'Connor
6 to Horace Traubel

              Ten   [Dollars]
    [Payable at]   Burlington, Vermont
    [Payable to]   Mrs: Hannah L Heyde
              21 Pearl   [Street]
          Burlington   Vermont
    [Sent by]   Walt Whitman
              328 Mickle   [Street]
        Camden   New Jersey[3388]

3388. This very last item in the *Daybook* is actually a postal money order, not dated except for the printed 188[ ], not signed by the postmaster, but filled out in Whitman's hand.
    The last few pages, after the diary entry ended, are at the end of the *Daybook*; and the pages in between, about two-thirds of the book, are blank.